I0753204

HISTORIC PHOTOS OF
KANSAS

TEXT AND CAPTIONS BY DAVID KNOPF

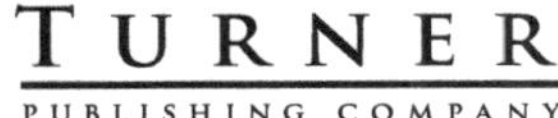

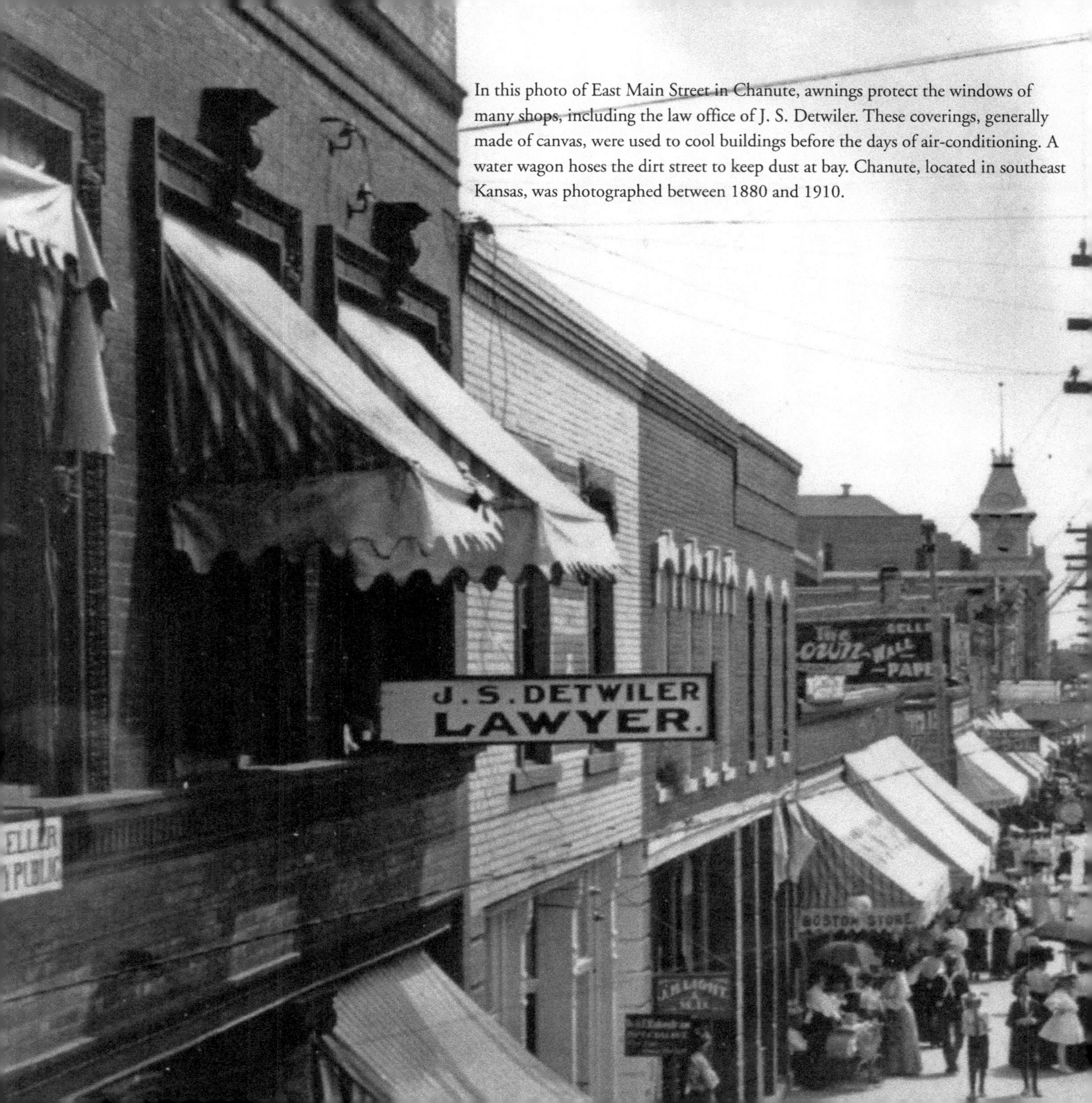

In this photo of East Main Street in Chanute, awnings protect the windows of many shops, including the law office of J. S. Detwiler. These coverings, generally made of canvas, were used to cool buildings before the days of air-conditioning. A water wagon hoses the dirt street to keep dust at bay. Chanute, located in southeast Kansas, was photographed between 1880 and 1910.

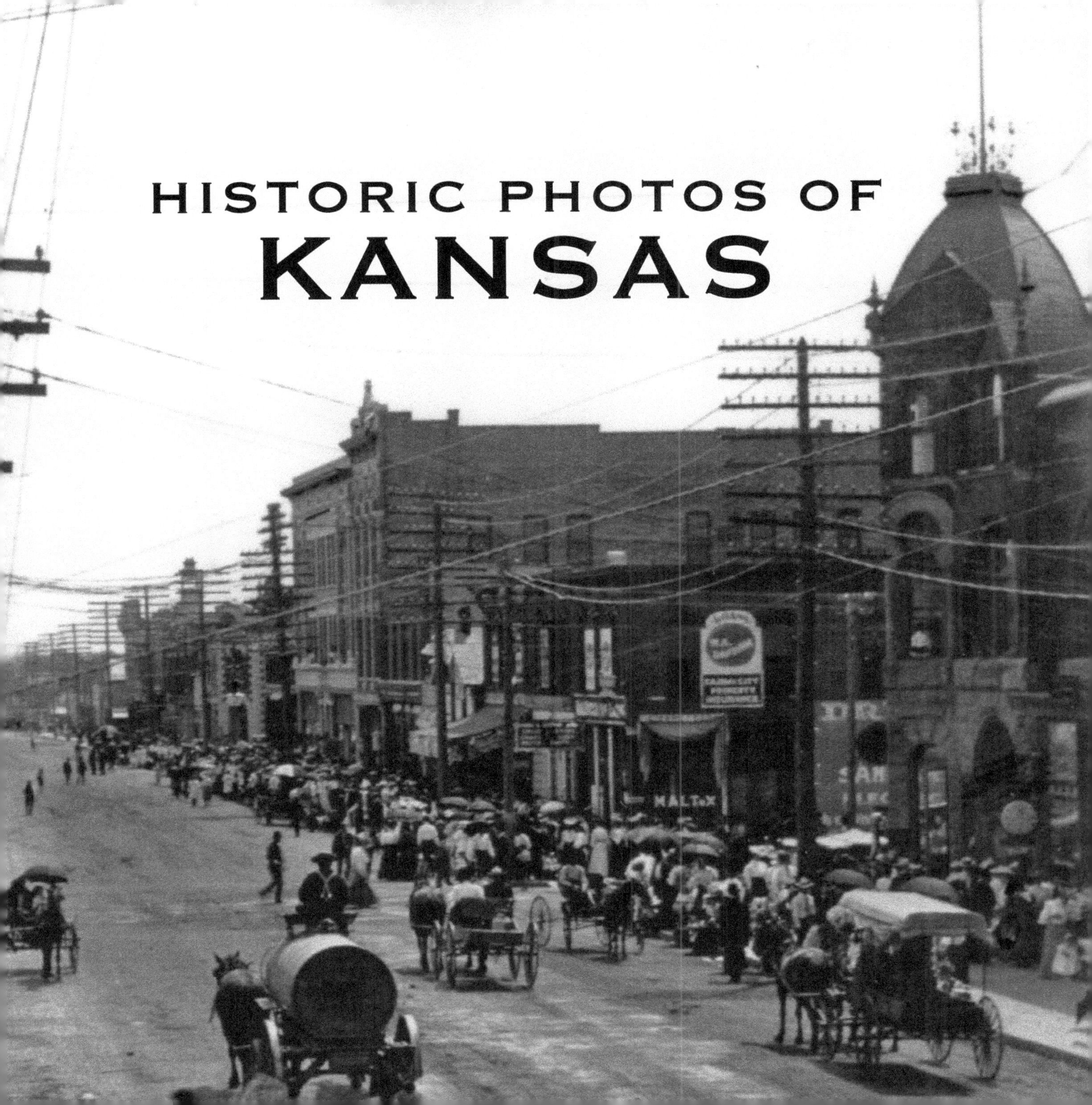

HISTORIC PHOTOS OF KANSAS

Turner Publishing Company
www.turnerpublishing.com

Historic Photos of Kansas

Library of Congress Control Number: 2009939248

ISBN: 978-1-59652-564-1

Printed in the United States of America

ISBN 978-1-68442-107-7 (hc)

Contents

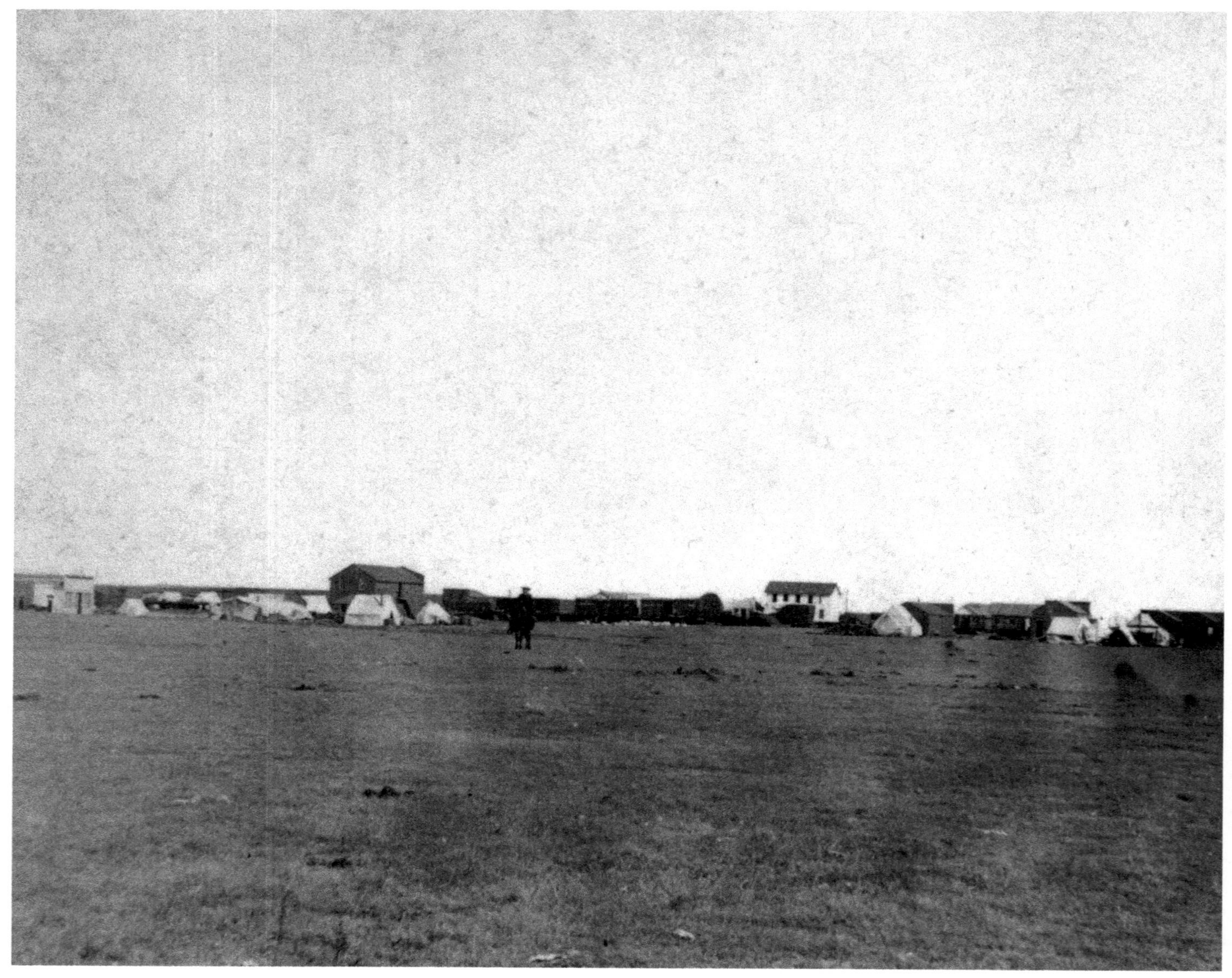

This photo of Hays City reinforces the popular—though sometimes misleading—image of Kansas having only flat terrain. The photo was taken by Alexander Gardner, who documented the path of the Missouri Pacific Railroad.

Acknowledgments

This volume, *Historic Photos of Kansas,* is the result of the cooperation and efforts of many individuals, organizations, and corporations. It is with great thanks that we acknowledge the valuable contribution of the following for their generous support:

Library of Congress
Kansas Historical Society

The writer would also like to thank Reference Librarian Marieta F. Knopf of Maple Woods Community College, Kansas City, Missouri, for her valuable contributions and assistance in making this work possible.

With the exception of touching up imperfections that have accrued over time and cropping where necessary, no changes have been made to the photographs. The focus and clarity of many photographs is limited to the technology and the ability of the photographer at the time they were taken.

PREFACE

Among the things that people tend to notice about Kansas is its location in the middle of the country. What few realize, however, is that the generalization has a factual basis: Geographically, the Great State of Kansas is precisely at the midpoint of the contiguous 48 states. So the next time someone casually refers to "Middle America," for accuracy's sake, make sure they tip their hat in the direction of the Sunflower State.

In the greater scheme, being in the middle of the country is more a matter of curiosity than anything of importance. What does matter is Kansas's unique role in the lead-up to the Civil War and the nation's westward push.

The epic struggle between abolitionists and pro-slavery forces may have reached its tragic flashpoint in the years between 1861 and 1865, but as early as the 1850s, it was in Kansas—then a territory—where tinder and spark first came together. One can say that the Civil War was played out in miniature, almost on a trial basis, in "Bleeding Kansas" years before shots were fired on Fort Sumter.

In *Historic Photos of Kansas,* almost 200 black-and-white photos document the state's position at the center of important historical events. The images and their captions touch on Kansas's contributions to the abolition of slavery, westward expansion, railroads, cattle drives, agriculture, the oil industry, aviation, and much more. And who can forget Dodge City, Kansas, and its role in the Wild West's colorful lore of outlaws, lawmen, and gunfights?

No discussion of Kansas would be complete without acknowledging the state's roots in Native American culture and, sadly, its role in the forced relocation of Indian tribes. The state's name, in fact, is derived from the Kansa, a tribe that inhabited the land.

As a neighbor of Kansas in Missouri—20 or so miles from the Kansas state line—I found the photos contained here not only visually compelling, but possessing the power to spark both the imagination and the desire to learn more. They drove my curiosity to follow a path of reading and research.

Although I worked in Kansas for a year, I know far more now than I did then. I owe a debt of gratitude to the many professional historians who have written about the state and helped broaden my knowledge and enabled me to inject substance to the captions contained here.

Charles C. Howes, author of *This Place Called Kansas,* deserves thanks for producing a highly readable introduction to the state's history and development within the pages of his book. Scholarly work by historians such as Kirk H. Beetz, Robert W. Richmond, William D. Baker, Malcolm J. Rohrbough, Craig Miner, Sanford Wexler, Catherine Reef, William H. Coogan, and others not only fleshed out my understanding of the photos, but left me in awe of the historian's commitment to fact-gathering, accuracy, and clear prose.

I can't claim to be smart enough to foresee that marrying a librarian might be a good career move. But dumb luck (and possibly a touch of dead reckoning) apparently was with me when I met my wife, Marieta, now a reference librarian at Maple Woods Community College in Kansas City. Not burdened by the writer's sometimes-cluttered mind, she found source materials on Kansas that I wouldn't have located without her. I'm also indebted to her wise guidance and ability to navigate the databases that only a librarian can fathom.

The irony here is that my wife grew up in Roeland Park, Kansas, a suburb of Kansas City. Perhaps the wagon trains that left Independence, Missouri, and followed the trail to Olathe, Kansas, and on to points west rolled past her future home.

Great things always seem to happen when you're in the middle of things.

—David Knopf

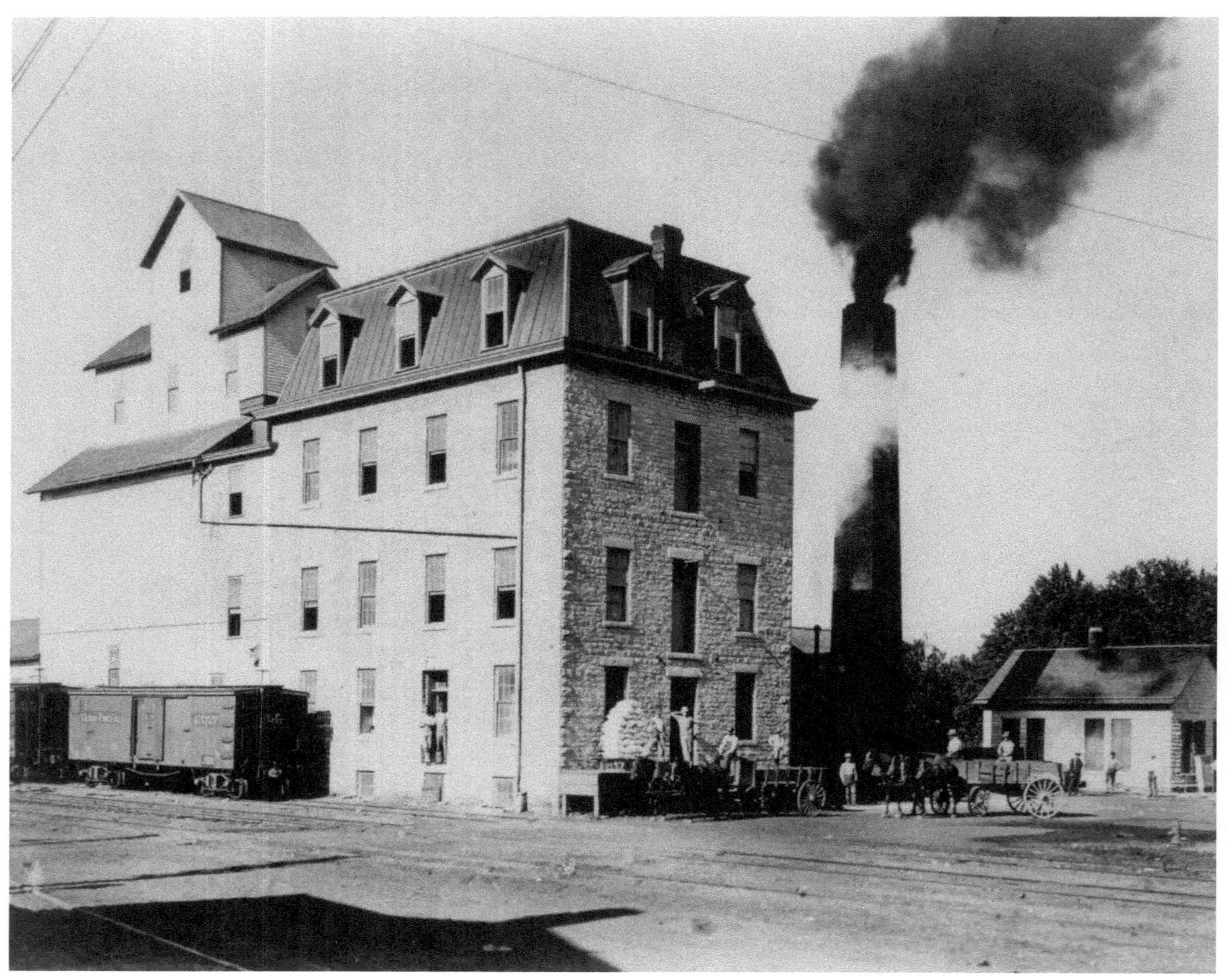

Kansas's agriculture-based economy produced a need for processing, storage, and transportation. A significant structure involved in production and distribution is the Manhattan Milling Company, pictured in this photo dated between 1870 and 1900.

From the Turbulence of "Bleeding Kansas" and the Civil War to the Plains and Beyond

(1860–1889)

It has been said that Kansas was in the path of history being made. But the mere coincidence of its location doesn't do justice to its role in deciding how history would be written.

Kansas Territory was acquired in 1803 as part of the Louisiana Purchase, and a year later, Lewis and Clark passed through. They found a territory that was home to Indian tribes, including the Kansa for whom the state was named. Then, in 1821, the Santa Fe Trail began crossing the future state, bringing settlers to the promise of a new life in the West. In 1860, the Pony Express began carrying mail over Kansas terrain.

Even as westward migration made Kansas its primary thoroughfare, the territory served to foreshadow the Civil War. "Bleeding Kansas"—a battleground for free-state abolitionists and pro-slavery advocates—has come to describe a period that determined the territory's future alignment. Would Kansas become a slave state like Missouri, its next-door neighbor, or a free state like Iowa, to the northeast?

When the Kansas-Nebraska Act opened the territory in 1854, it was decided that settlers would determine its position on slavery. Advocates for both sides immigrated and the result was violence, including an 1856 sack of the abolitionist town of Lawrence and subsequent reprisals that left five dead on both sides. The border war continued up to and during the Civil War with William Clarke Quantrill's pro-Confederate raiders devastating Lawrence in August of 1863.

Free-state sentiment prevailed, and Kansas became the 34th state on January 29, 1861. Although most of the Civil War was fought outside its borders, Kansas sent a larger percentage of its citizenry to fight for the Union than any other state.

With the war's conclusion in 1865, the state settled into its role as a nexus for westward migration. Railroads bought land and laid tracks; communities developed, serving those who stayed and those who passed through; settlers and the indigenous peoples clashed, pushing entire tribes farther west or south; Texas cattle drove across the state to railheads for the trip to stockyards in Chicago and the East; freed slaves, so-called Exodusters, migrated north and west to make their home in Kansas. It was a period of passion and exploration, one in which Kansas was never merely a conduit or passive observer.

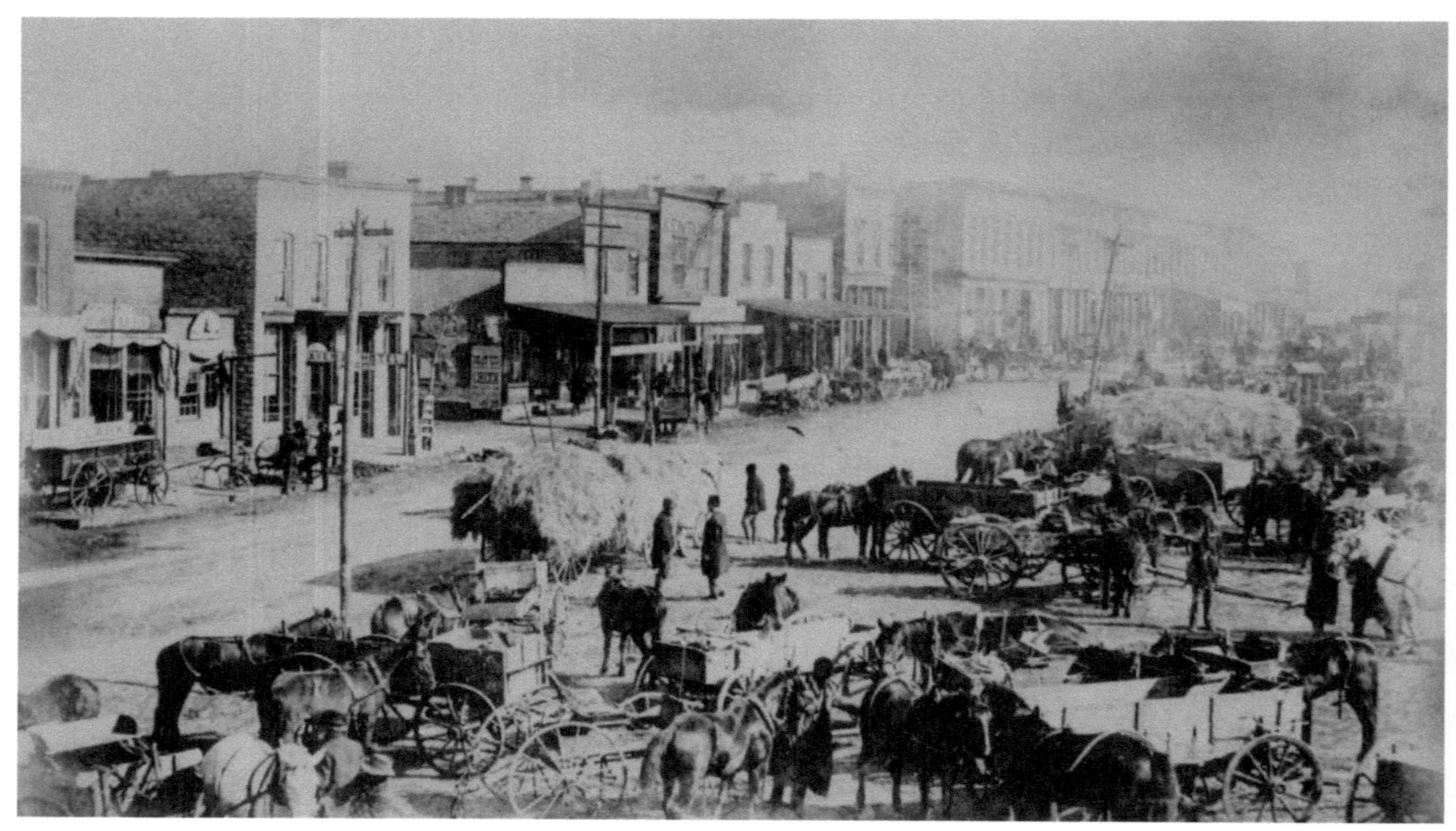

Founded in 1842, Fort Scott was one of several army posts built to provide frontier defense and to protect travelers on the Santa Fe Trail. Pictured in this early photo is the east side of Market Square, a triangular area bounded by Market, Oak, and National avenues. Market Square is at the heart of Fort Scott's historic business area.

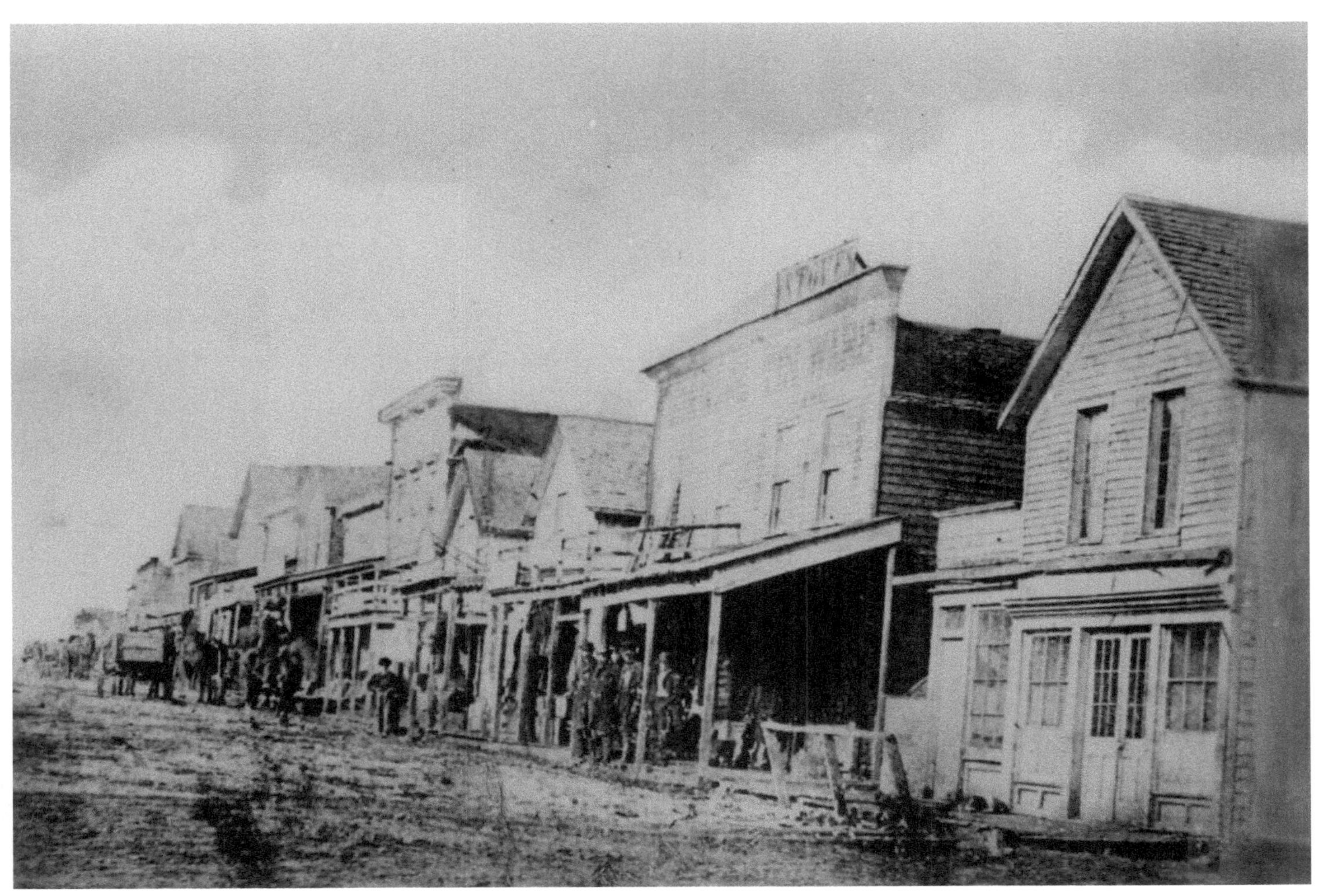

Fort Scott's early Main Street, pictured here, was located adjacent to the fort and parade grounds. It was also the site of the nearby Wilder Hotel, which served as the center of Fort Scott nightlife in the 1860s. Local lore has it that when asked by a traveler if the structure was the Wilder House, the innkeeper would reply, "You stay here awhile and you'll find there ain't a wilder house in the country."

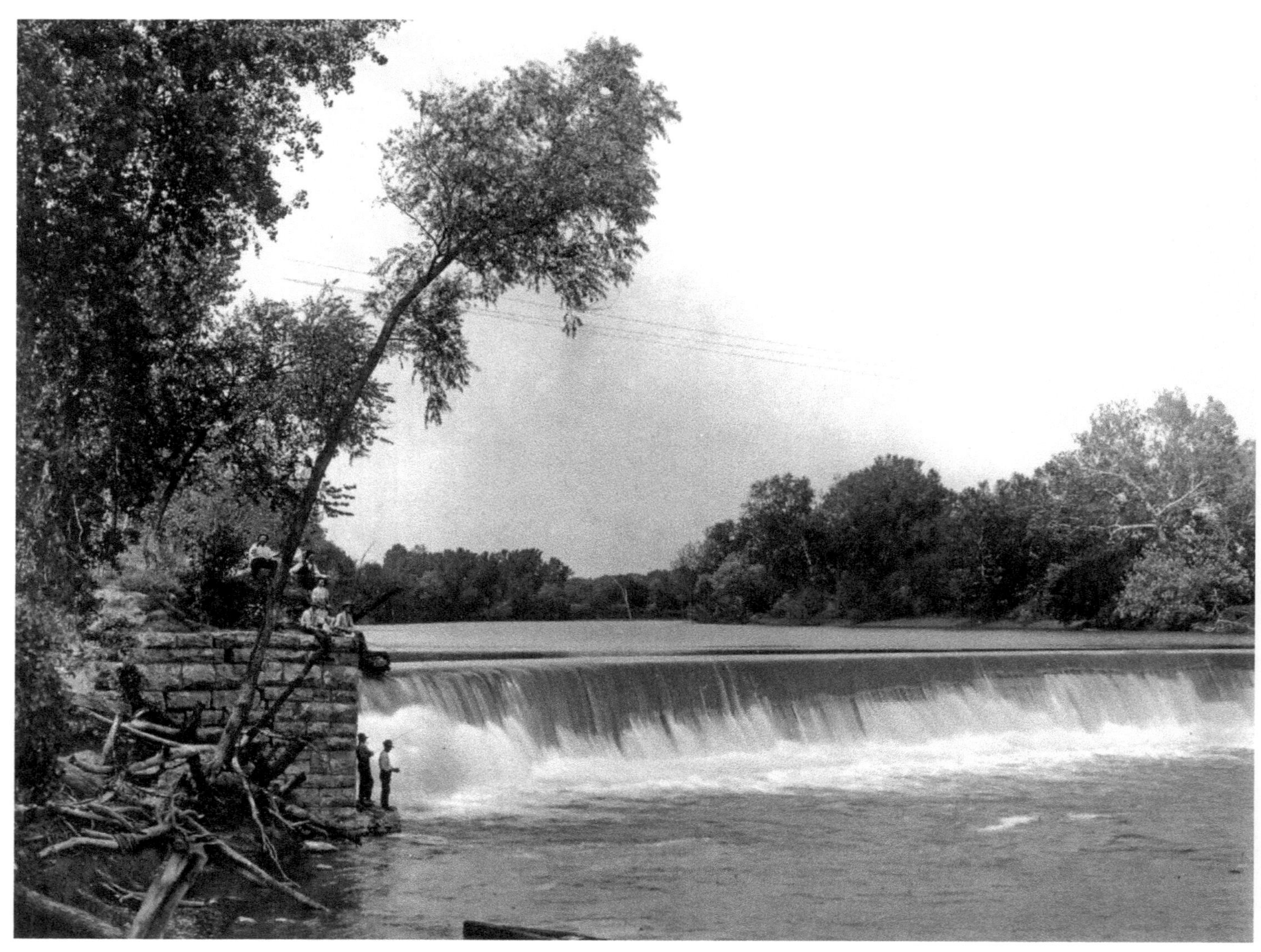

Rocky Ford Dam, which spans the Big Blue River north of Manhattan, helped create what is known today as the Rocky Ford State Fishing Area. In this 1866 photo, adults and children are seen fishing in the river.

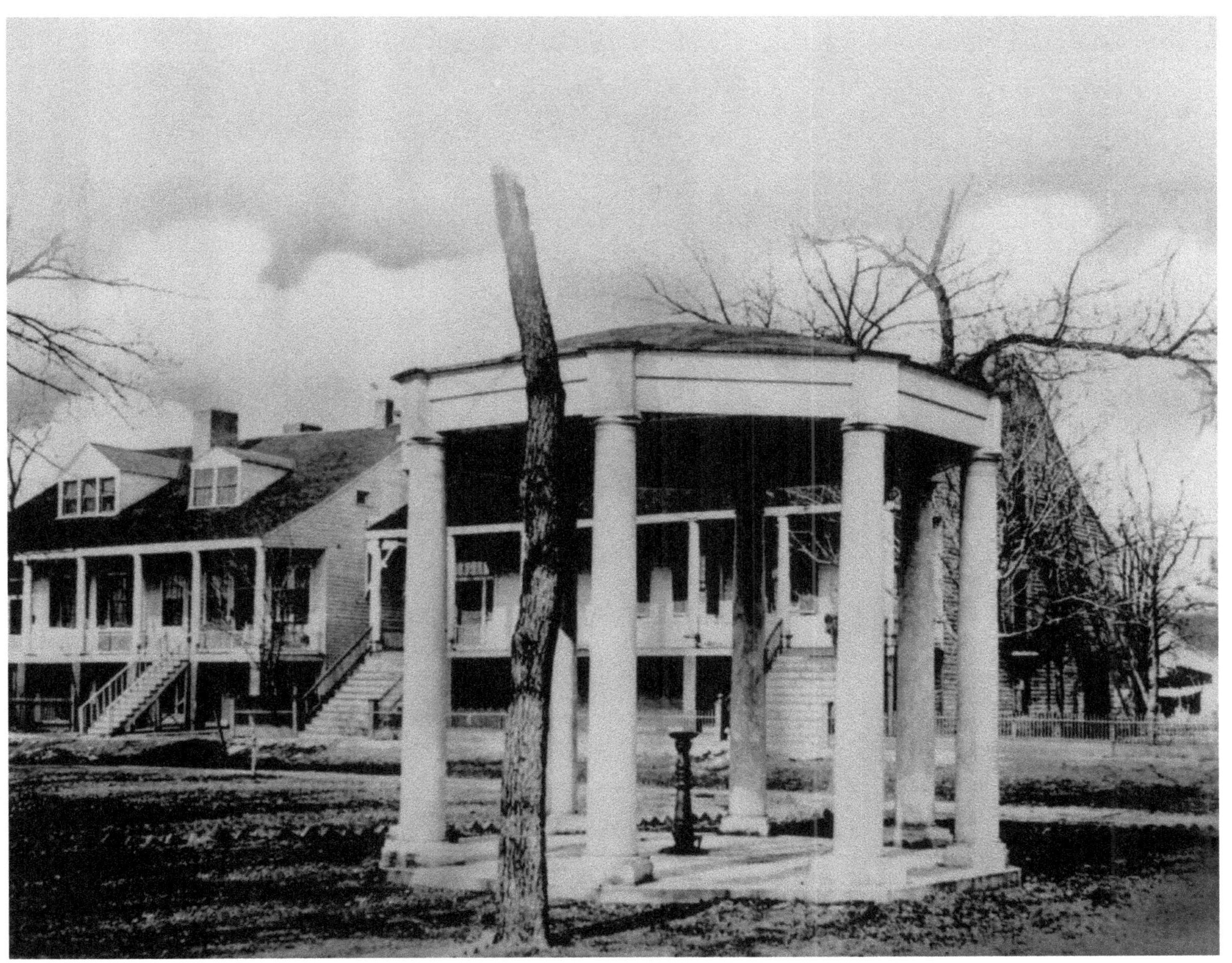

The site of the Old Fort Well in Fort Scott is marked with a stone canopy near a bandstand that served troops at the fort. The original well was dug soon after the fort was established in 1842.

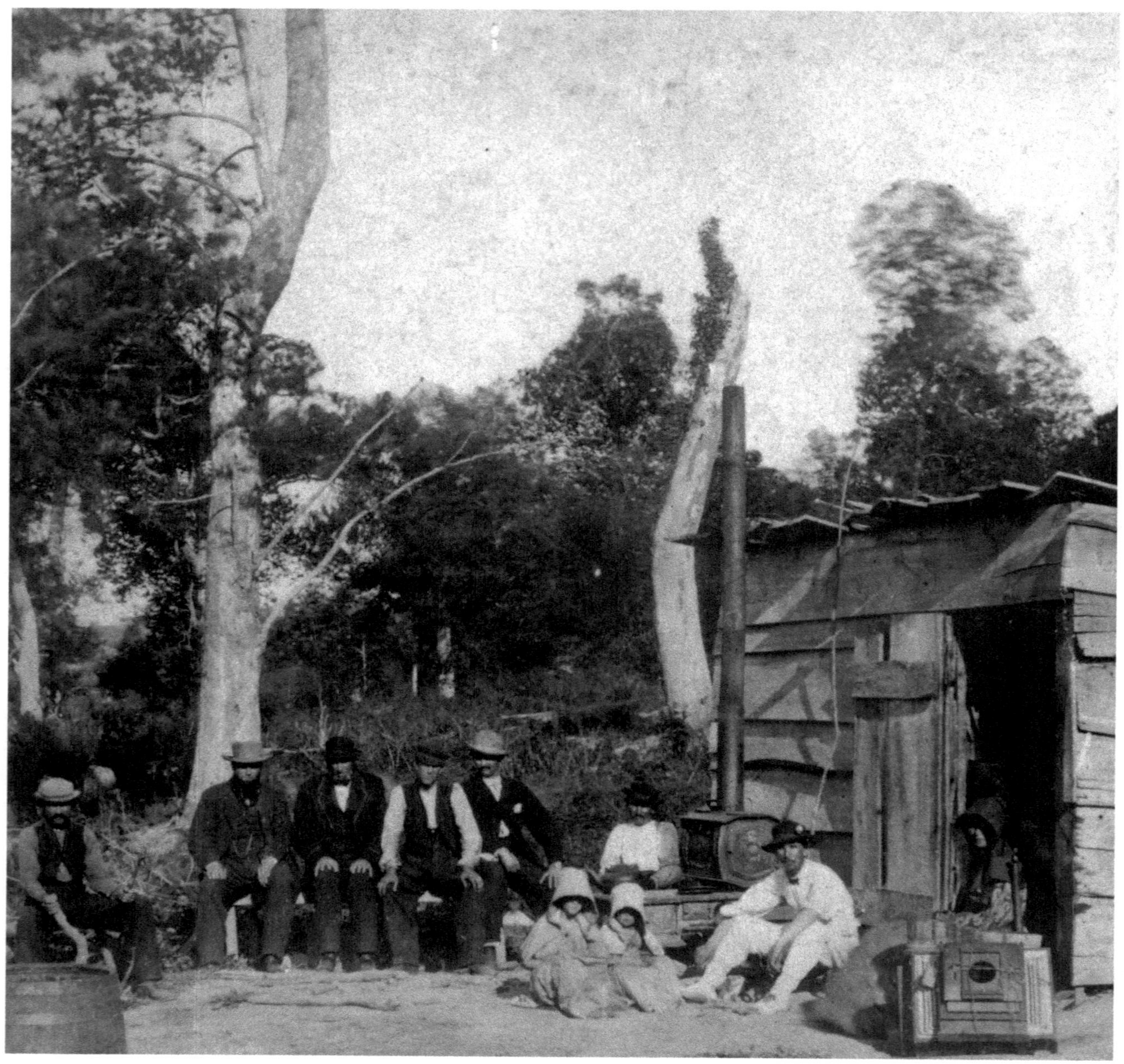

Not much is known about the Hotel de Dutton, other than its location near what is referred to as State Line, Kansas, 284 miles west of St. Louis. Alexander Gardner captured this image of adults and children in 1867.

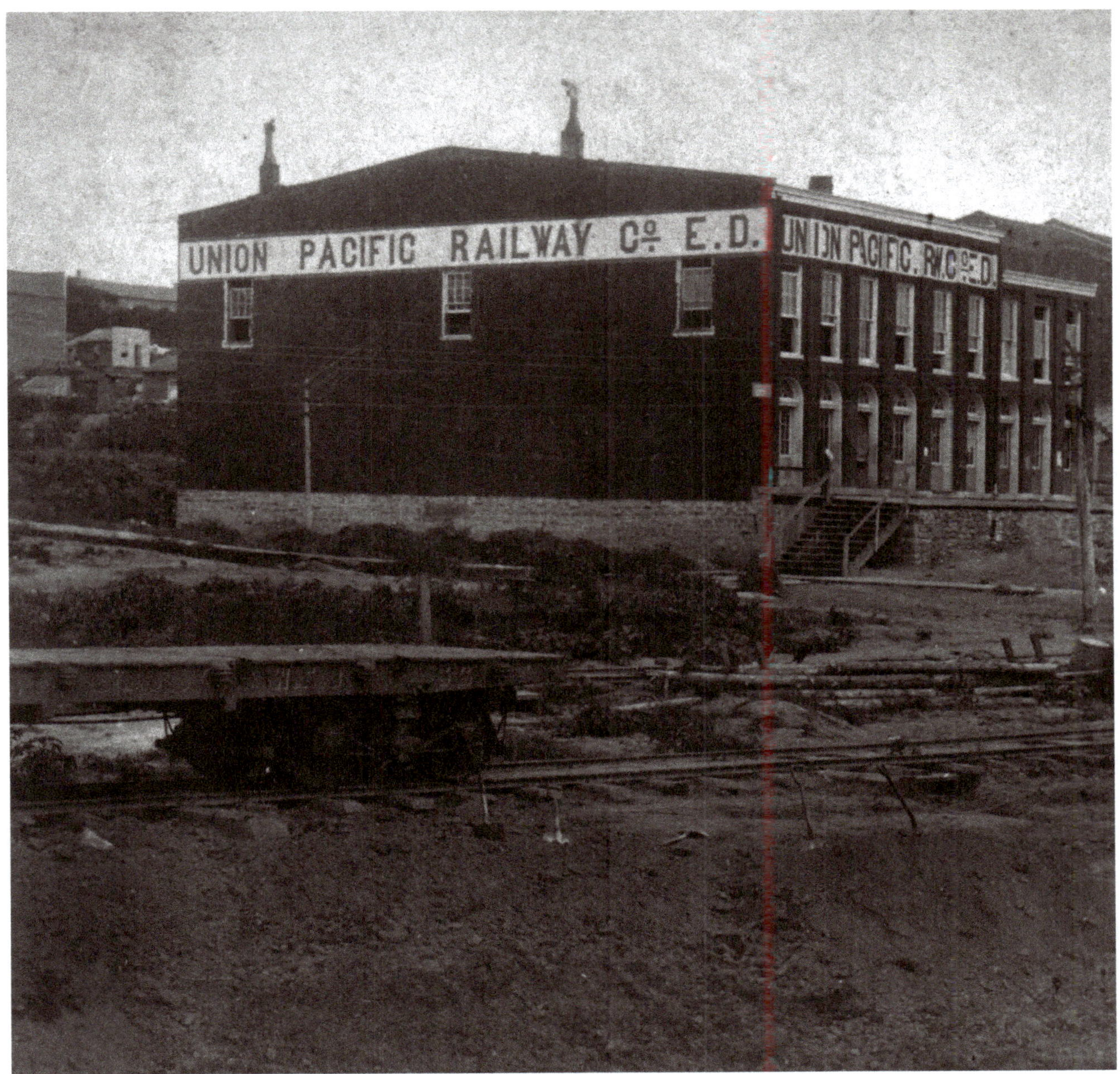

The Union Pacific Railway building in Wyandotte, Kansas, was documented by a photographer in 1867. Today, Wyandotte is the county in which Kansas City, Kansas, is located. Wyandotte Township was formally dissolved in the 1970s.

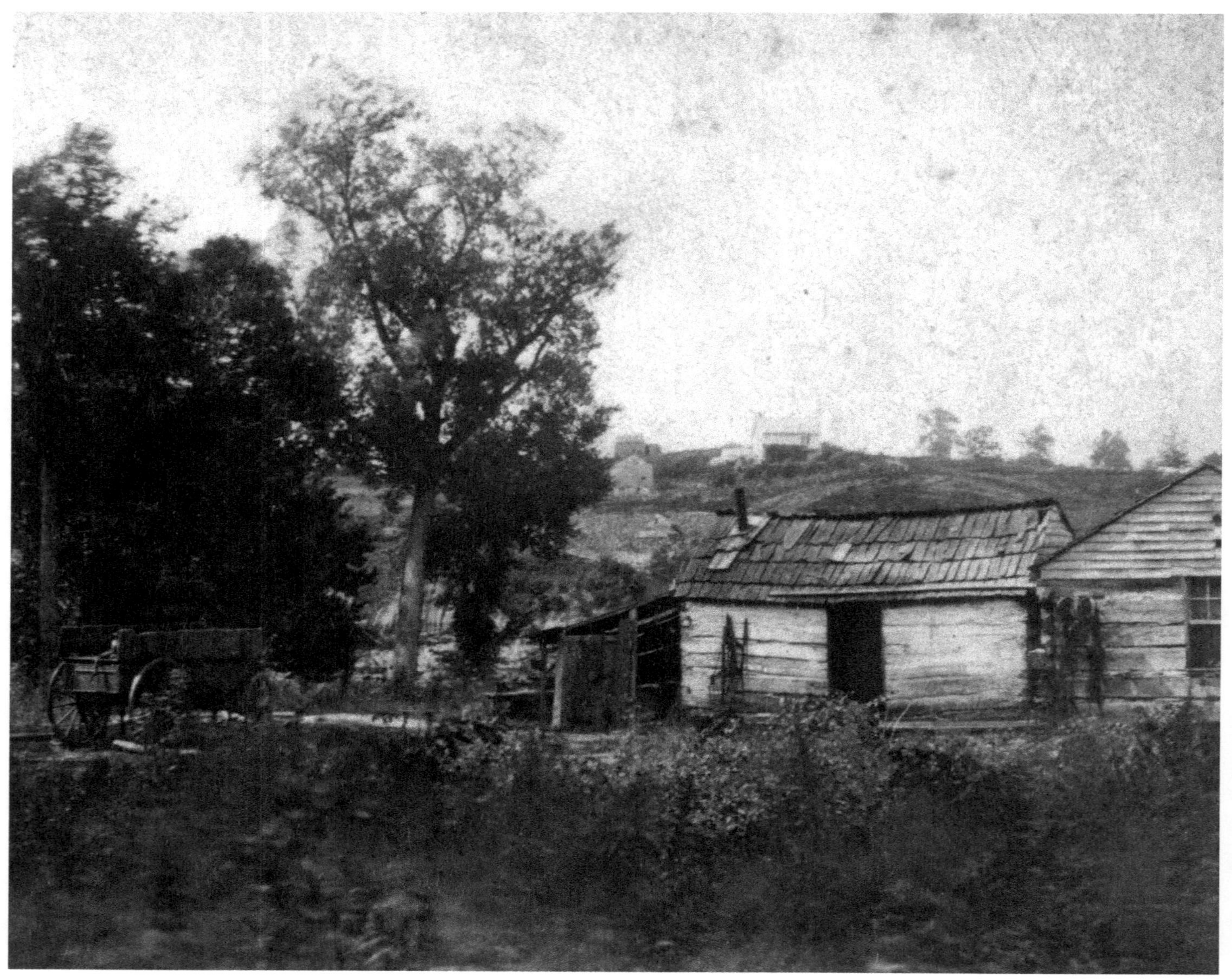

The photographs of Alexander Gardner helped document battles during the Civil War. Two years after the war was over, he photographed this primitive farmhouse near the Missouri state line. The photo was part of a series charting the path of the Union Pacific Railroad's Eastern Division.

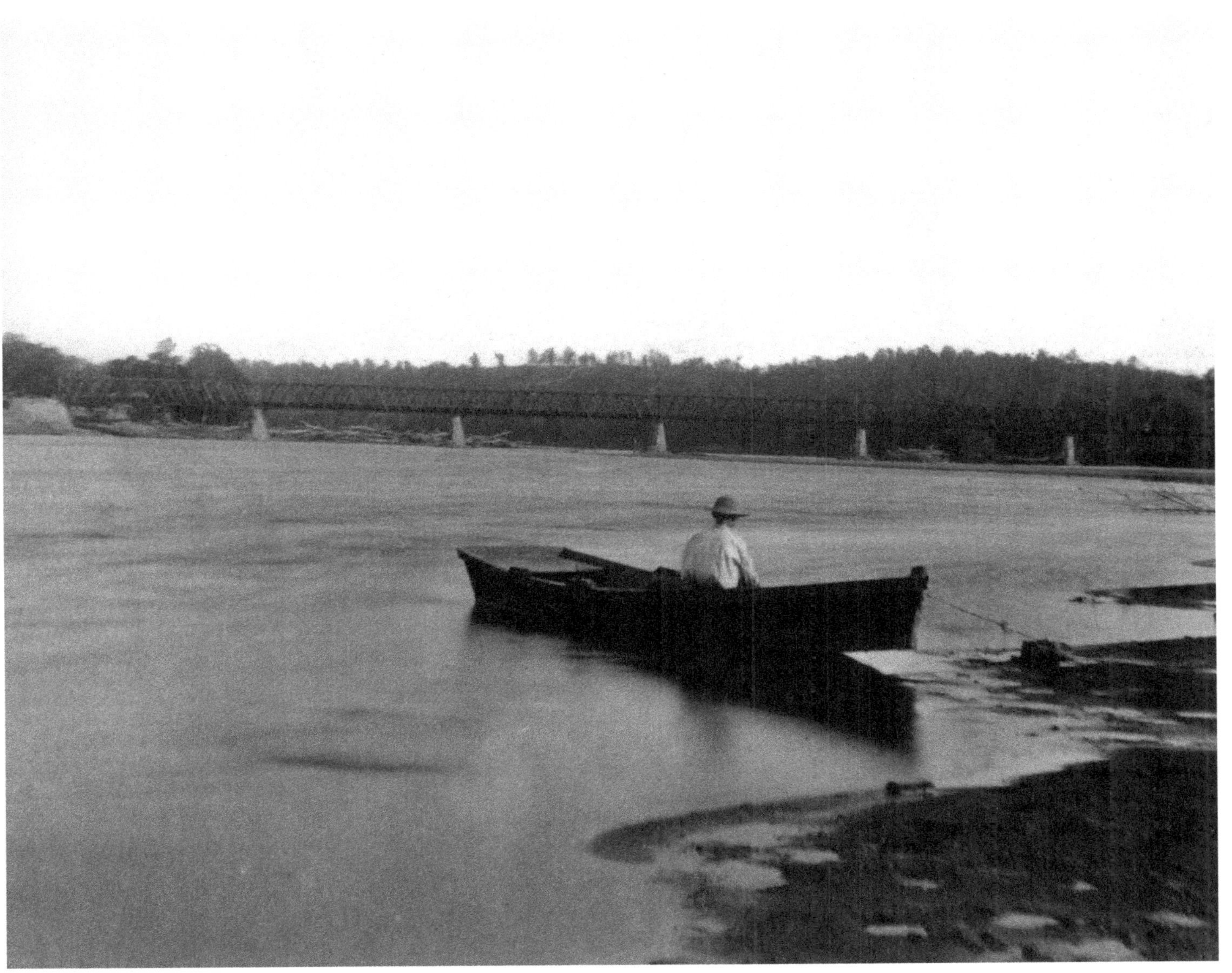

In this 1867 photo in Wyandotte, the occupant of a boat faces the turnpike bridge spanning the Kansas River. The river, often referred to as the Kaw, empties into the Missouri River near Kansas City.

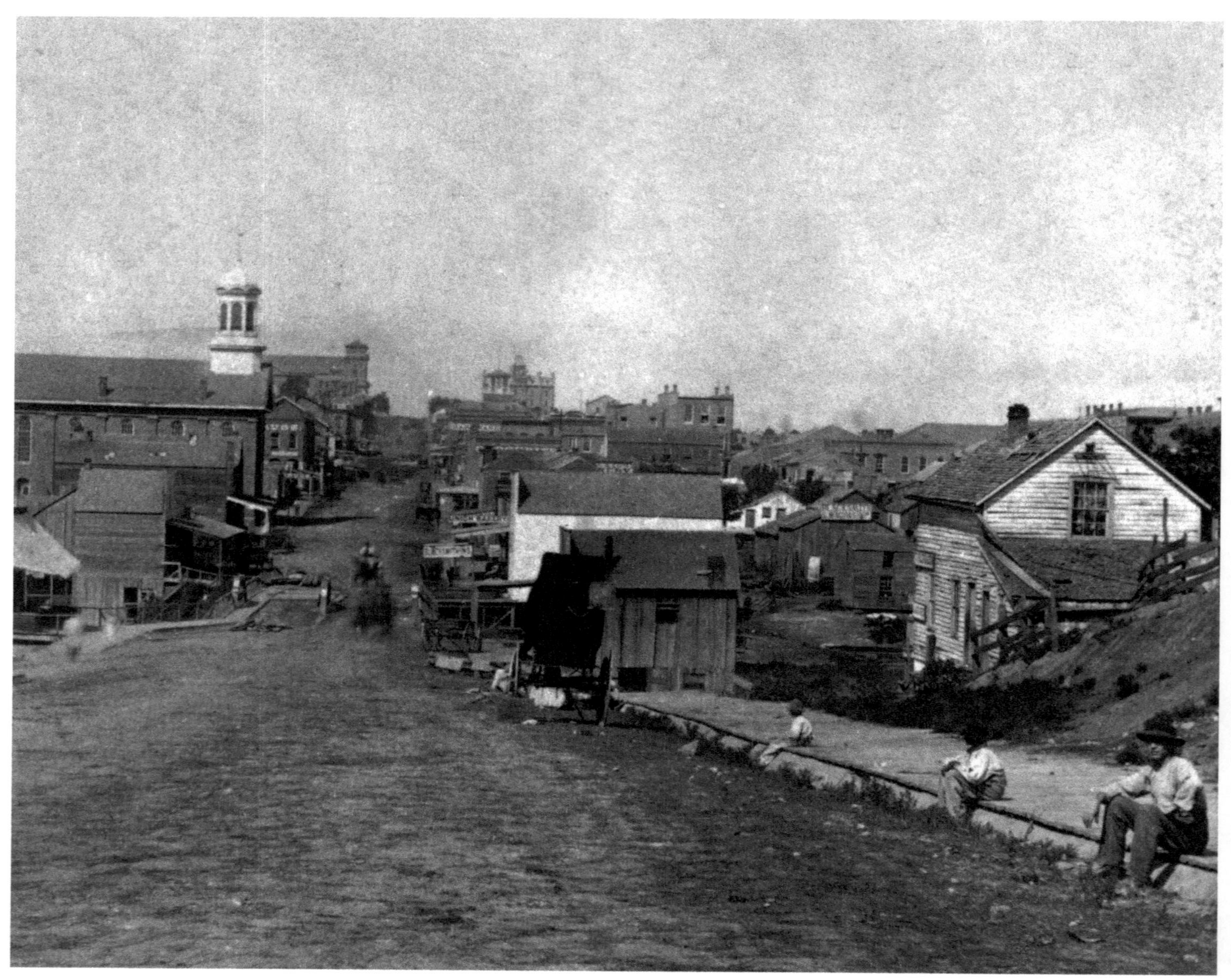

Several people rest on the curb in Leavenworth. The small wood-frame structures in the foreground contrast with several larger buildings in the background including what appears to be a church, on the left, and Leavenworth Public School across the street on the right.

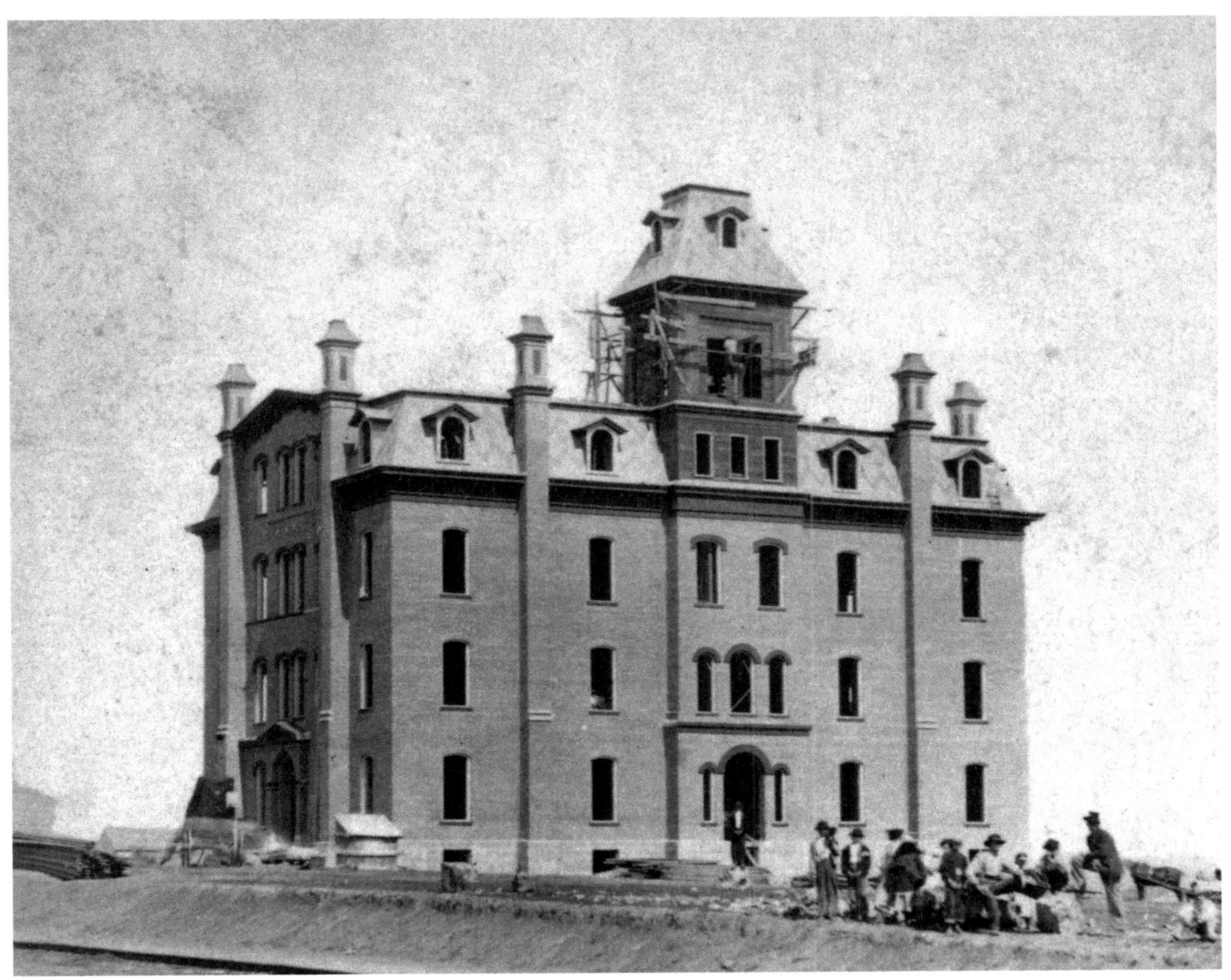

A group of men gather in front of the new Leavenworth Public School, an impressive structure that was under construction when this photo was taken. Scaffolding is visible around the tower at the center of the building.

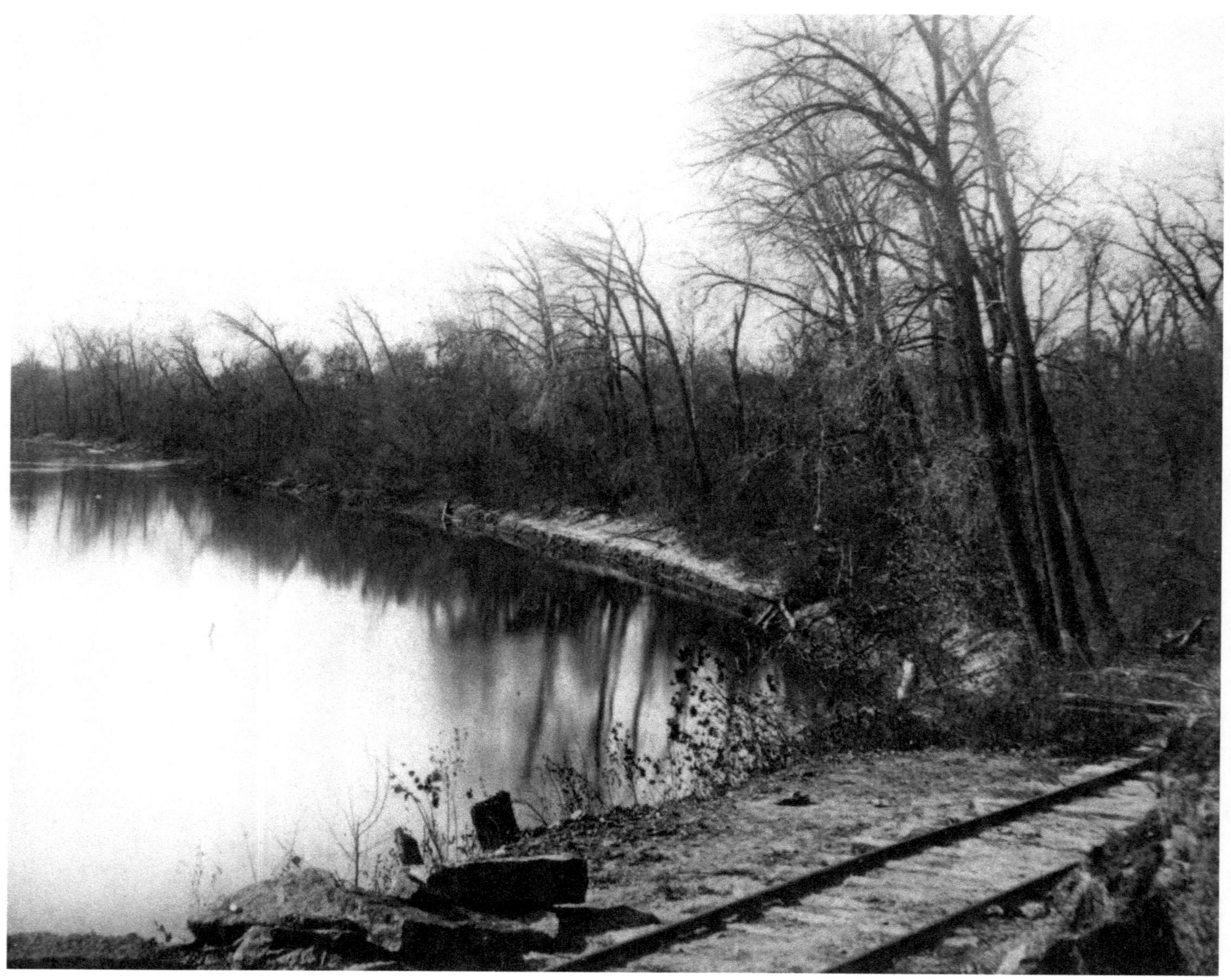

In 1867, Alexander Gardner documented train tracks running along the edge of the Kansas River in the Delaware Indian Reservation in eastern Kansas. The Delaware tribe was forcibly moved to Kansas from the East, then later migrated to what is now the state of Oklahoma.

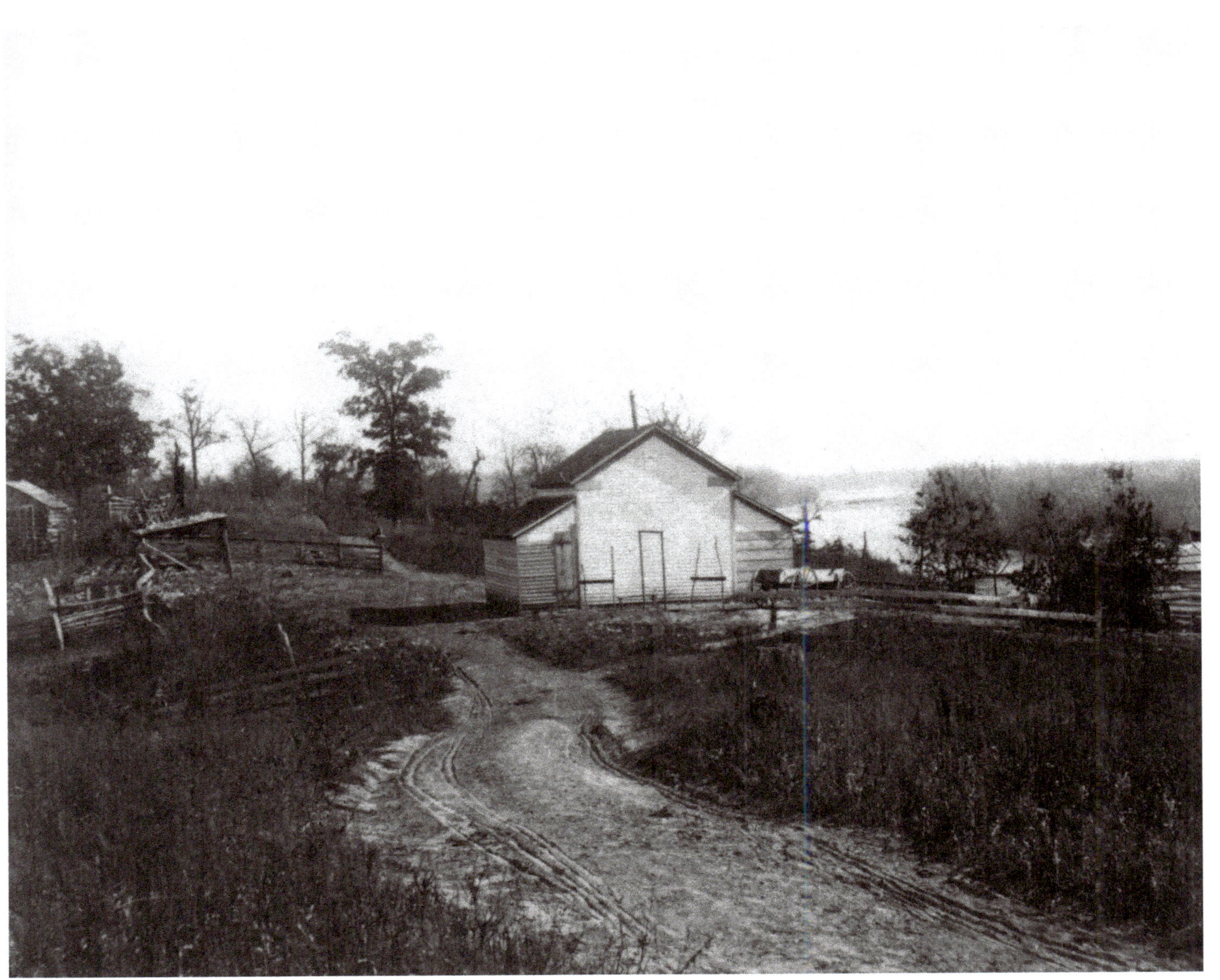

This Native American farm was situated in the eastern section of Kansas on land designated as the Delaware Indian Reservation. The photo was displayed in a gallery in Washington, D.C., in 1867.

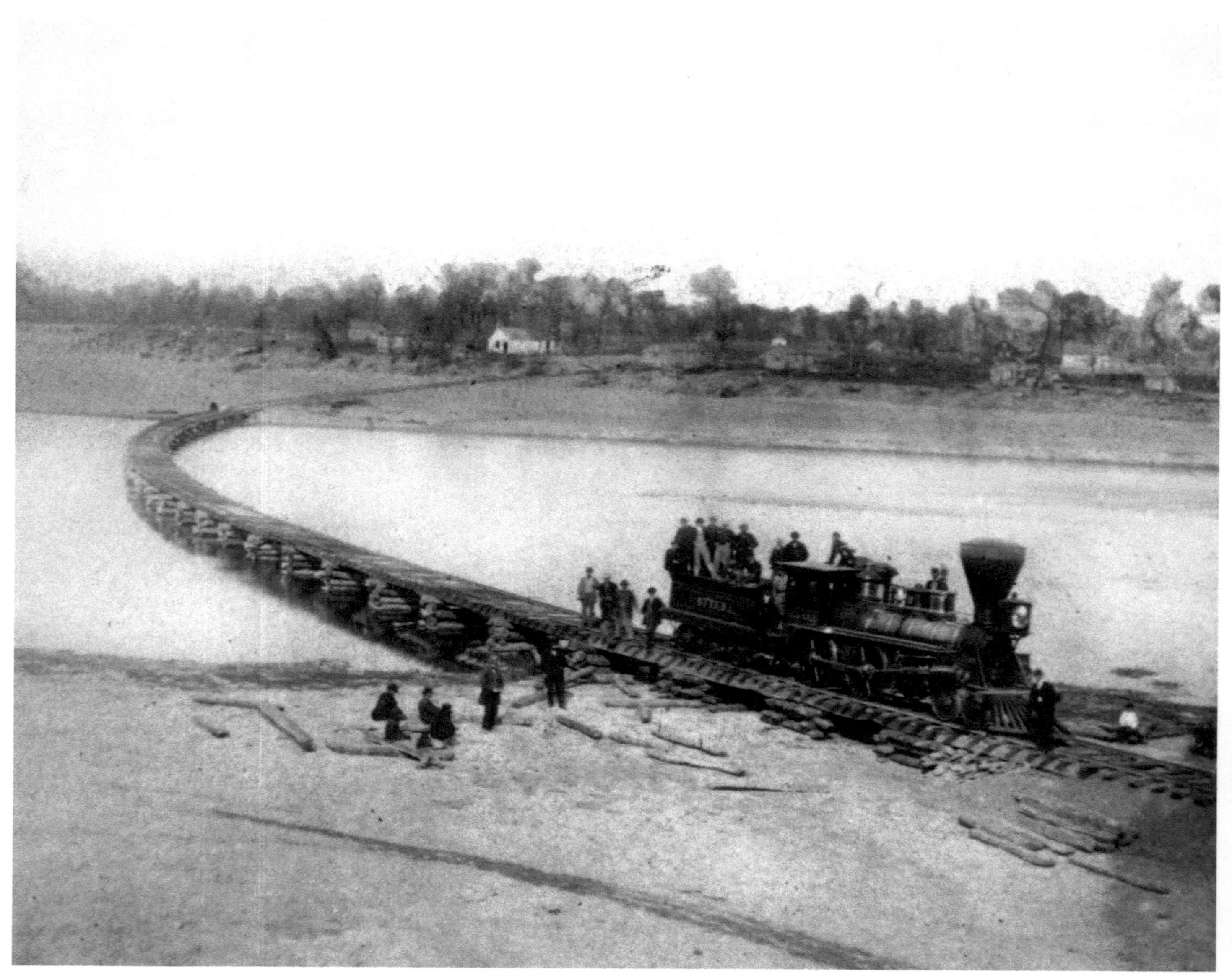

Completion of the Leavenworth, Lawrence and Galveston Railroad bridge across the Kansas River near Lawrence enabled the railroad to meet a deadline to receive the proceeds from county bonds. The requirement was that track be completed between Lawrence and Ottawa.

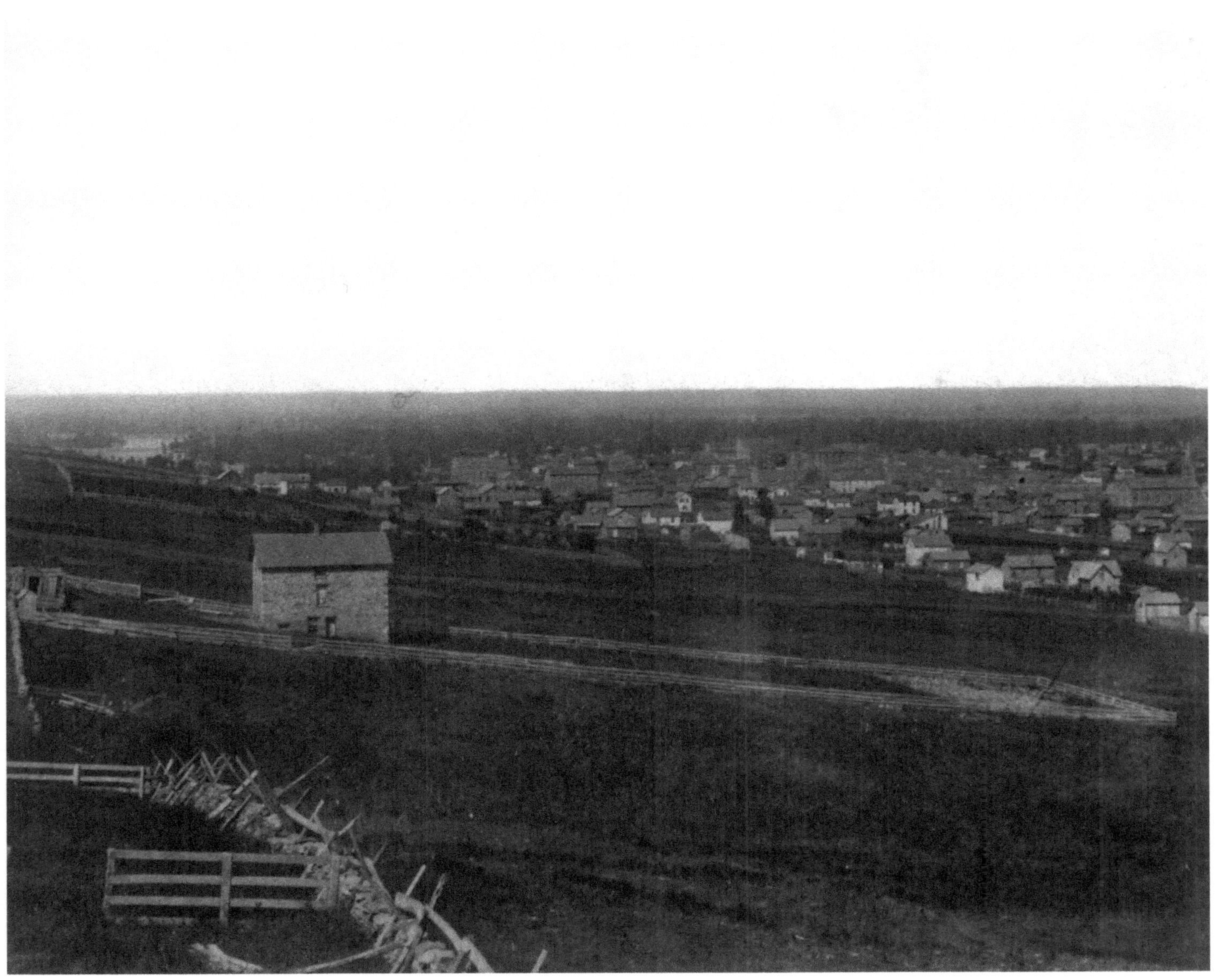

This Alexander Gardner photo identifies the scene as Fort Union in Lawrence. Because there is not sufficient evidence that a Fort Union existed in Lawrence, Gardner may have been referring to Fort Wakarusa, established in 1857 five miles southeast of Lawrence, or possibly Camp Ewing. Camp Ewing, a Civil War installation, later became Camp Lookout and then Fort Ulysses. It was built on Mt. Oread, current site of the University of Kansas.

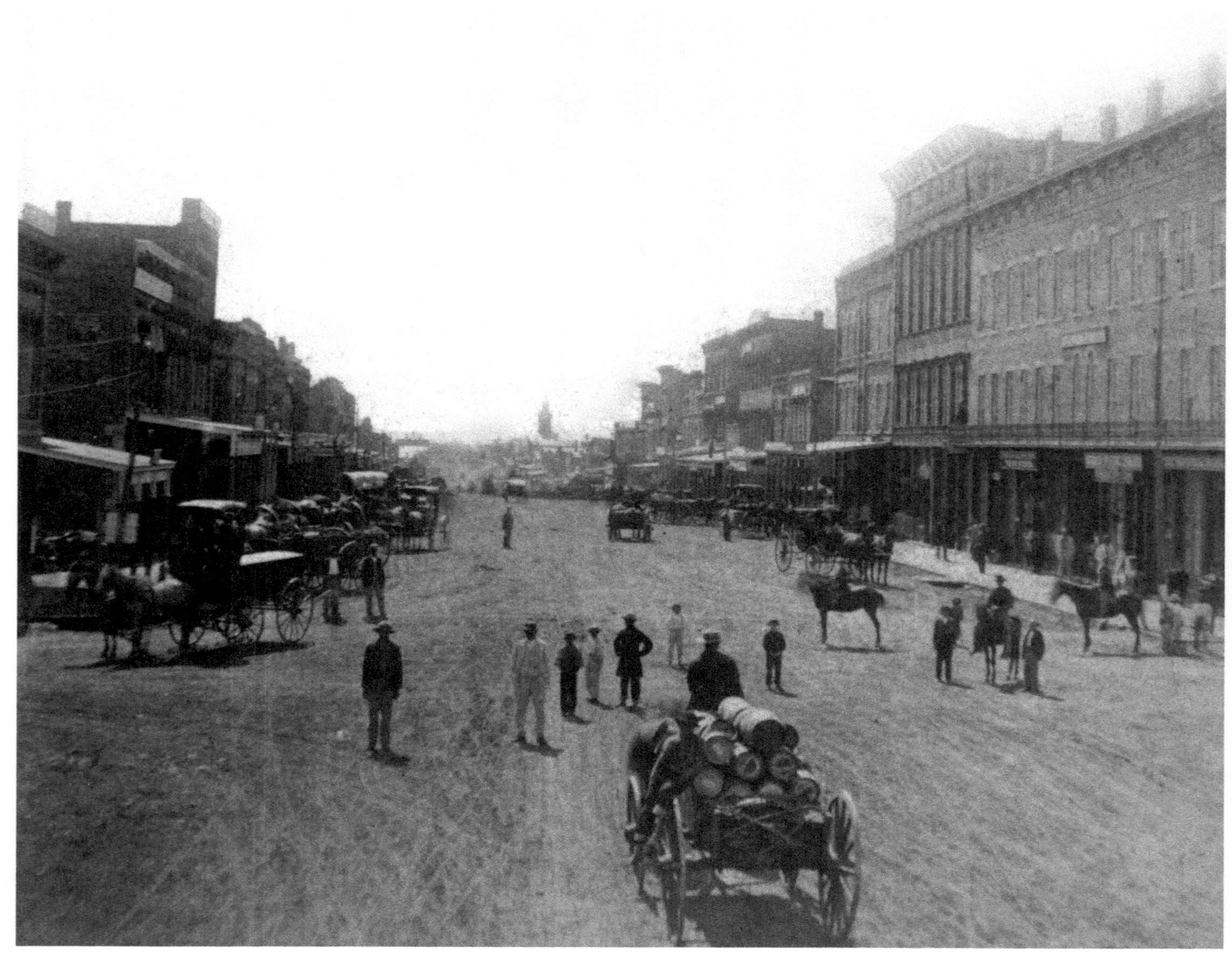

Pictured is an unpaved Massachusetts Street, the business center of Lawrence, in 1867. The thoroughfare was named to honor the Massachusetts Emigrant Aid Society, or Company, which founded Lawrence to bring antislavery proponents—so-called Free-staters—to the Kansas Territory.

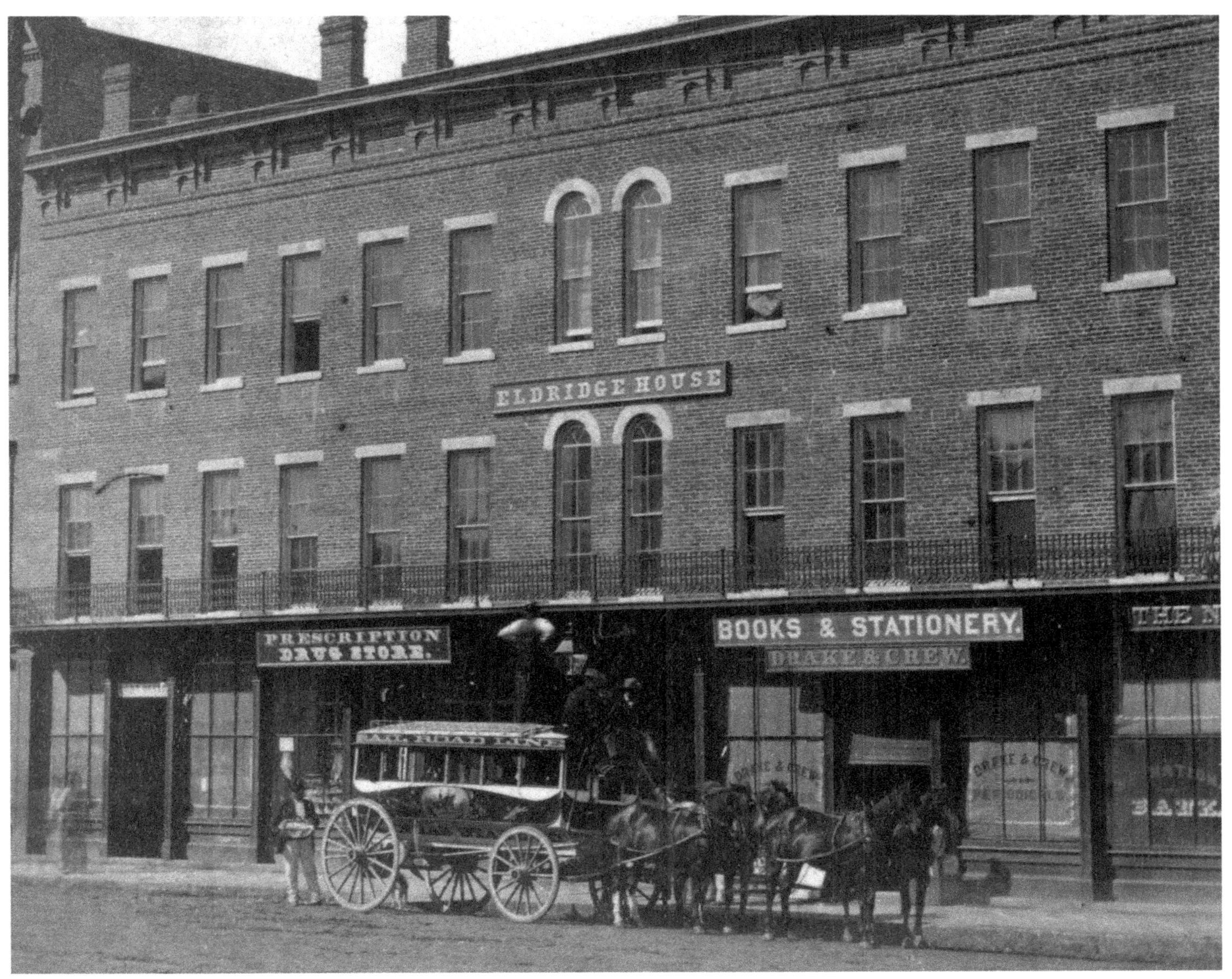

The Eldridge House, a Lawrence hotel with roots predating the Civil War, appears here in 1867. An institution in the city, it began as the Free State Hotel in 1855, was twice destroyed by pro-slavery forces, and then was rebuilt by Colonel Shalor Eldridge. The hotel still operates, although it underwent major restorations and modification in 1925 and 1985.

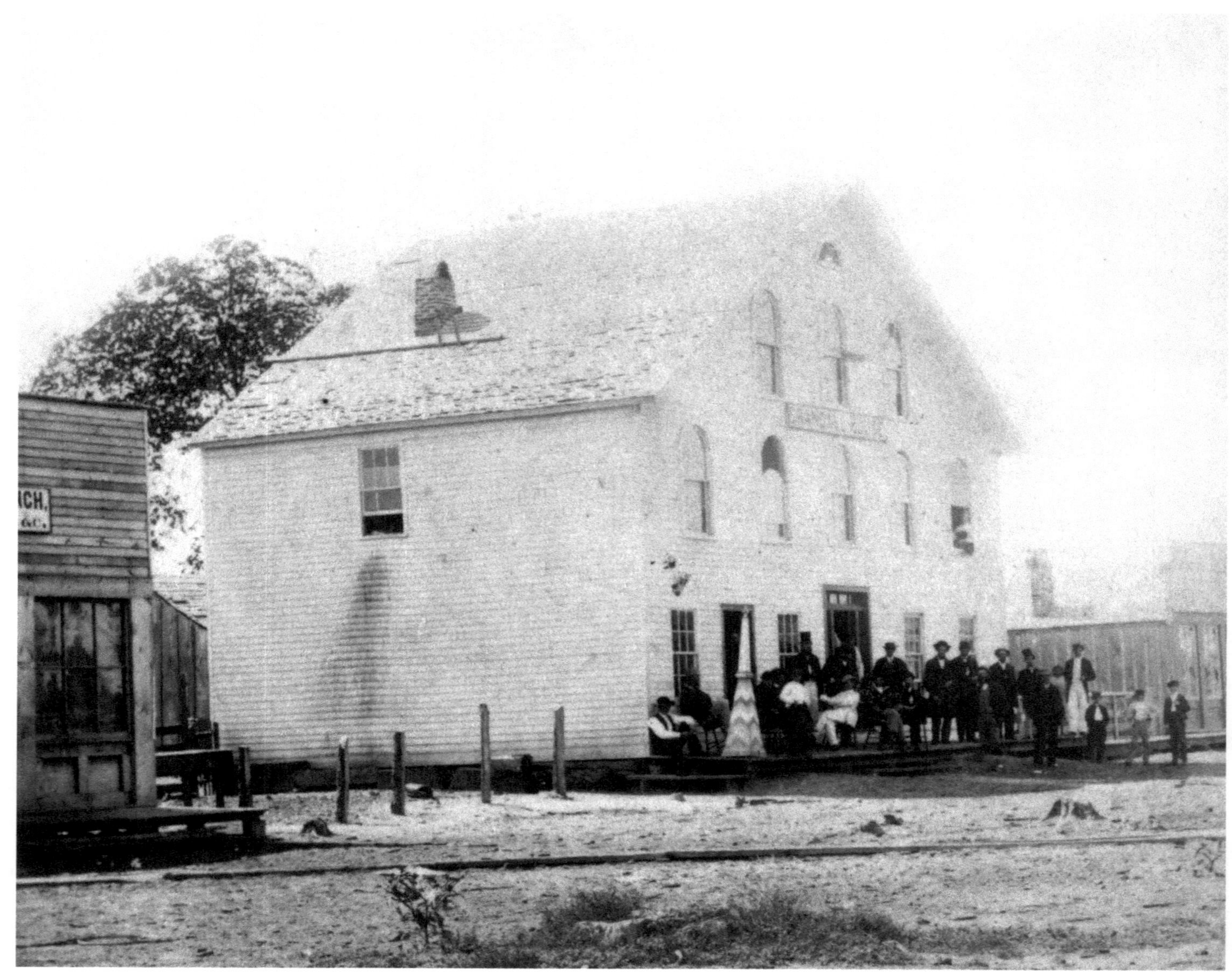

The Crandall House, termed by one historian as "the leading hotel in North Lawrence," as it stood in 1867. The hotel was located across the street and south of the Kansas Pacific Depot. The history of North Lawrence—located on the north bank of the Kansas River—is explored in *North Lawrence, Kansas: A Brief History* by Lynn H. Nelson (1995).

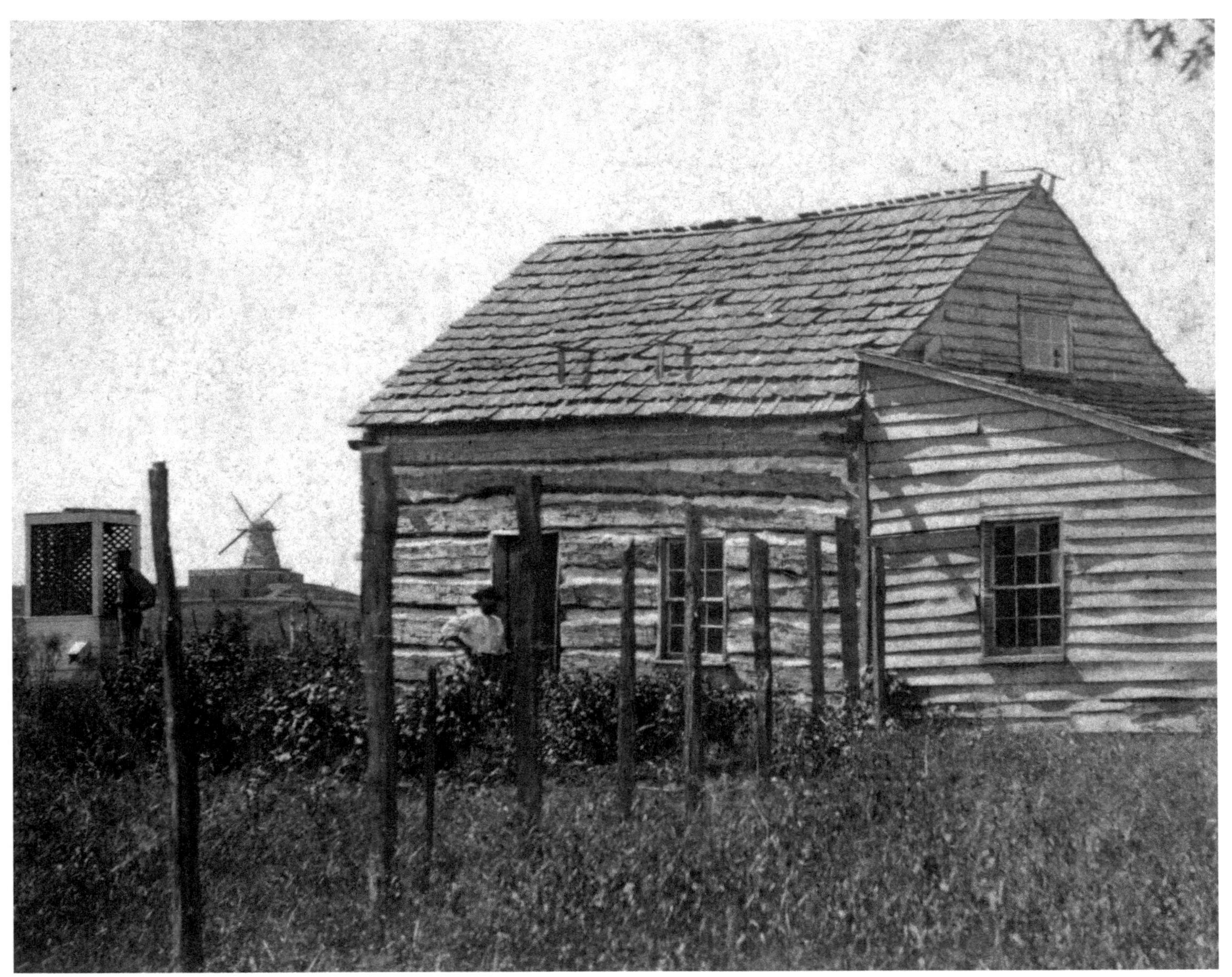

Pictured are the house and well where, in 1858, abolitionist Jim Lane killed Captain Gaius Jenkins, a neighbor and fellow Free-stater, over a boundary dispute. Lane was elected one of Kansas's first senators and served as a Union general during the Civil War.

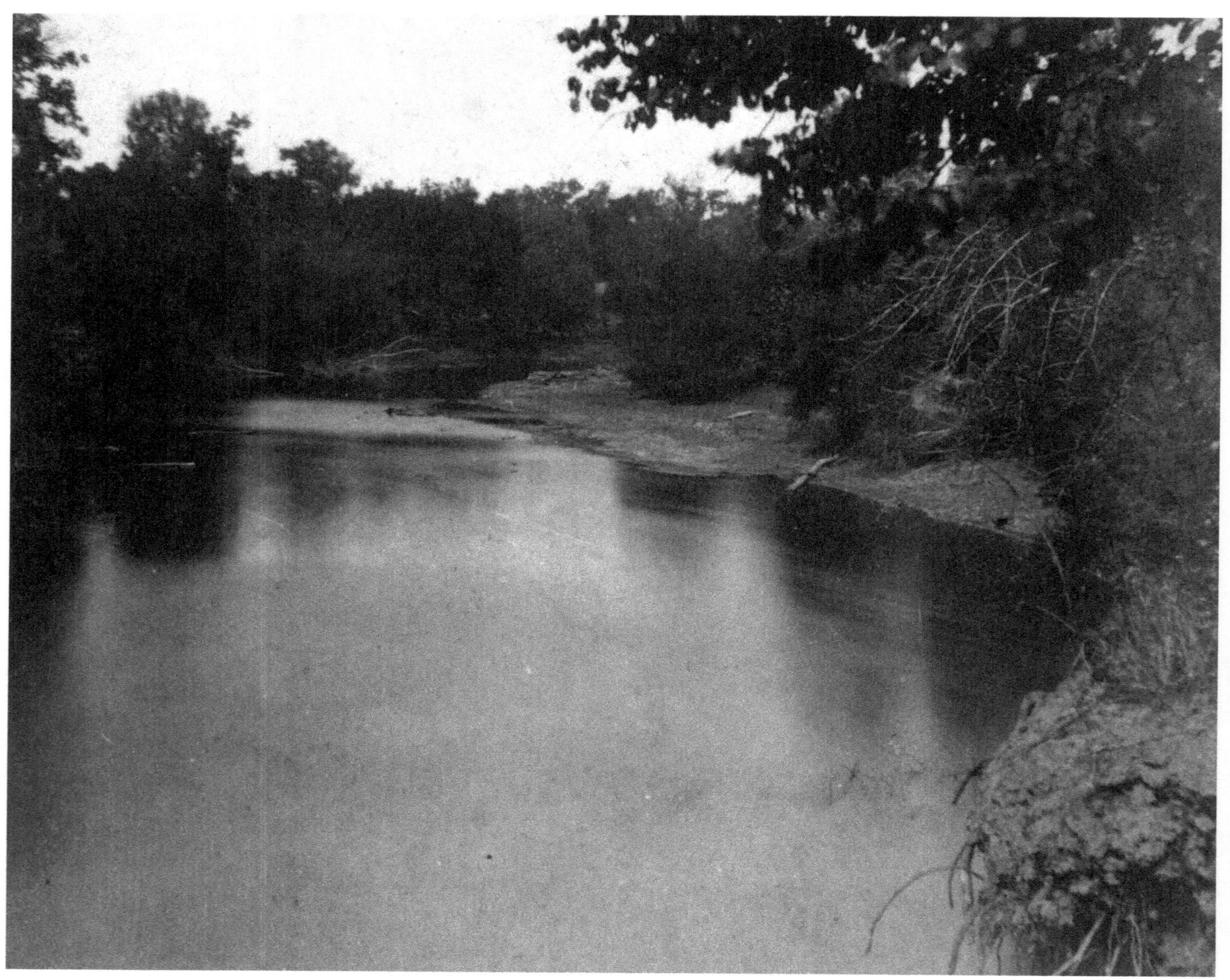

Grasshopper Creek, identified as being located 336 miles west of St. Louis, fed into the Delaware River. Grasshoppers have a significant place—though not always positive—in Kansas history. Grasshopper plagues, dust storms, drought, floods, and tornados were among the hardships endured by early settlers.

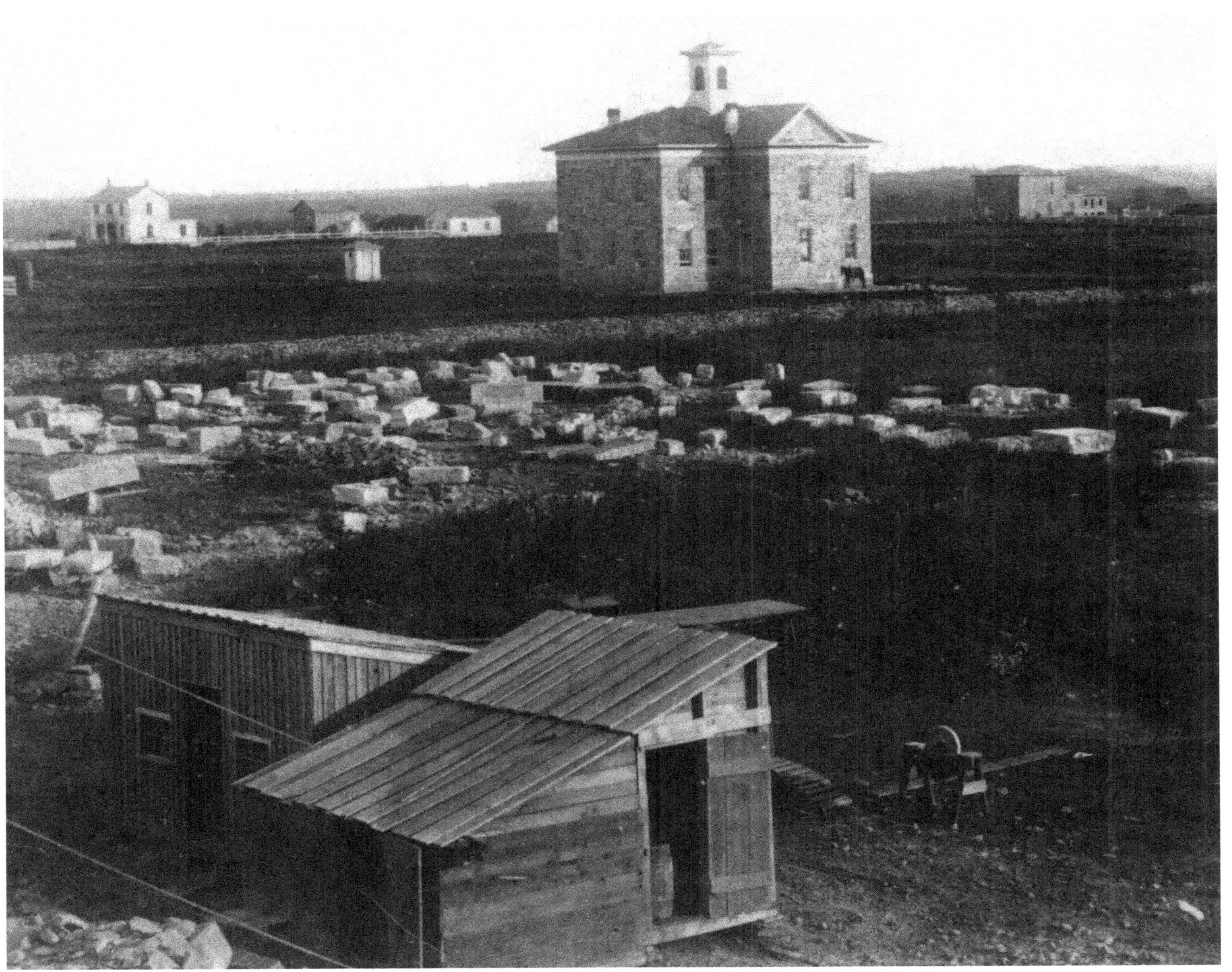

Lincoln College, also referred to as Congregational College, stands tall in an 1867 Alexander Gardner photograph. It became Washburn College in 1868 and has since become a university. The original Lincoln College building pictured in the background no longer exists.

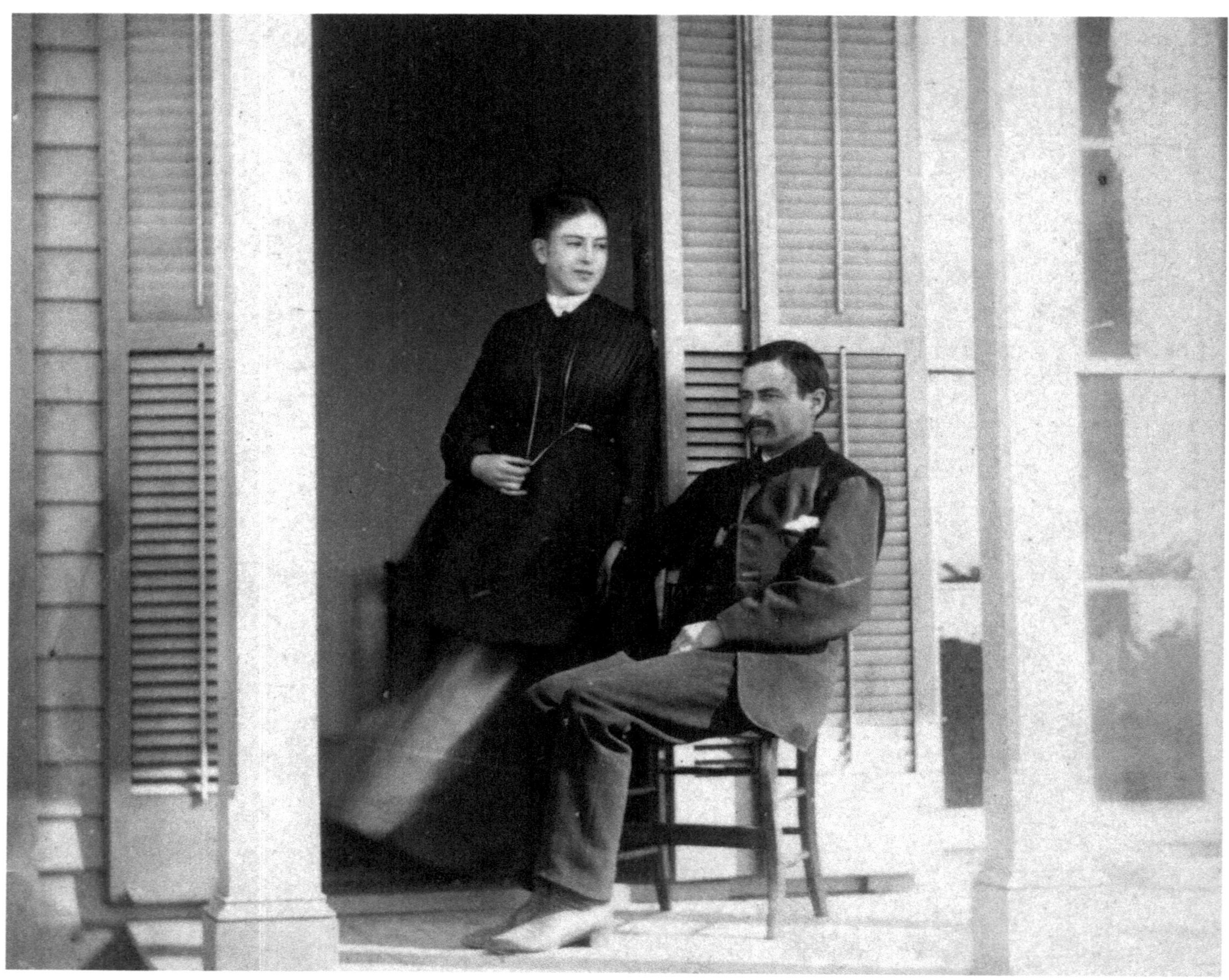

This photo described simply as "View at Mr. Wetherall's, Topeka, Kansas" is reproduced in many histories of early Kansas. But nothing is known about the portrait's background or the people in it. The picture was part of a display in Washington, the nation's capital, in 1867.

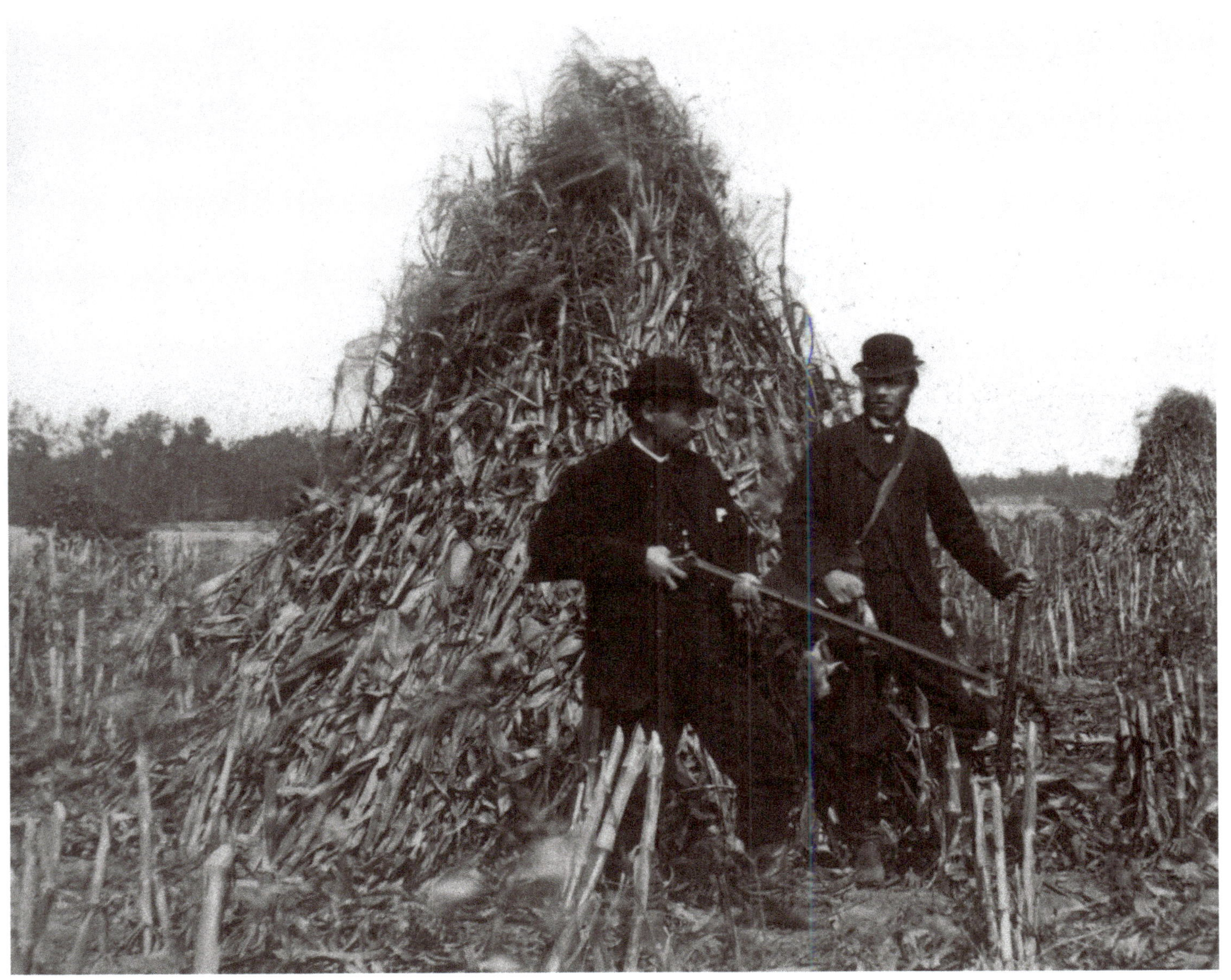

Hunting has been an important part of Kansas culture from the time indigenous peoples hunted for food until the present. These two men, in a cornfield amid shocks of corn, are prairie hunting in the 1860s.

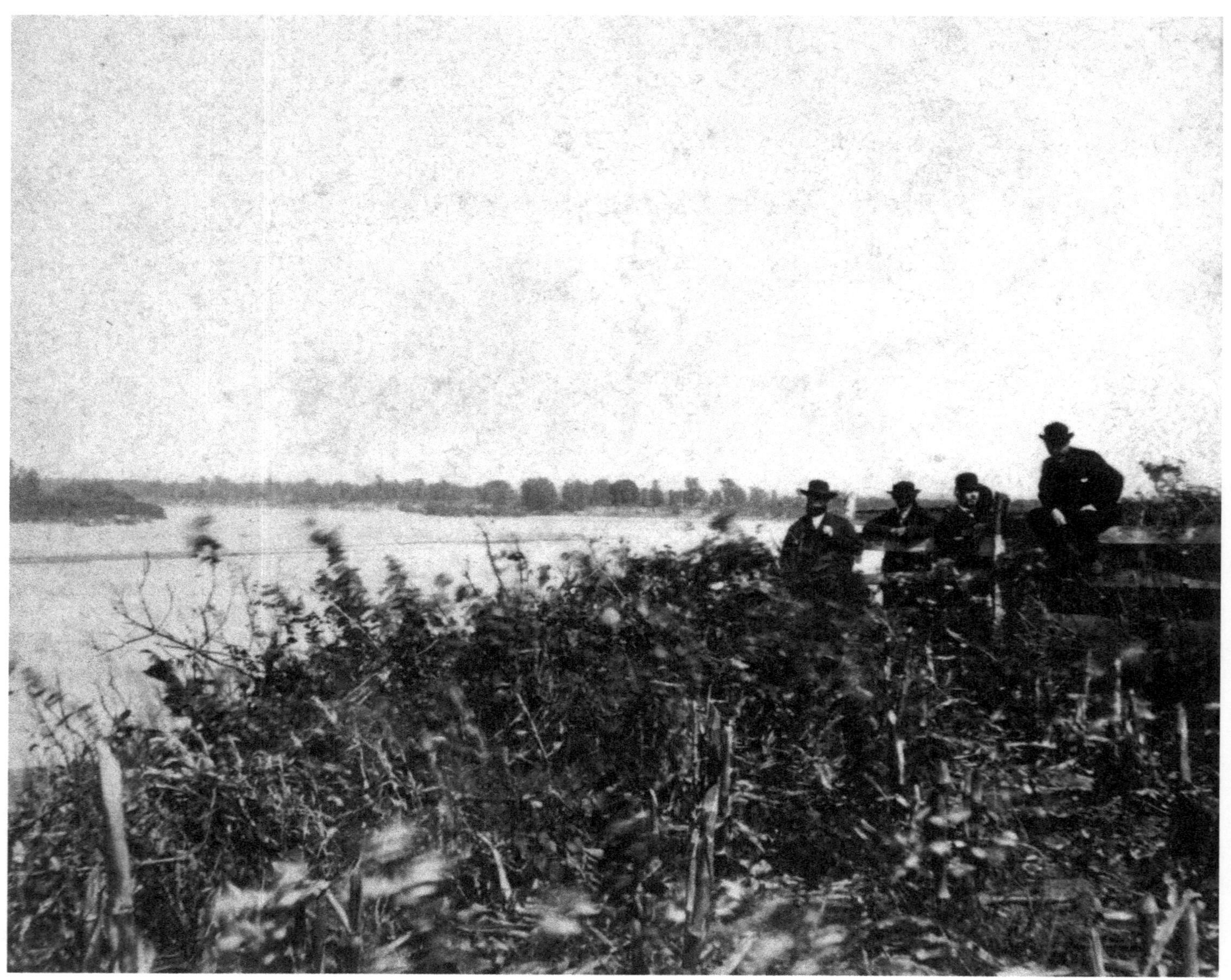

When Alexander Gardner photographed the frontier in 1867, the idea was to return with images of the West, not detailed written descriptions. Gardner's notes for this image identify it as a view of the Kansas River in Topeka. The notes do not mention the four men in suits and hats along the fence, who look somewhat out of place.

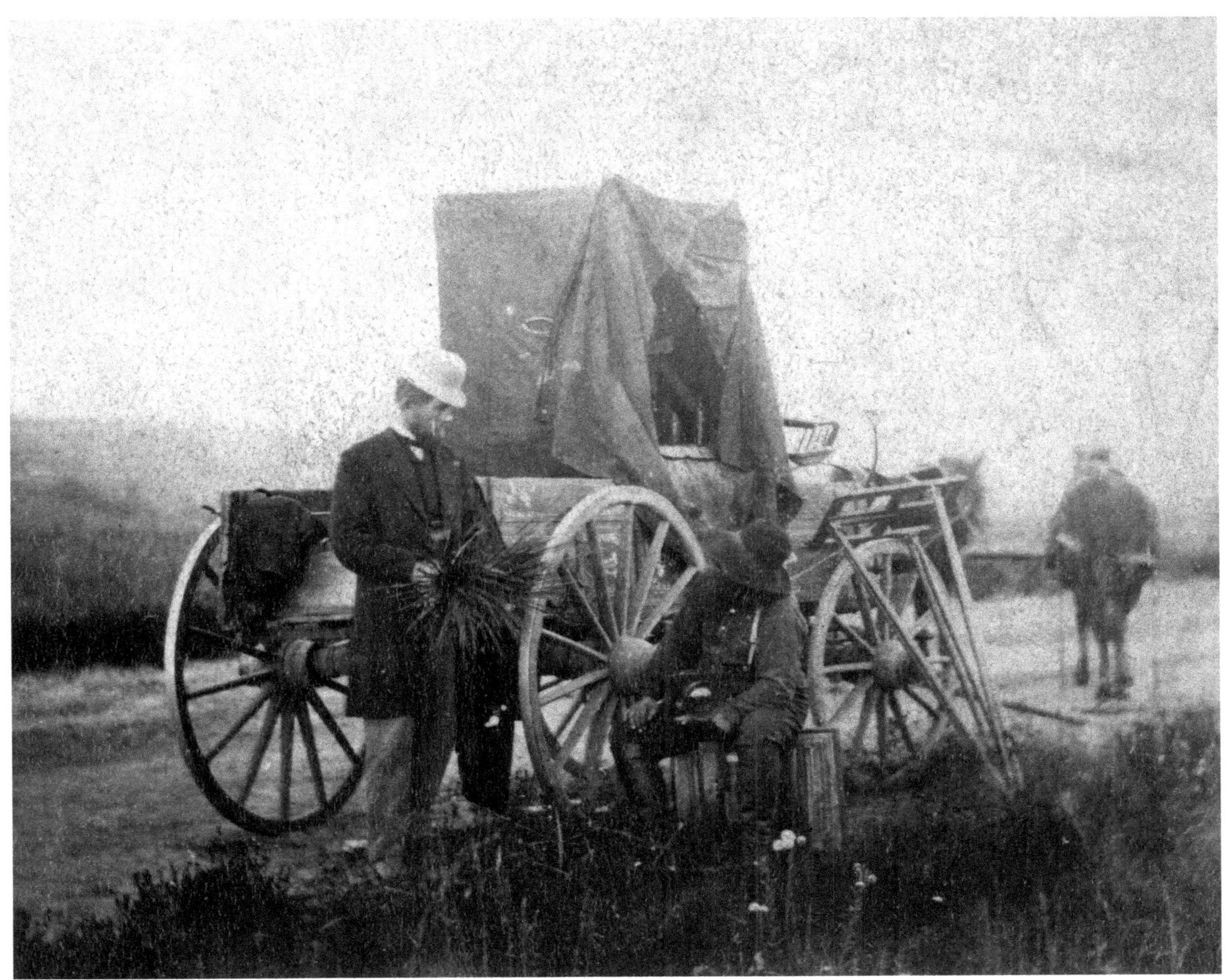

A man stops to examine a rare specimen found by the road on a hill above Fort Riley. A curiosity of the picture is that Alexander Gardner, the photographer, is seated next to the wagon. Many of the existing photos of the state's early days were taken by Gardner.

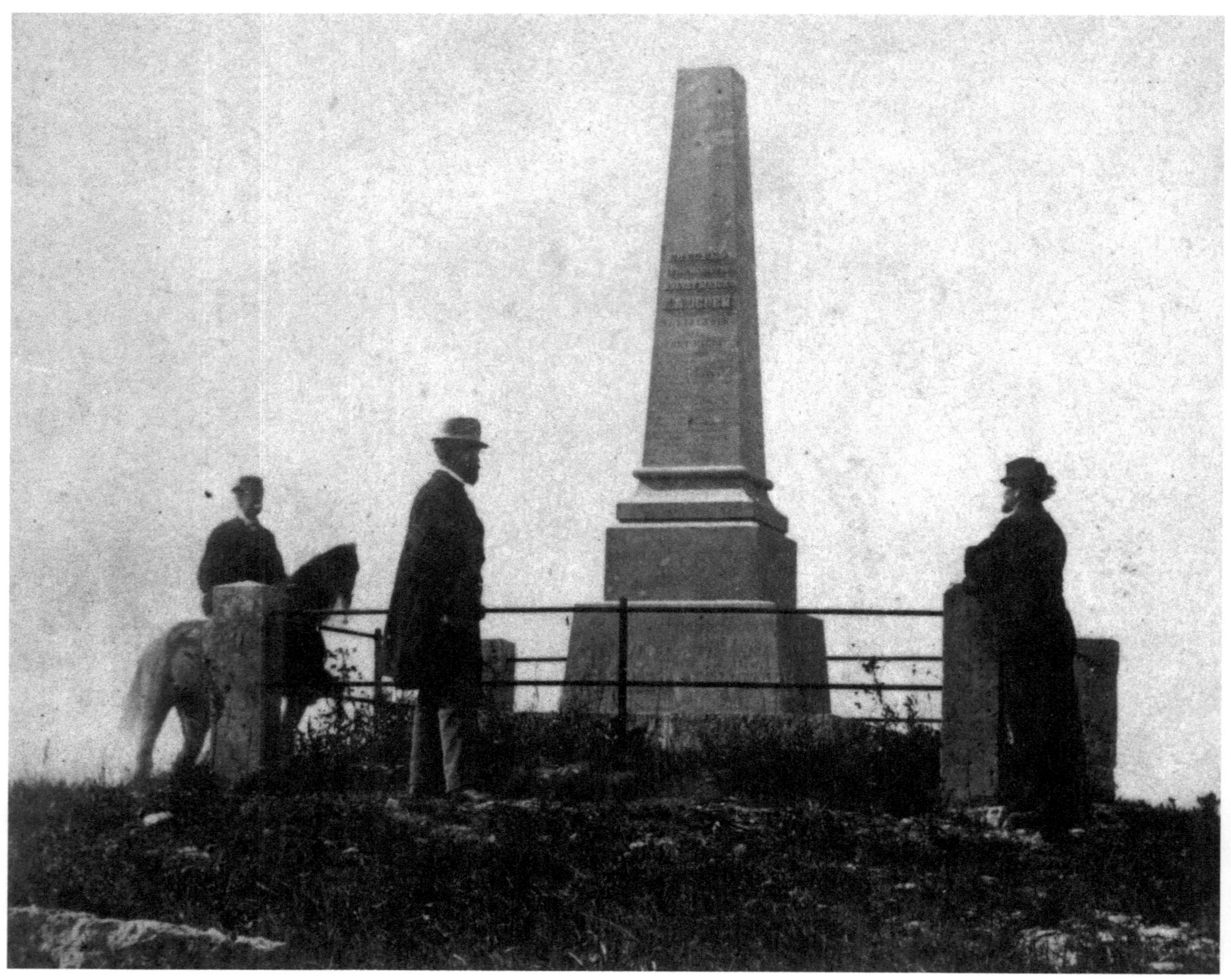

Several men stop to examine a monument erected to honor Major E. A. Ogden near Fort Riley. Ogden is credited with supervising the construction of the fort. Ogden, the town named in his honor, is in Riley County near present-day Manhattan.

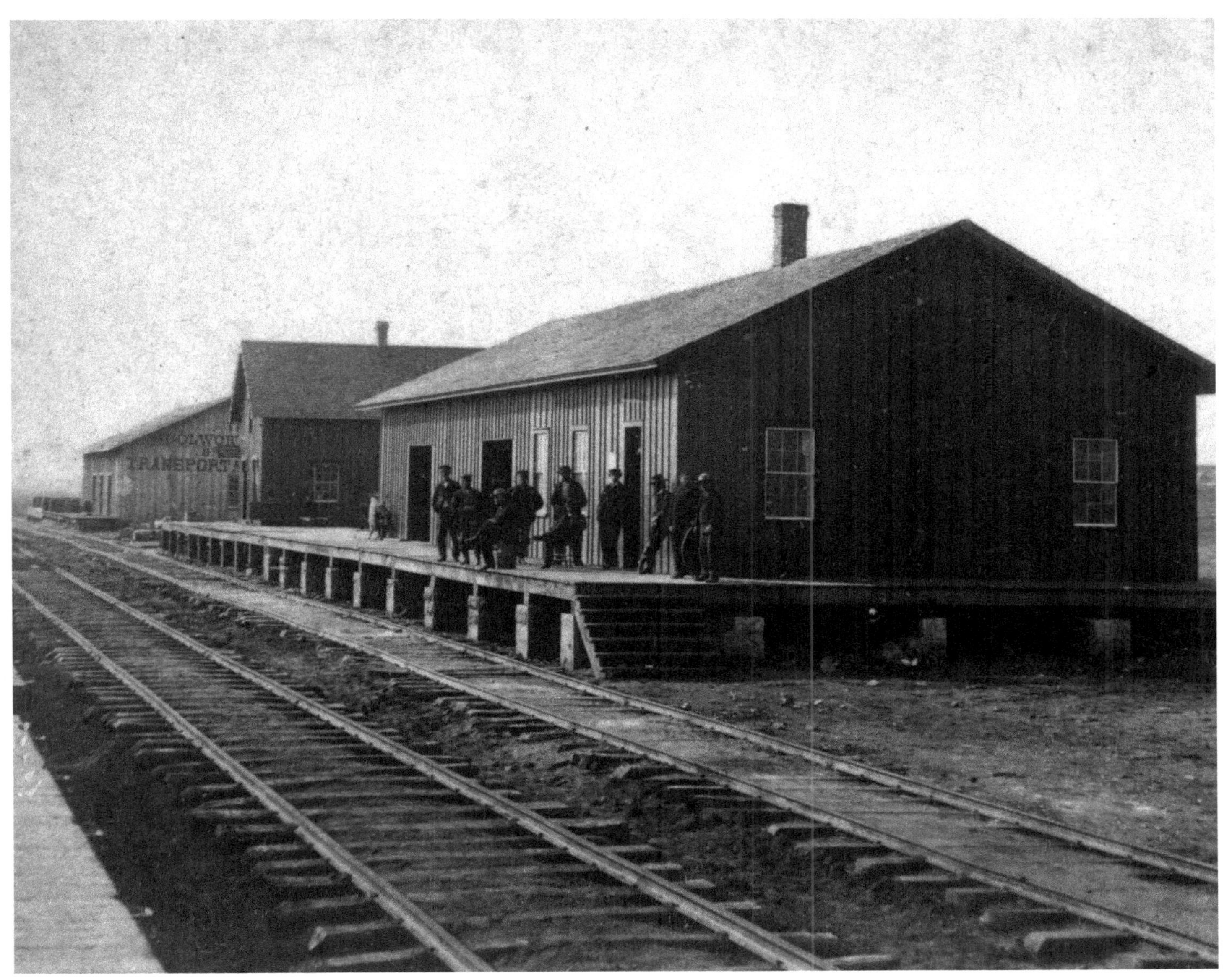

Junction City's Kansas Pacific Railroad depot, pictured in 1867, served as a destination for soldiers stationed at Fort Riley. Just a year earlier, trains began taking passengers from Leavenworth, site of another fort, to Junction City.

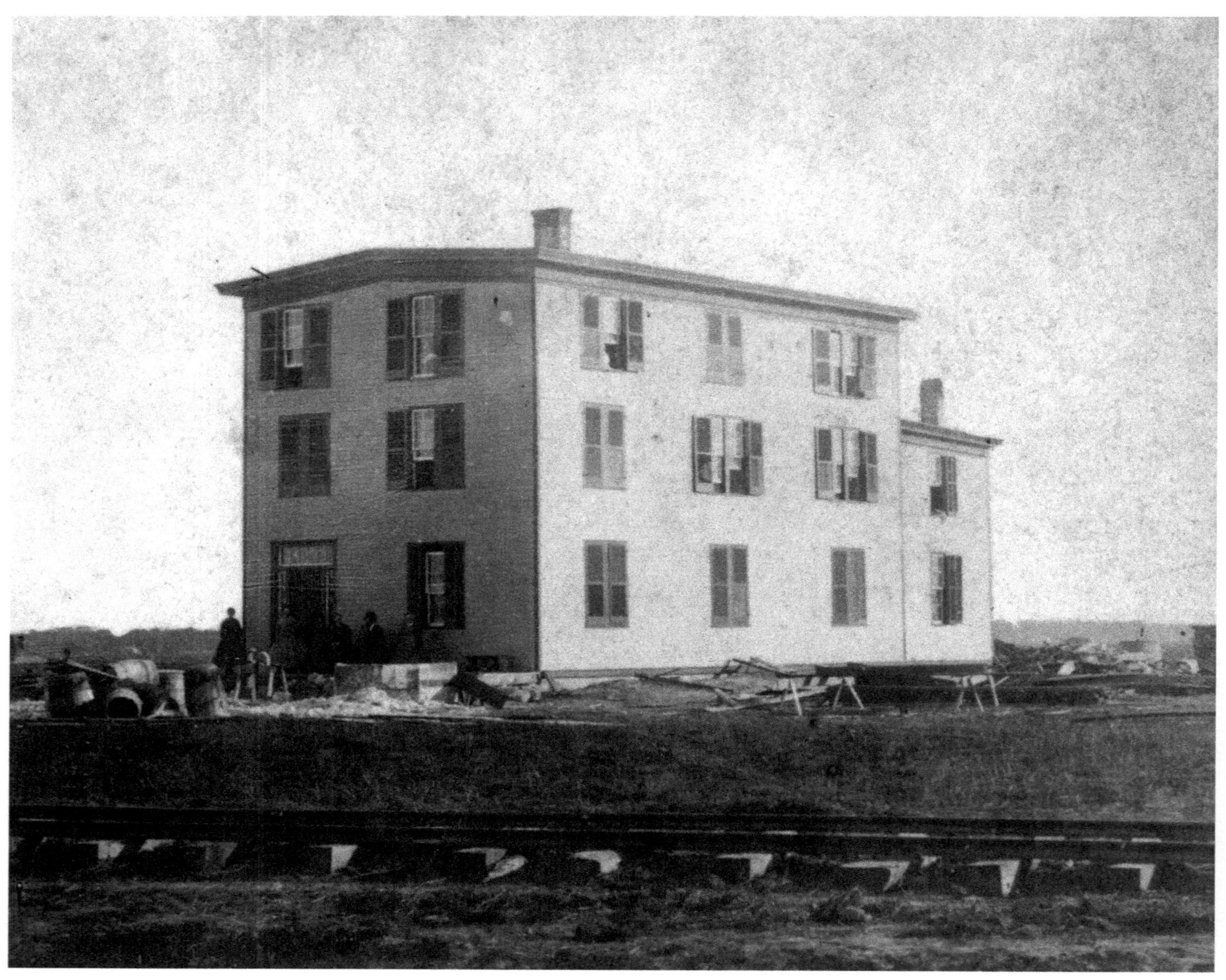

Rail transportation and cattle were key elements in the development of Abilene. Pictured is a photo of Abilene's Drover's Cottage at McCoy's Stock Yard. The women standing in front of the door are wearing skirts supported by crinolines, popular cage-like accessories that gave skirts dome-shaped silhouettes.

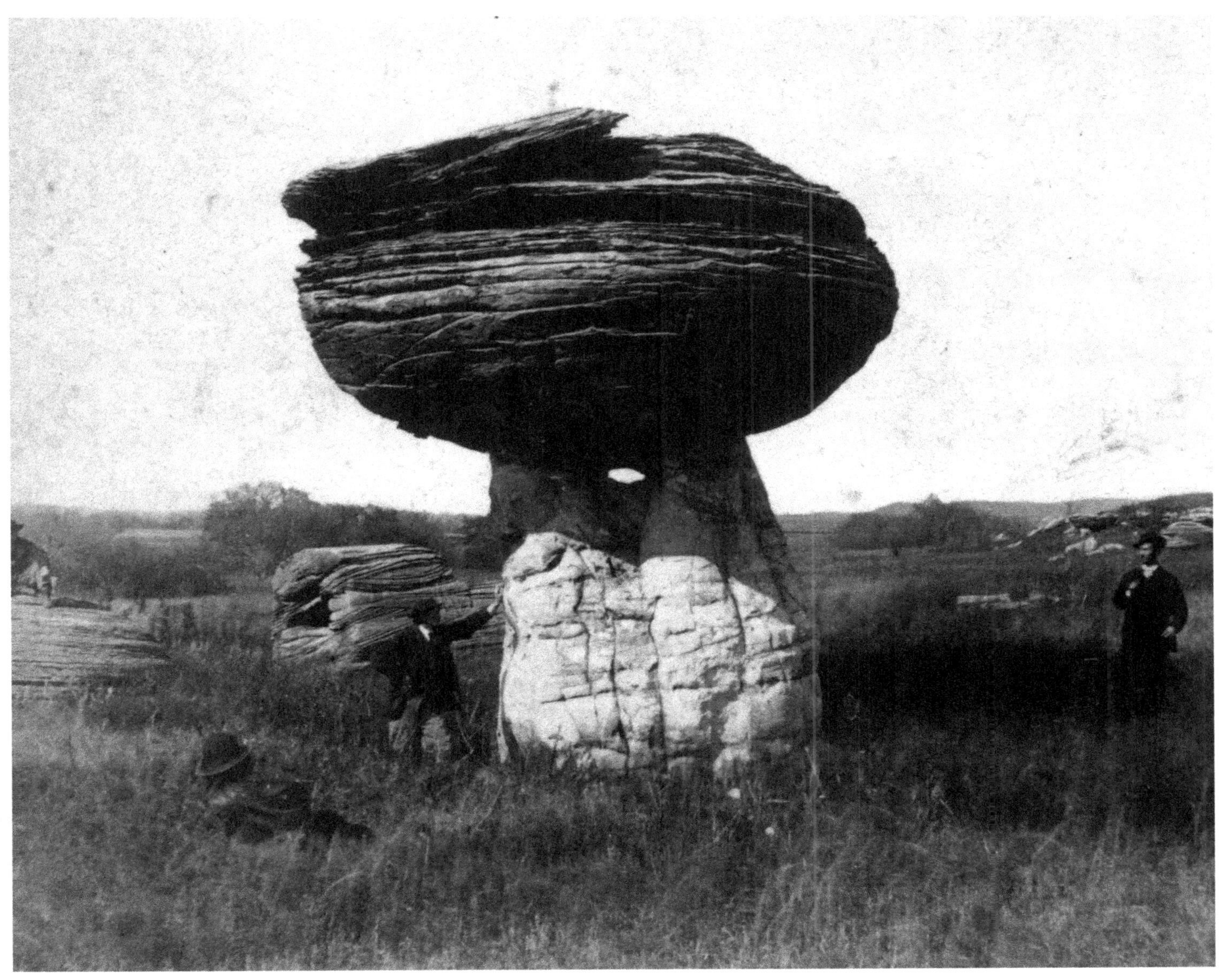

Described as "mushroom rock" by photographer Alexander Gardner, this unusual formation was found on Alum Creek, seven miles east of Fort Harker. Fort Harker, located in Kanapolis, was an active military installation from 1866 to 1872.

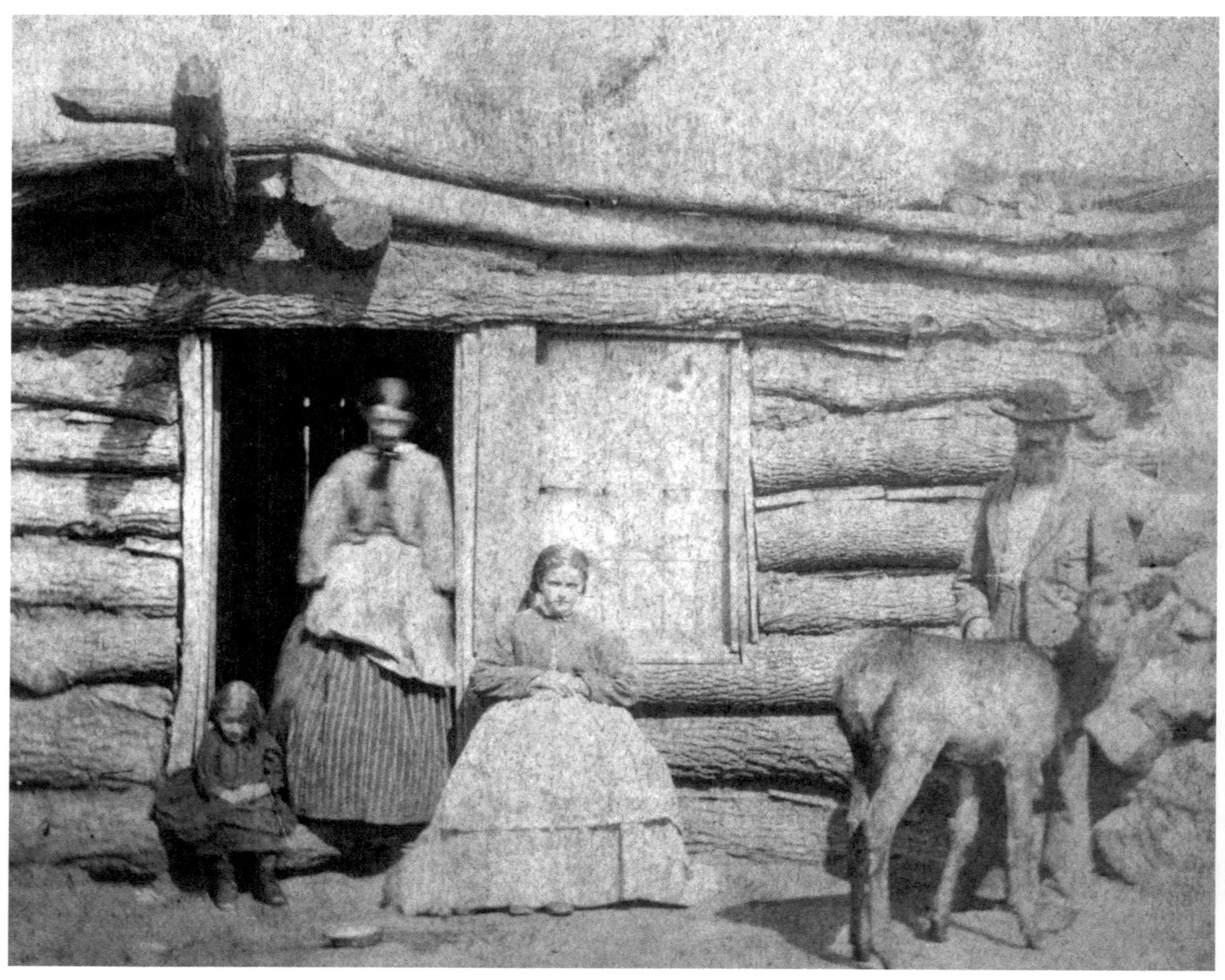

Not all game in central Kansas was hunted or even wild. This pioneer ranch family in Clear Creek, an Ellsworth County township, is pictured with a tame elk calf.

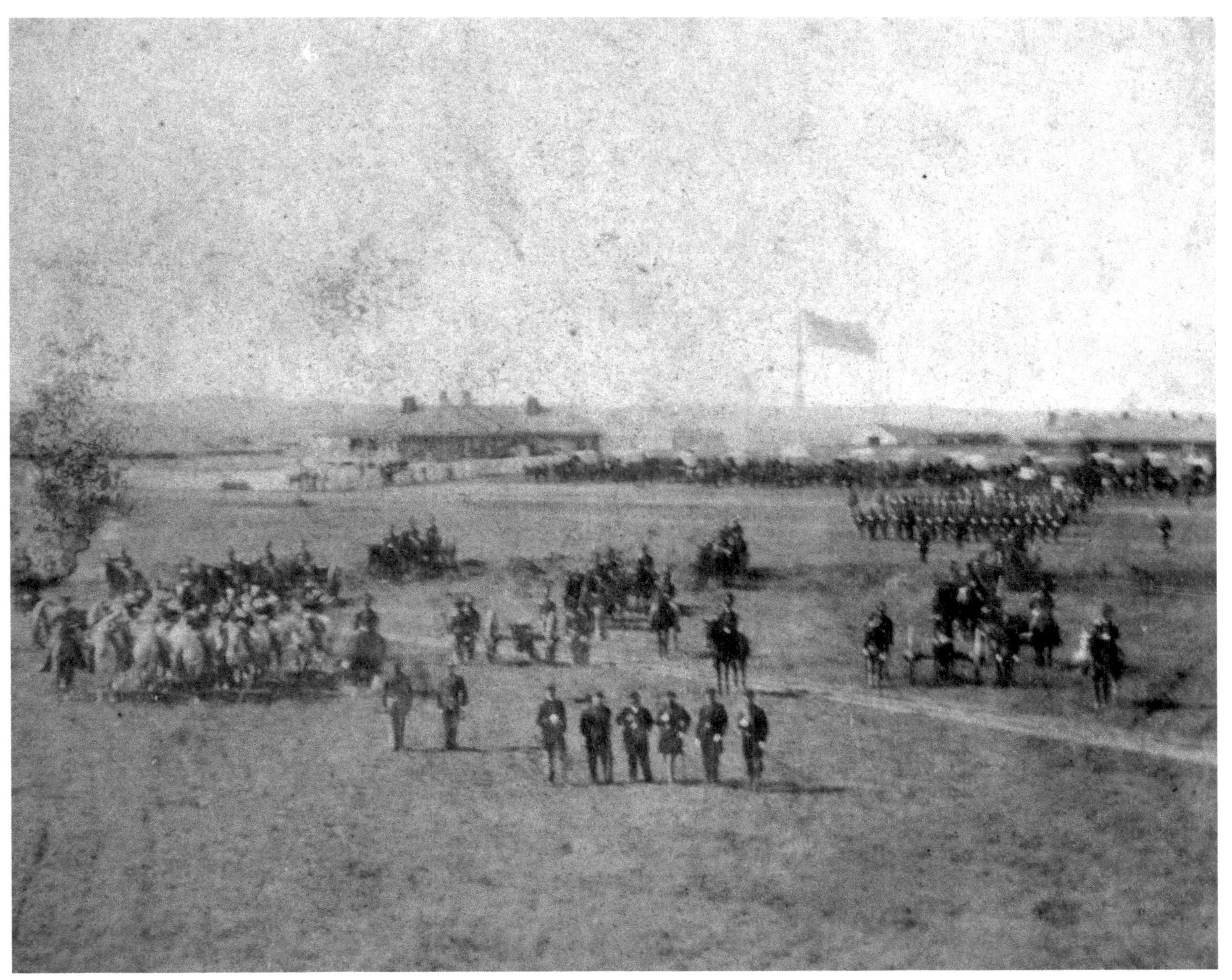

Two years after the conclusion of the Civil War, troops conducted field exercises at Fort Harker. One of several forts created to protect westward travelers and Kansas communities, it was located in Kanapolis and completed by the Union Army in 1866.

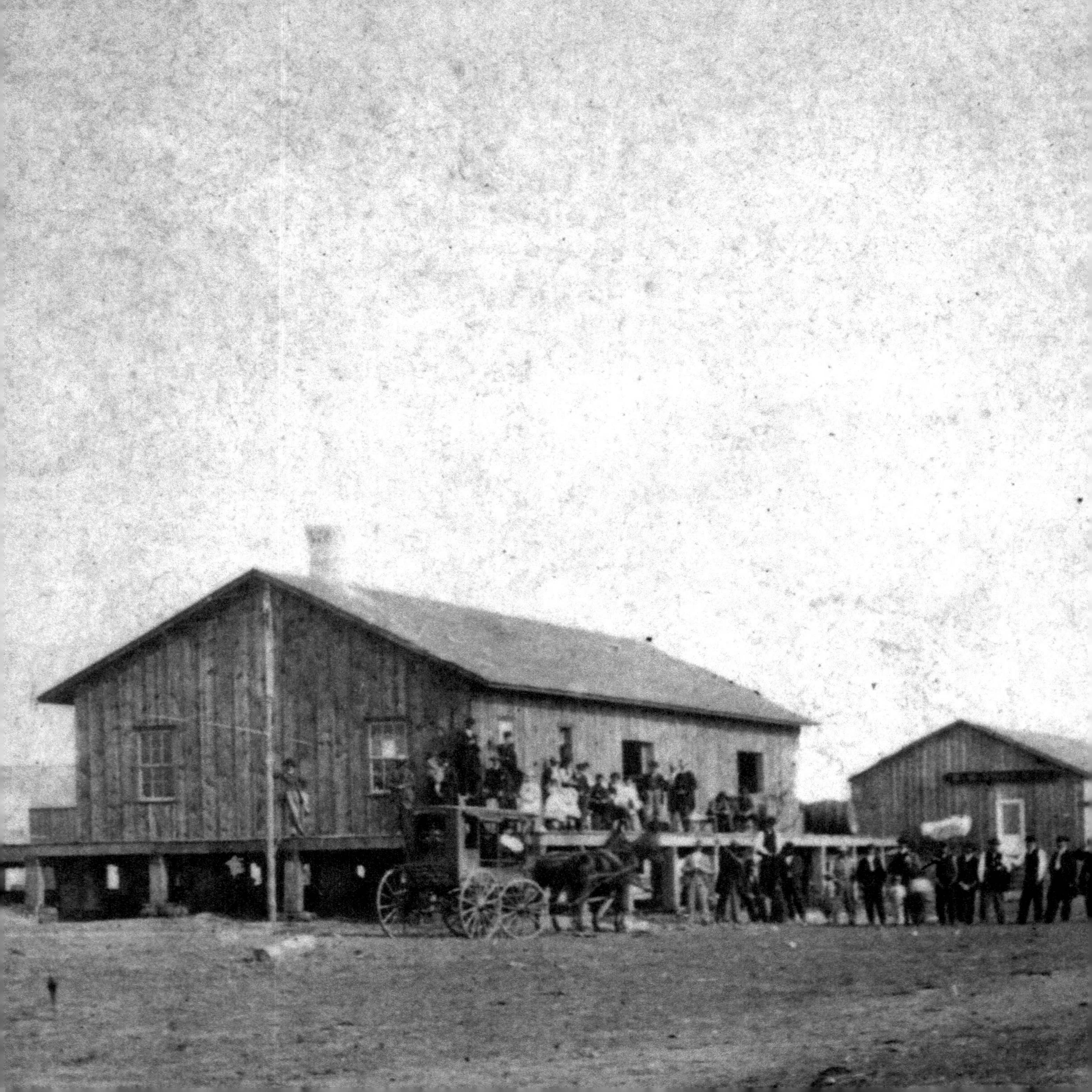

With the arrival of the railroad, Ellsworth and its military fort were soon overflowing with what one source (www.droversmercantile.com) described as “soldiers, gamblers, bullwhackers, railroaders, Texas cowboys, and the inevitable unruly women that made up the character of doing business in an ‘end of the line’ town.” When the depot was photographed in 1867, the town was a wide-open, often violent settlement at the edge of the frontier.

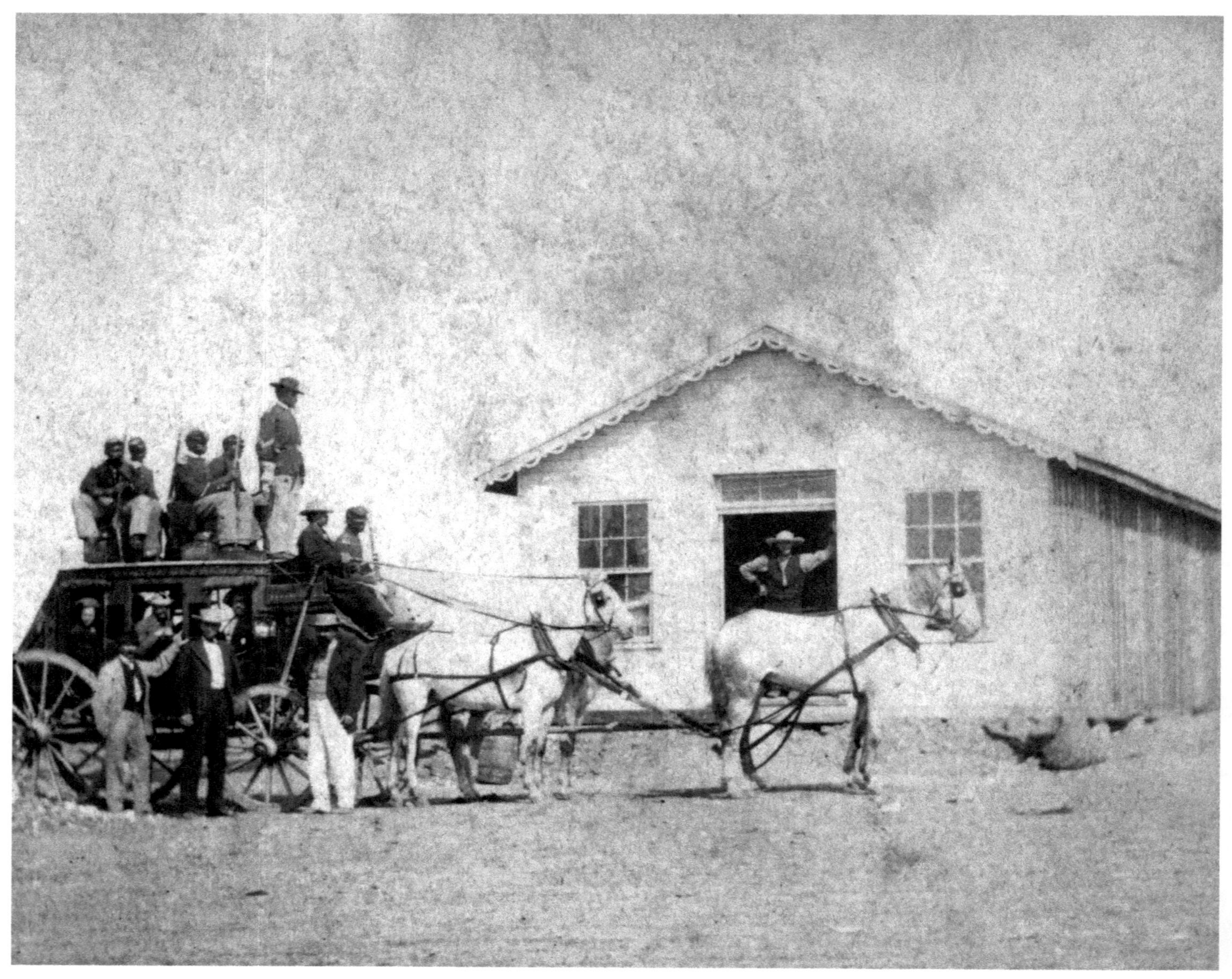

Passengers on the United States Express overland stage board in Hays City in the 1860s for the journey to Denver City, Colorado.

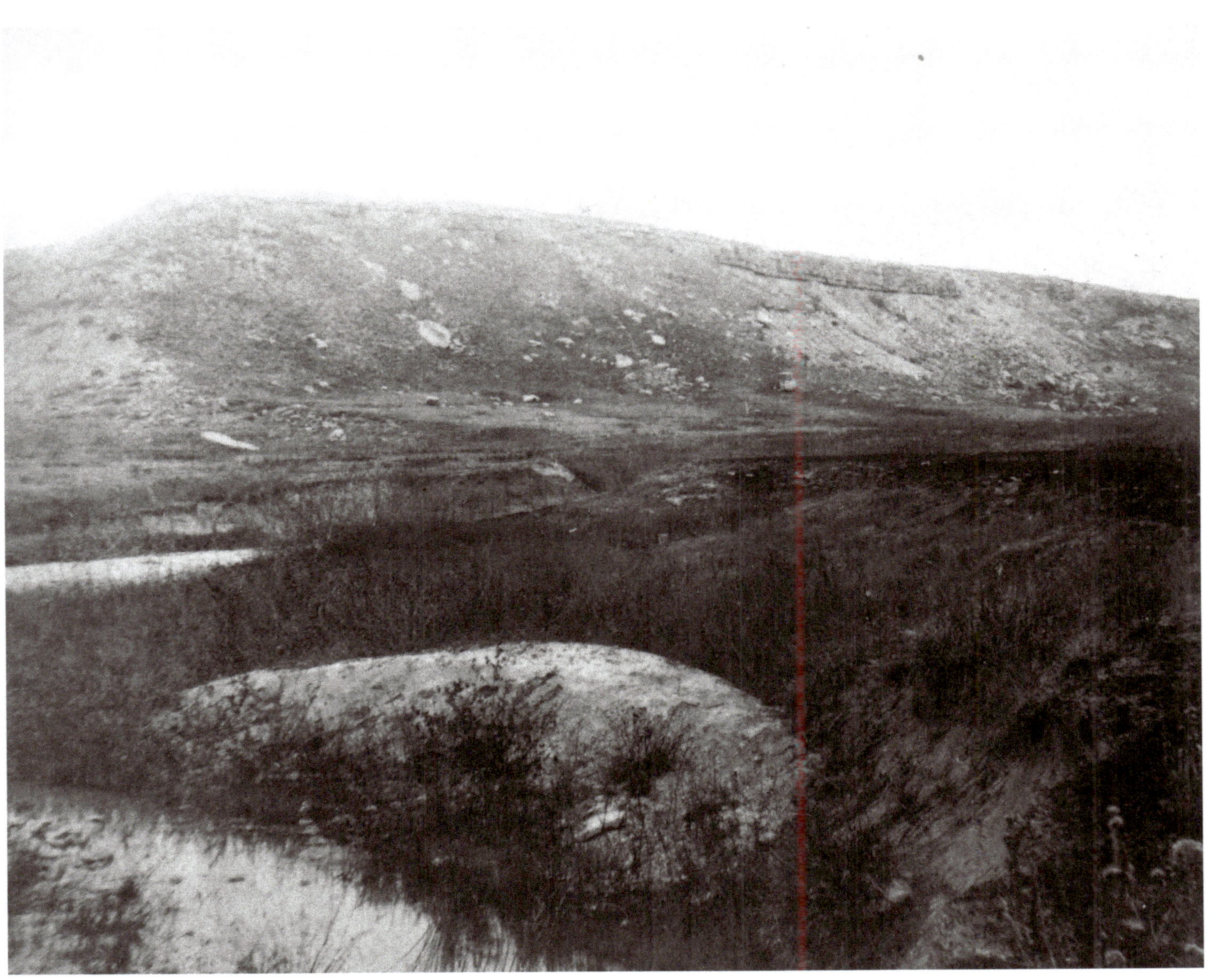

The central plains of Kansas were often far from flat. It's this topography that wagon trains encountered during their sometimes treacherous journeys from Fort Harker to Denver City, Colorado. The route was inhabited by Cheyenne Indians, who resented the encroachment of pioneers and often attacked their wagon trains.

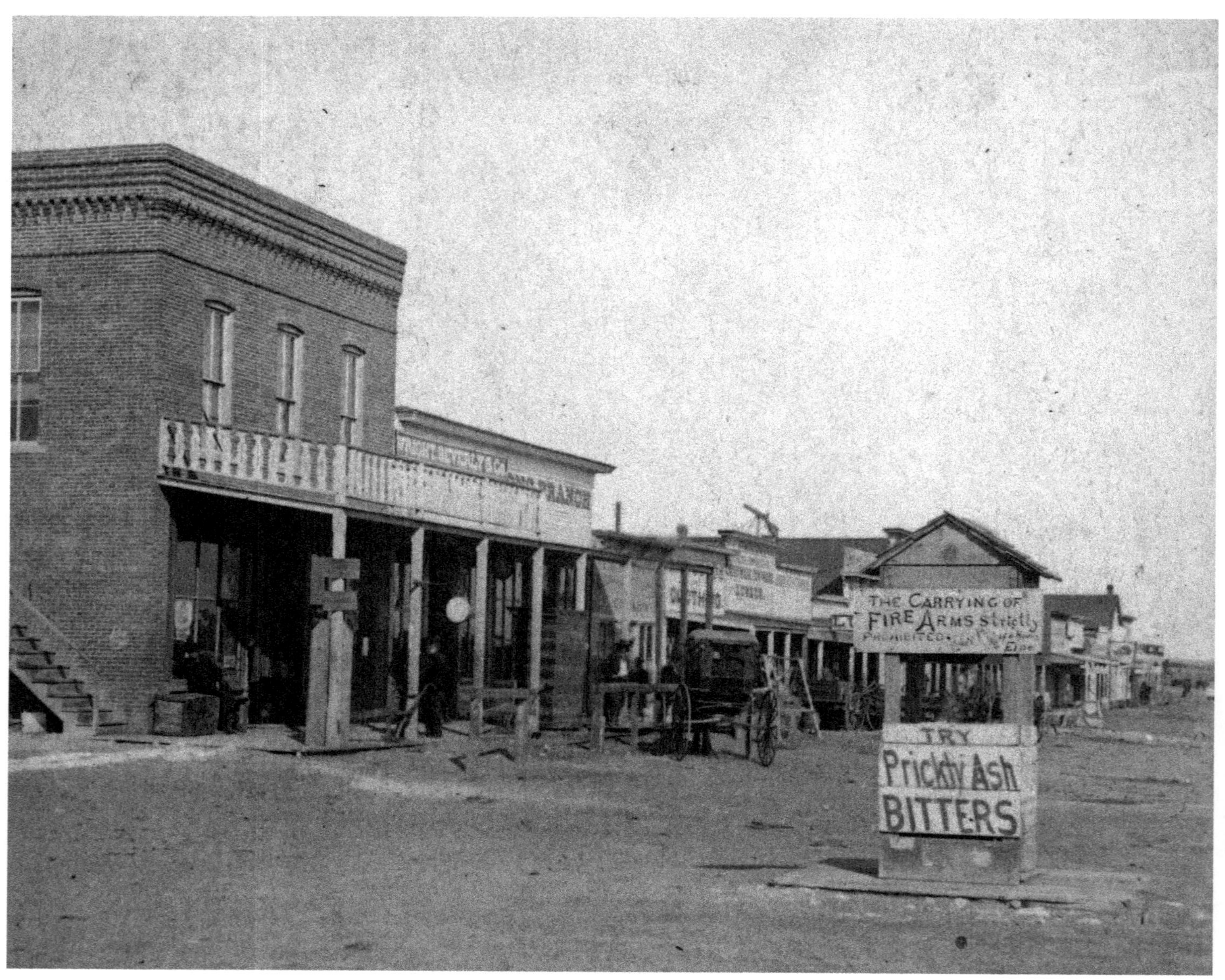

Today, Dodge City is mid-American, both geographically and culturally. In the mid to late nineteenth century, however, it epitomized the Wild West and the struggle between outlaws and lawmen. That's reflected in this photo, taken between 1880 and 1885, and a sign that reads "Try Prickly Ash Bitters" and "The Carrying of Fire Arms Strictly Prohibited." Bitters, medicinal concoctions of alcohol and herbs, were thought to cure stomach problems and other maladies.

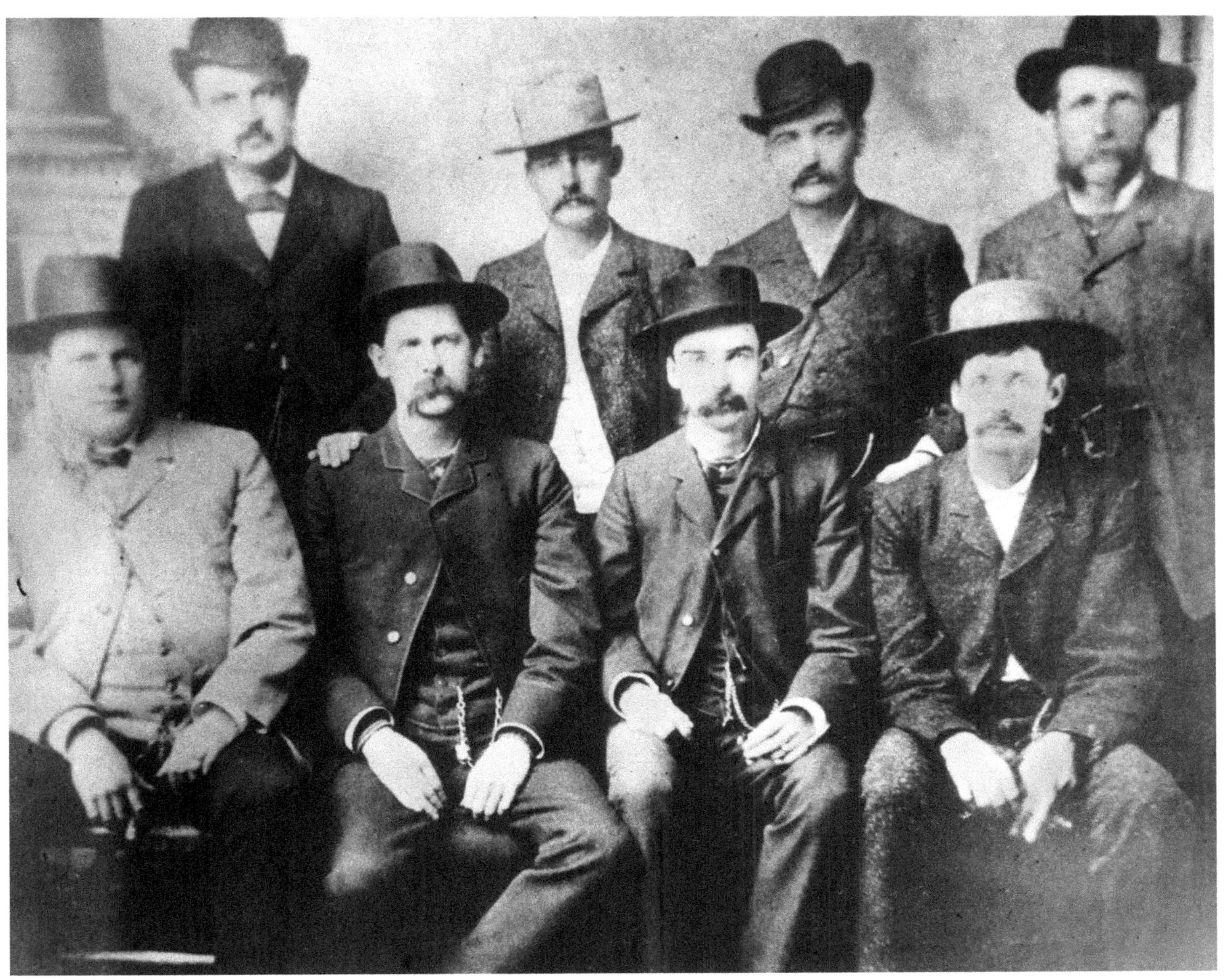

Pictured in an 1883 photo is the Dodge City Peace Commission, whose members are identified as (back row, left to right) William H. Harris, Luke Short, William Bat Masterson, W. F. Petillon, and (front row, left to right) Charles E. Bassett, Wyatt Earp, Frank McLain, and Neil Brown.

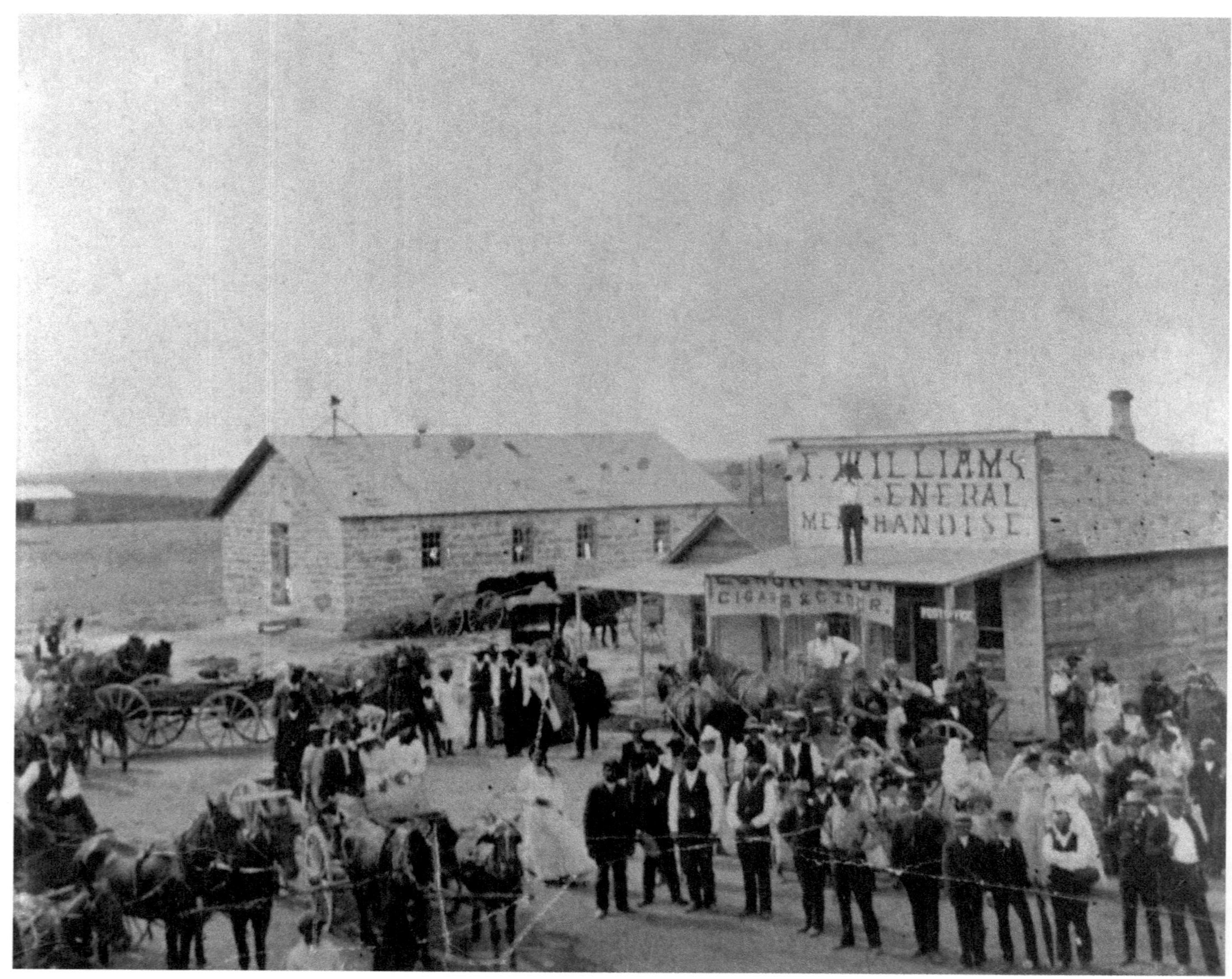

In a photo taken of Washington Street in Nicodemus around 1885, the African-American community's first stone church and F. Williams General Merchandise store form the backdrop for a large gathering. The church is the Nicodemus African Methodist Episcopal Church, which is built from limestone. The general store was Nicodemus's first two-story structure.

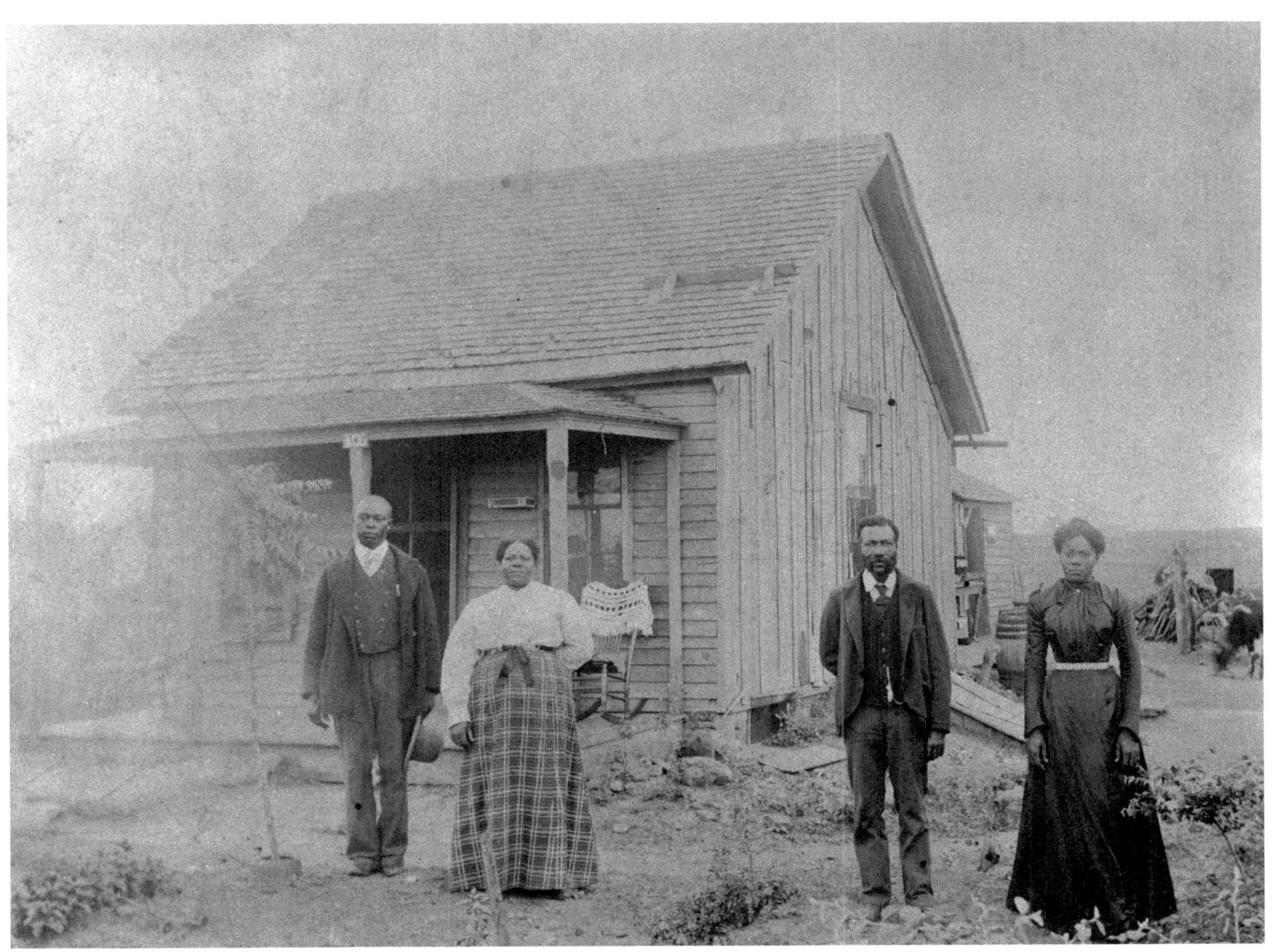

Several years after the Civil War, freed slaves migrated from the South to Kansas. Known as the Exodusters, many black sharecroppers settled in rural and some urban areas in eastern Kansas. Pictured are four settlers in Nicodemus, located in Graham County.

Henry Baden's grocery and dry goods store in Independence attracted customers on horseback and in wagons. The scene dates to between 1880 and 1910. According to the Independence Convention and Visitors Bureau, Baden walked from Kansas City to Independence, settled there, and with his sons owned and operated four different stores.

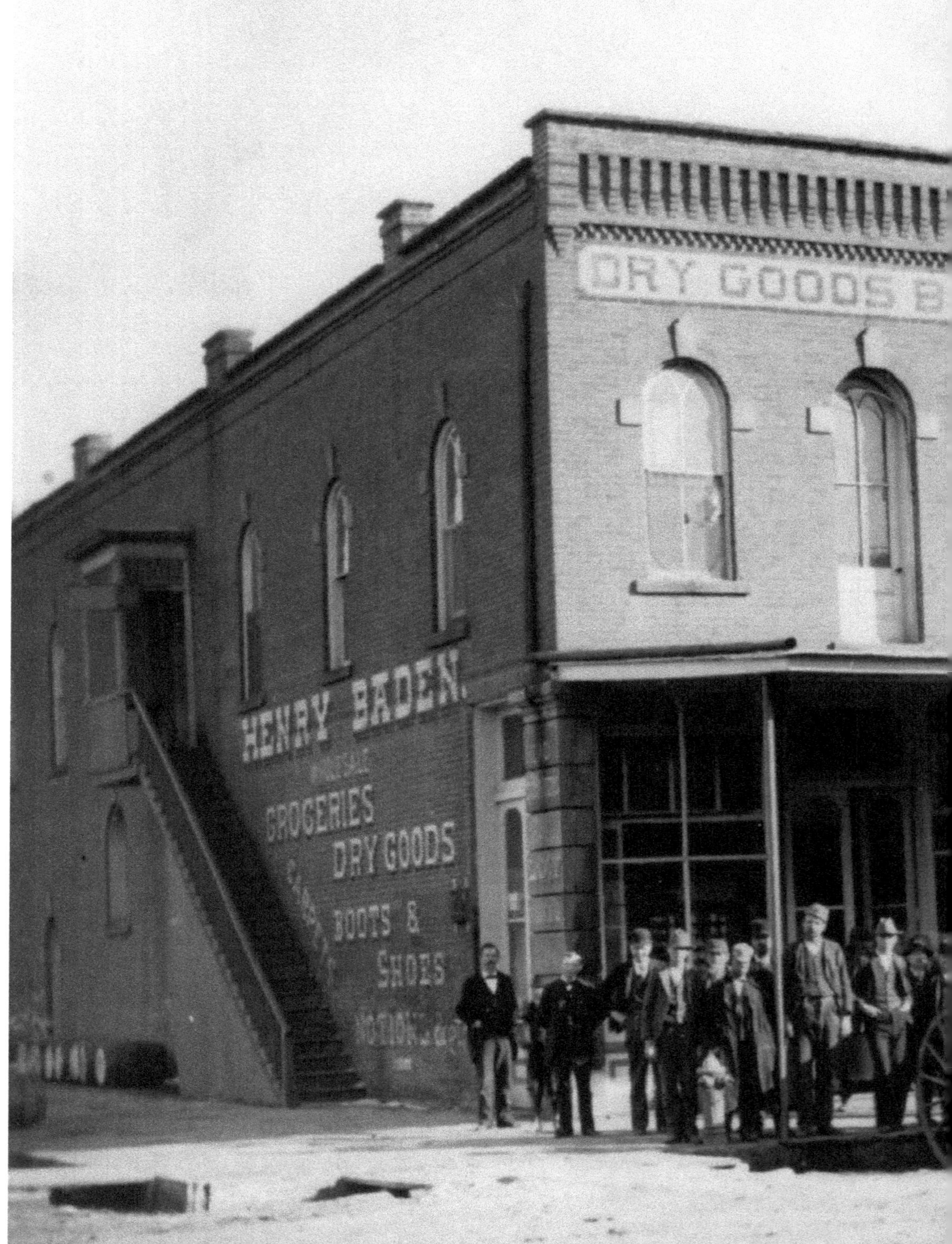

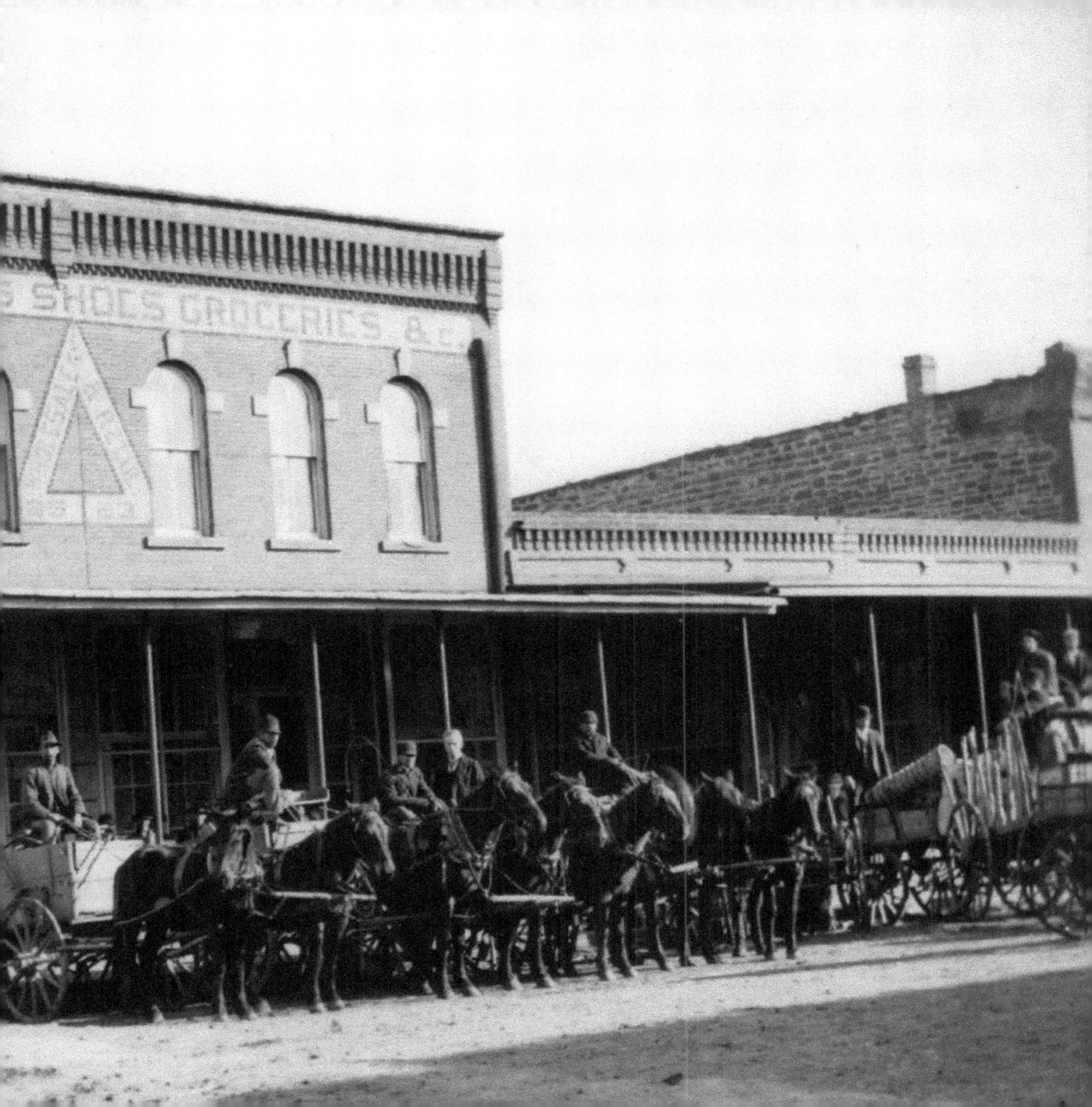
SHOES GROCERIES &

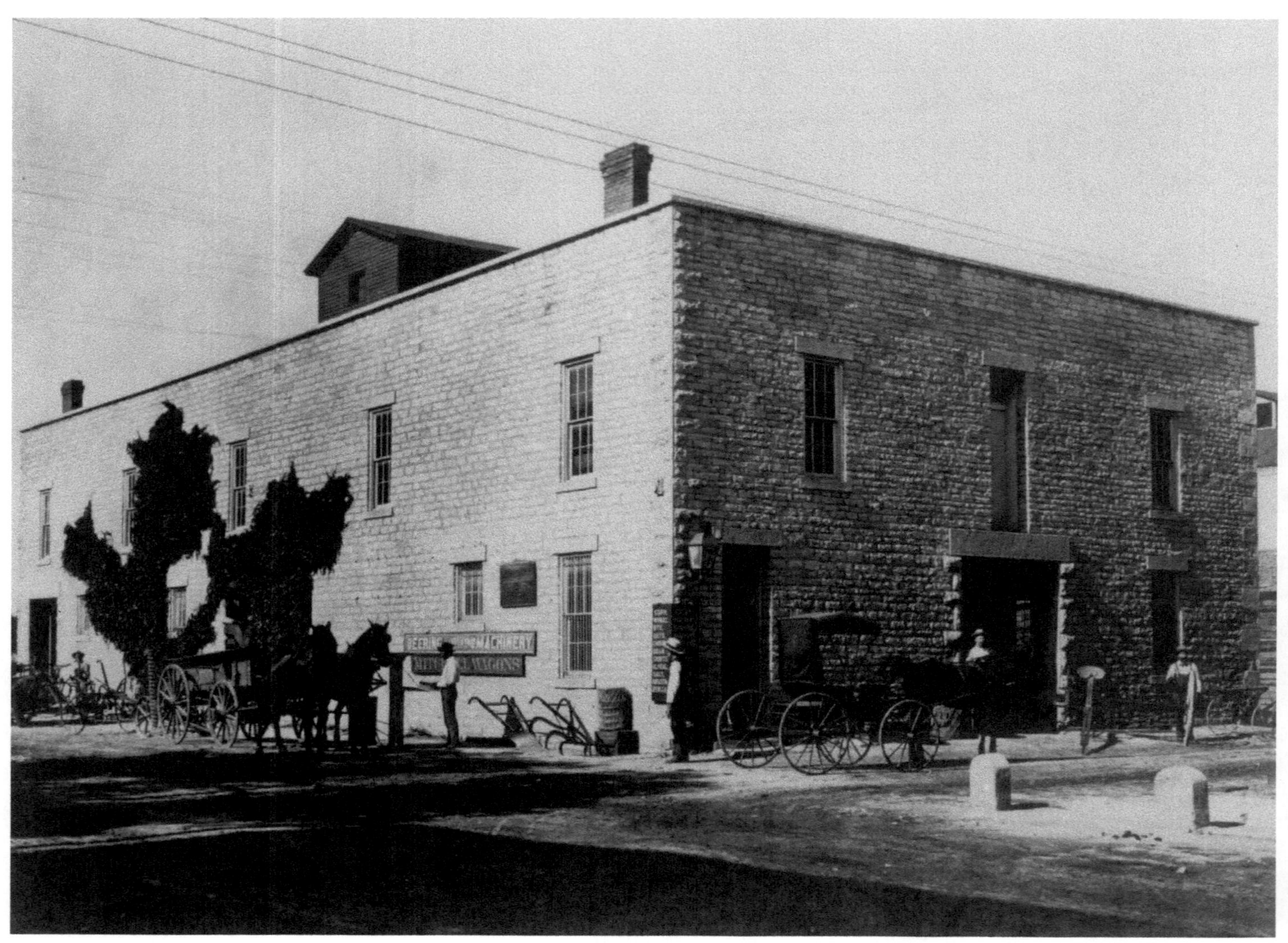

Kansas farmers needed equipment, supplies, and repairs, and businesses like the E. B. Purcell Trading Company in Manhattan sprang up to serve them. Pictured is the company's implement warehouse, with a sign on the corner advertising items for sale, from food products such as corn, wheat, rye, oats, bran, and salt, to buggies and wagons.

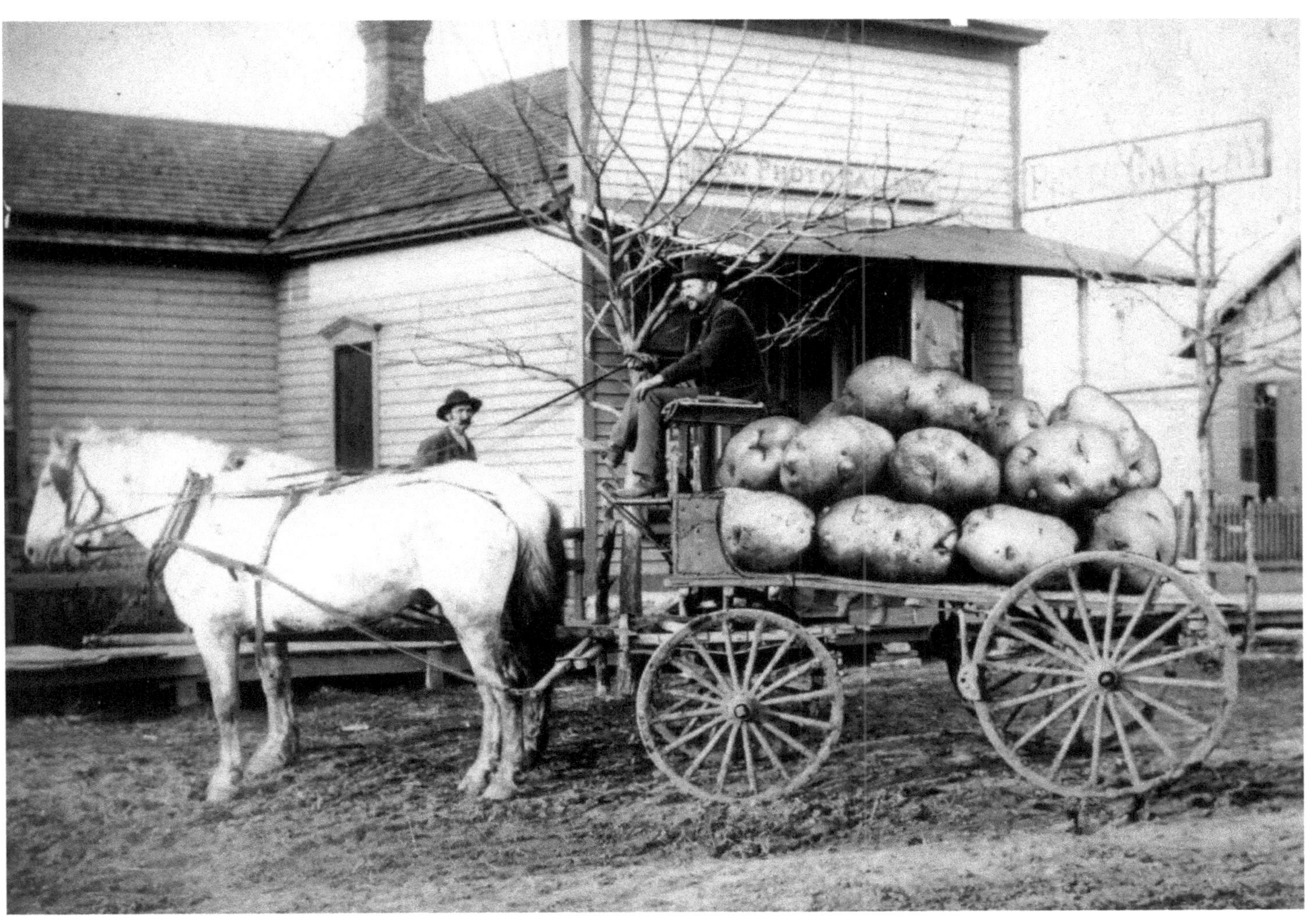

How do you like them potatoes? In 1889, photographer W. H. Martin produced a lighthearted photo of some exceptionally large potatoes on a wagon in Blue Mound, located in Linn County. Around the turn of the century, Martin sold several postcards with exaggerated images like the one above.

Erie, in southeastern Kansas in Neosho County, is known as "Beantown, U.S.A." In the late nineteenth century, much of Erie's bean counting must have taken place in the Bank of Erie Block, pictured on the corner. Banks and churches were often the most impressive buildings in Kansas during that period.

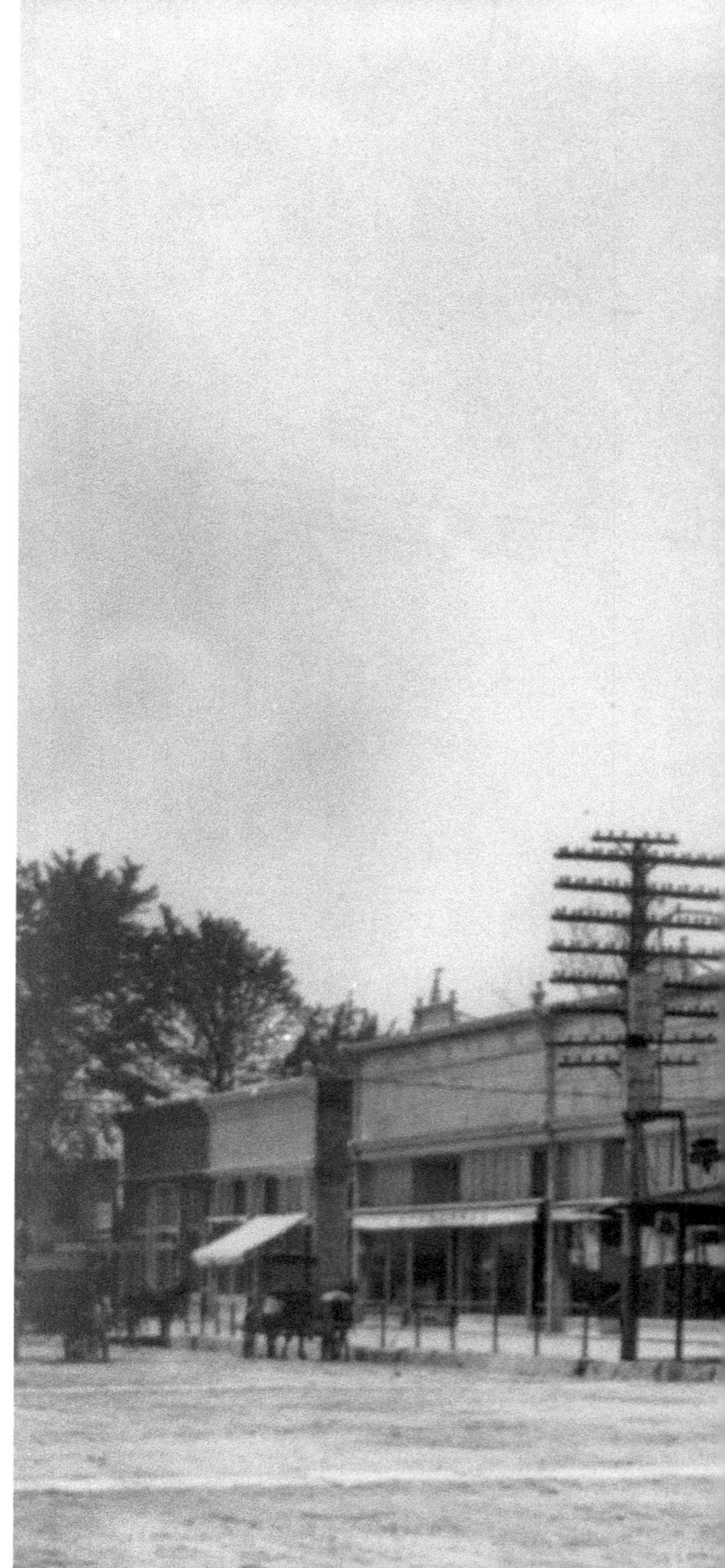

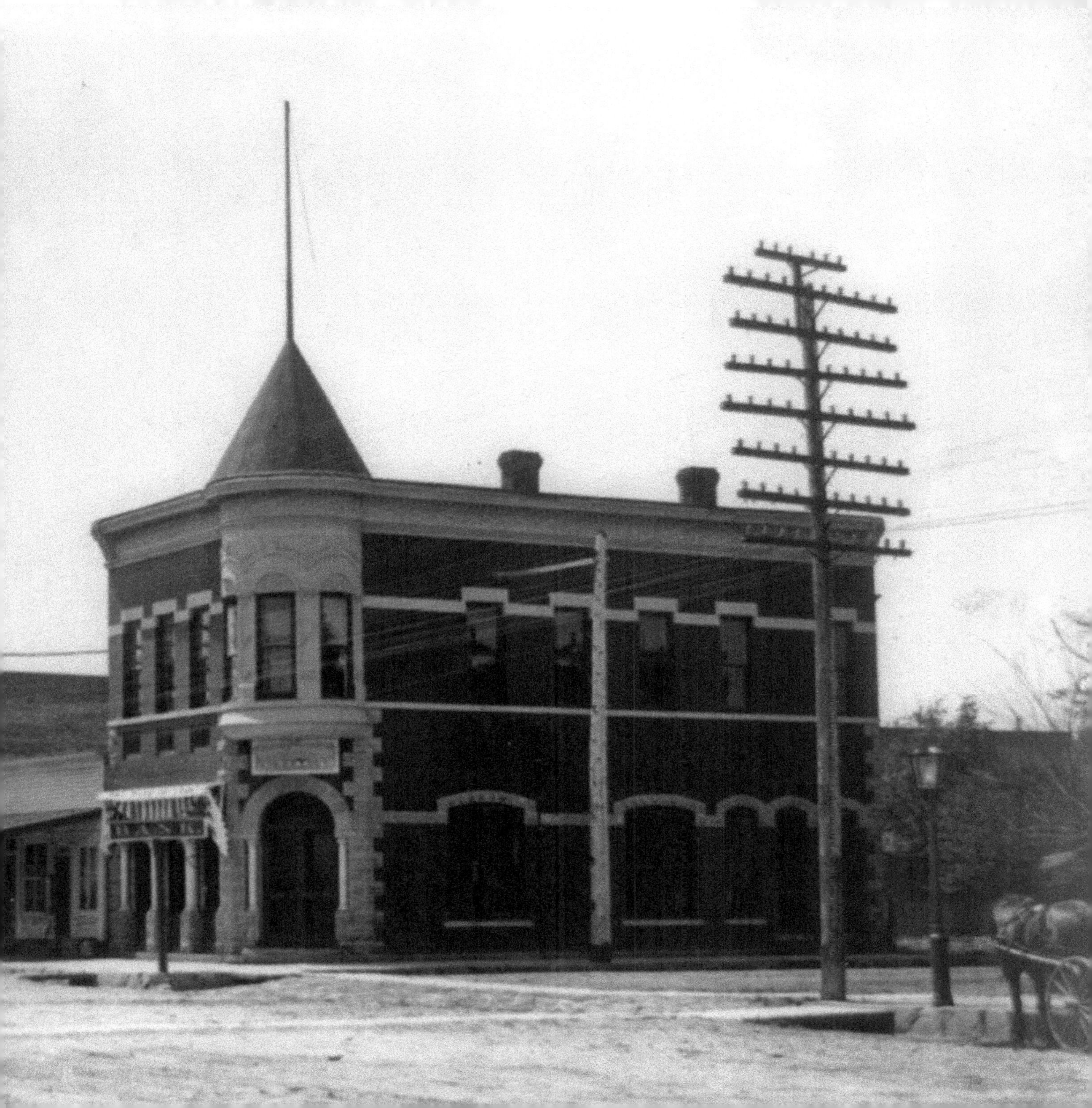

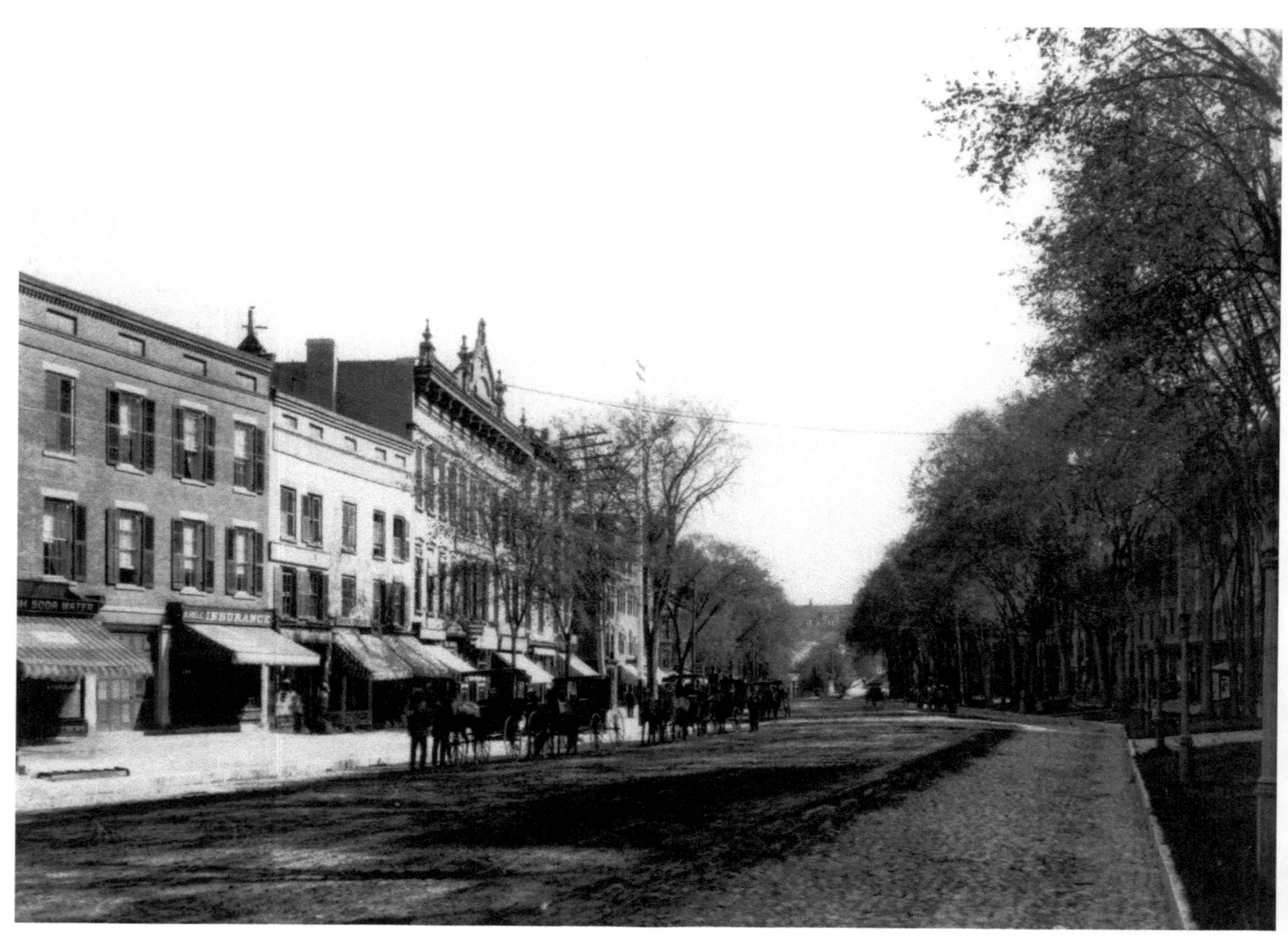

Horse-drawn carriages line a street in Ottawa's business district. Like so many towns, Ottawa's commercial growth accelerated in the wake of railroad construction. The Solomon Valley branch of the Kansas Pacific came first in 1877. Now the Union Pacific, it was eventually joined by a second line built by the railroad and later by track built by the Atchison, Topeka and Santa Fe.

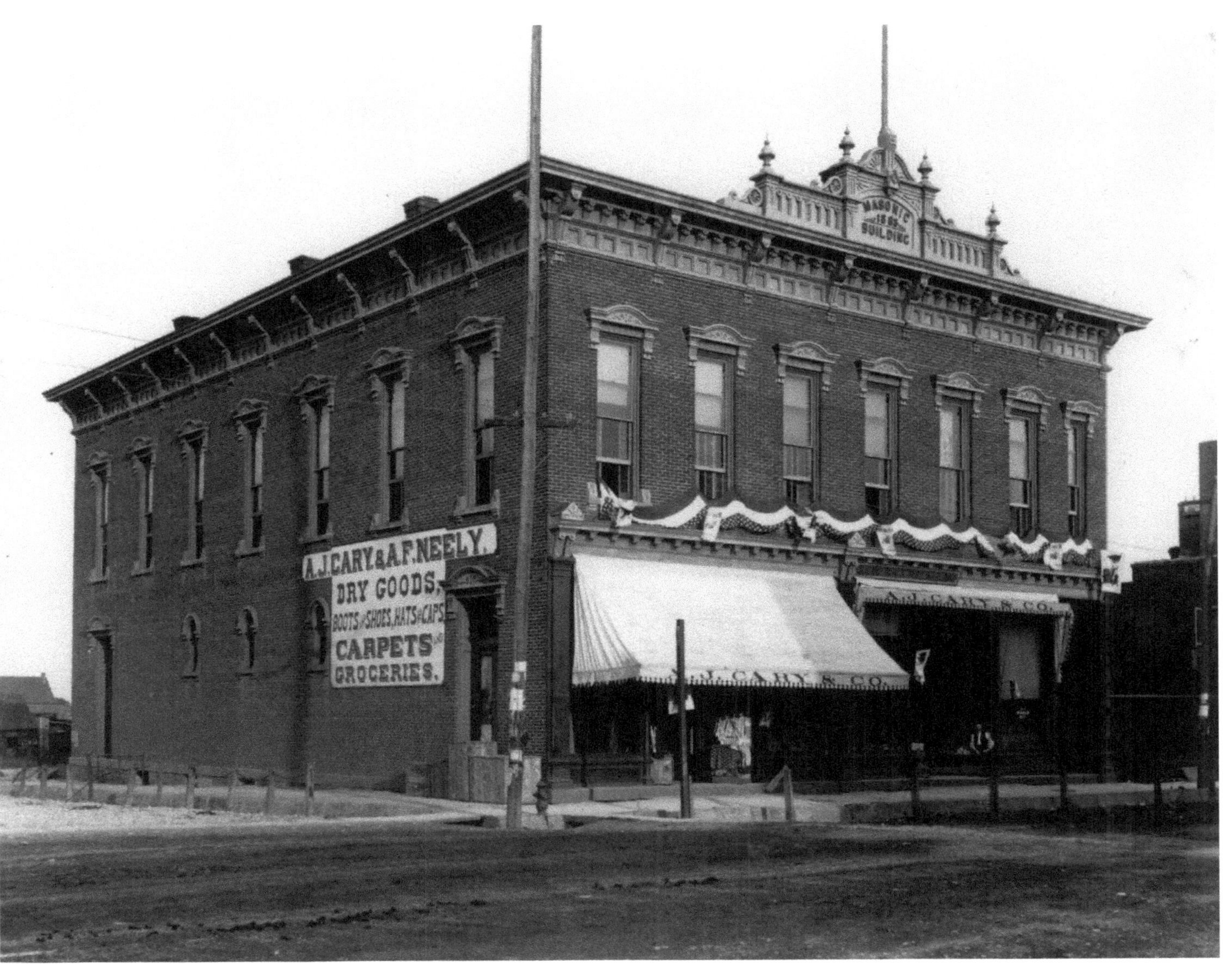

The Masonic Temple is among Parsons' most historically prominent structures. The building was constructed by Hezekiah A. Wade, a banker and bricklayer by trade, who also was a Mason with the rank of Knight Templar. Tenants at the time of this photo operated a dry goods store that sold a broad range of merchandise.

Located on the navigable Arkansas River, Arkansas (pronounced Ar-KAN-sas) City grew prosperous as a shipping point for Kansas flour and other agricultural and industrial goods. Land rushes—then referred to as land races—started four miles south of Arkansas City and brought settlers to what is now Oklahoma.

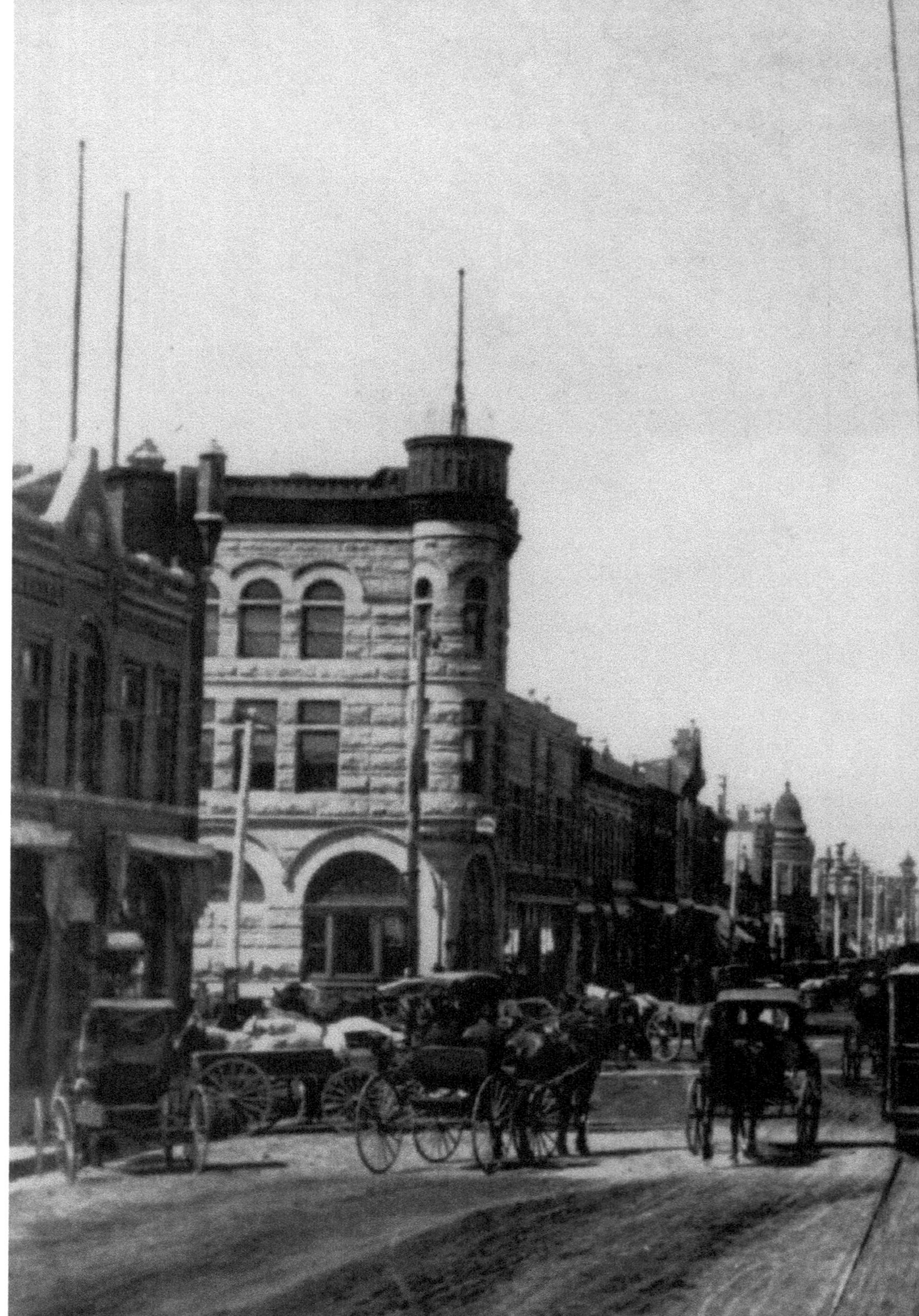

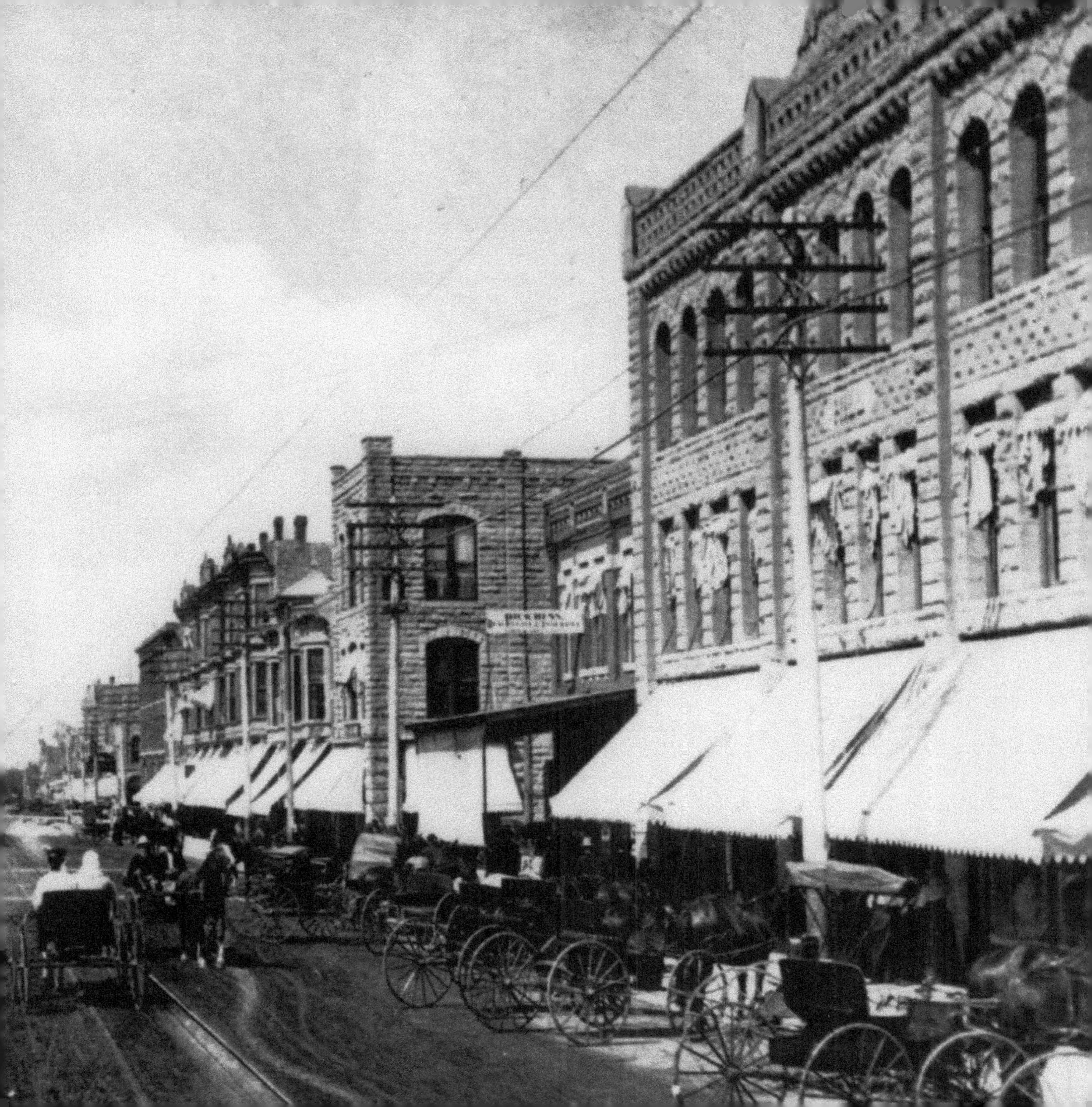

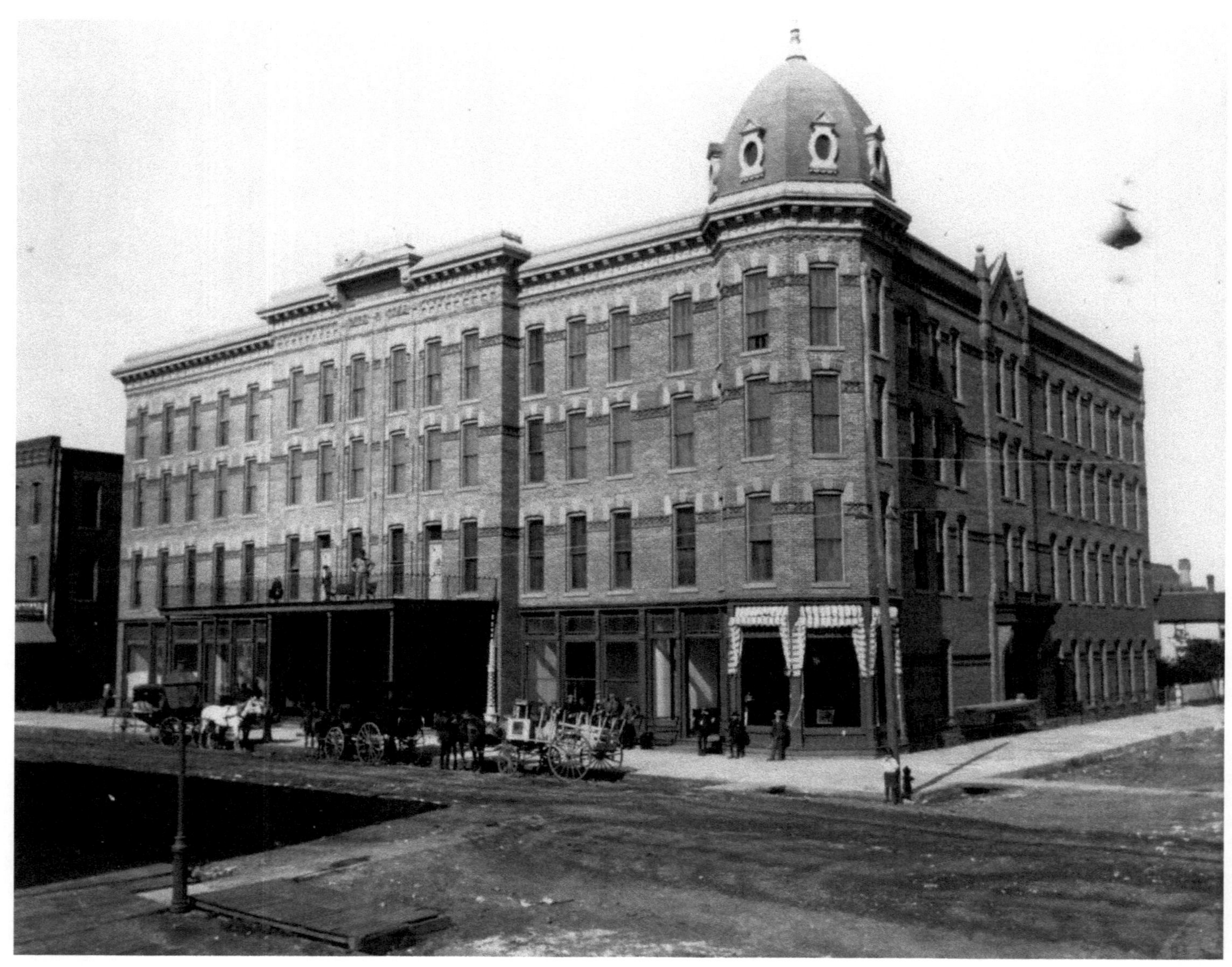

Parsons, the largest city in LaBette County, is the site of the Rasbach, an impressive hotel photographed between 1880 and 1910. The city was named for Levi Parsons, president of the Missouri-Kansas-Texas Railroad, popularly referred to as "the K-T" and later "The Katy."

Industrial Expansion and Financial Corruption

(1890–1909)

Leave it to Kansas farmers to put railroad magnates, financiers, and industrialists in their place. Farming's unpredictable nature—and the endless, hard work it demanded—led those who worked the fields to pull no punches when it came to describing the lust for power and wealth.

The instinct for unadorned truth led Kansas farmers to coin the expression "robber barons" to describe those who wielded unbridled power from 1870 to 1914. It was a period that historian Catherine Reef aptly describes as a time when "power and affluence form[ed] a glittering surface over a core of cheating and corruption."

So it made sense that Kansans, down-to-earth by nature and occupation, would see through it all. In 1905, Kansas governor Edward Wallace Hoch termed monopolistic Standard Oil as "the greatest socialistic corporation now doing business on earth." And, in a March 2, 1905, article in the *Independent,* a popular periodical, Hoch noted that "if we can force the Standard Oil Company to a basis of fair play what an achievement for the intelligent patriotism of the country!" This bold, populist stance came from a Kansan the editors lauded for being "an example of rugged honesty and courage." Values forged from hard labor tend to do that to you.

But the period between 1890 and 1909 wasn't only about fighting excess. The rapid growth of industrial America in the two decades spanning the turn of the century left its mark on a largely rural, agricultural state. The continued growth of railroads meant that cities along the tracks would develop, giving birth to industries and commercial bases of their own. Electricity was becoming more common, streetcars were ferrying passengers to and from business districts, and the automobile was about to become the newest phenomenon.

The world—and Kansas along with it—was changing. But beneath the storm of progress, Kansans could still be counted on to stand up and tell it like it is.

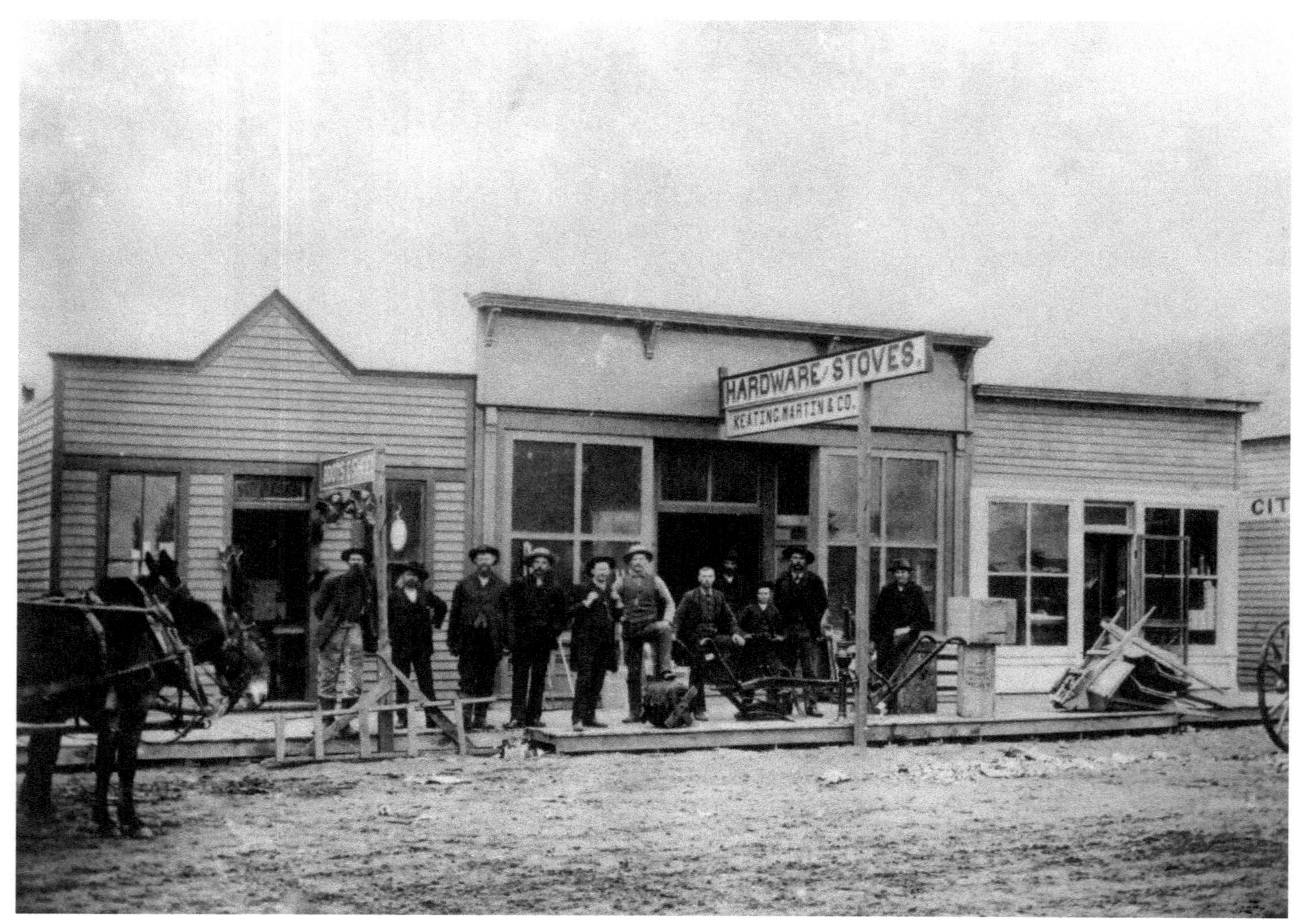

A group gathers for a photo in front of a Liberal hardware store managed by Clarence Y. Martin, father of Glenn L. Martin. In its early days, Liberal was a boomtown whose prosperity was linked to the Rock Island Railroad. Its population dipped to around 400 people by 1900, but Liberal, the county seat of Seward County, now has around 20,000 residents.

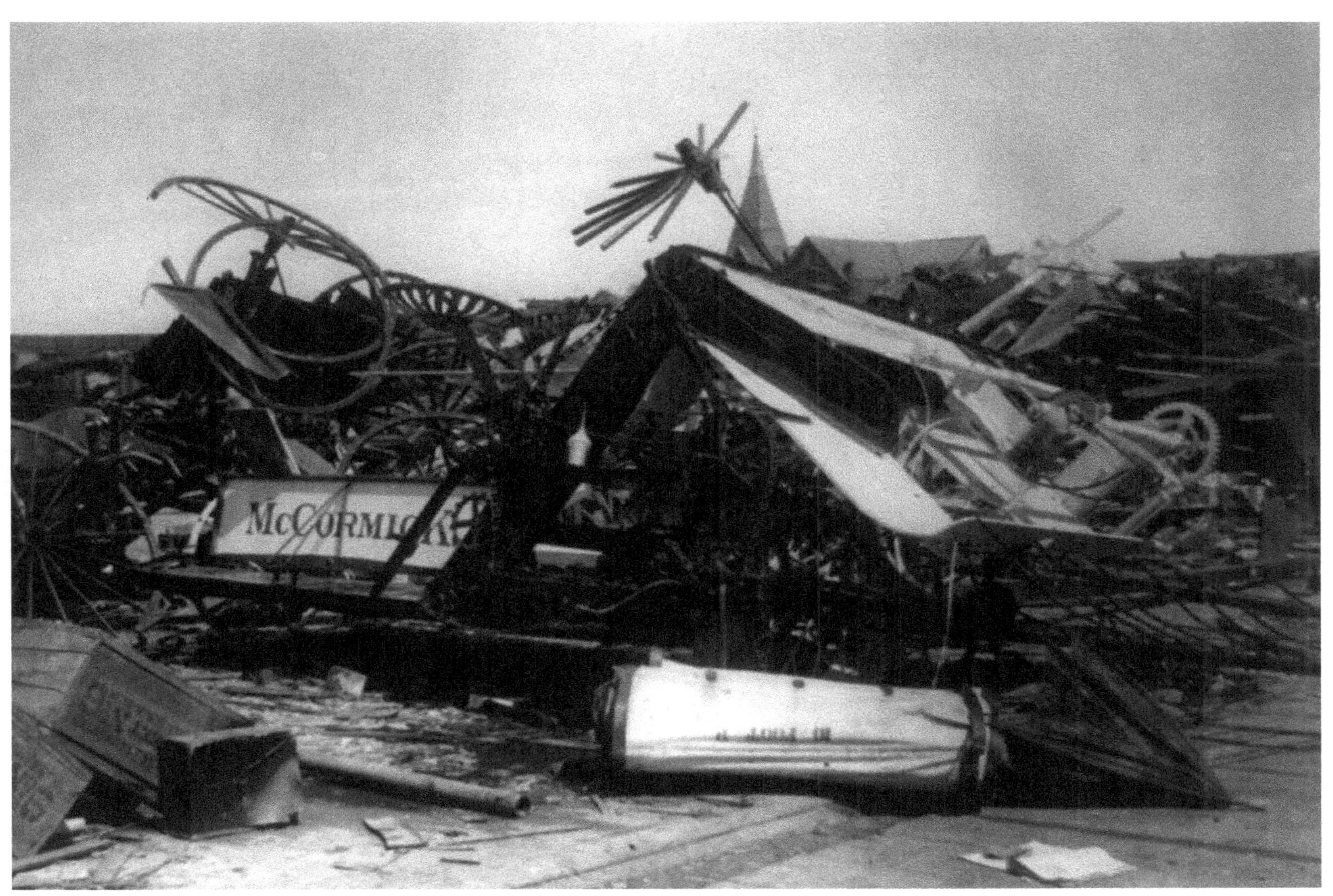

A May 27, 1892, tornado demolished a piece of McCormick farm machinery outside R. J. Smith's Implement House in Wellington. Although storms of this kind often were referred to as cyclones at the time, a Colorado newspaper noted that "never in the history of Kansas was there anything like it." According to the account, 17 people died and many buildings were destroyed.

Following Spread: Pictured is Central Avenue in the business district of El Dorado. The economic health of the community, the county seat, and the most populous city in Butler County had long been tied to an oil refinery that was one of the largest in the plains states.

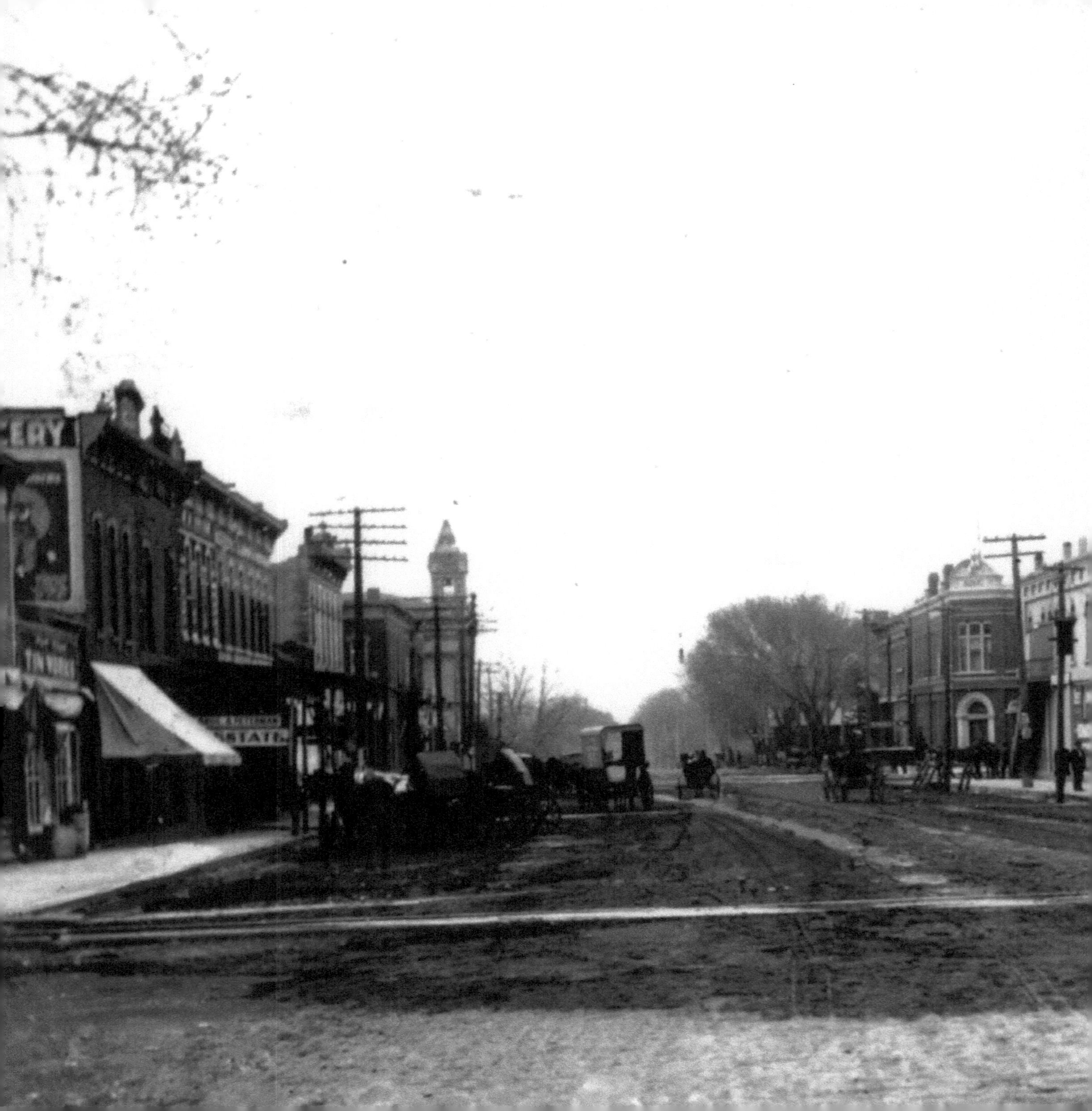

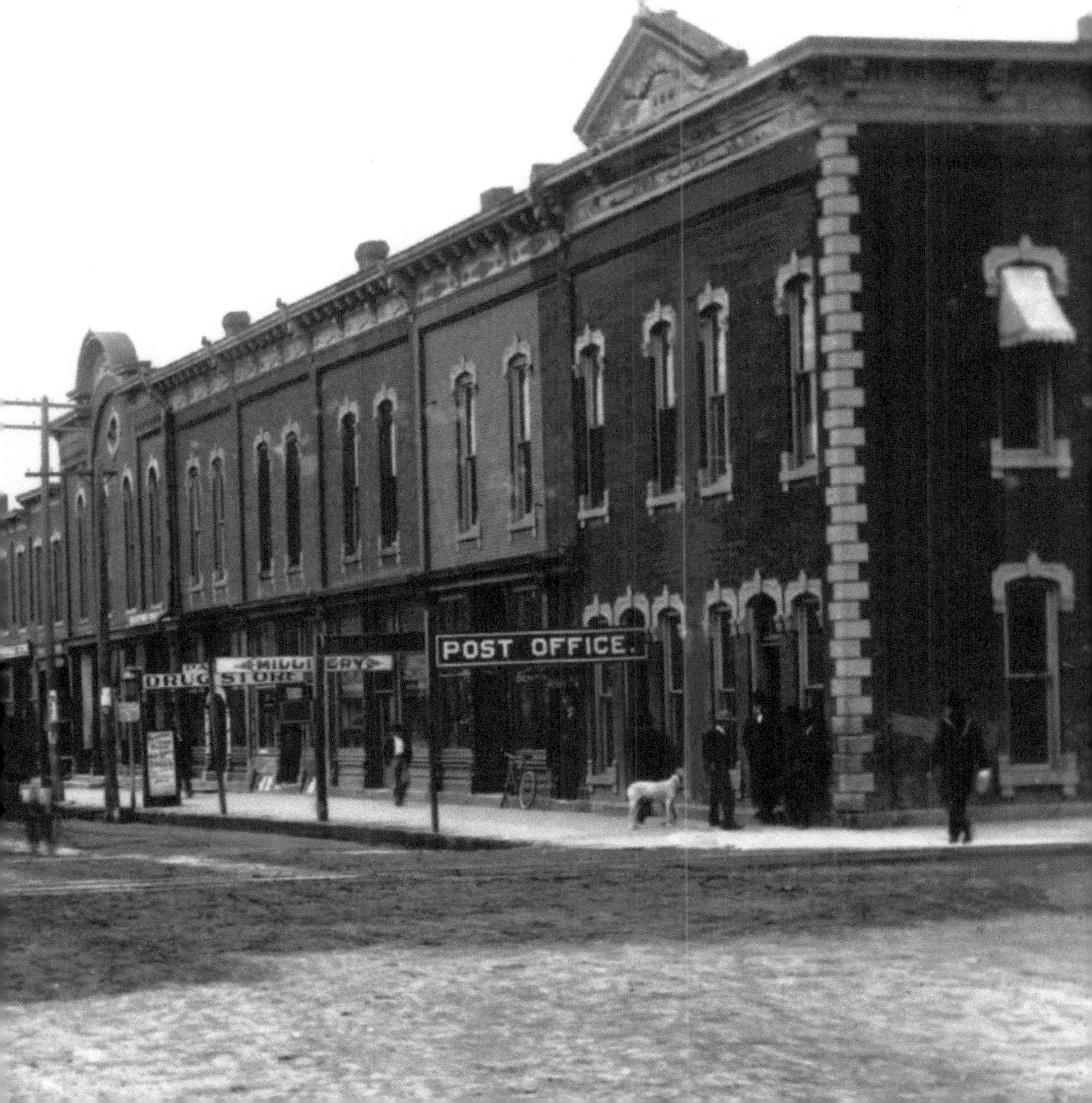
POST OFFICE.
DRUG STORE

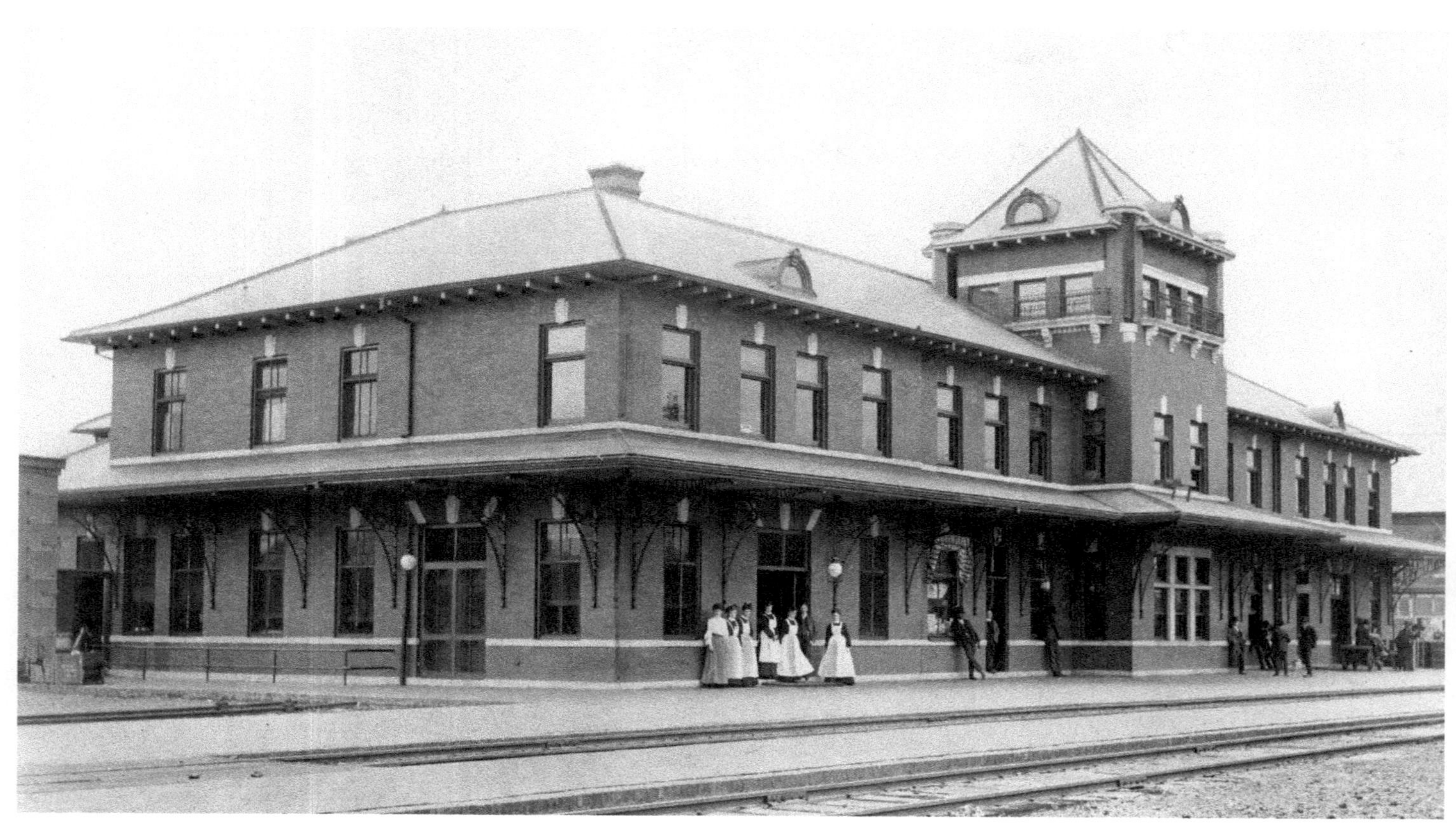

Thriving depots, Fred Harvey restaurants, and the Harvey Girls who served meals to hungry travelers were commonplace during Kansas's railroad heyday. Harvey Girls are pictured in front of Chanute's Santa Fe station around the turn of the century.

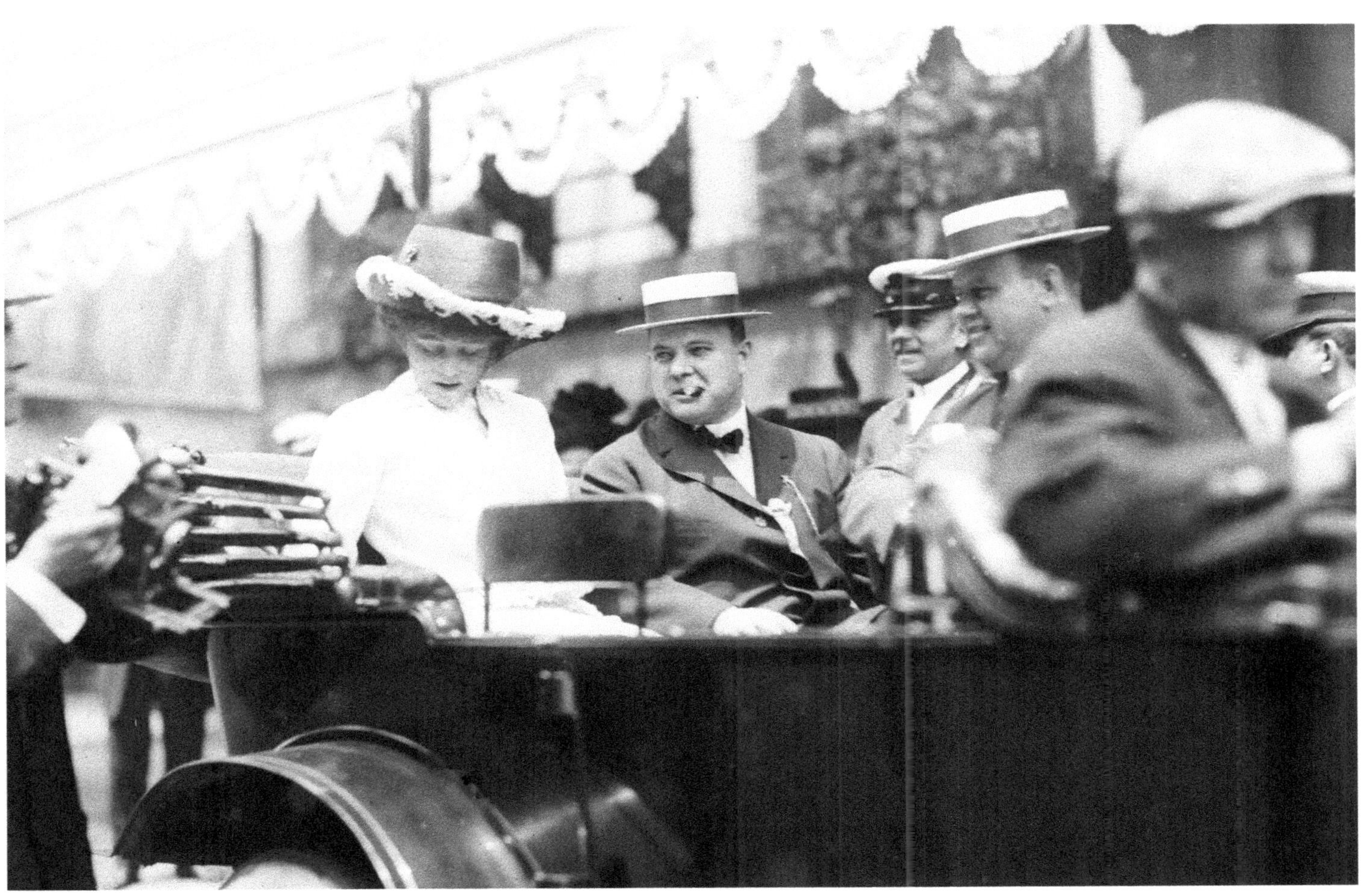

Not much is known about the couple pictured in a news photo taken around 1900. The event appears to be a parade or political rally. The couple is only identified as "Wm. McLaughlin & Wife, Kansas." The photo is from a collection attributed to George Grantham Bain, one of America's earliest news-photo agencies.

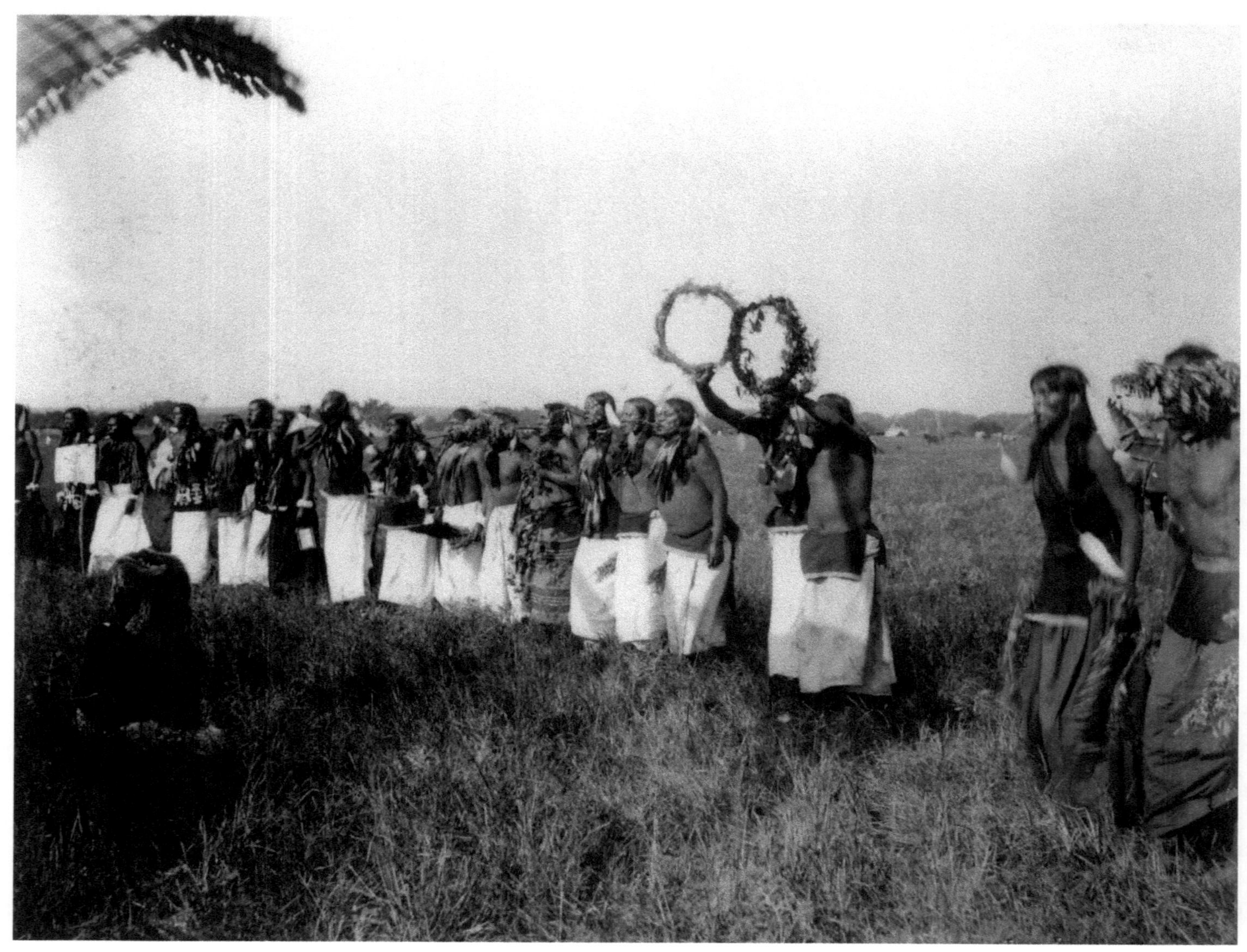

A sun dance is performed on the Ponca Indian Reservation near Arkansas City. Native Americans played an important role in the development of the city and of Indian territory to the south in what is now Oklahoma.

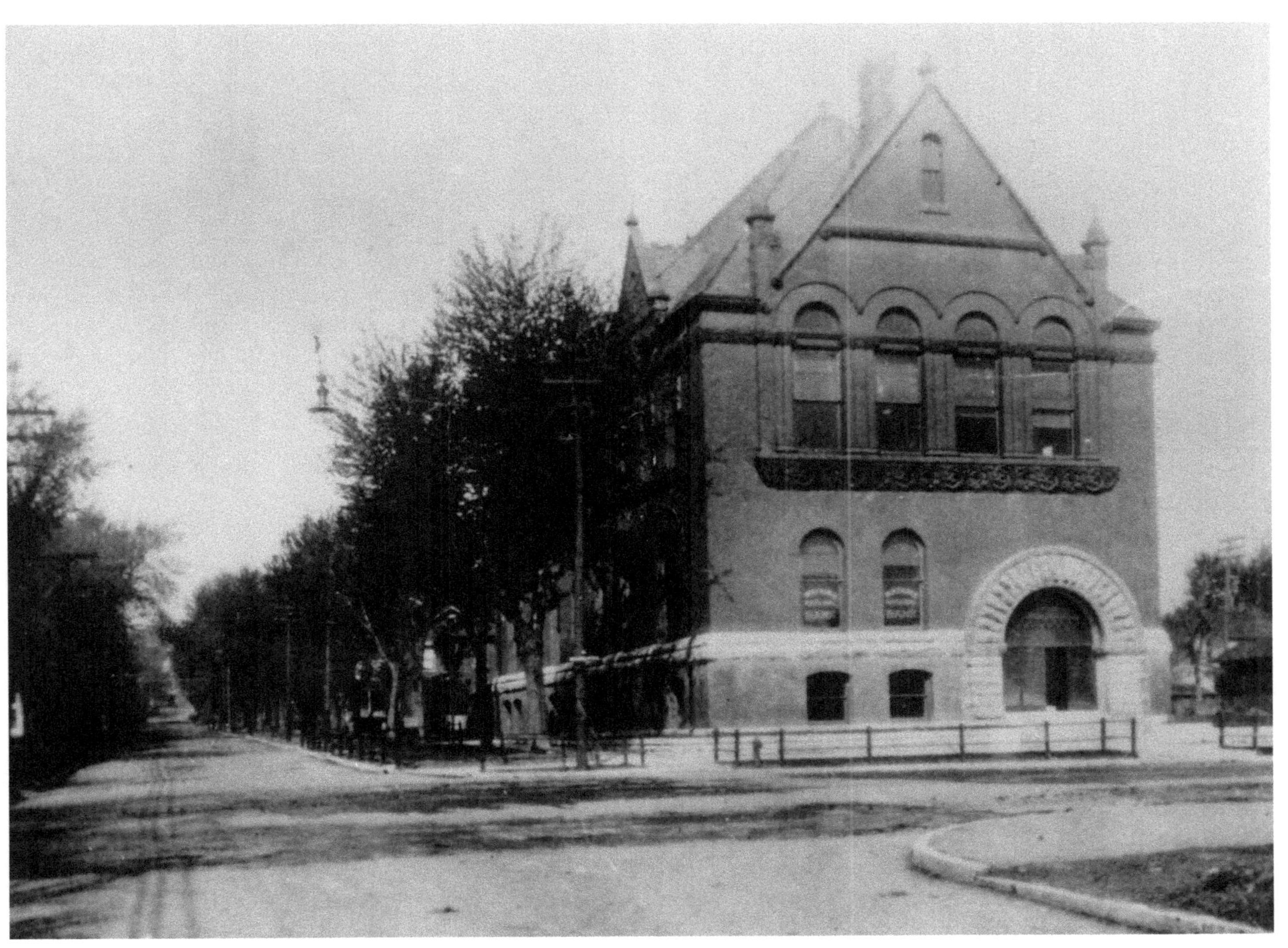

J. B. Watkins Land Company, 1047 Massachusetts Street in Lawrence, is pictured from the southeast in a photo taken around 1895. The building currently houses the Watkins Community Museum of History.

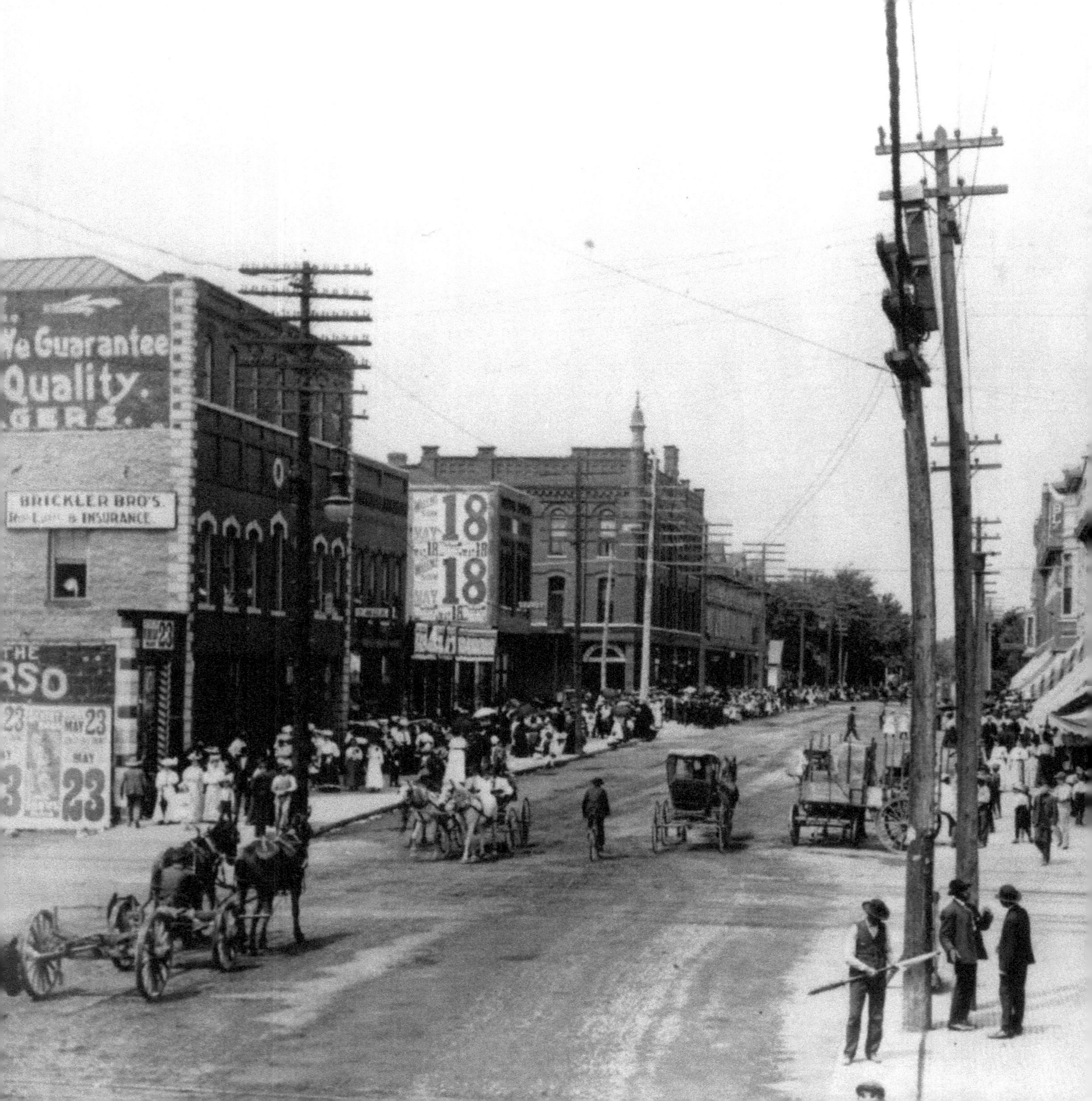

Quality
BRO'S
INSURANCE
18
MAY
18
23
MAY 23
23

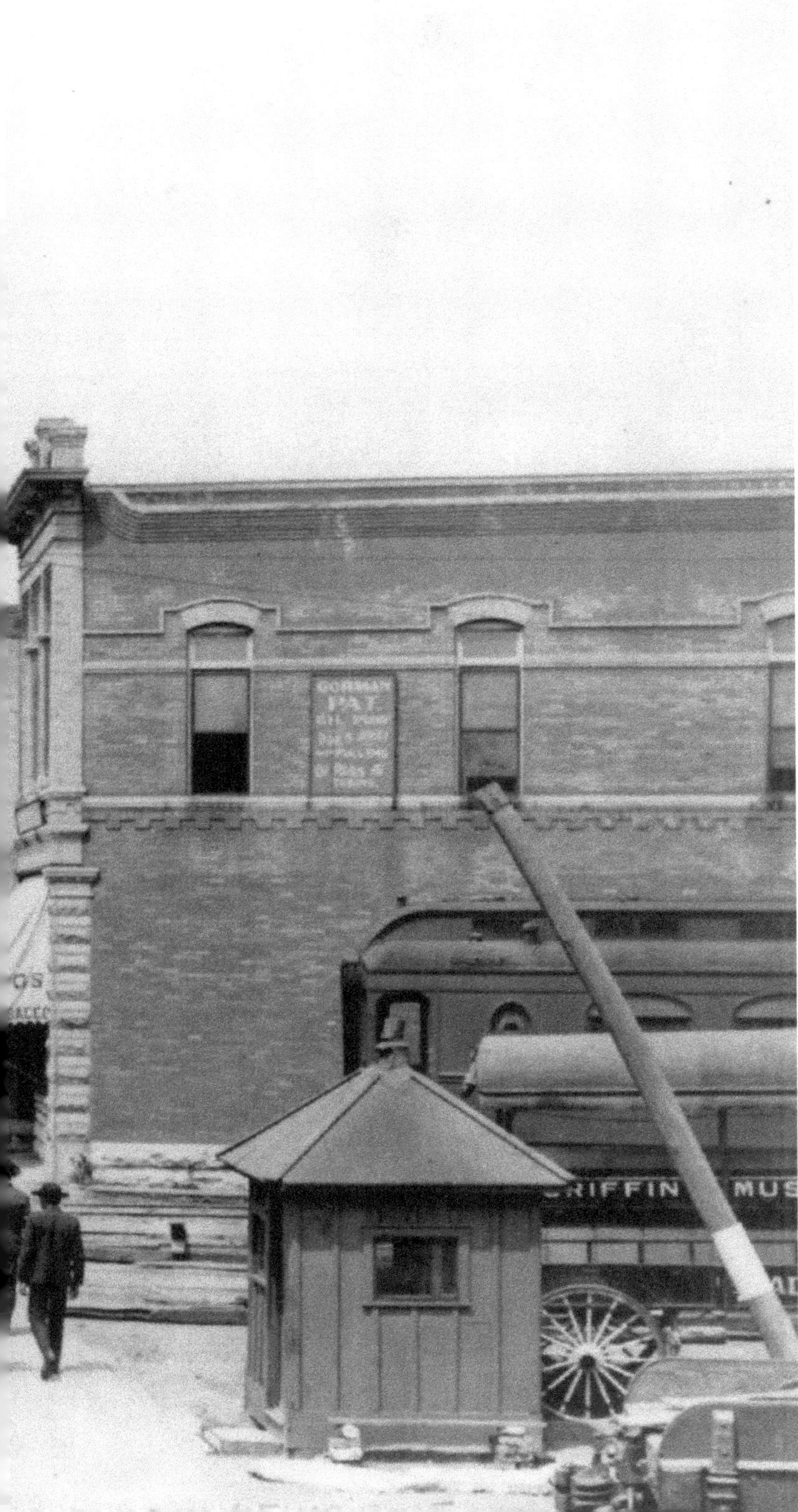

An early-twentieth-century photo depicts West Main Street in Chanute. Chanute was a thriving railroad town and business hub in southeast Kansas. The building at left advertises a Gentry Brothers show on May 23. The Gentry Brothers, "the World's Best Trained Animal Exposition," was a popular traveling circus whose performances featured mainly dogs, horses and ponies, and elephants.

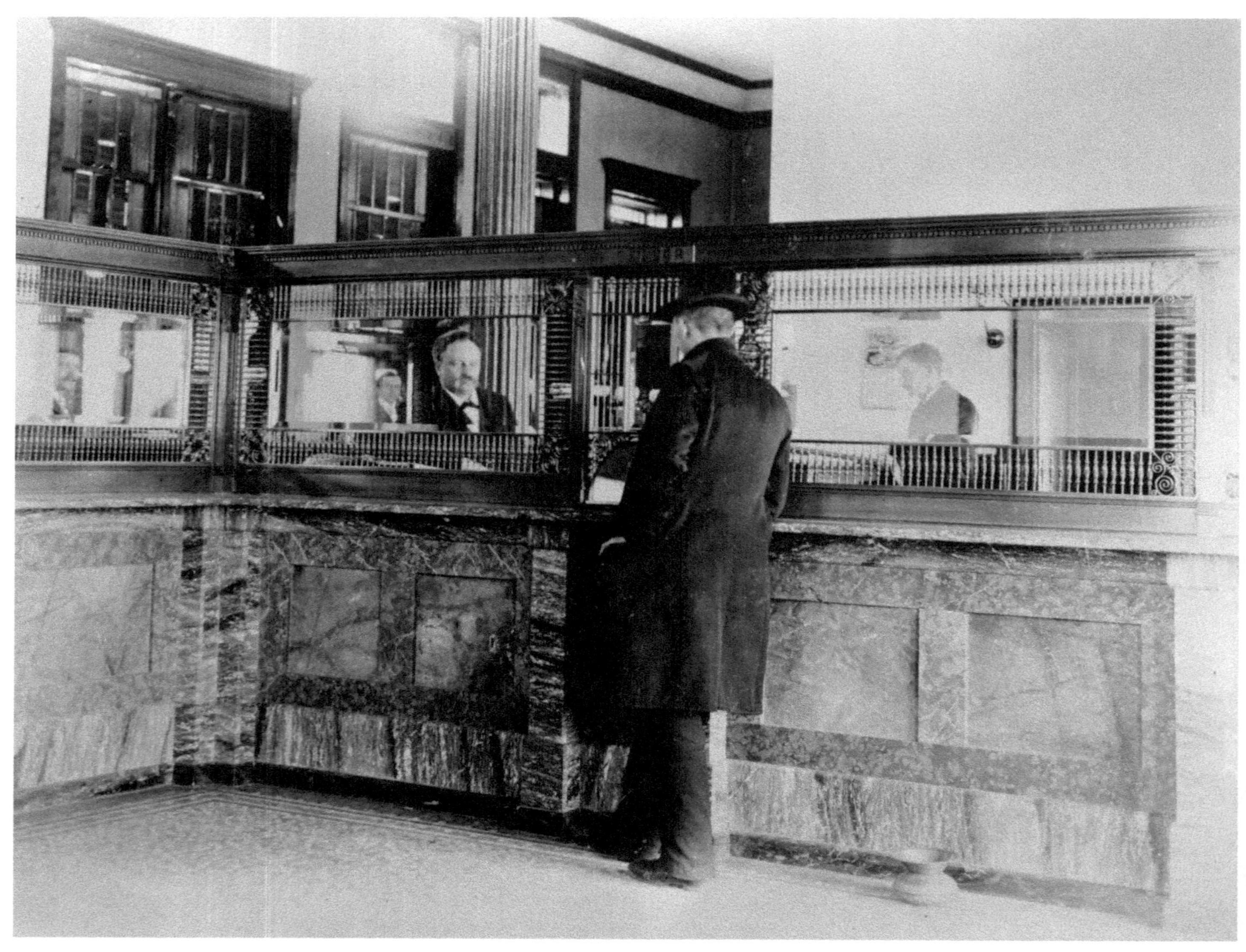

A transaction takes place between a customer and a representative of the J. B. Watkins Land Company and Watkins National Bank in Lawrence. The building was originally commissioned by Lawrence financier Jabez Bunting Watkins and was completed by 1888.

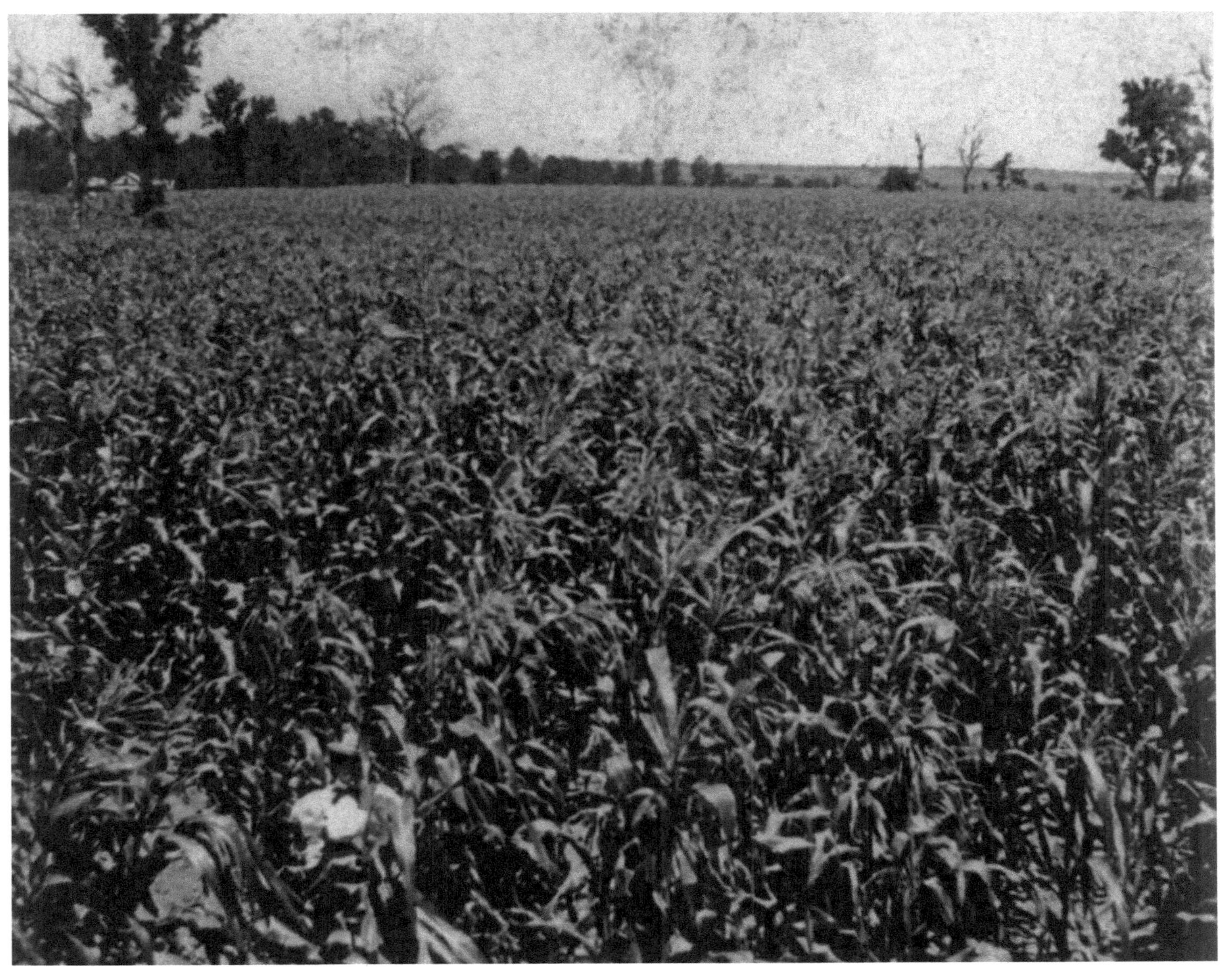

A woman (front left) is all but dwarfed by a field of corn in eastern Kansas. Today, Kansas ranks among the top 12 corn-producing states in the U.S.

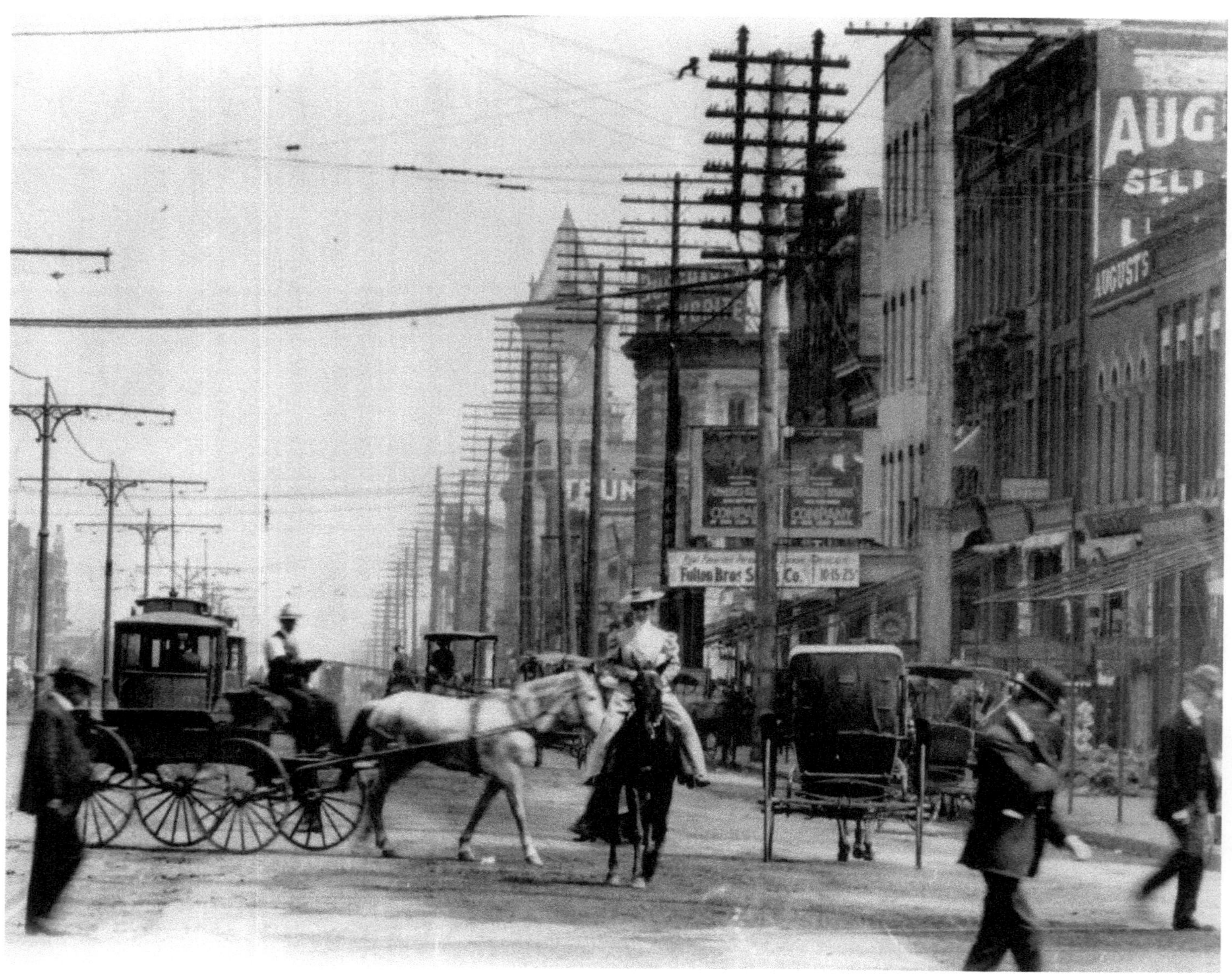

By 1900, this street in Topeka's business district was bustling with streetcars, wagons, carriages, and pedestrians. A boom period in the late 1880s doubled the city's population, and Topeka survived a period of economic depression in the 1890s.

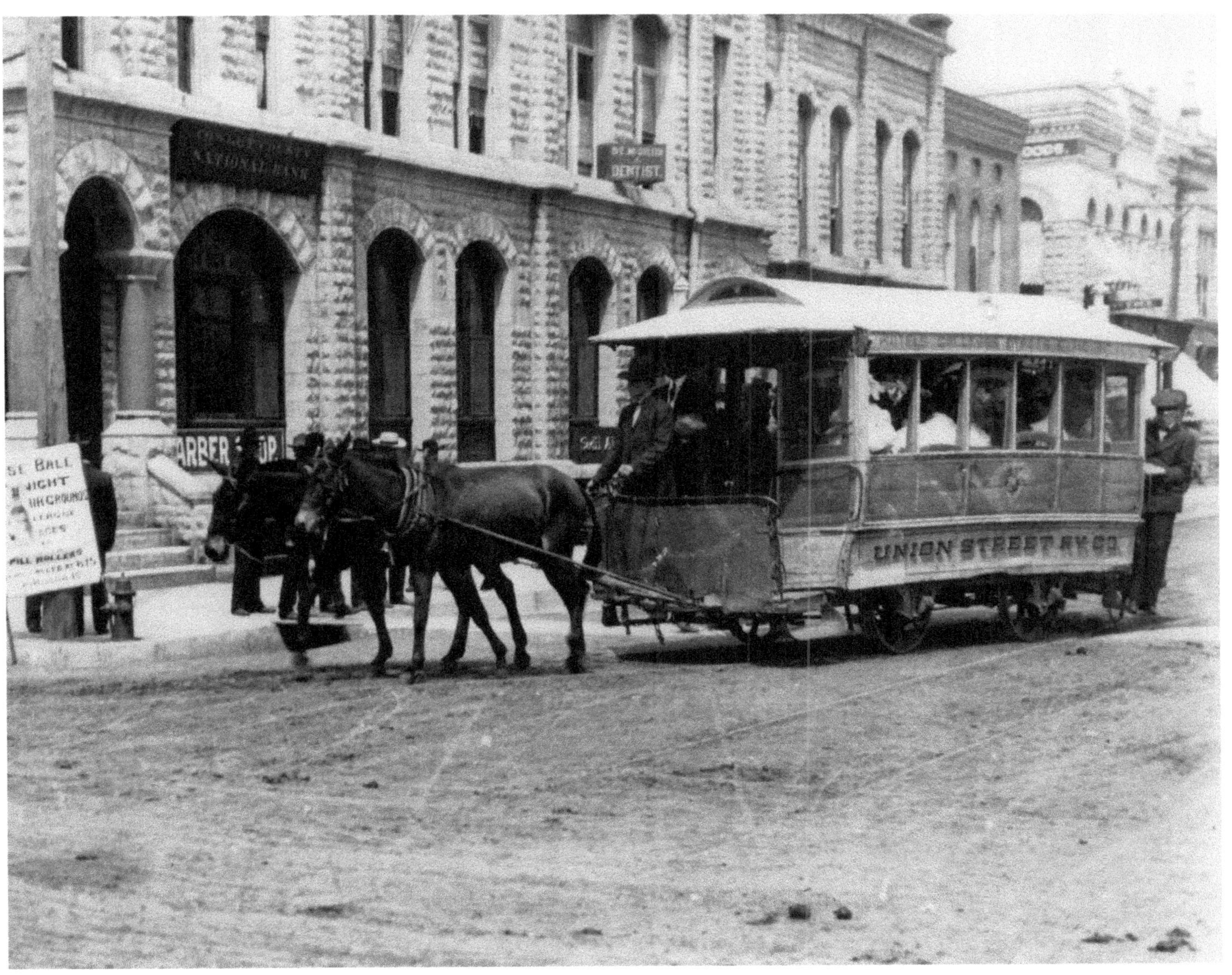

Mules might still have been pulling streetcars around the turn of the century, but the development of the railroads made Winfield a business hub and helped the population grow to more than 5,500 people by 1900.

A 1902 tornado approaches Lebanon, which in 1898 had been established as the geographical center of the contiguous 48 states. Lebanon, in north-central Kansas, is no stranger to tornados. They strike the area at a slightly higher average than the rest of Kansas and at 185 percent of the national average.

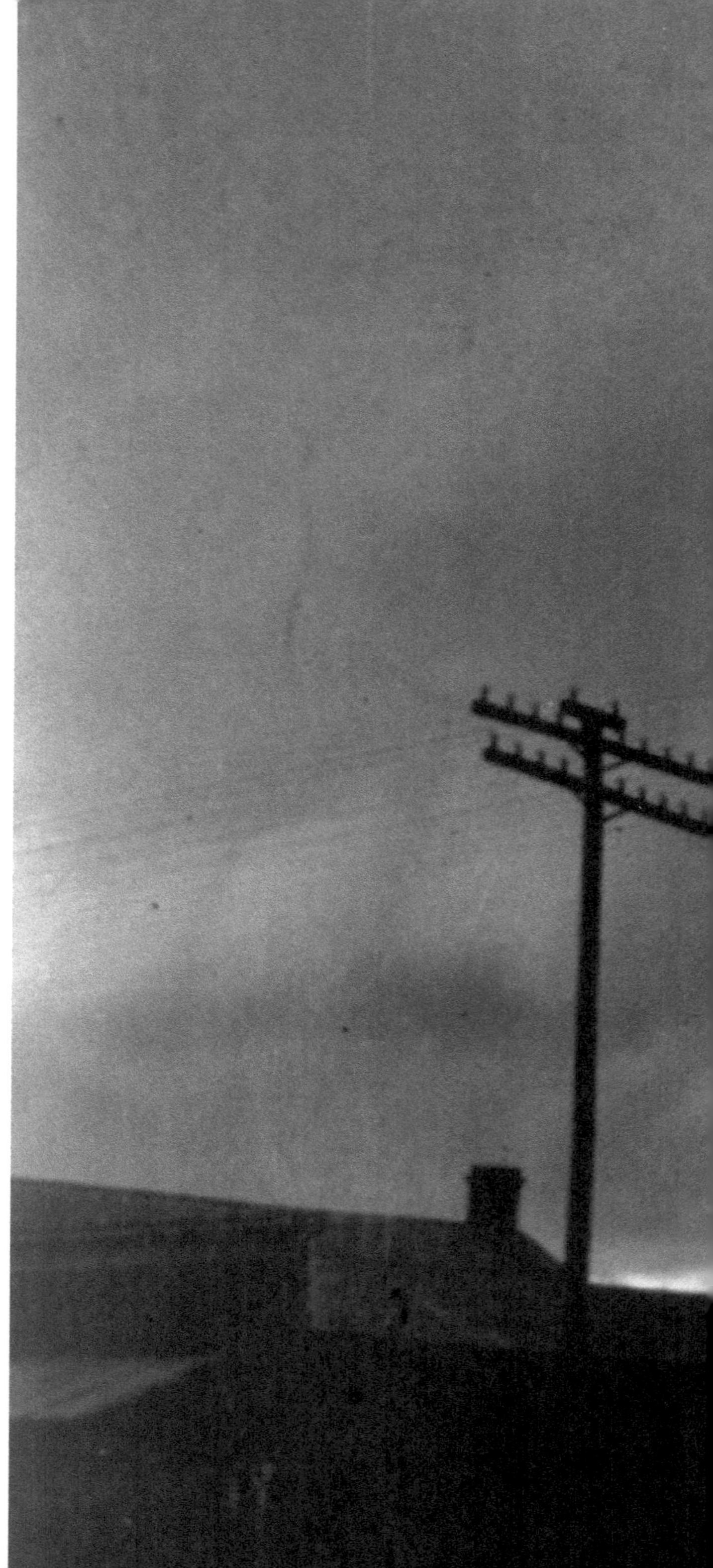

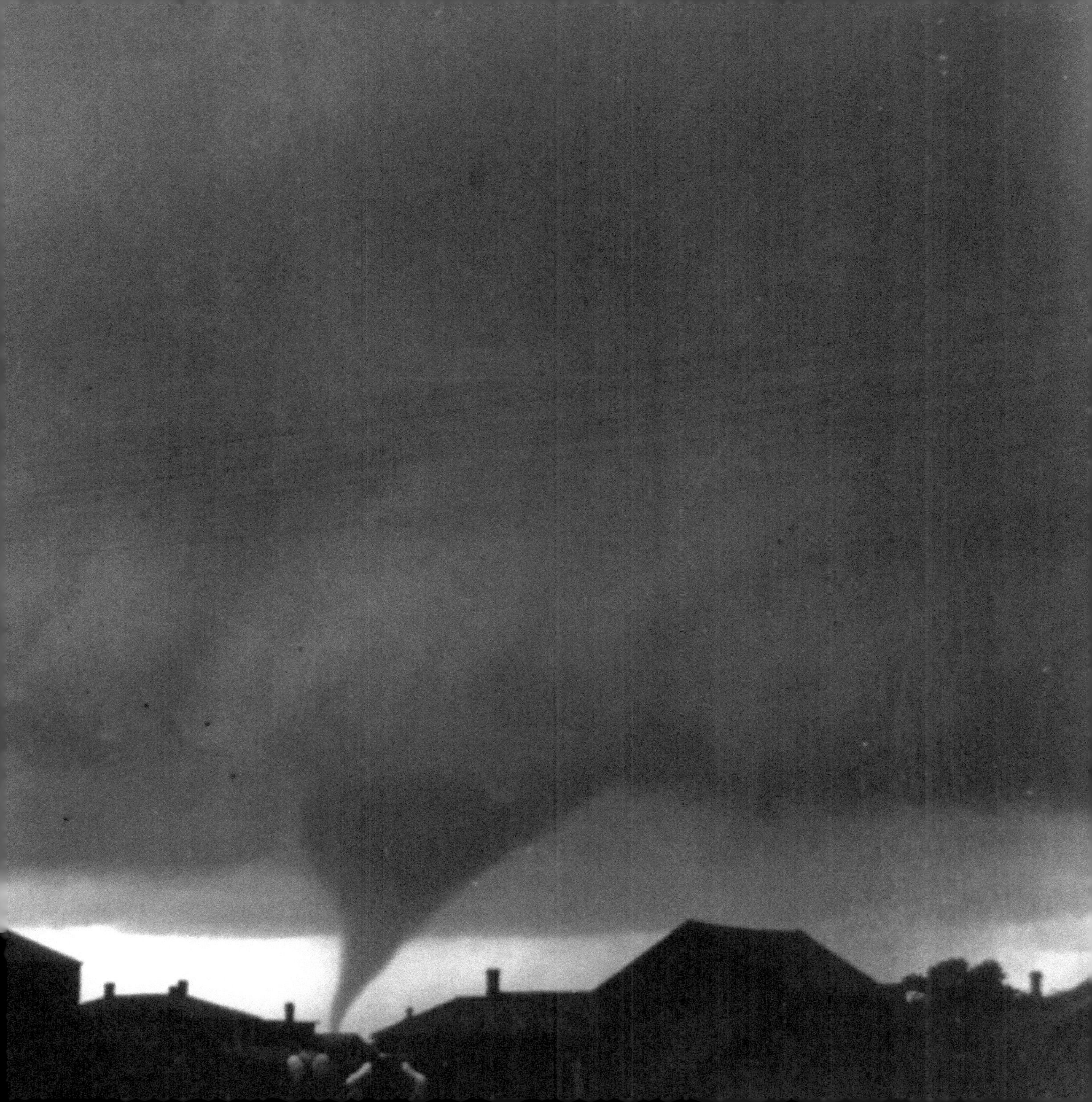

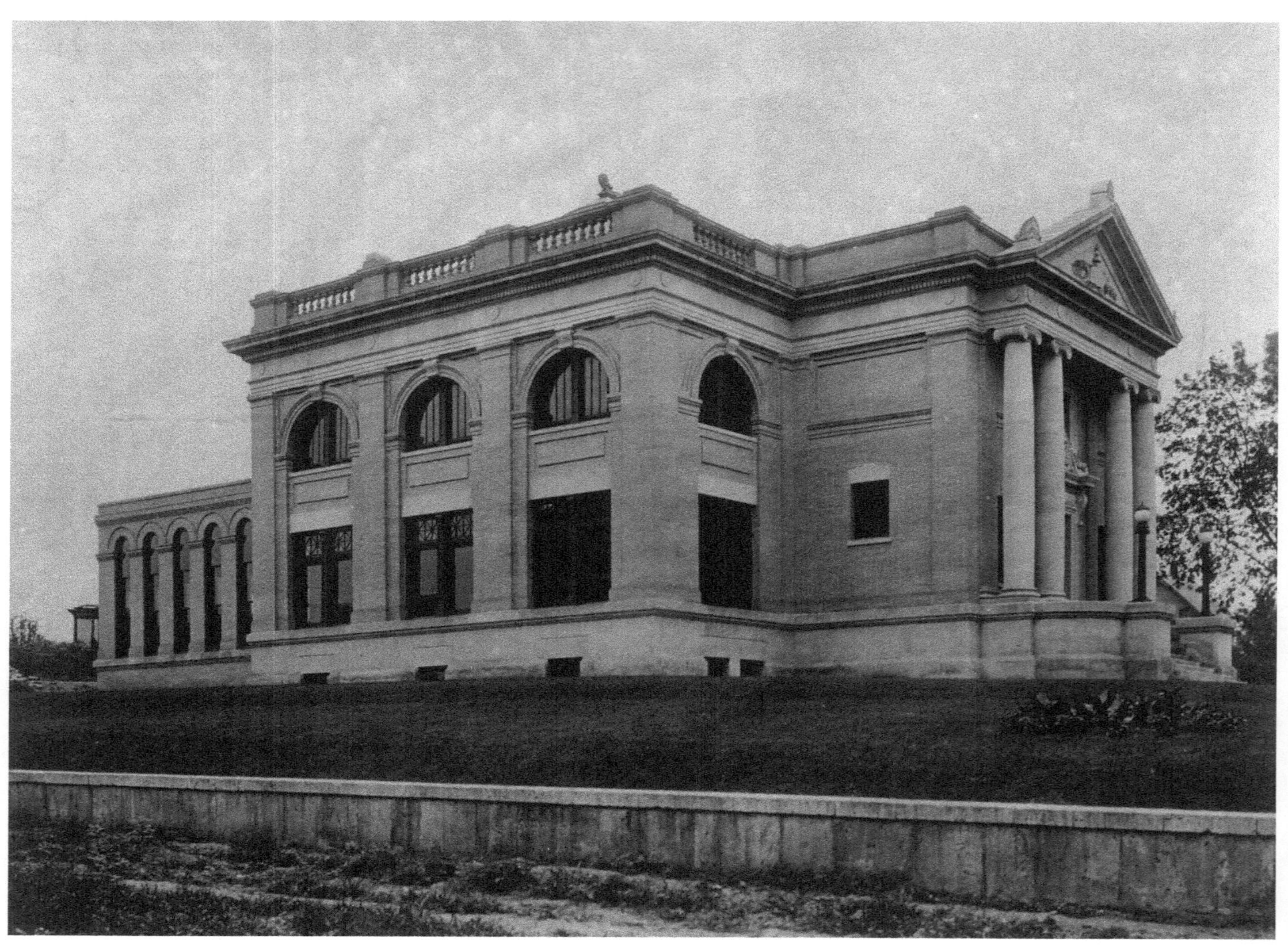

Many of the 1,689 Carnegie Libraries built in the United States from 1883 to 1929 were smaller than Leavenworth's. The building was photographed in 1902. Scottish-American businessman and philanthropist Andrew Carnegie—considered a robber baron by many—donated the money to build the libraries.

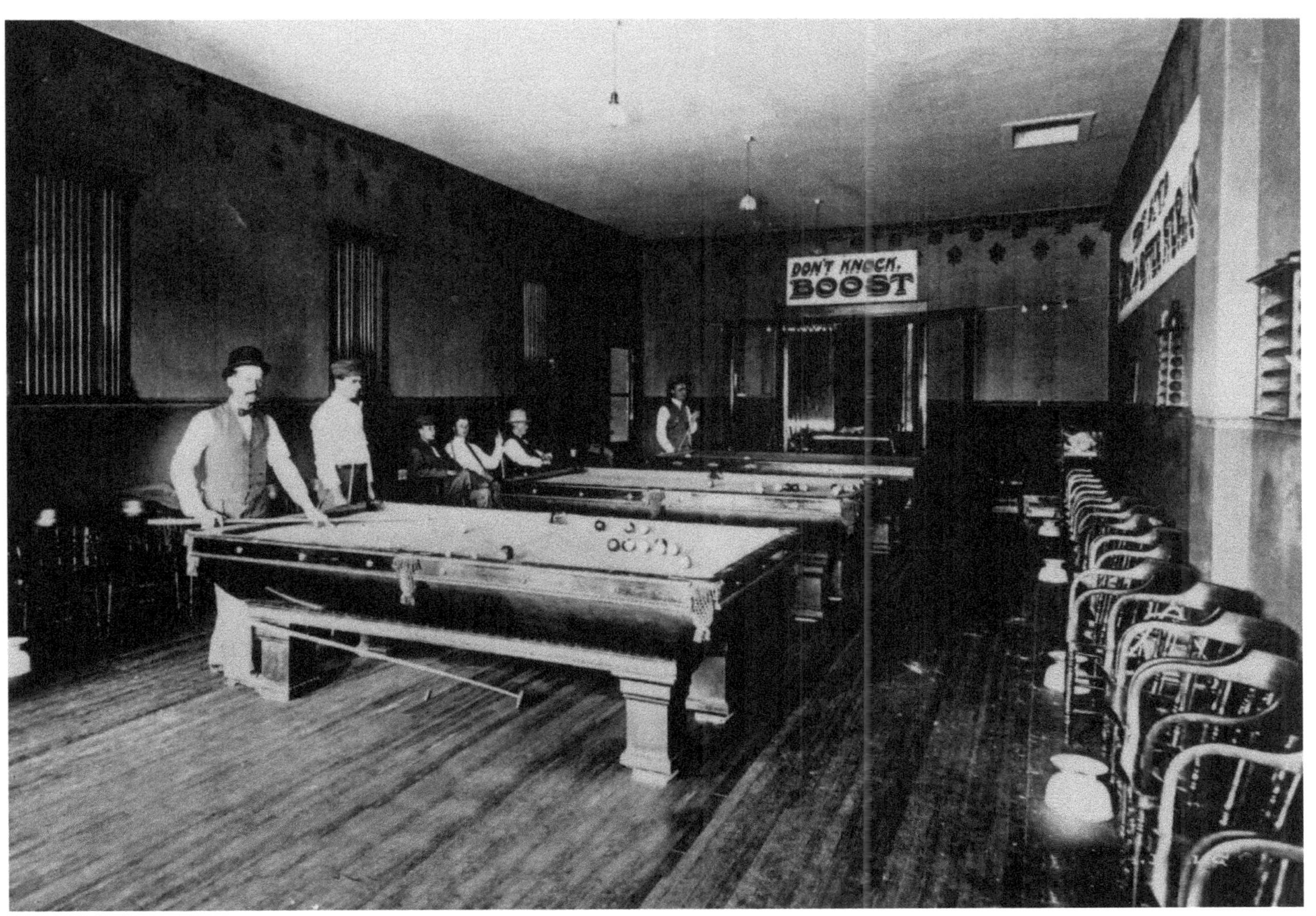

Encourage, not criticize, was the word of the day in the recreation room of the Young Men's Commercial Room in Sterling. A sign on the wall suggests that players should encourage each other and show respect for their opponents.

Pictured are Northern Surprise and Jessamy at Lowes Kennels in Lawrence. They're described as the sire and mother of America's best coursing hounds—dogs that pursue rabbits by sight, not scent. Included in this category are greyhounds, Afghans, borzois, whippets, and salukis.

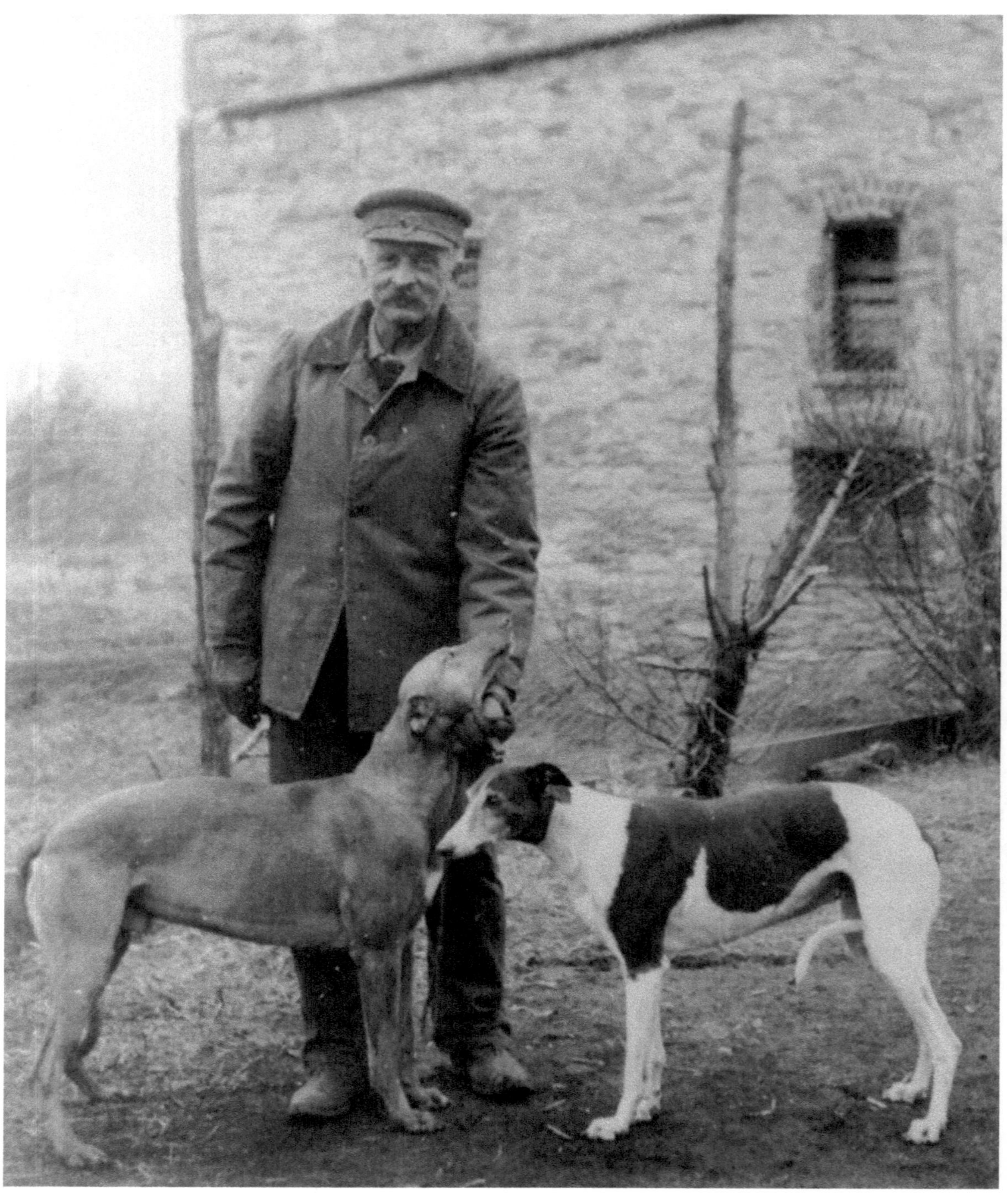

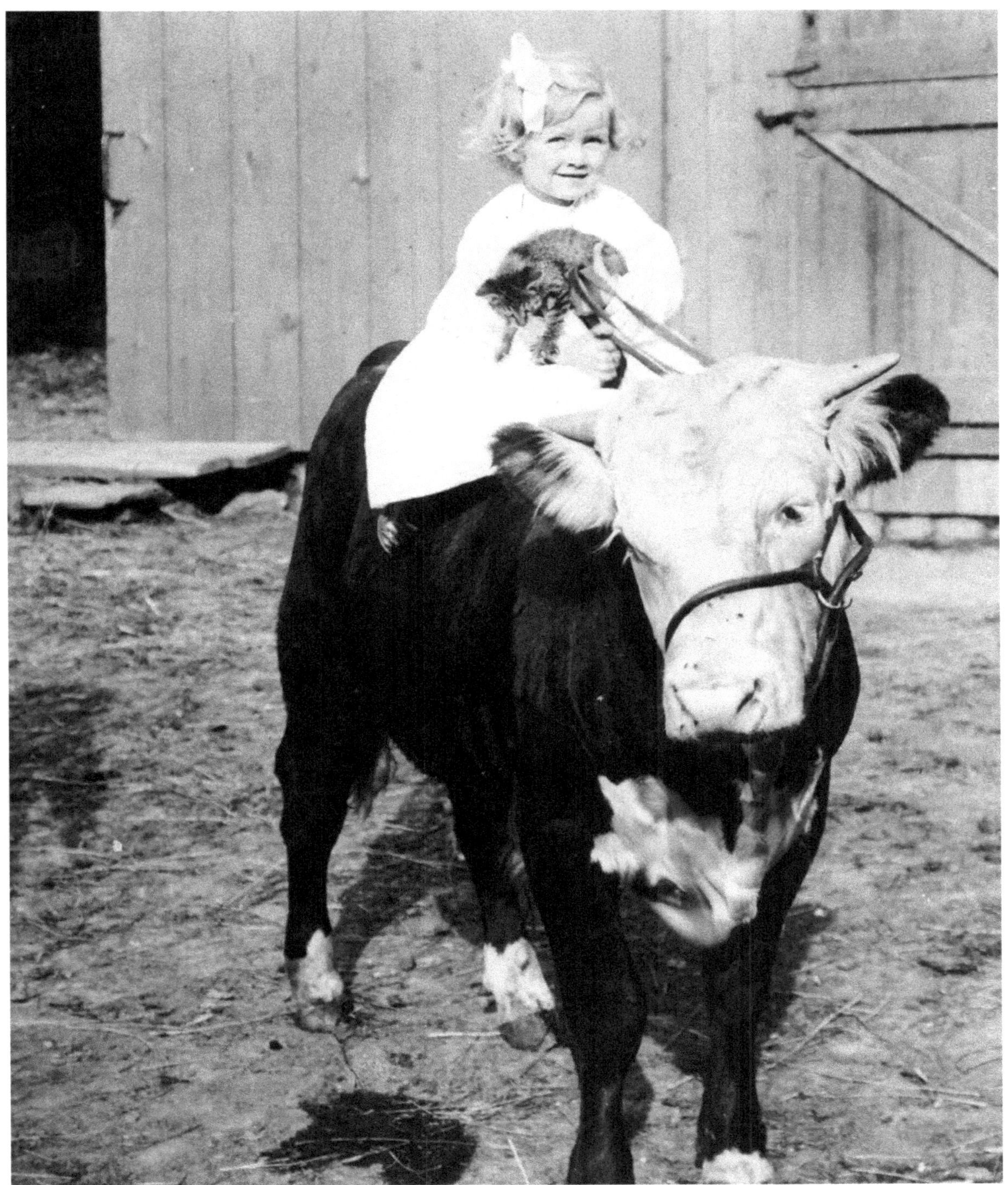

Taken on a stock farm in western Kansas, this photo draws on two classic elements of cuteness—an attractive young girl holding a kitten—and adds the surprise element of her being seated on a cow.

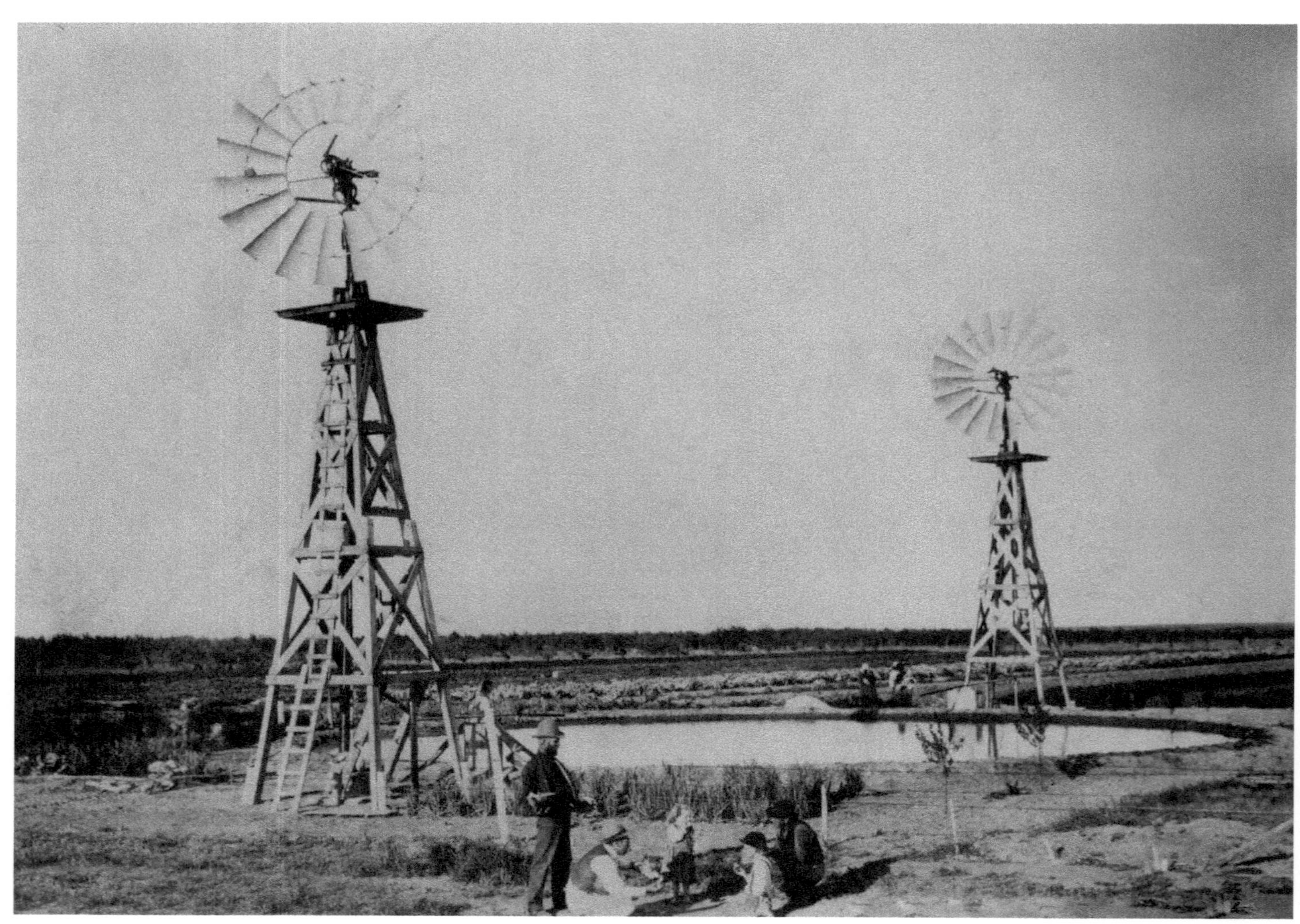

Well before Kansans began viewing wind power as an energy source, farmers, geologists, and engineers devised a system in which windmills helped pump water from deep wells to irrigation ponds. In a photo titled "The Garden of the Desert," windmills and a pond in Goodland are used to irrigate fields.

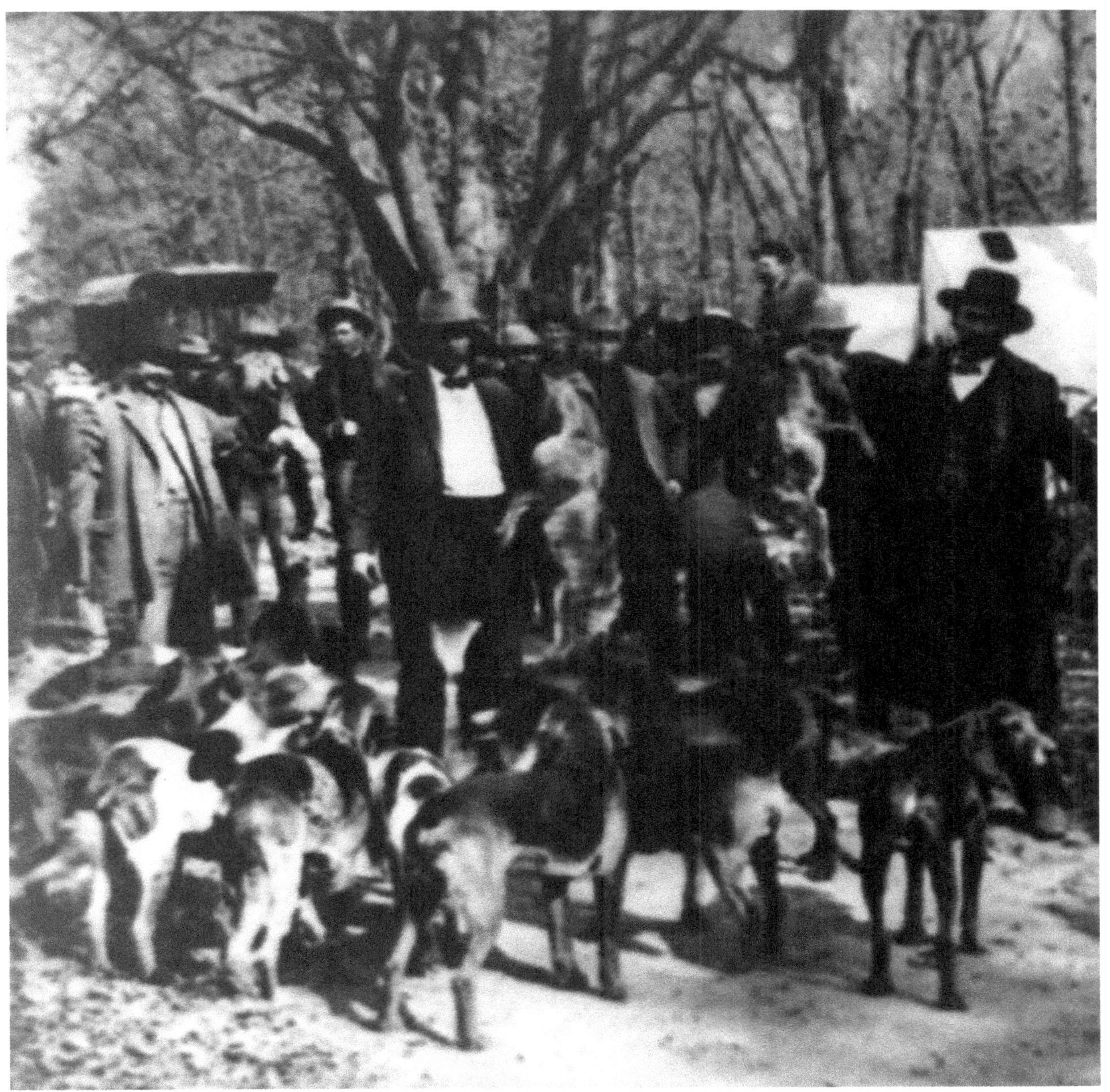

In a photo dating sometime between 1900 and 1910, hunters and a pack of foxhounds are pictured with their prey—two prairie wolves and a grey fox.

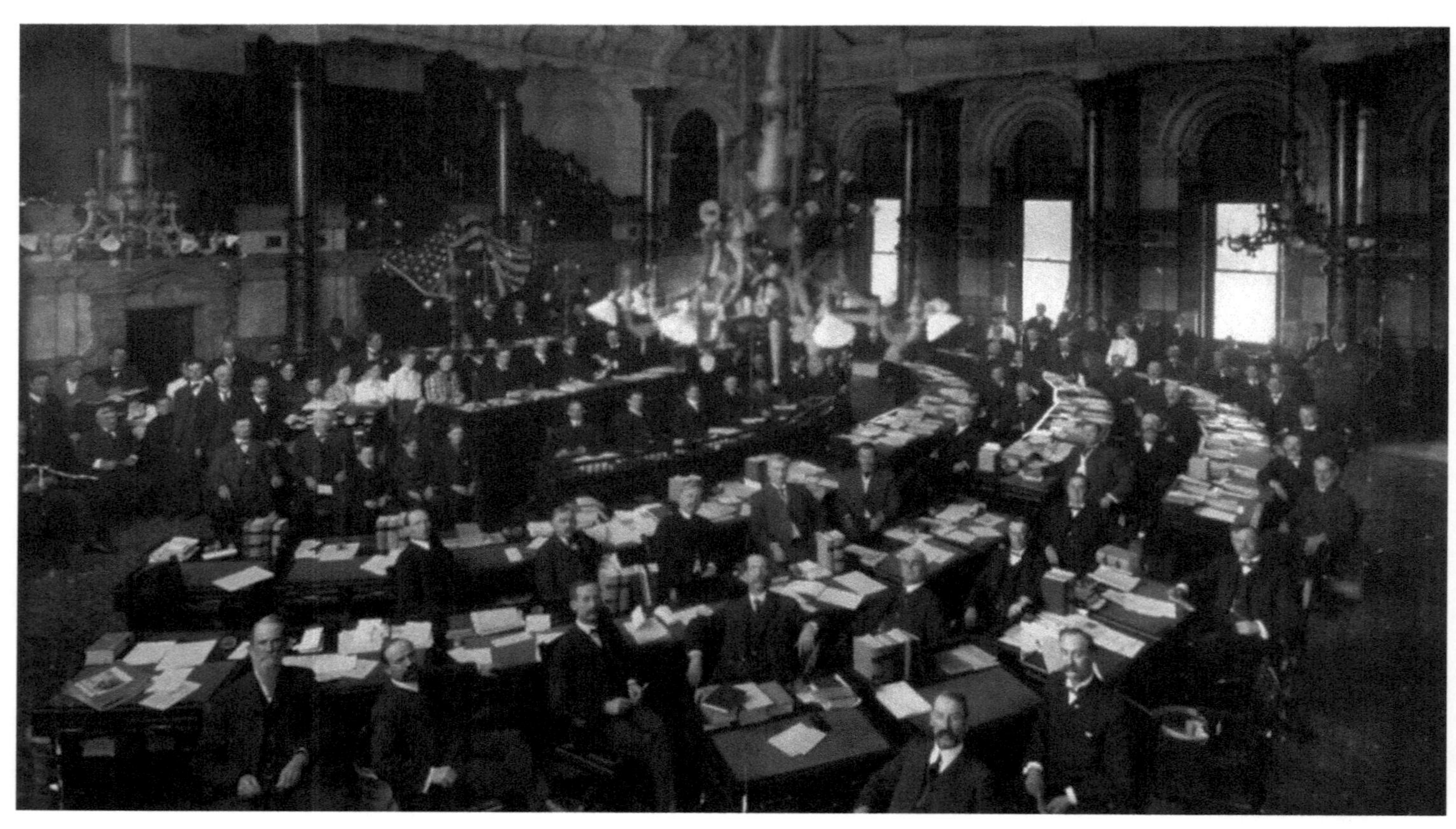

In 1905, Kansas senators face the camera for a formal portrait taken in their chambers at the Capitol in Topeka. The American flag displayed in the background featured 45 stars; Alaska, Arizona, Hawaii, New Mexico, and Oklahoma were not yet part of the Union.

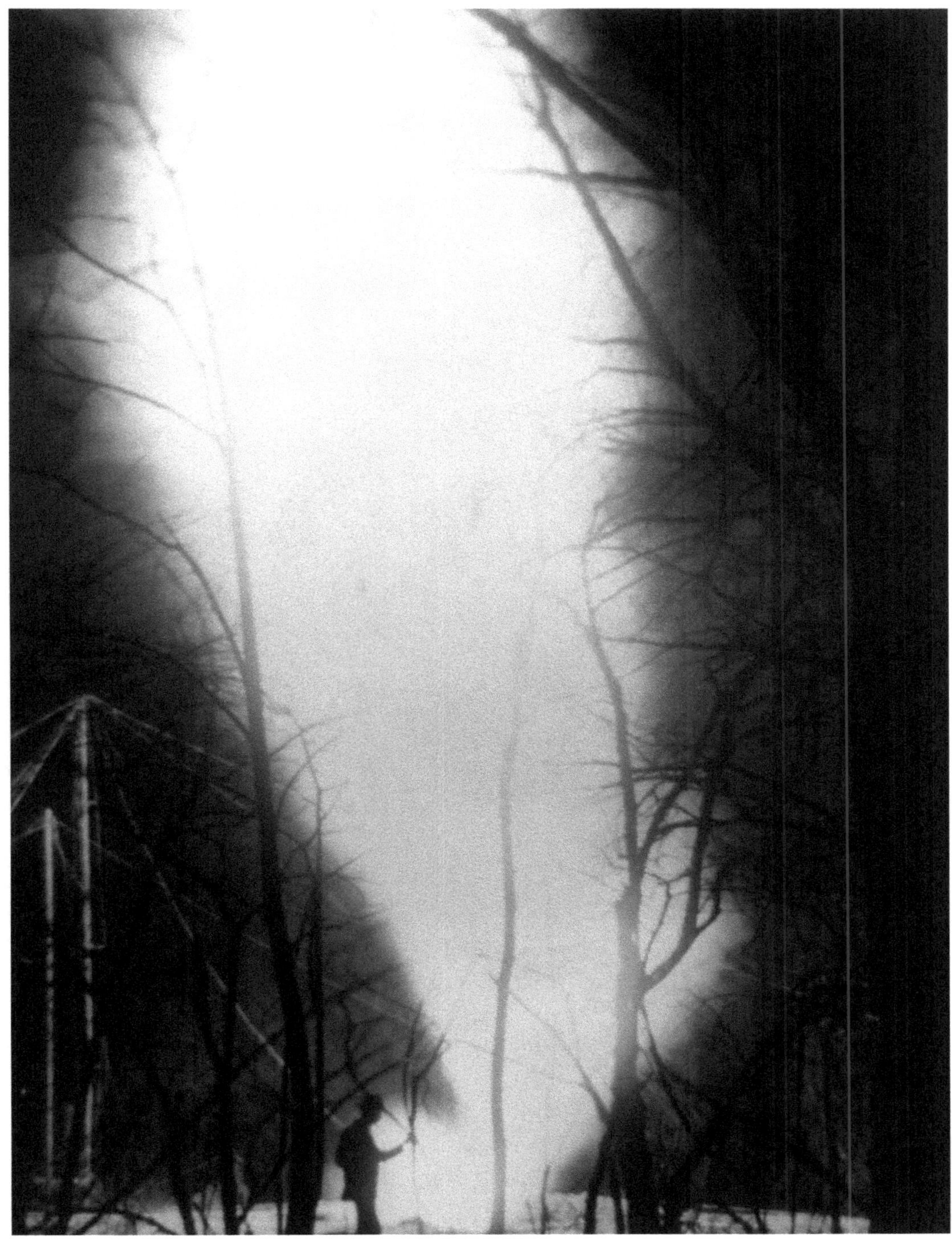

In 1906, a gas well in Caney caught fire and became something of a tourist attraction. W. E. McKinney, a Coffeyville photographer, snapped the shot, which was soon depicted on postcards. Although the fire was in Caney, Independence and Coffeyville also claimed it, as did Bartlesville, Oklahoma.

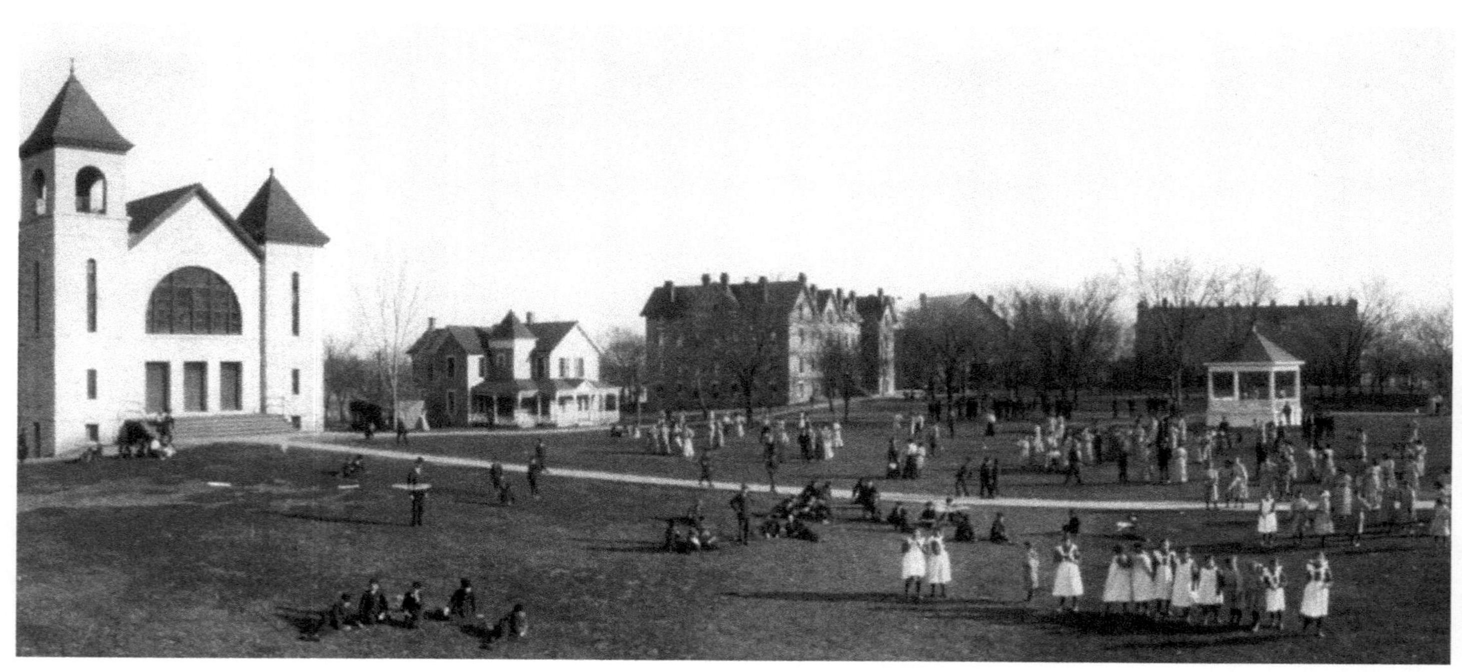

Lawrence's Haskell Institute, the predecessor of Haskell Indian Nations University, was founded in 1884 to educate Indian children. The first students were 22 members of the Ponca and the Ottawa tribes.

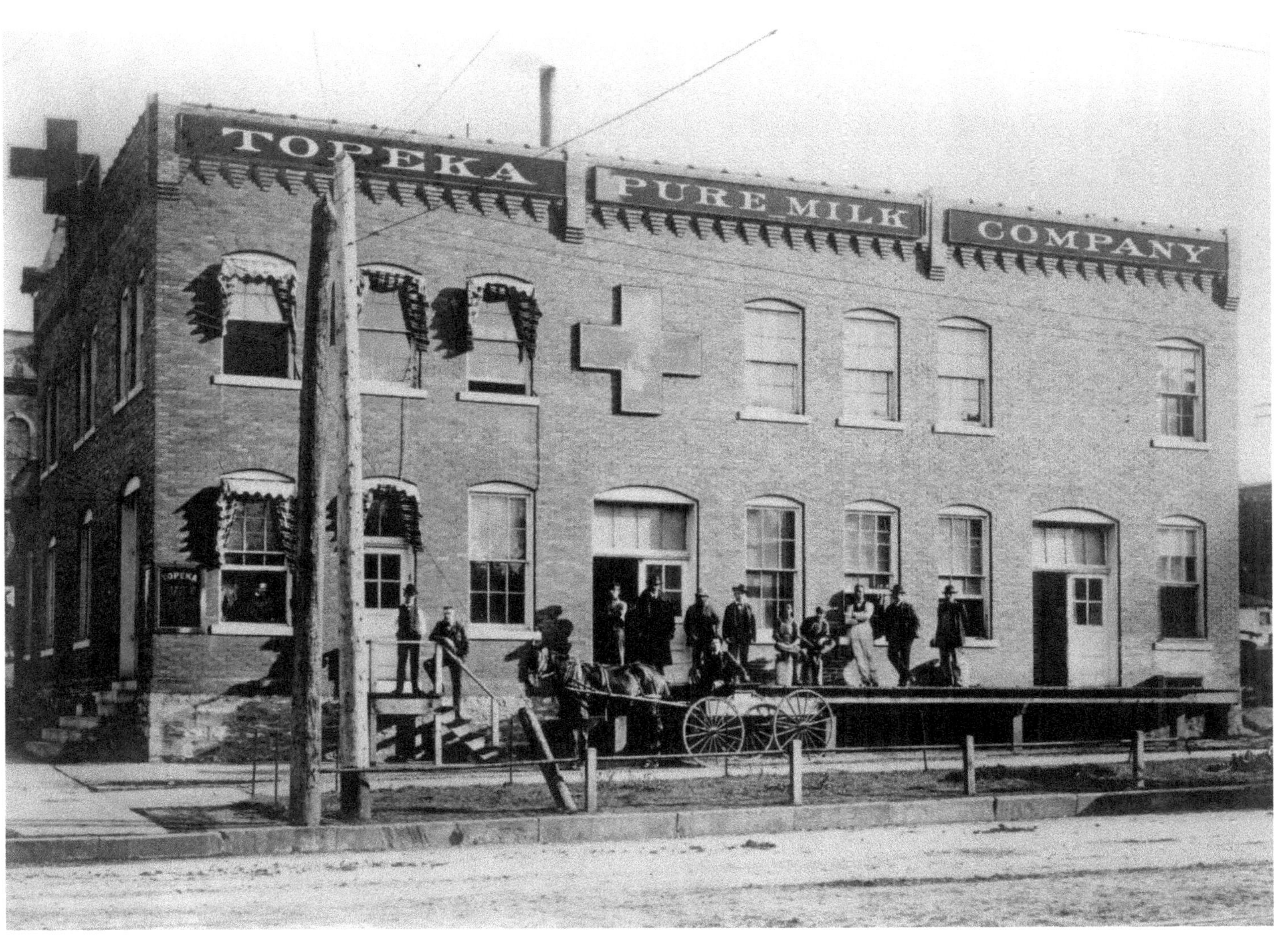

The exterior of the Pure Milk Company of Topeka is pictured in this photo. It's among the visual materials contained in the Library of Congress's Booker T. Washington collection in Washington. A *Kansas City Journal* article published on August 10, 1907, noted that Washington was to speak in Topeka the following week before the Business League, a Negro organization.

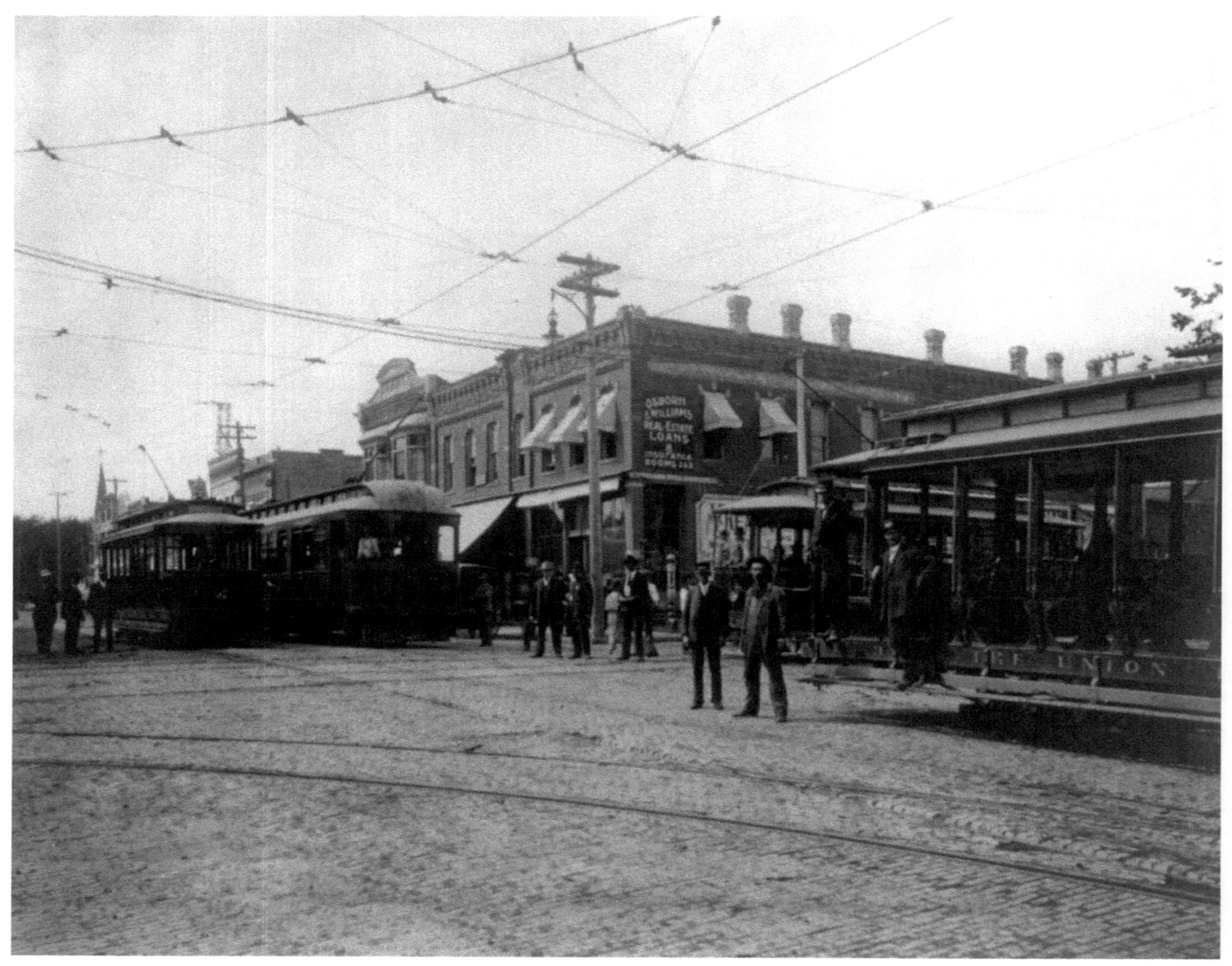

Four streetcars converge at an intersection and transfer hub in Coffeyville in 1907. First established as a trading center for a rich farming area, the city diversified with several new industries in the early 1900s and had a population of 18,500 by 1915. The town was founded in 1869 by Colonel James A. Coffey.

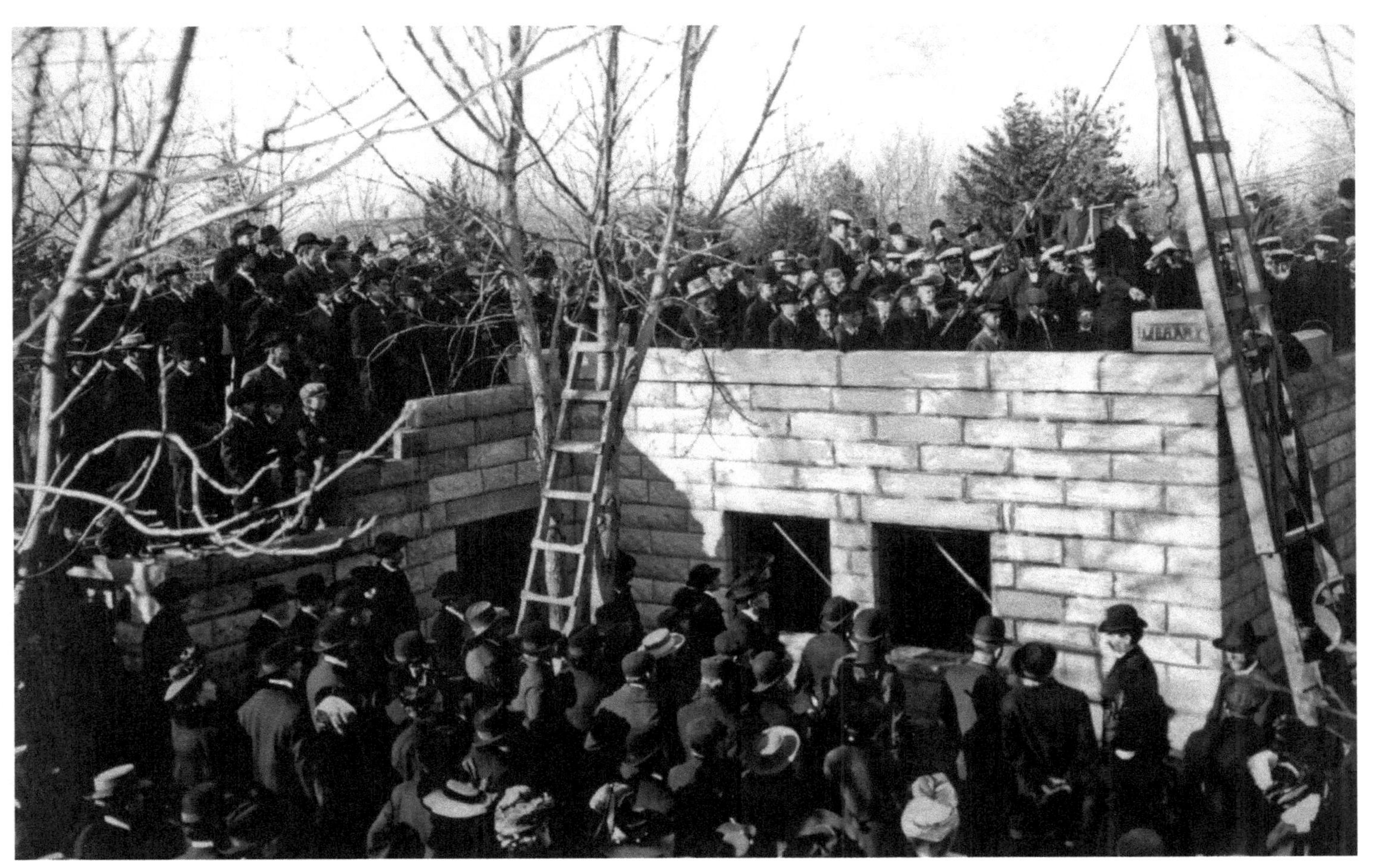

Workers lay the cornerstone for Bethany College's Carnegie Library in or around 1908. Founded in 1881 in Lindsborg, a Swedish-immigrant community, the college has counted many Lutheran students among its enrollment.

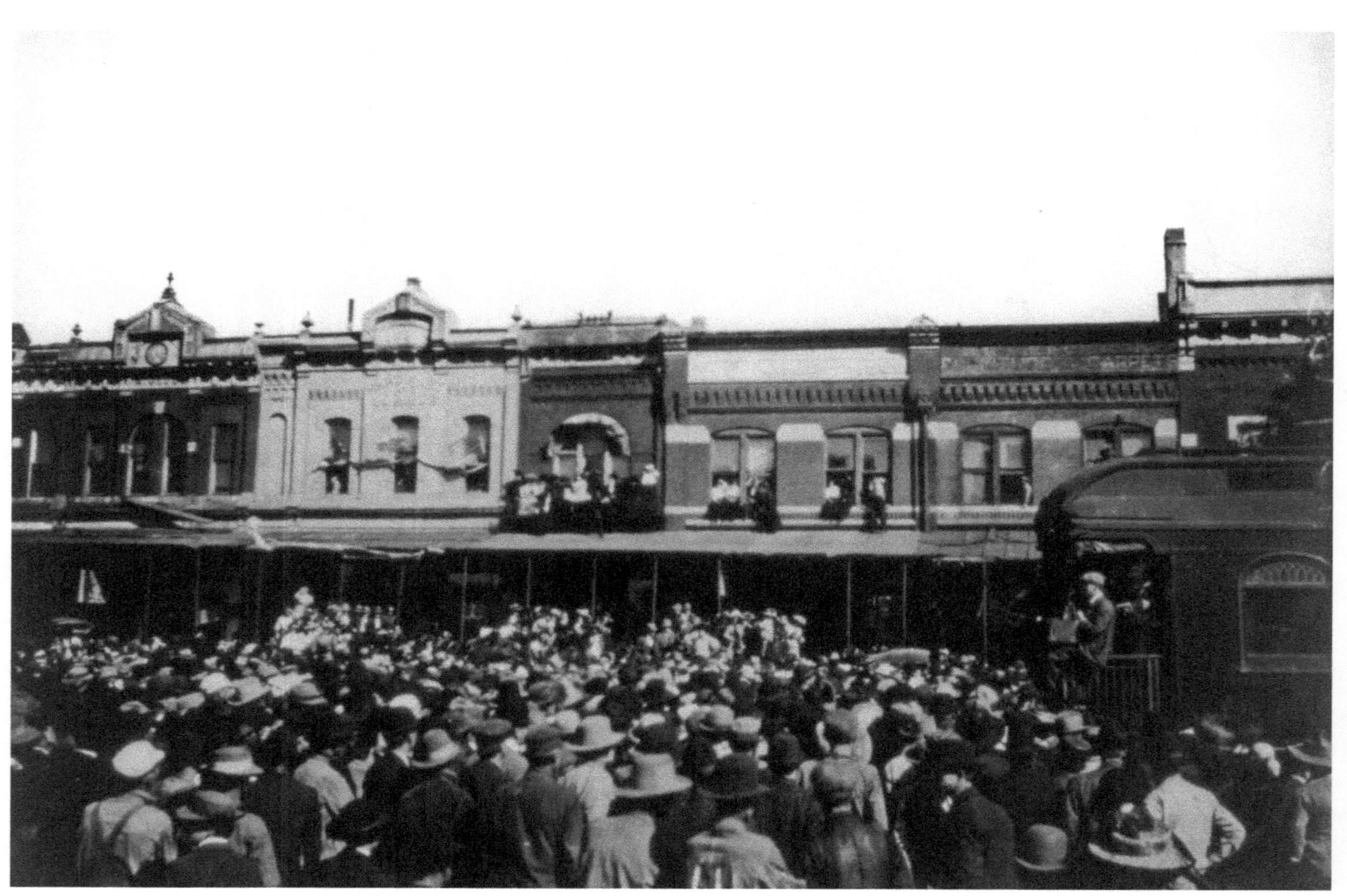

During an October 1908 campaign trip to Kansas, soon-to-be president William Howard Taft addresses an audience from the back of a train. Taft was the 27th president and served one four-year term. He was defeated by Woodrow Wilson in 1912.

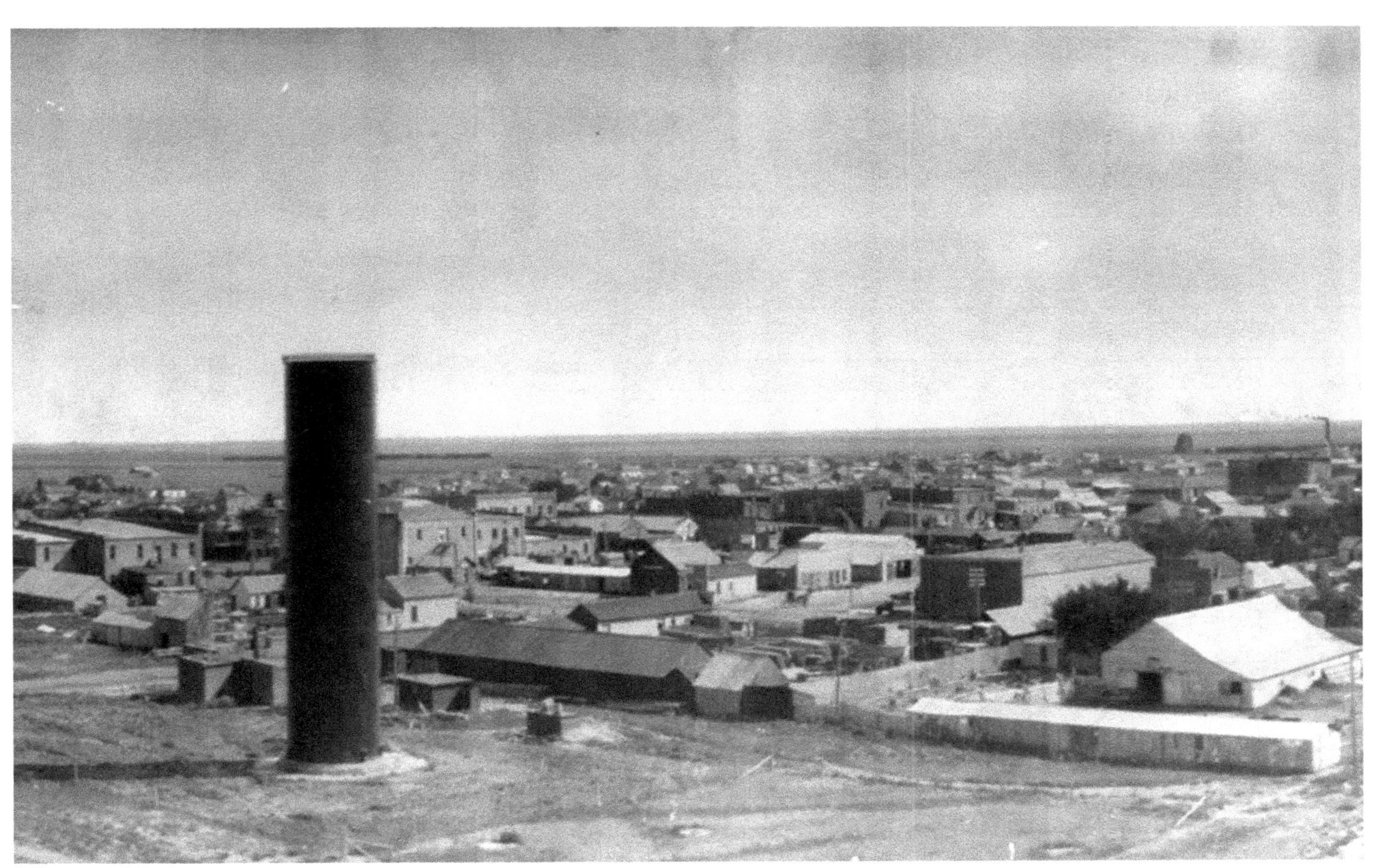

A panoramic view of Goodland taken in 1907 shows the community's growth, but also offers a stark image of the flat terrain and vulnerability to wind and dust storms.

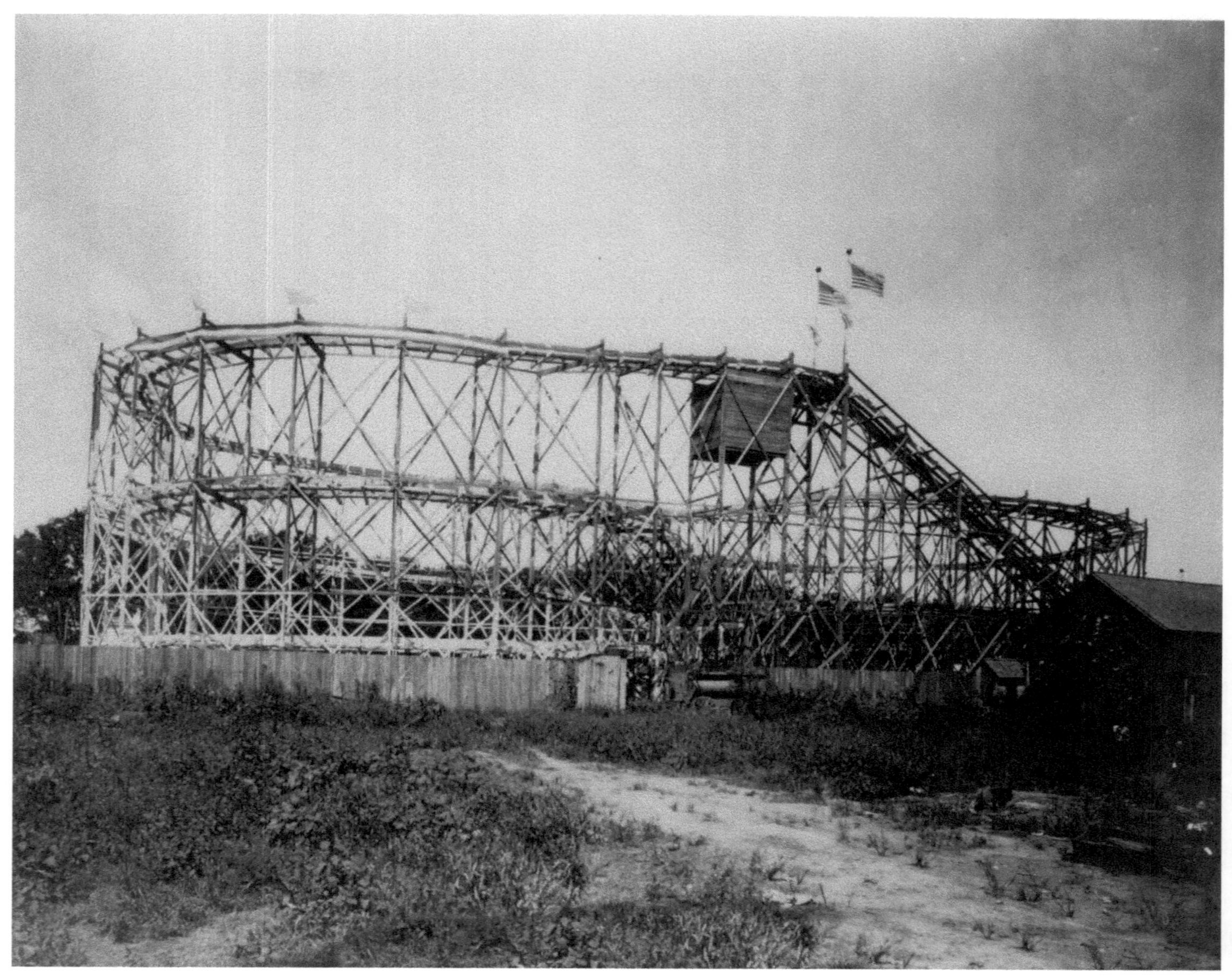

By today's standards, a 1907 roller coaster in Coffeyville may not be a match for Worlds of Fun or Six Flags, but it did bring modern thrills to fairgoers in southeast Kansas.

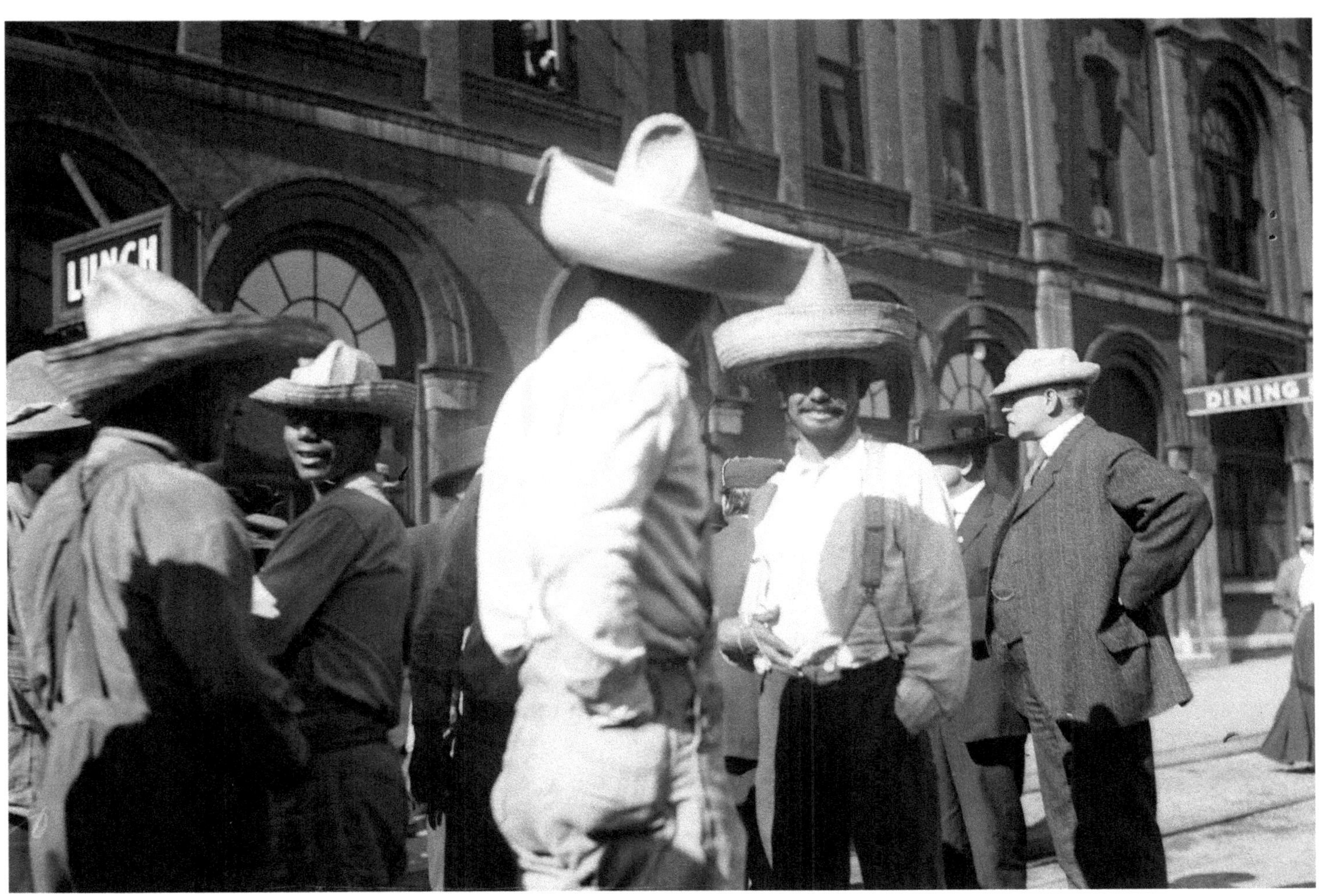

As far back as 1908, when this photo was taken in Newton, Kansans relied on seasonal laborers. Guest Mexican workers came north to help with harvests and other work.

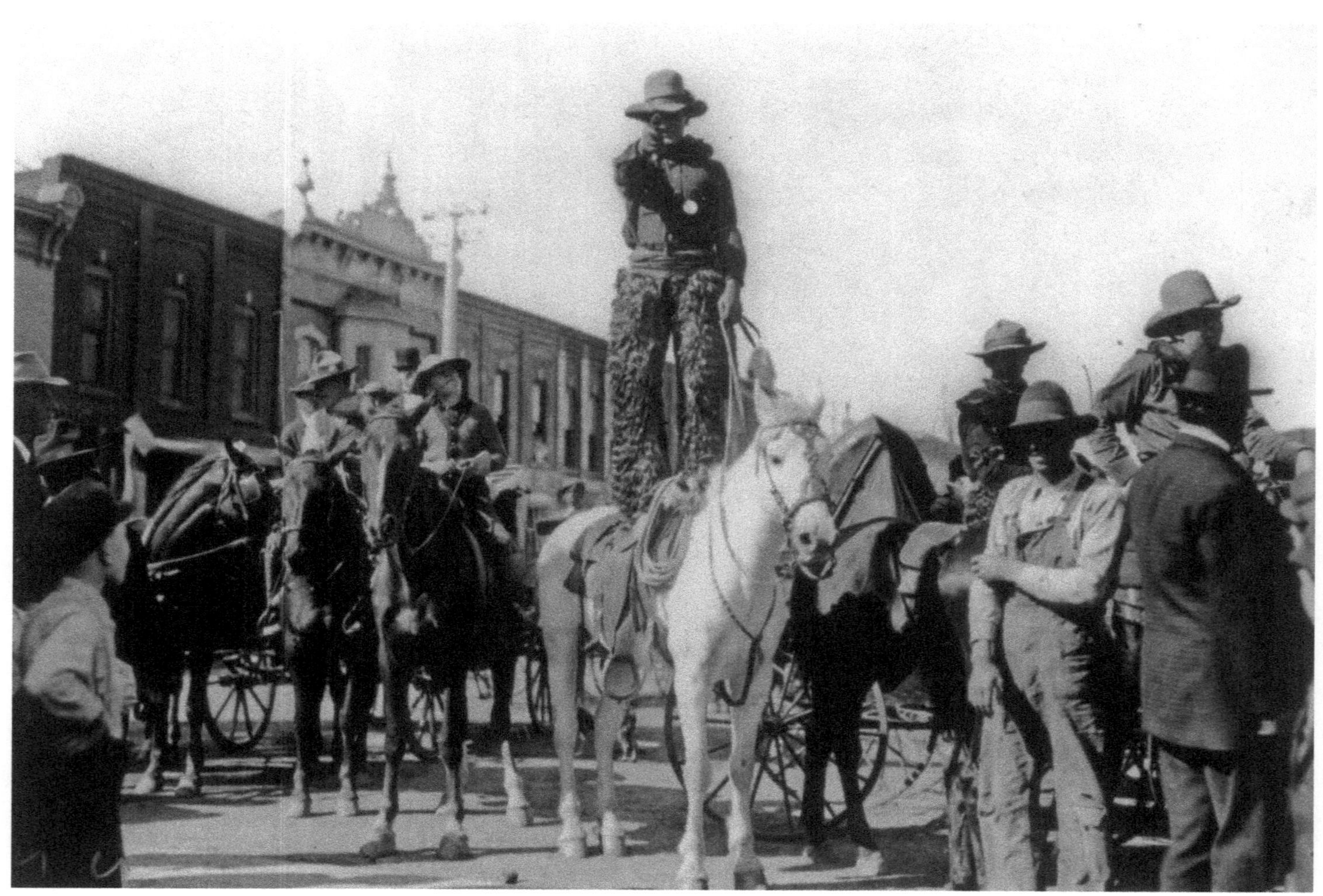

The image of a cowboy standing on his horse and pointing a revolver at the camera in Newton has a farcical air, but cowboys, Indians, cattle drives, and the colorful struggle between lawmen and outlaws played a significant role in nineteenth-century Kansas.

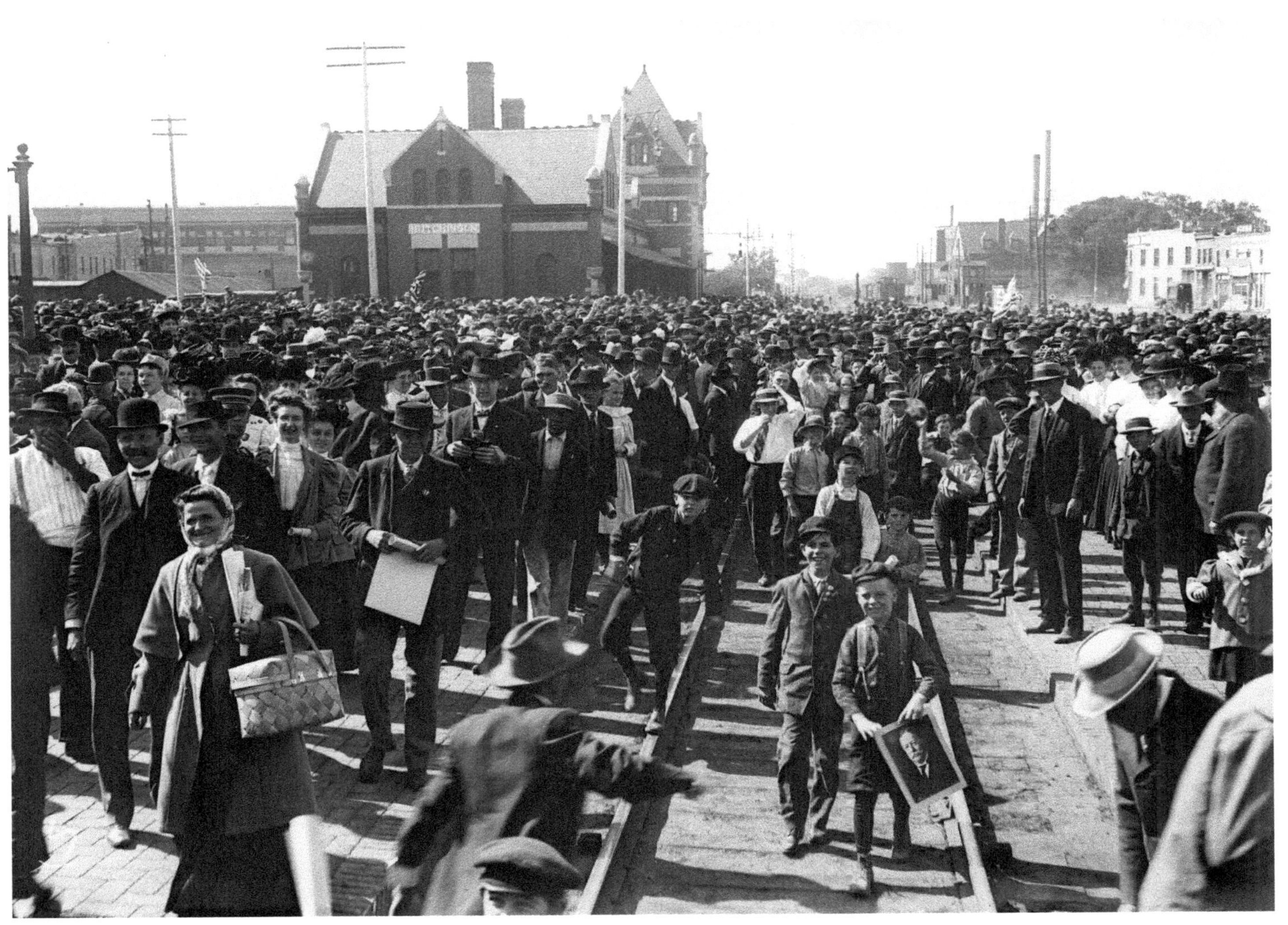

Before the television age, Kansans came out in force to see their presidents and presidential candidates in person. In Hutchinson, a crowd gathers to see William Howard Taft, the 27th president. Taft was elected in 1908.

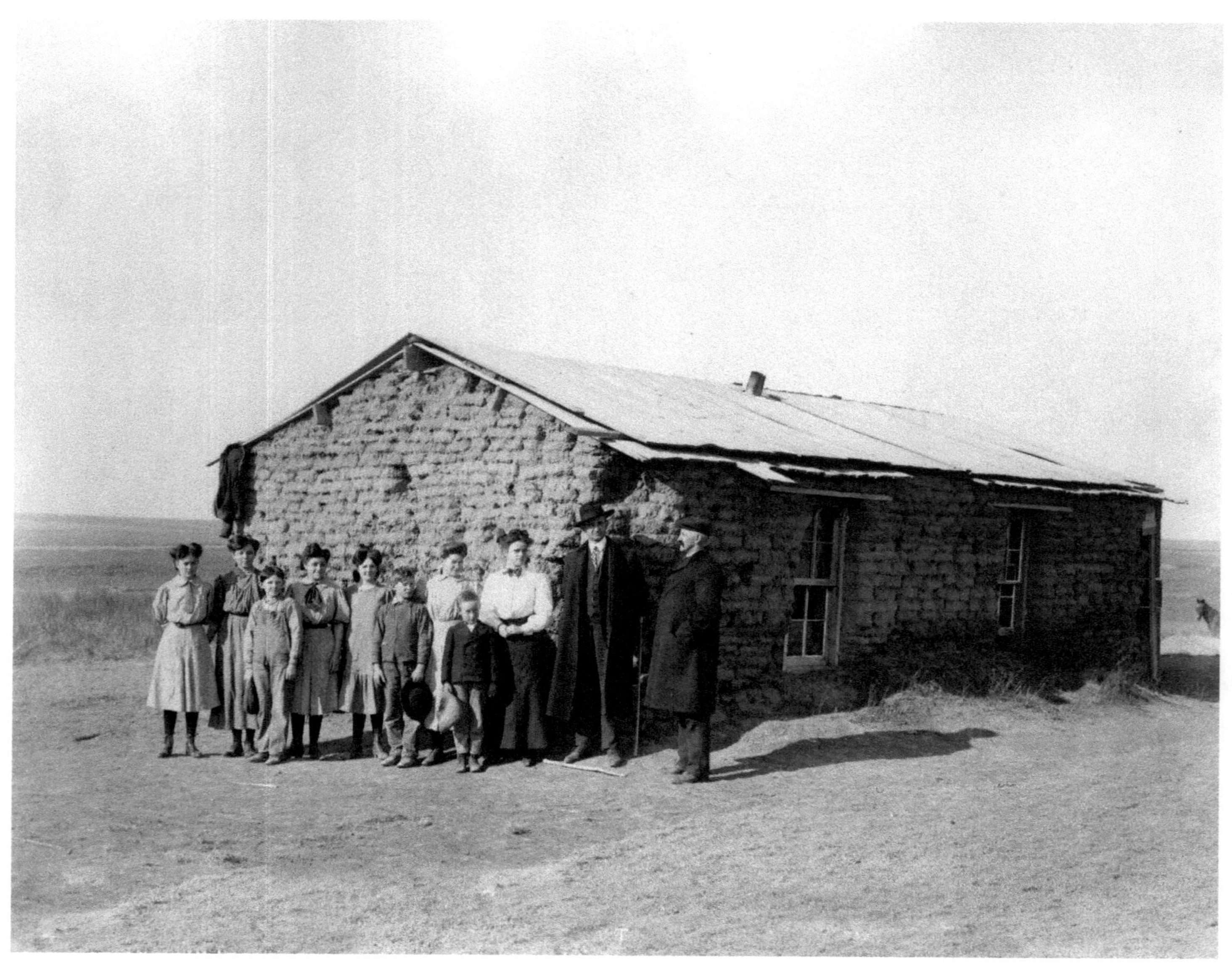

What's described as "the only remaining sod schoolhouse in Oberlin County" serves as the backdrop for a group of adults and children in Oberlin, located in Decatur County. The females' updos, probably Gibson Girl styles, reflect the fashionable hairstyles at the time the photograph was taken.

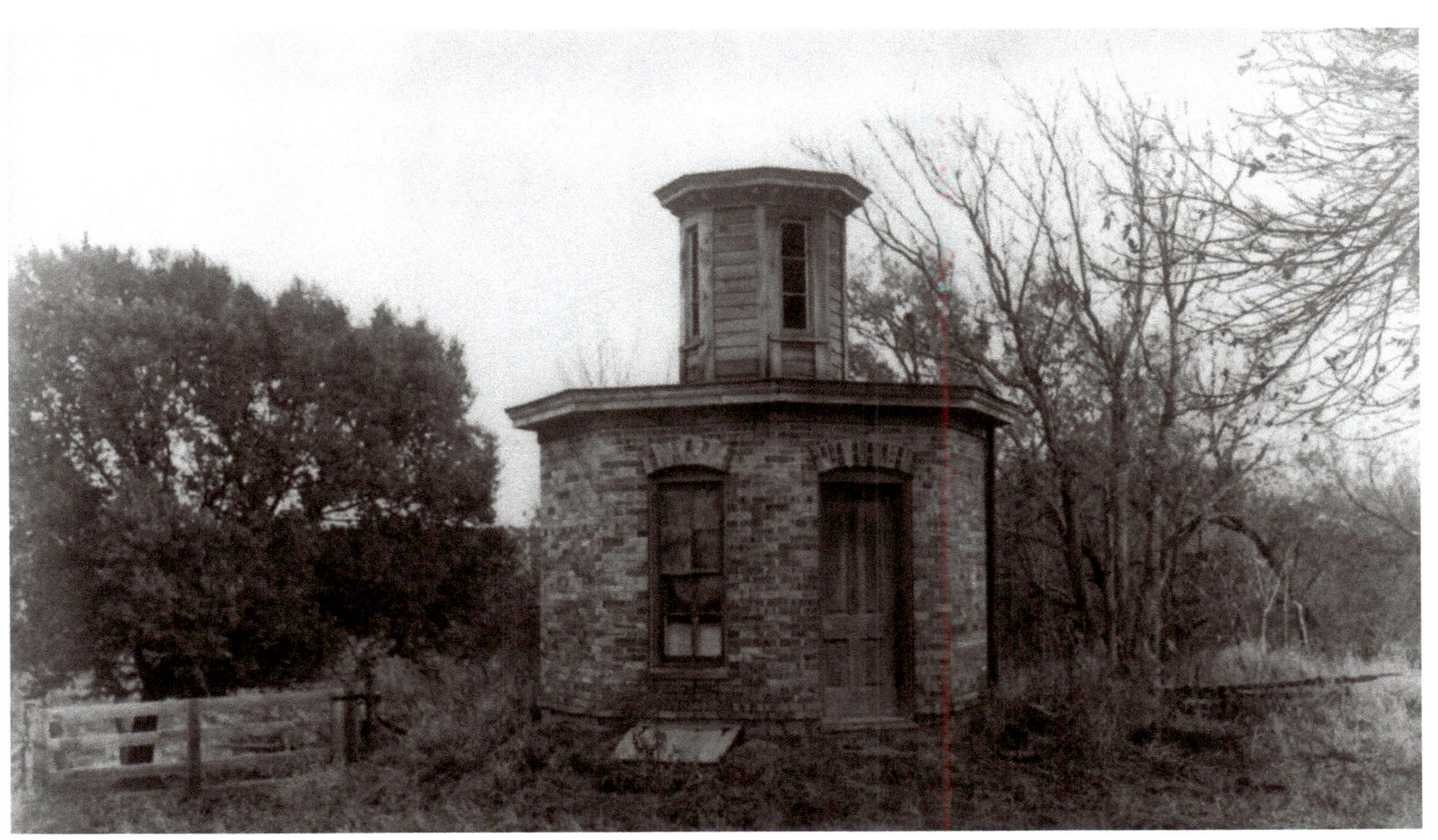

This unusual building, an octagonal brick structure with an octagonal wooden tower, served as the office of a Justice Holmberg. Taken in 1908, the photo notes that the building served as the "Office of Justice Holmberg in Sveadahl, 3 miles SW of Lindsborg." It also notes that Holmberg kept liquor in the building, and that he used the tower to keep watch over his workers and to "look out for Indians from across the river."

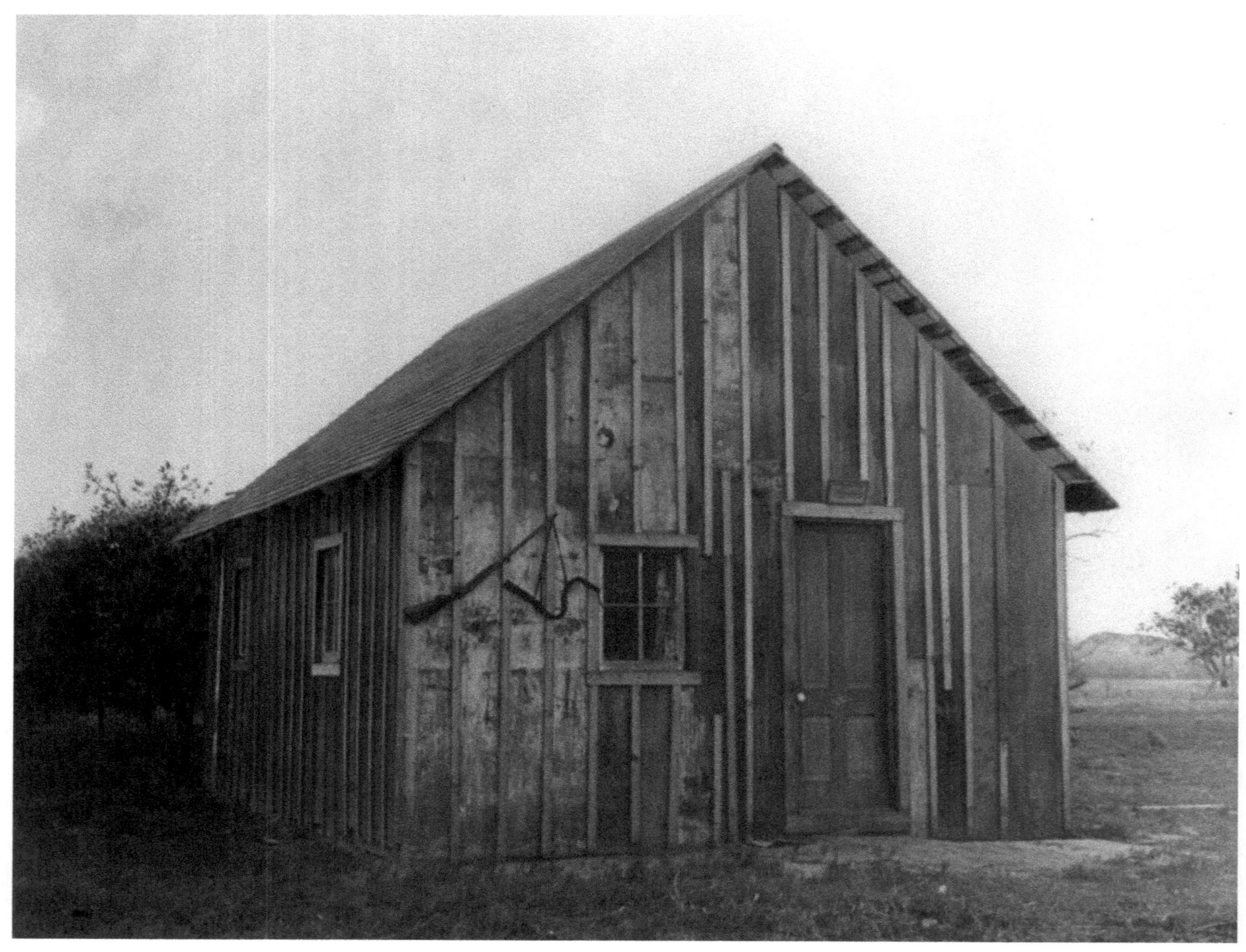

Sveadahl, a community three miles southwest of Lindsborg, was home to McPherson County's first courthouse. It's believed that the building also served as a post office and general store.

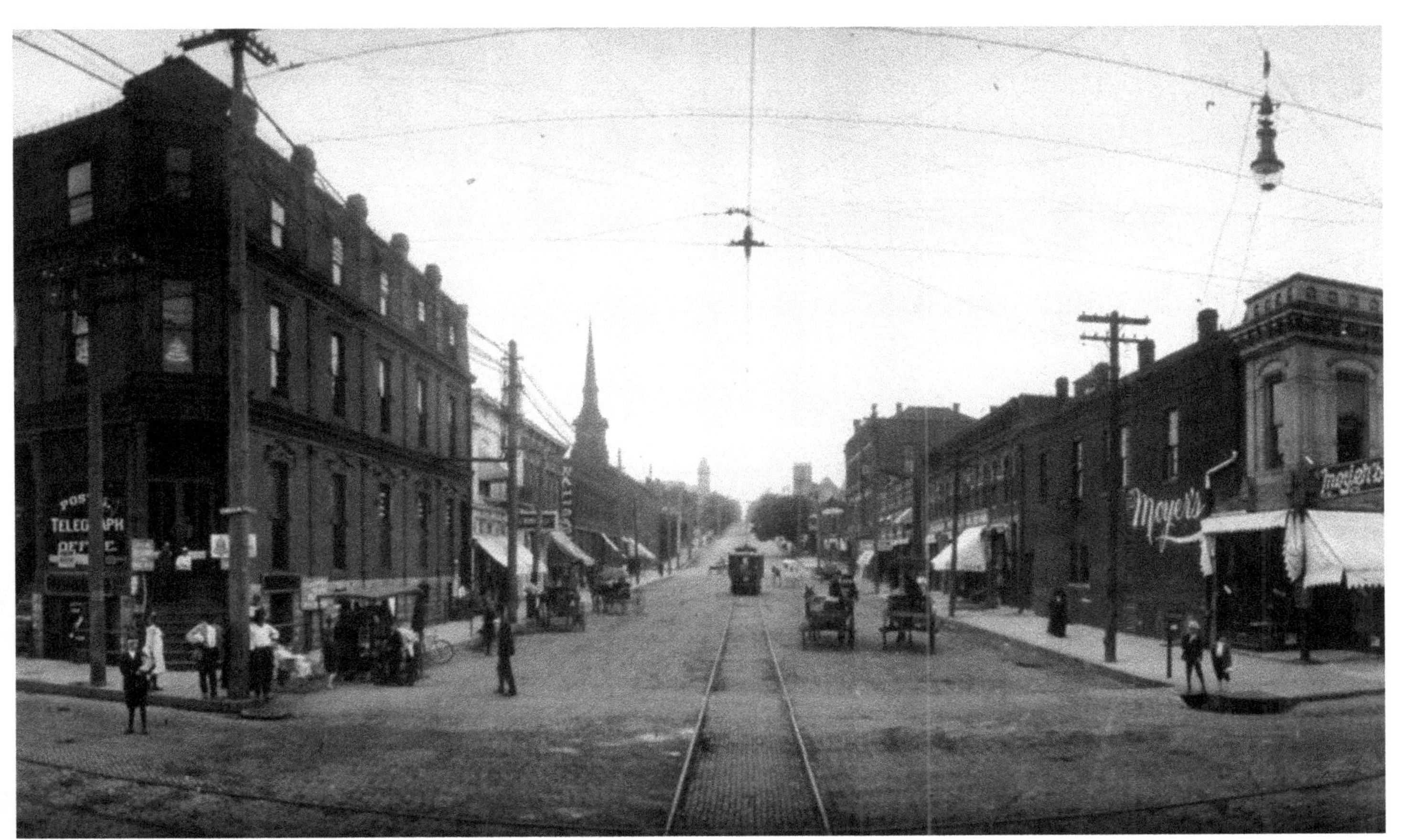

During the boom years of 1870 to 1900, railroads helped Atchison evolve from a bustling steamboat port on the Missouri River to an industrial-commercial center in northeast Kansas. Part of Atchison's business district is pictured here in 1909.

Pennsylvania Avenue and Myrtle Street in Independence intersect in this 1909 photo by F. J. Bandholtz, an Iowan who photographed the business districts of many Kansas cities and towns. Just miles away from Independence's downtown was one of several childhood homes of Laura Ingalls Wilder, who based part of her book *Little House on the Prairie* on the town.

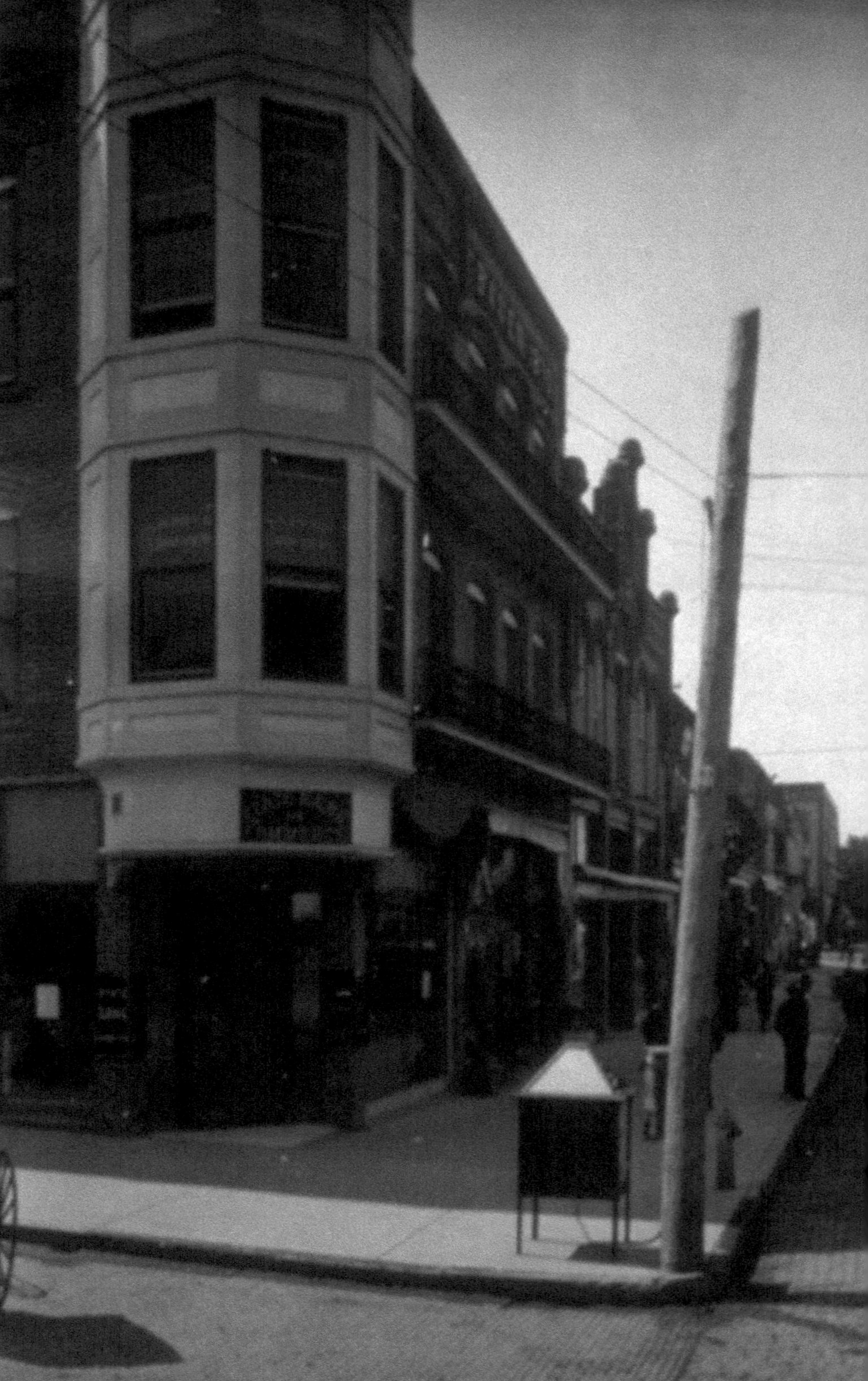

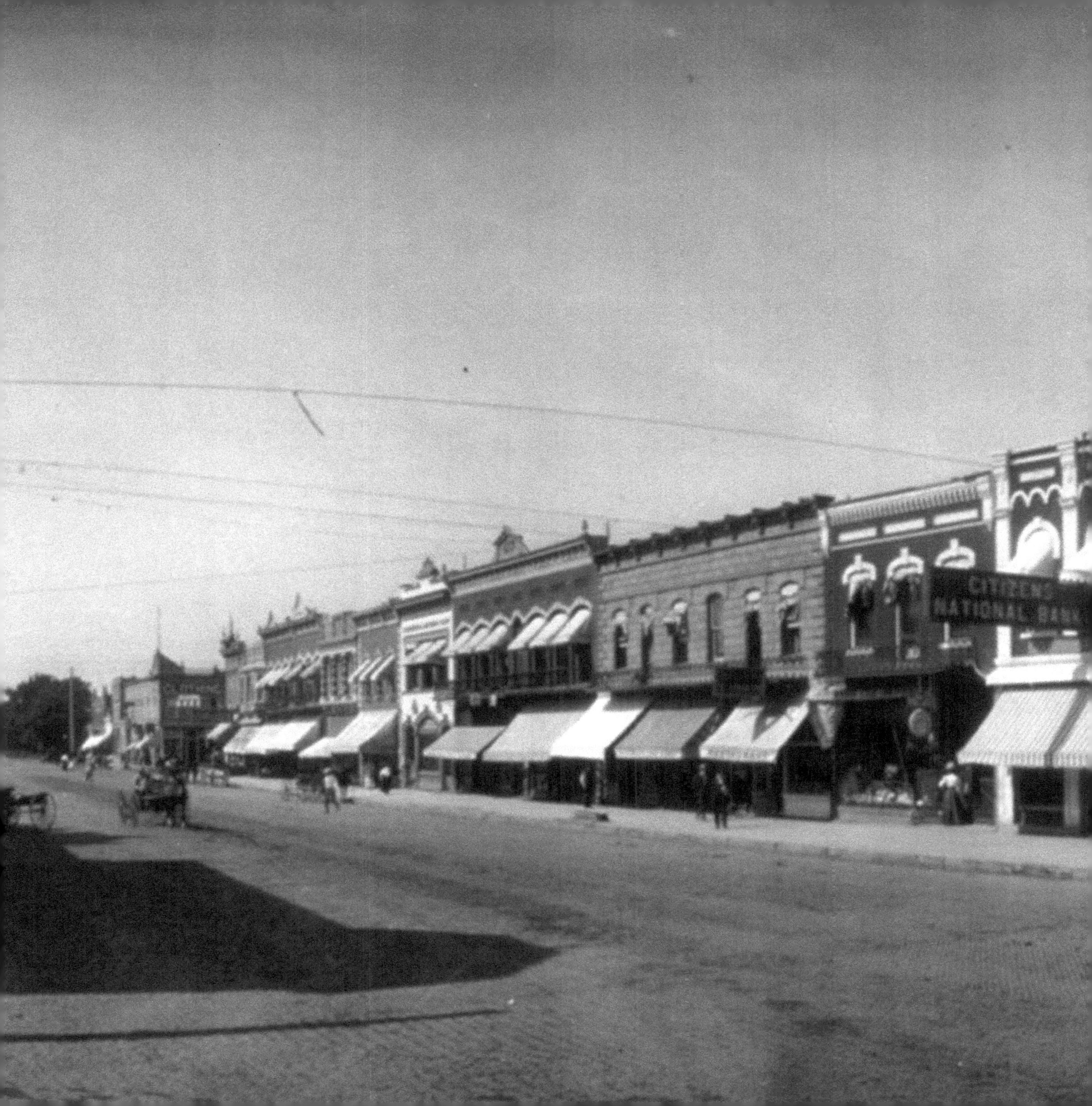
CITIZENS
NATIONAL BAN

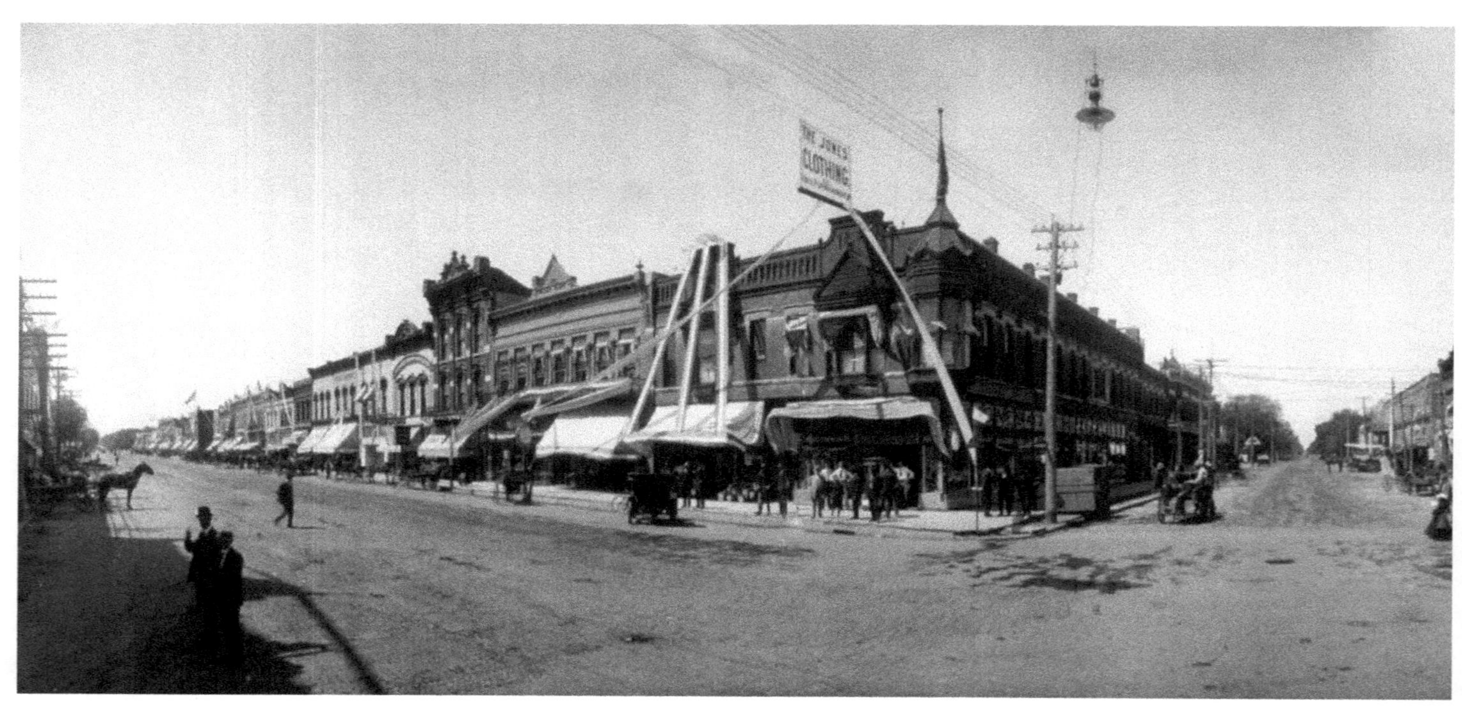

Horse-drawn wagons and carriages were still the primary mode of transportation when Ottawa's intersection of 2nd and Main streets was photographed in 1909.

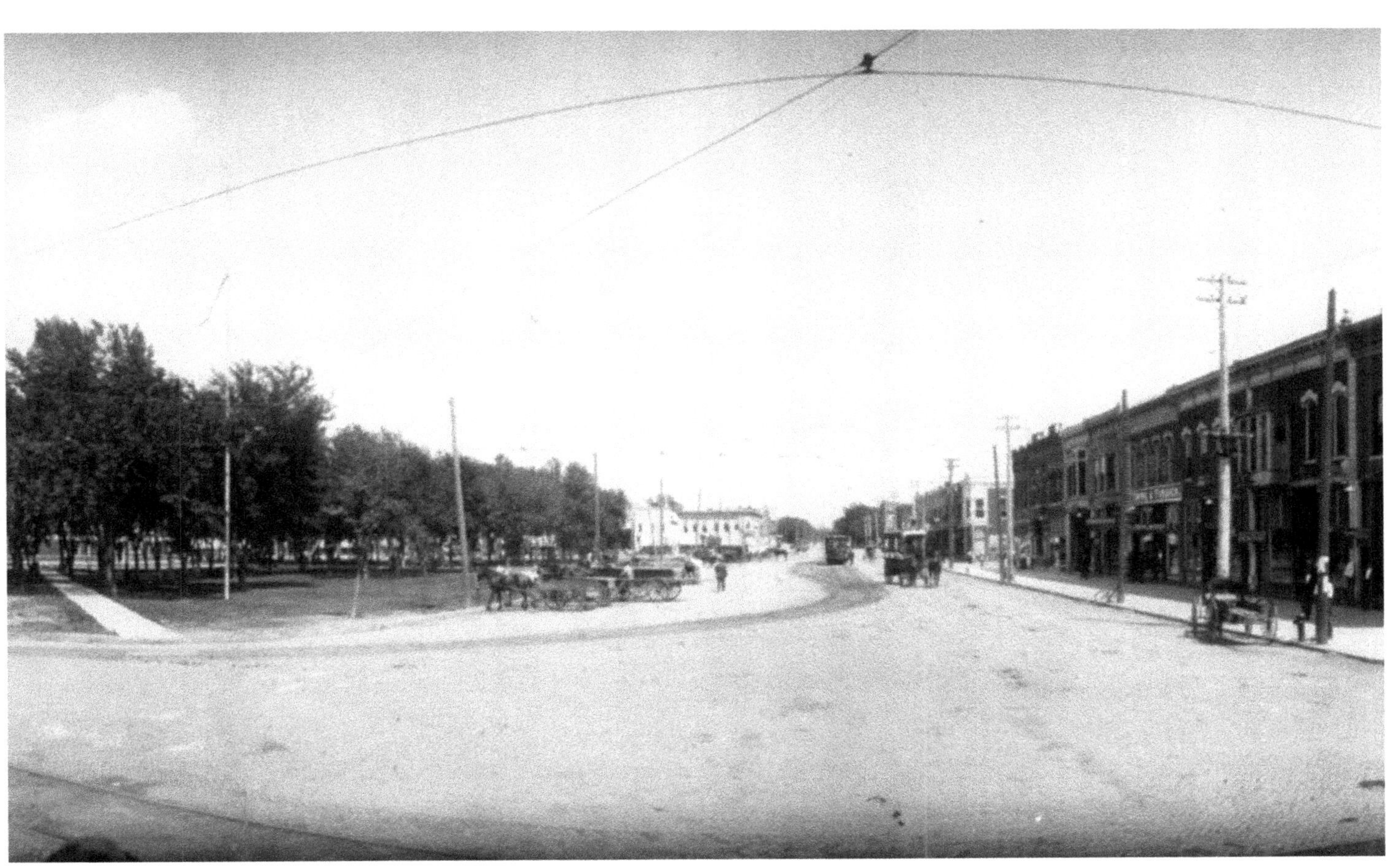

After years of political battling with the town of Humbolt, Iola was voted the government seat of Allen County. Securing county offices and rail service in the post–Civil War years provided stability for Iola's business district.

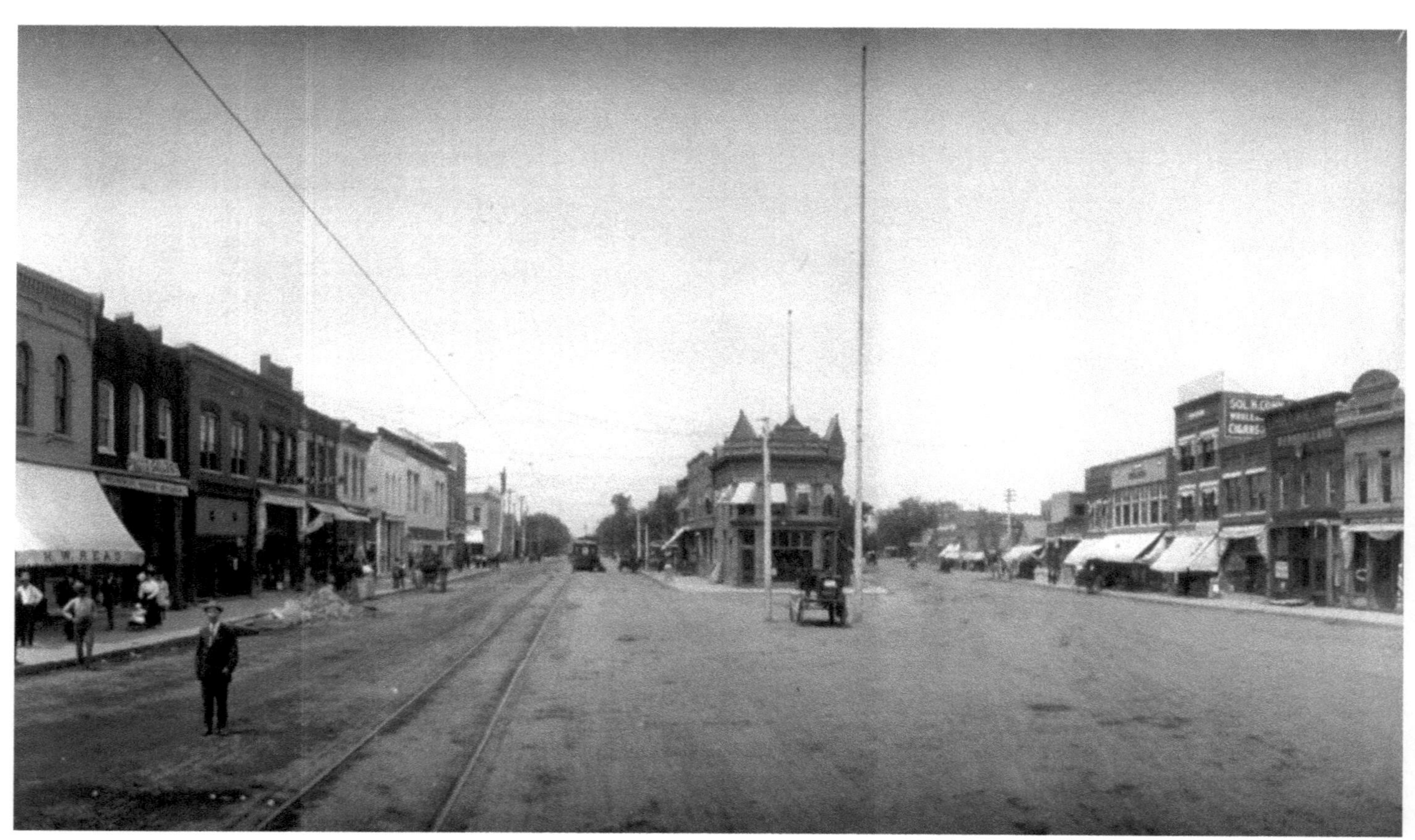

By 1909, Coffeyville's business district was beginning to support new industries that produced glass, brick, and tile.

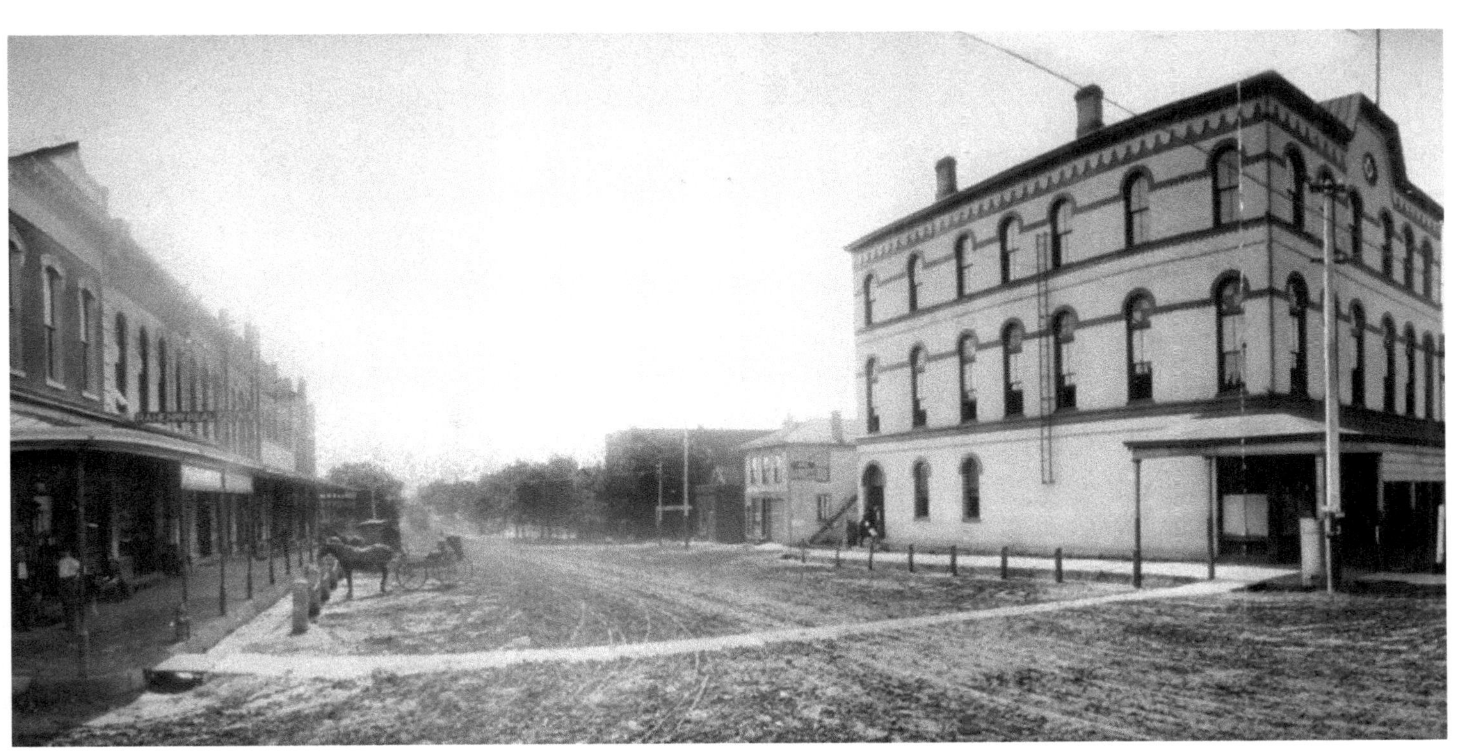

The largest city in Brown County, Hiawatha is the county seat, and its commercial base has long served area farmers with supplies, farm equipment, and service. It's believed that Hiawatha was named for the young Indian in Henry W. Longfellow's poem "Song of Hiawatha."

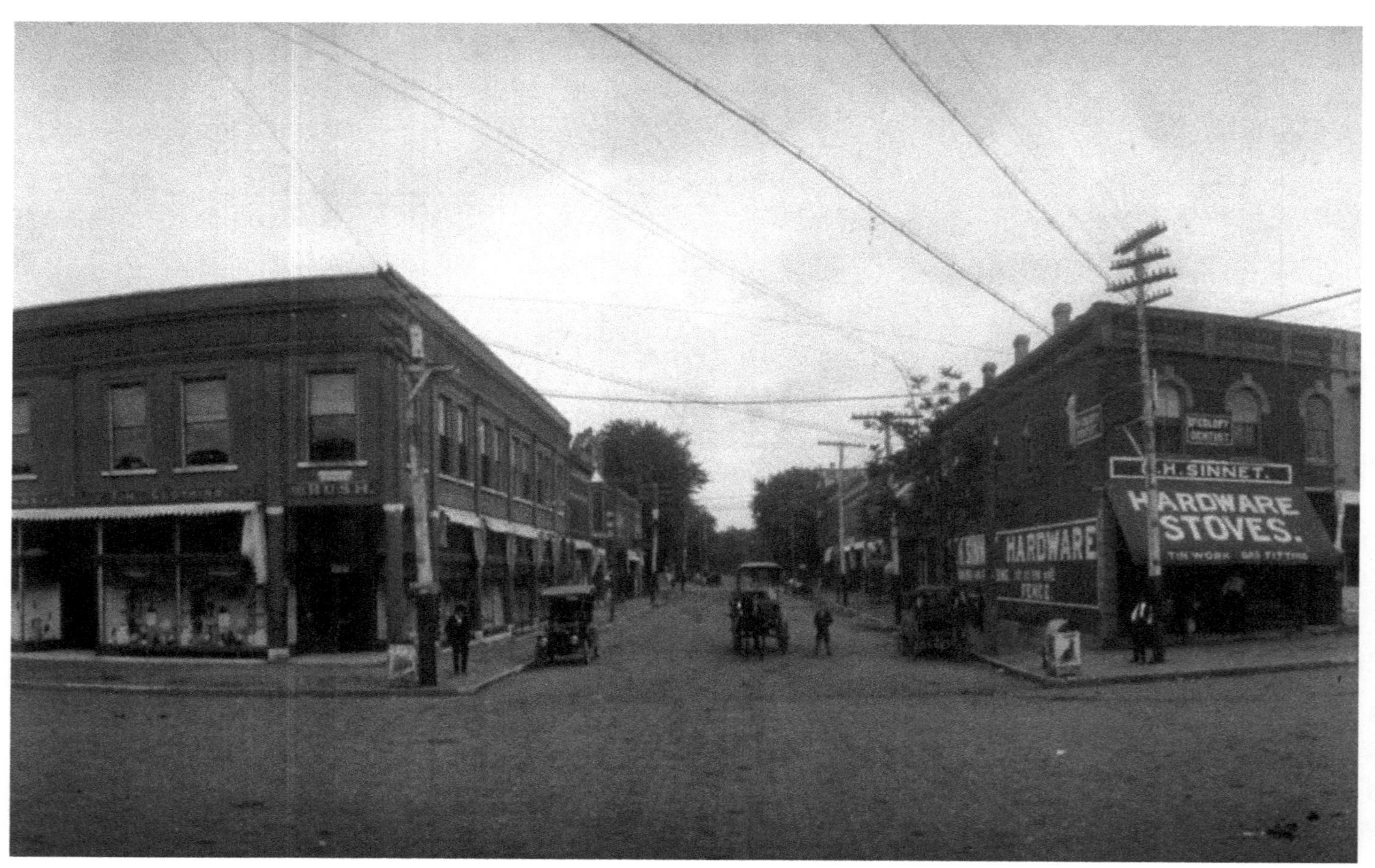

Cherryvale's Globe Street is recorded here in 1909, a year before the city's first trolley went into operation. Located in Montgomery County, Cherryvale's early economic vitality was the result of natural gas production; a popular cigar factory; glass, shovel, and barrel factories; and two grain elevators serviced by railroads.

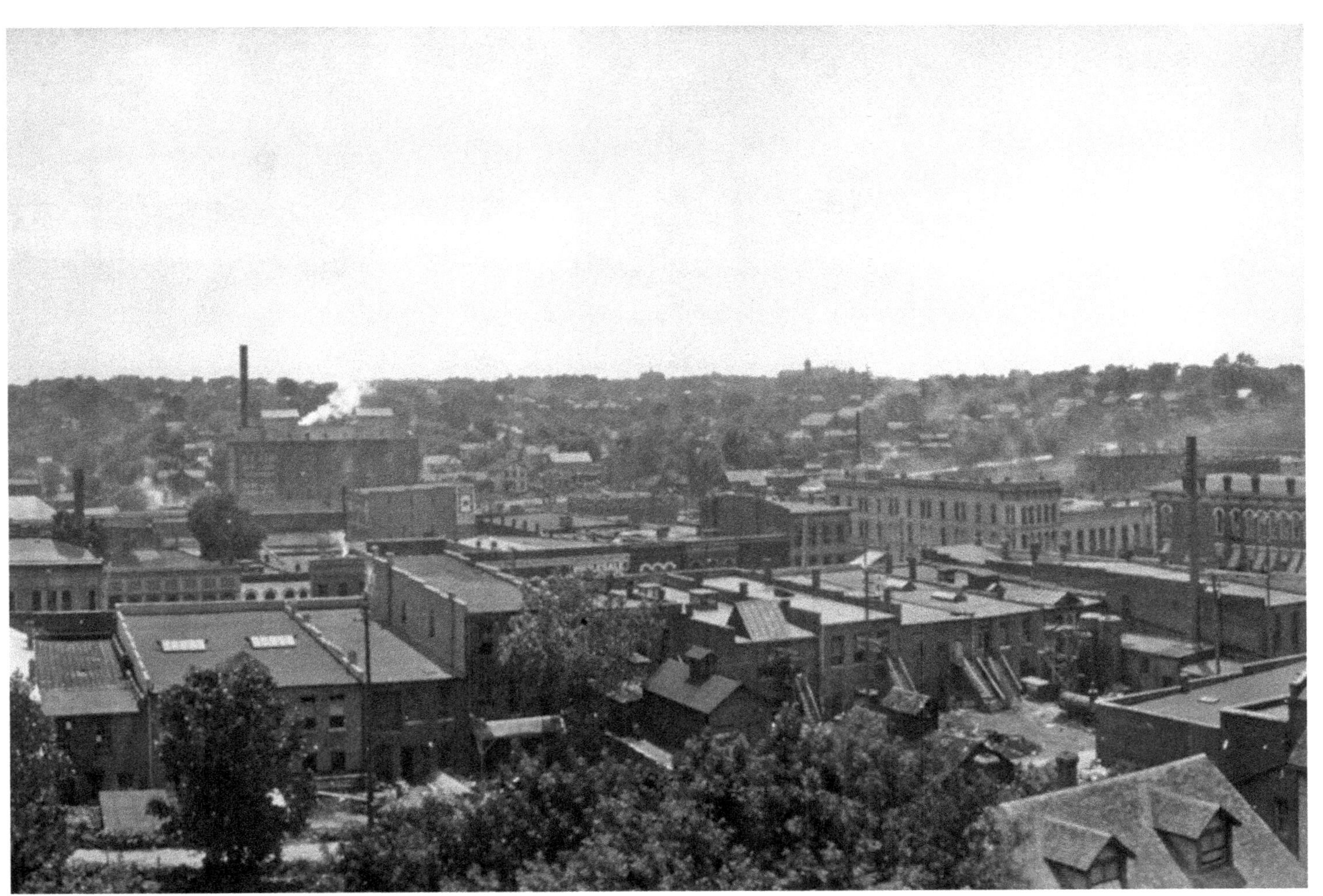

Its location on the Missouri River made early Atchison a center for steamboat traffic and trade. By the time this bird's-eye view was recorded in 1909, the city had diversified with a growing industrial and commercial base.

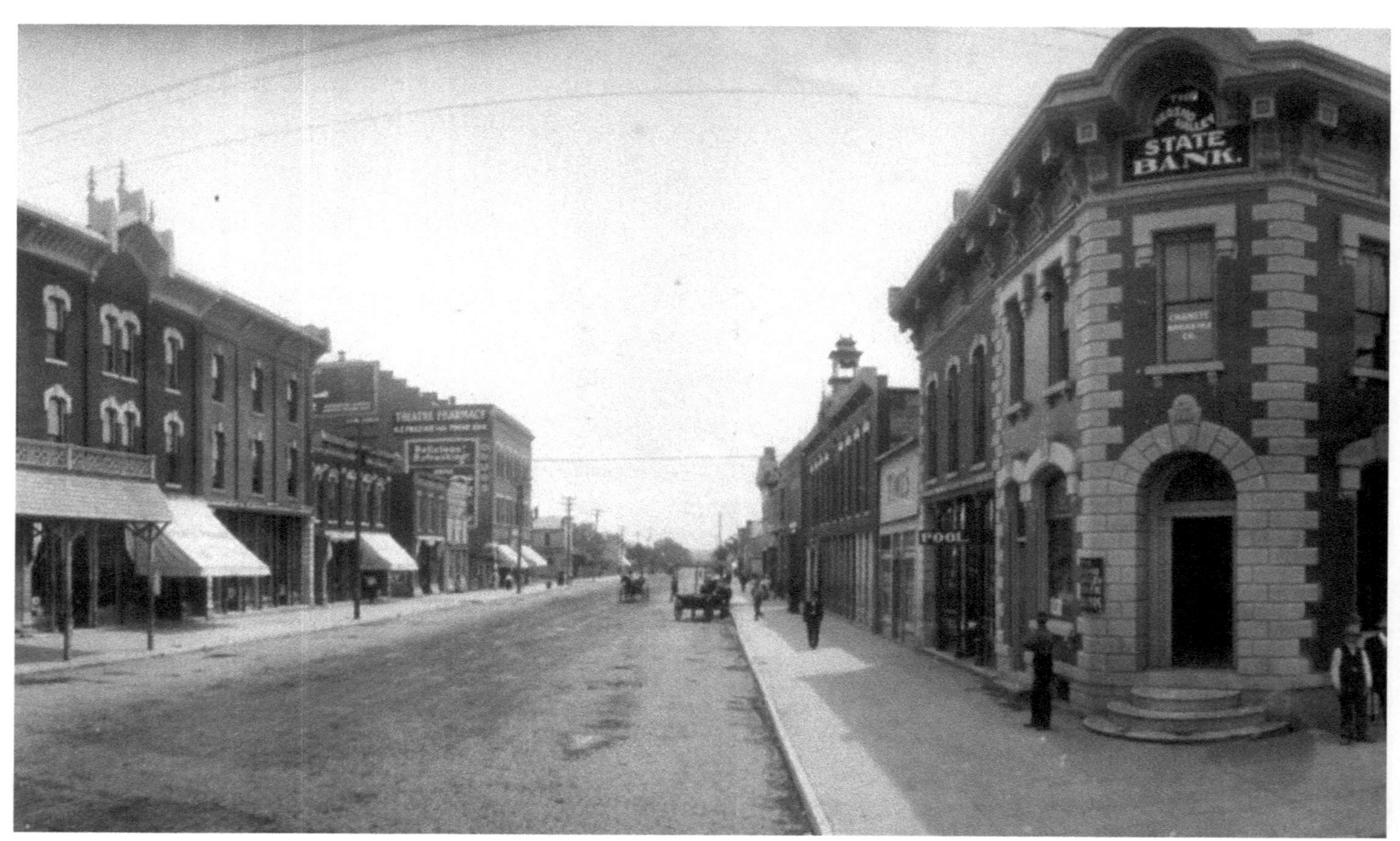

Iowan F. J. Bandholtz photographed a nearly deserted Main Street in Chanute in 1909. A painted advertisement on the brick Theatre Pharmacy building in the background reads “Delicious! Refreshing! Drink Coca-Cola.”

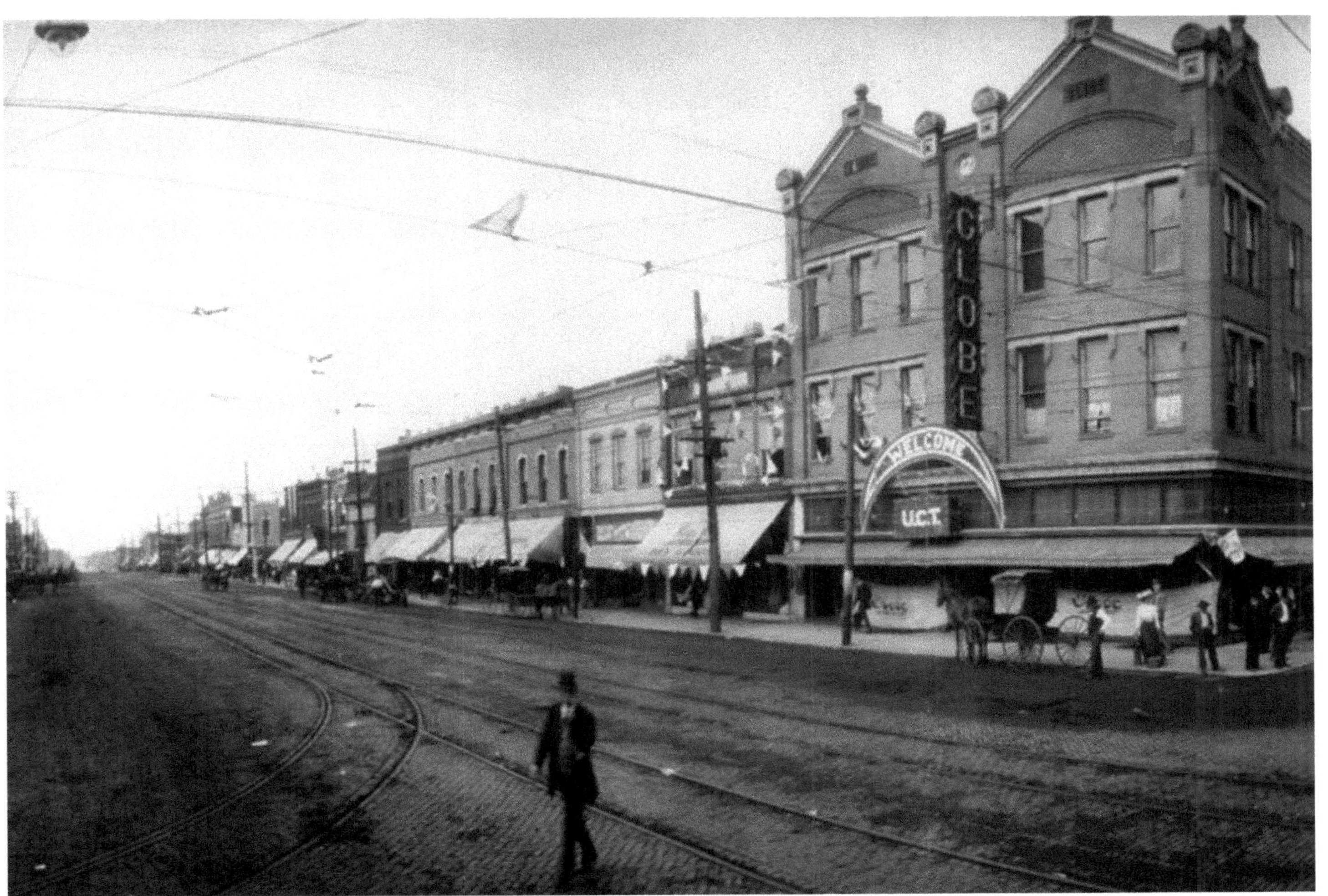

Tenants of Pittsburg's impressive Globe office building, with its three stories and a theater-like marquee and facade, were served by an extensive network of trolleys when this photo was taken in 1909. Advertisements, such as the one for ice cream at left, line the streets on wooden electric poles.

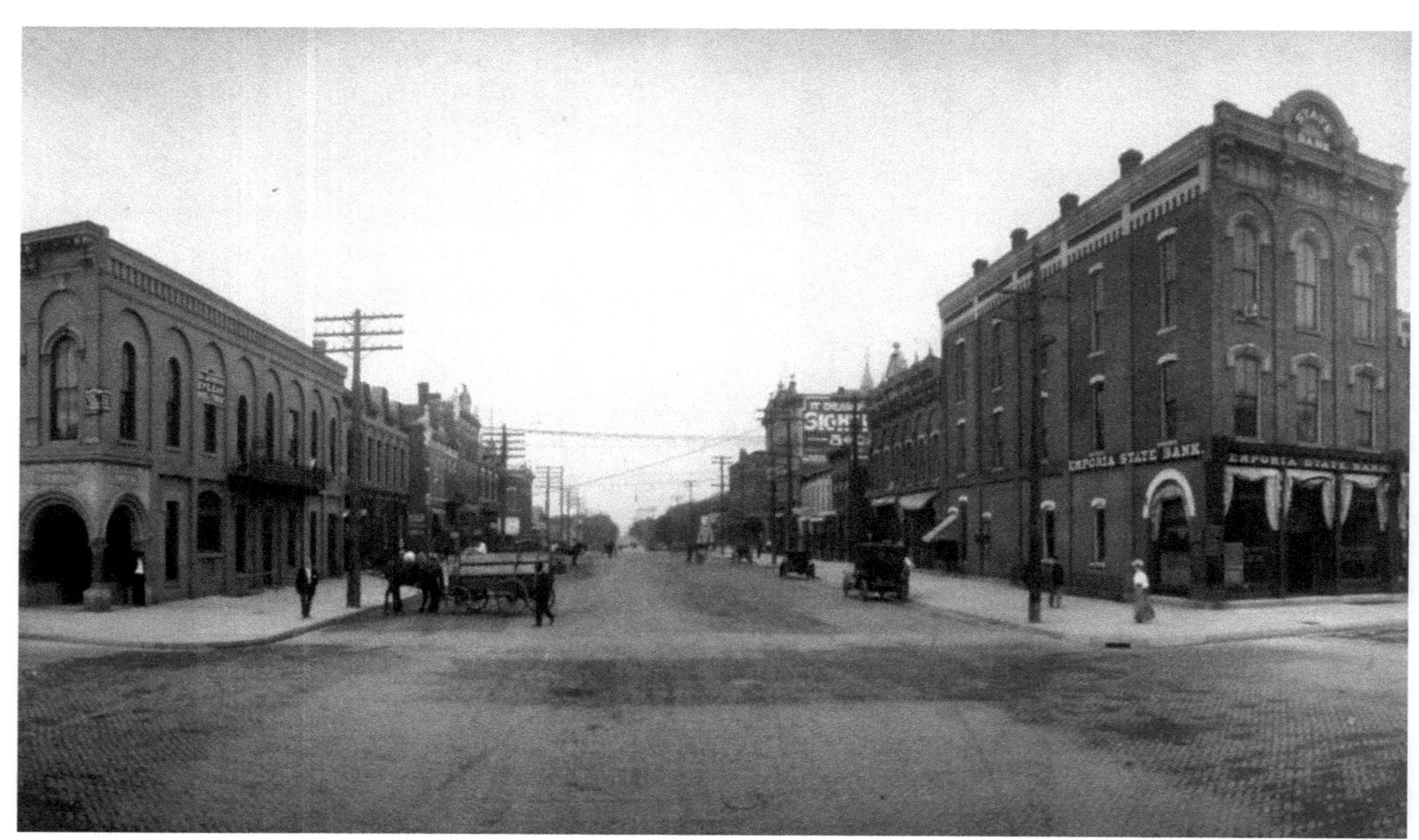

Emporia is the county seat of Lyon County. In addition to the state college of the same name, Emporia is well known for its *Emporia Gazette,* published by legendary journalist William Allen White after he purchased the paper in the 1890s.

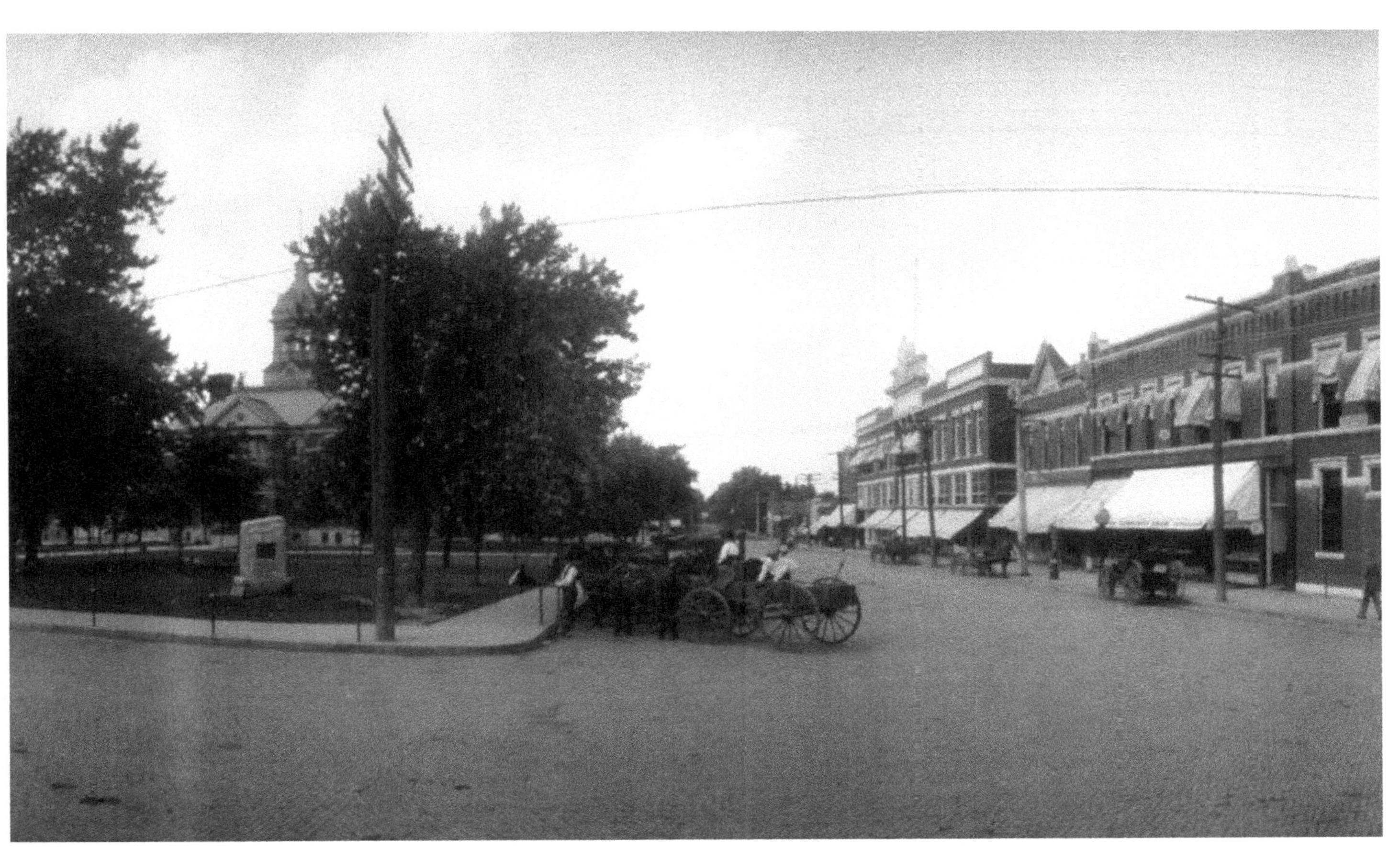

Olathe, county seat of Johnson County in eastern Kansas, was a stop on the Oregon, California, and Santa Fe trails. Although all seems quiet in this 1909 photo of a business district, Olathe's early commercial vitality was rooted in westward expansion. Located not too far from the pictured district is the preserved Mahaffie House, a resupply point for wagon trains that remains a focal point for visitors.

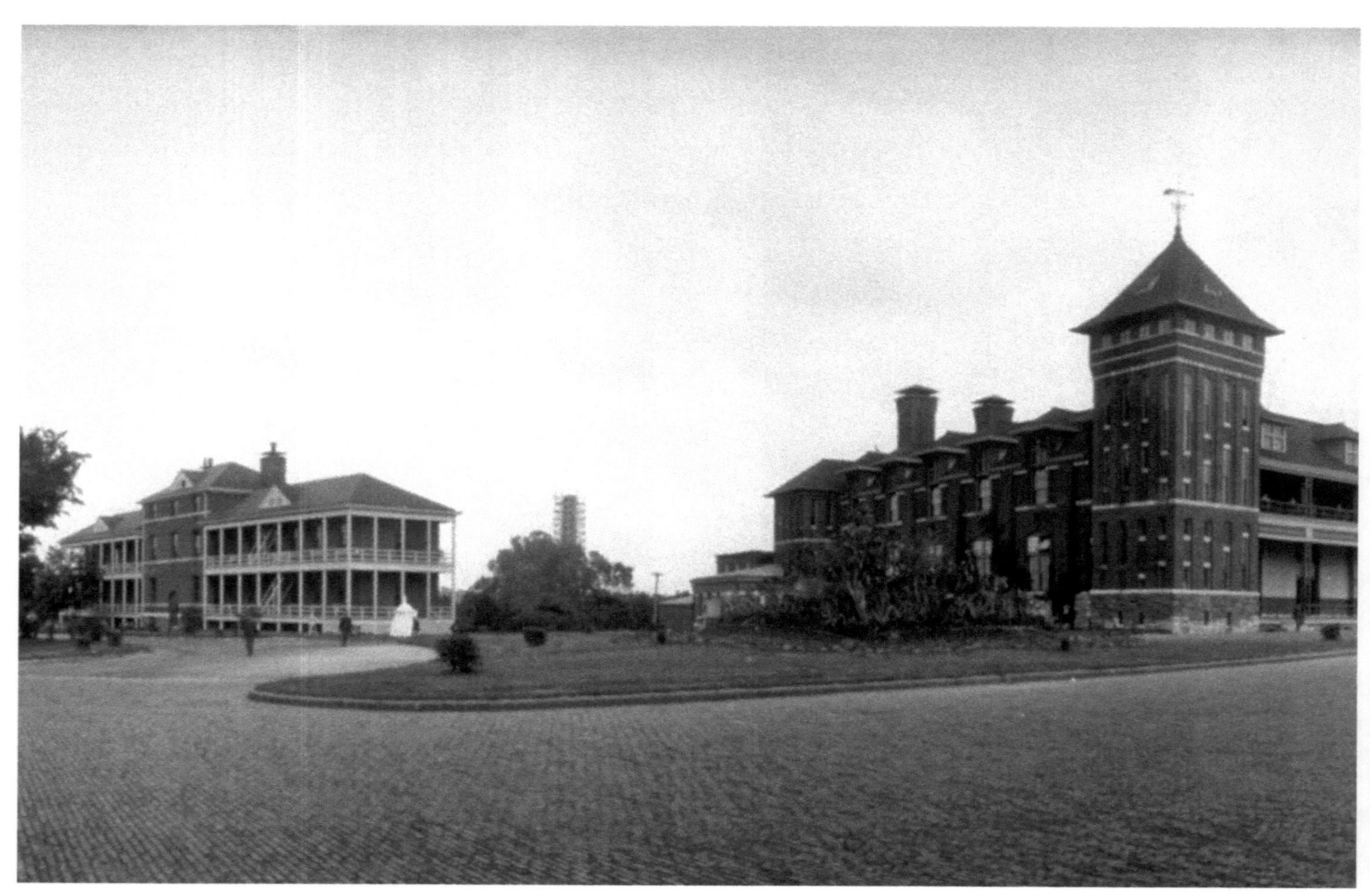

A beautiful Victorian building served as the Soldier's Home in Leavenworth. The building was photographed in 1909.

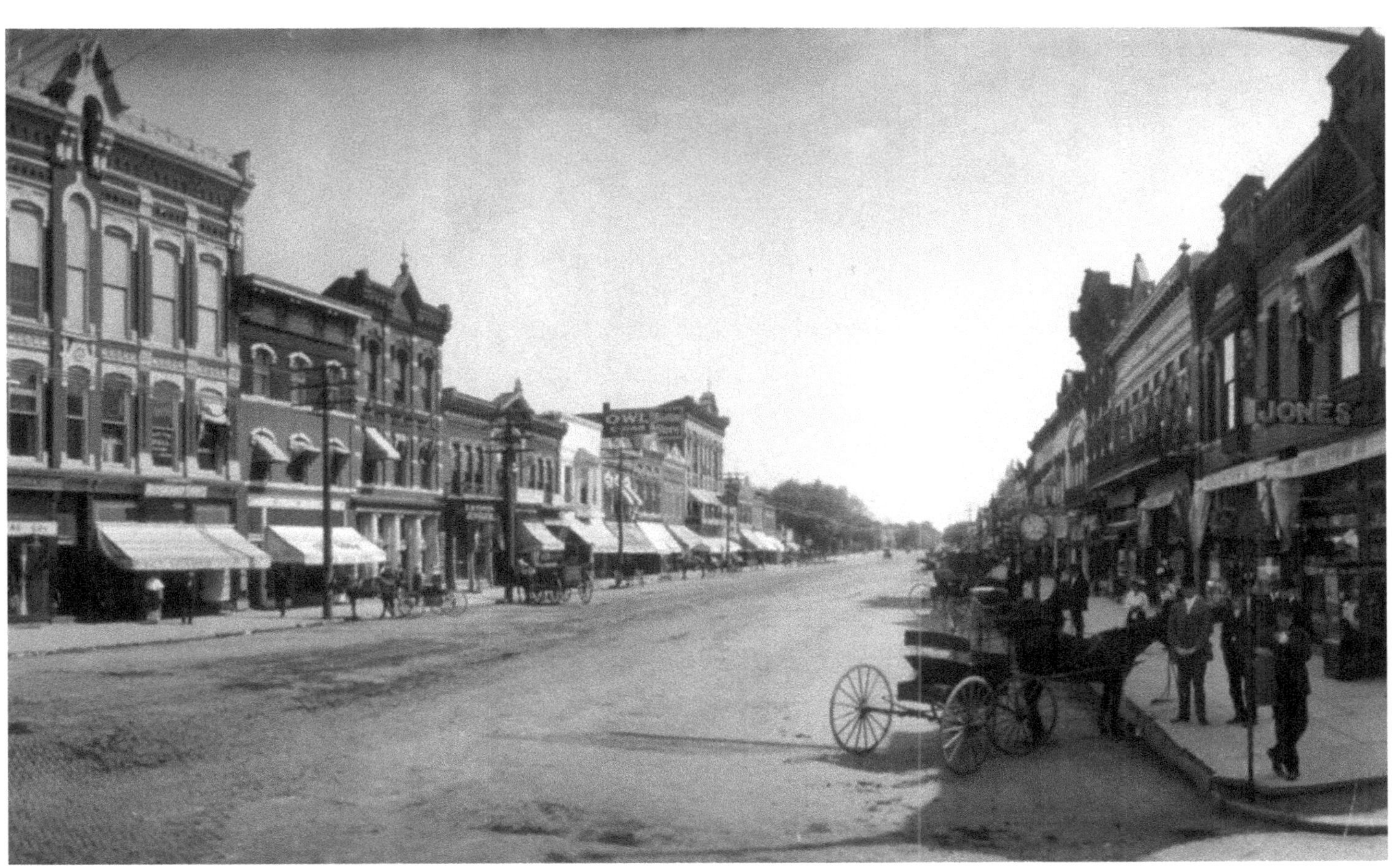

Ottawa, the county seat of Franklin County, traces its roots and name to the Ottawa Indian tribe. Photographed in 1909, the city's downtown served the local college—now Ottawa University—as well as the area's agricultural and commercial needs.

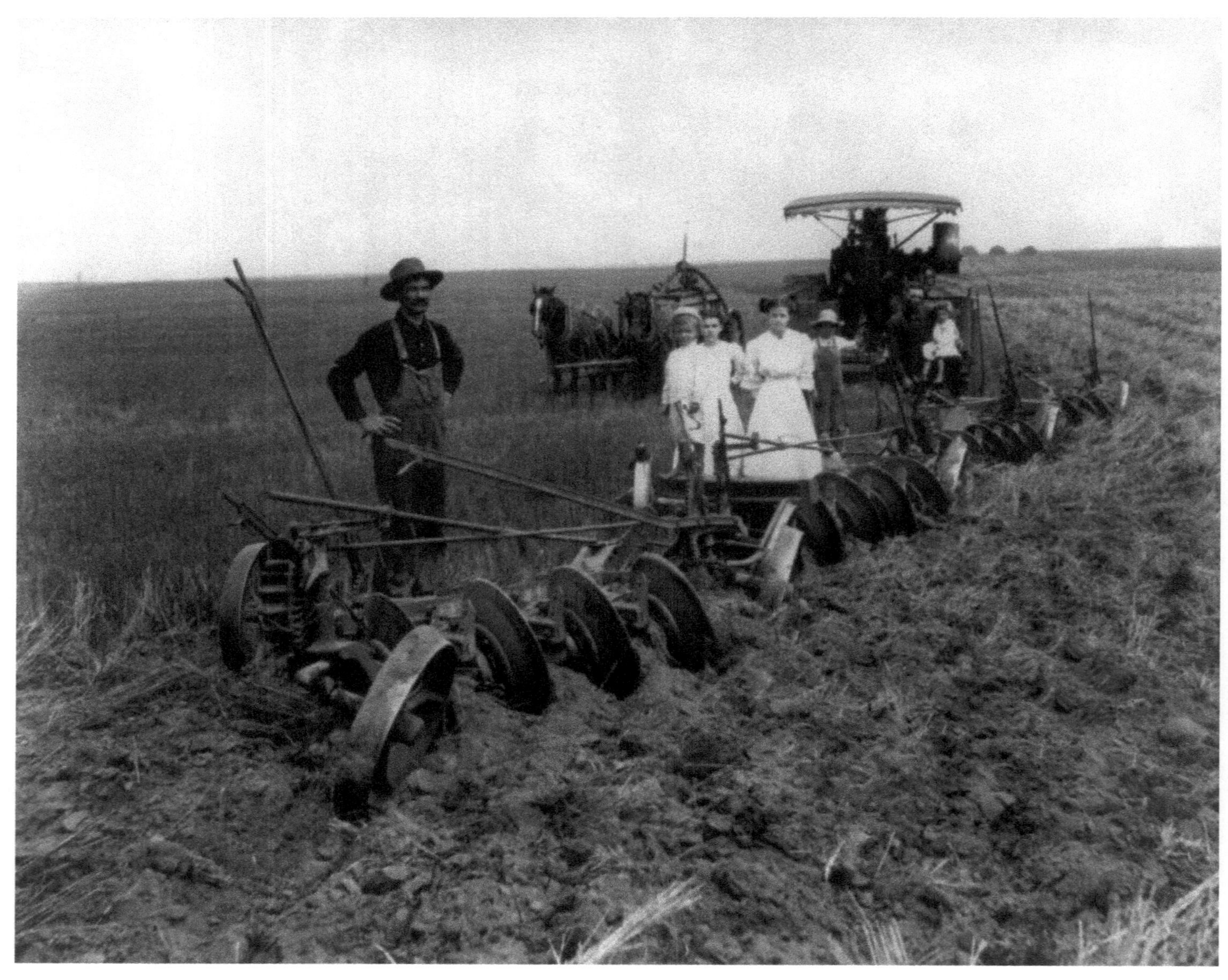

A farming family in Belpre gathers for a photo in a field worked with a steam-powered William Phillips plow.

World War I, Prohibition, the Stock Market Crash, and Energy Production

(1910–1929)

After seeing its population grow quickly from 1860 to 1890 in relation to the nation as a whole, Kansas experienced a final spurt from 1900 to 1910. But even with that 15 percent increase—census figures show 1,690,949 people in 1910—it remained a sparsely populated, rural place.

Kansas has never accounted for more than 2.7 percent of the nation's population—that occurred in 1890, after an influx of European immigrants—and it continued to lose people during the nation's urbanization. By 1930, Kansas was home to just 1.53 percent of America's population.

And while urban and industrial growth was experienced in Wichita and Kansas City, as a whole Kansas continued its roles as a food producer and transportation hub. What the state lacked in numbers it more than made up for with numbers of people fed and transported.

On October 6, 1915, oil deposits were discovered in El Dorado, Kansas. Finding oil was significant, but the way in which it was found was even more important. According to the Kansas Oil Museum, Stapleton well #1 was the first oil deposit located using scientific and geological methods. Geologists not only helped find oil, they had accurately pinpointed specific acreage in the El Dorado field in which to drill. That attracted the attention of major oil interests, including affiliates of Standard Oil and Gulf Oil, who turned the 34-square-mile El Dorado field into the largest single field in the country. By 1920, the population of Butler County nearly doubled from 23,000 people to 43,000 people as oil towns, offices, and support businesses sprang up.

By 1918, a year after the United States entered World War I, the El Dorado field was producing 12.8 percent of the nation's oil and 9 percent of the world's. At the time, it was said that the field helped "float" the country to victory on a sea of oil. Fort Riley, 100 miles to the north, was one of just 16 bases training soldiers for the Great World War. It could accommodate nearly 50,000 of them—many of whom were transported with oil-based energy.

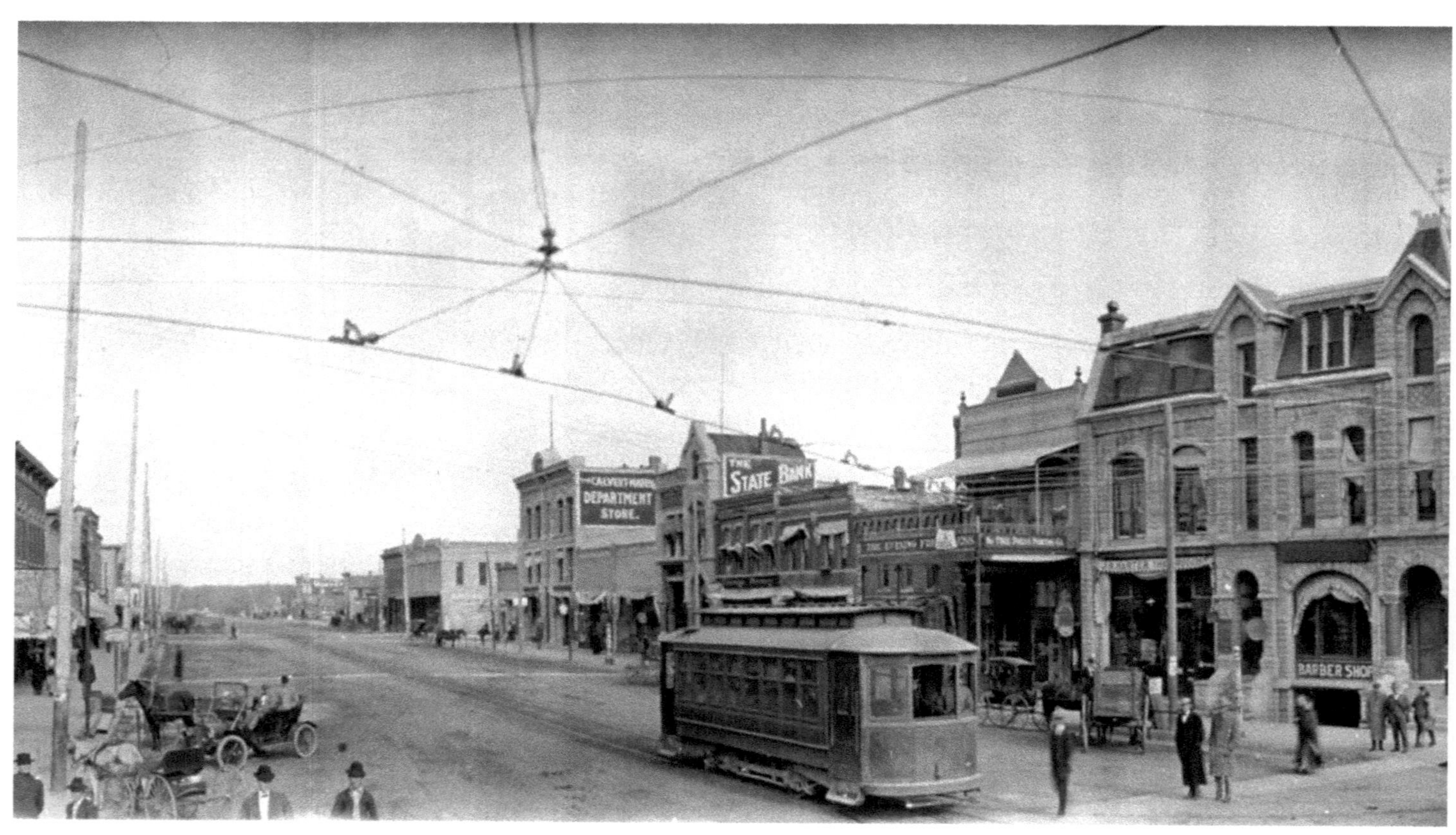

The area of 9th Avenue and Main Street in downtown Winfield reflects the changing modes of transportation in 1910. Pictured are an automobile (left), an electric streetcar, and horse-drawn carriages and wagons (right). Located in Cowley County in the heart of the Flint Hills, Winfield was in the path of the Old California Trail, which led southern adventurers to California for the 1848 gold rush.

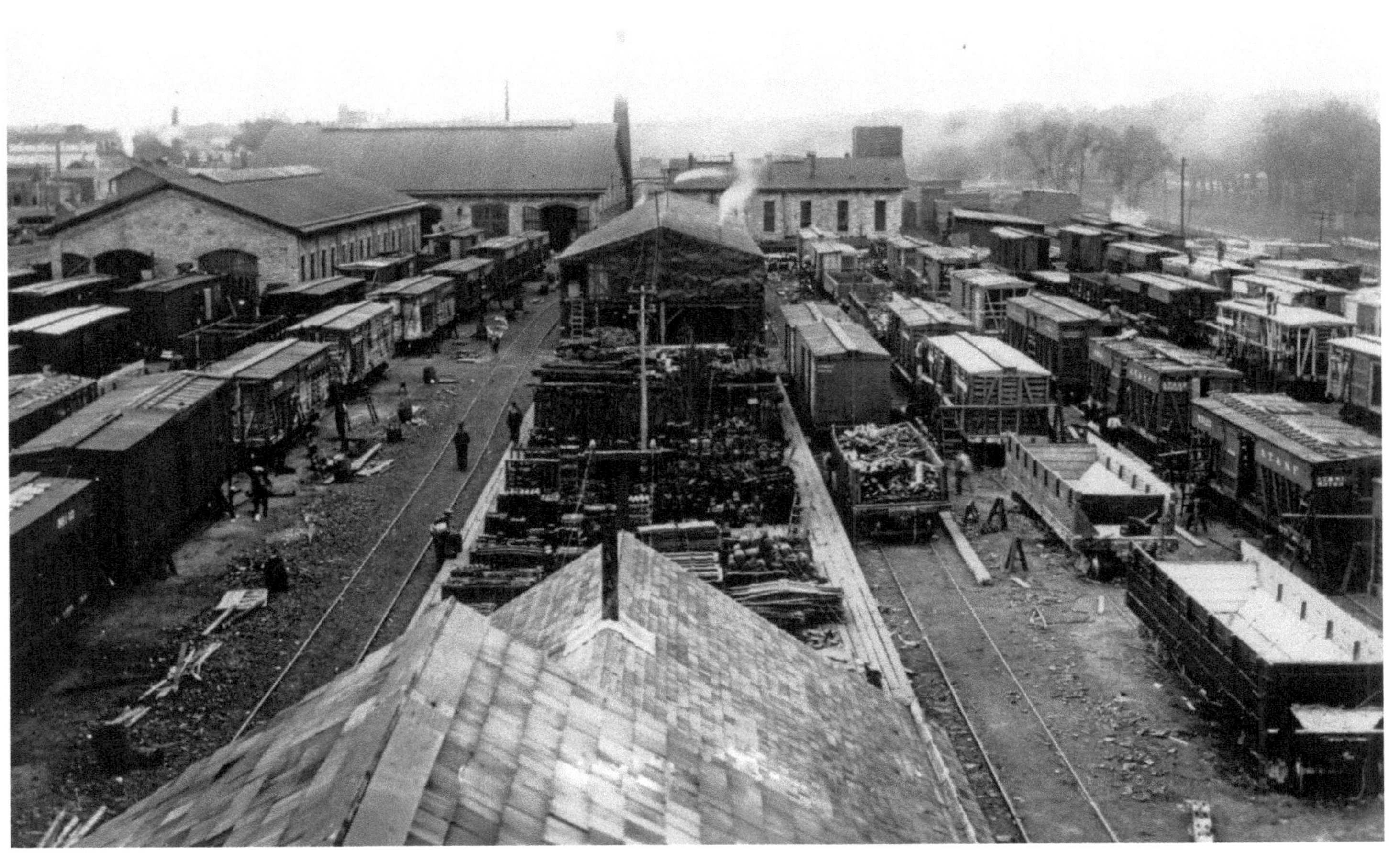

When this photo of Ottawa's railroad works was taken in 1910, shipping by rail had become a driving force in Kansas's economy.

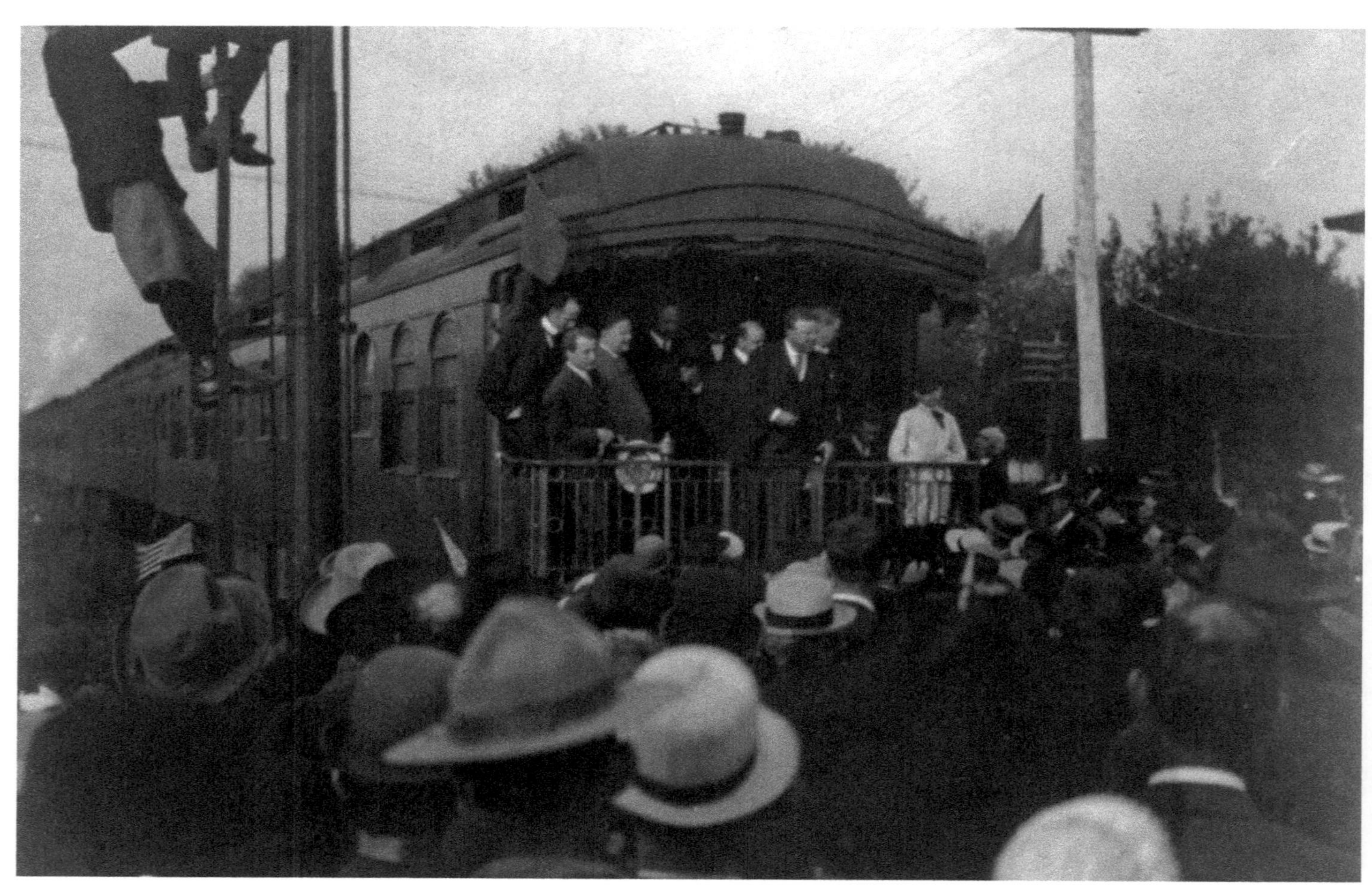

In 1910, Teddy Roosevelt stops in Baldwin during a whistle-stop tour on the *Roosevelt Special*. The 26th president, Roosevelt served from 1901 to 1909 and ran again as a third-party candidate in 1912.

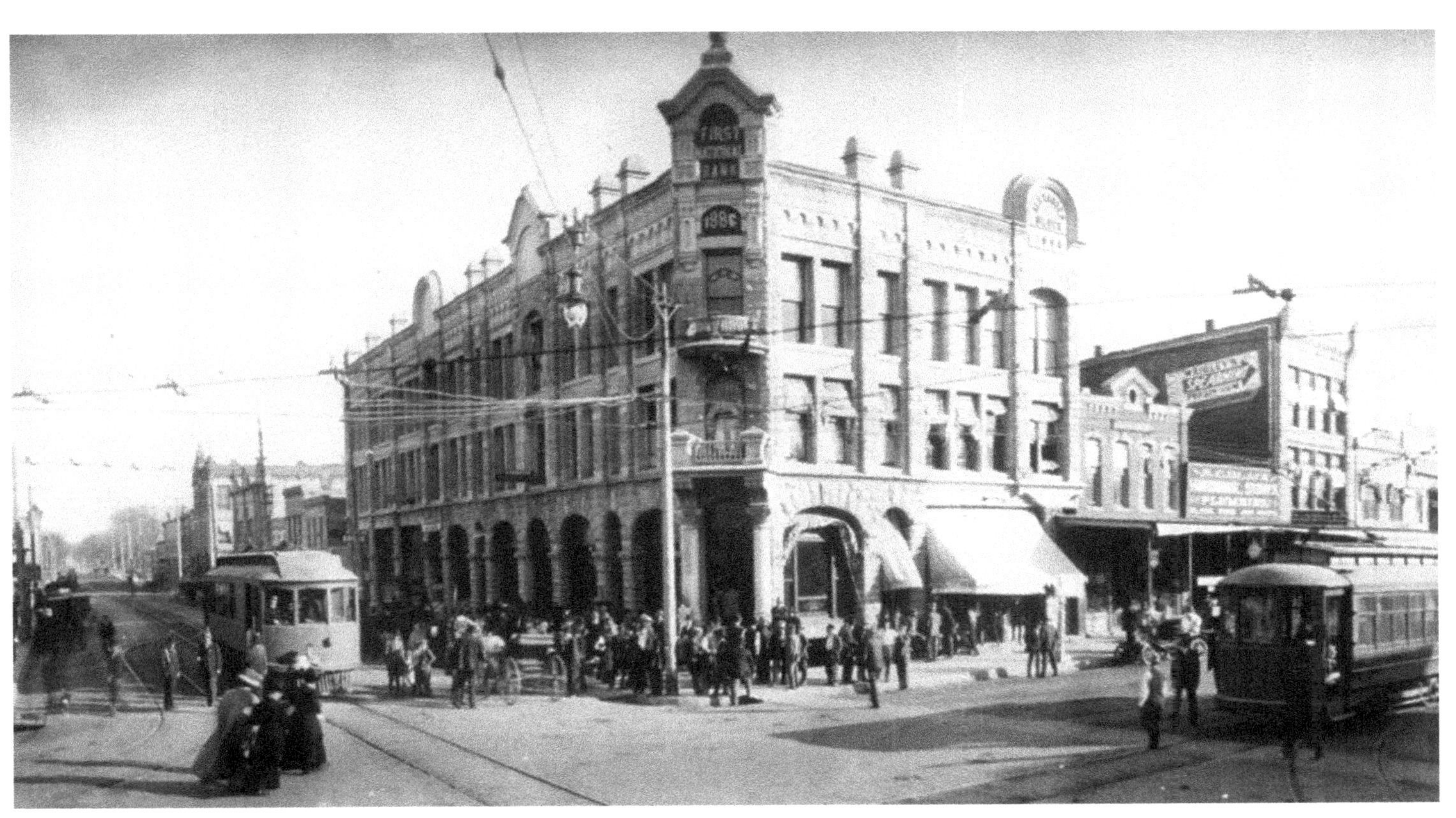

This 1910 photo documents bustling activity in downtown Winfield. Streetcars, wagons, and buggies were still the primary modes of transportation. A sign painted on one of the buildings advertises Wrigley's spearmint gum.

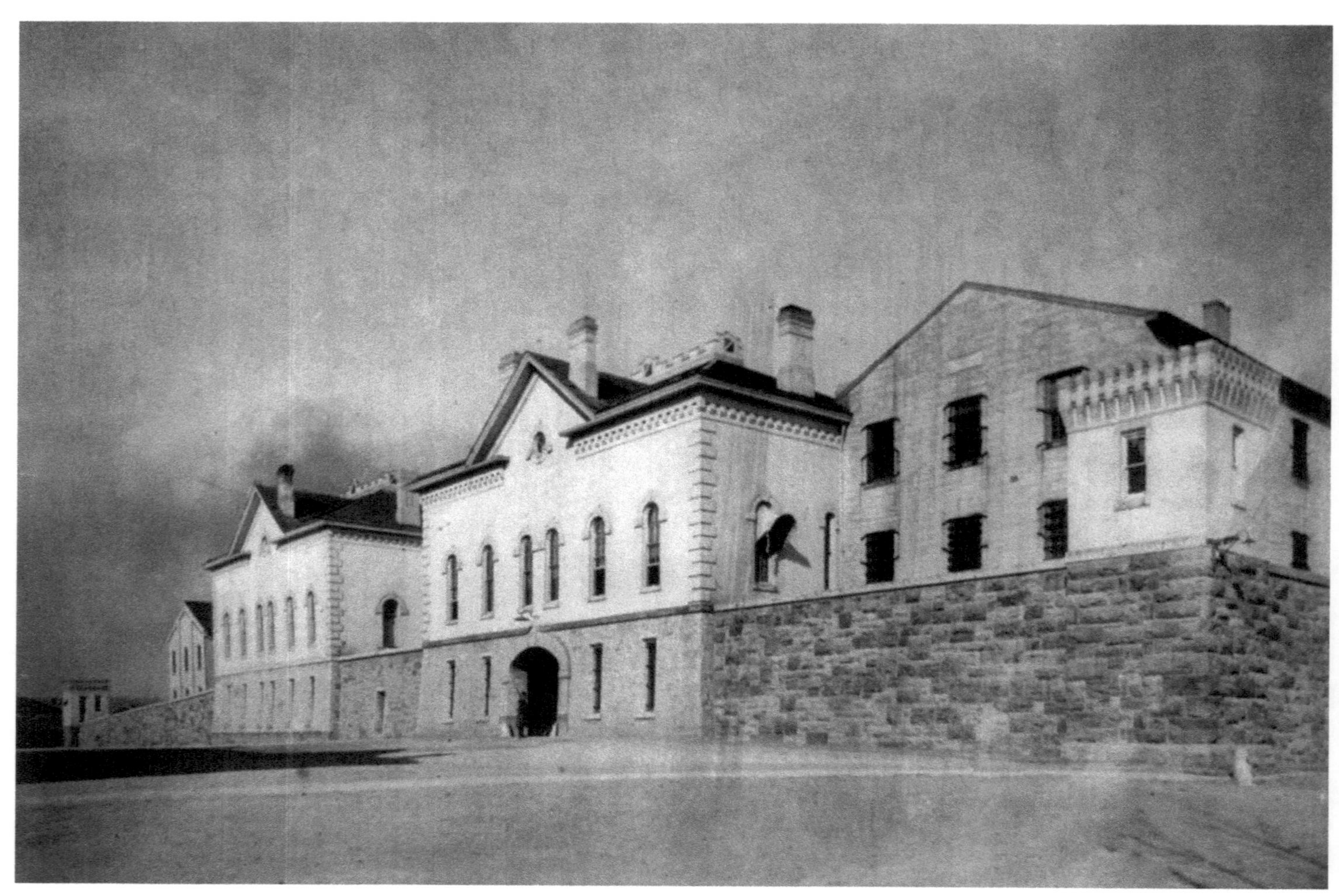

The U.S. Military Prison at Fort Leavenworth . The prison, still in operation today, began over 100 years ago as one of the country's first federal prisons.

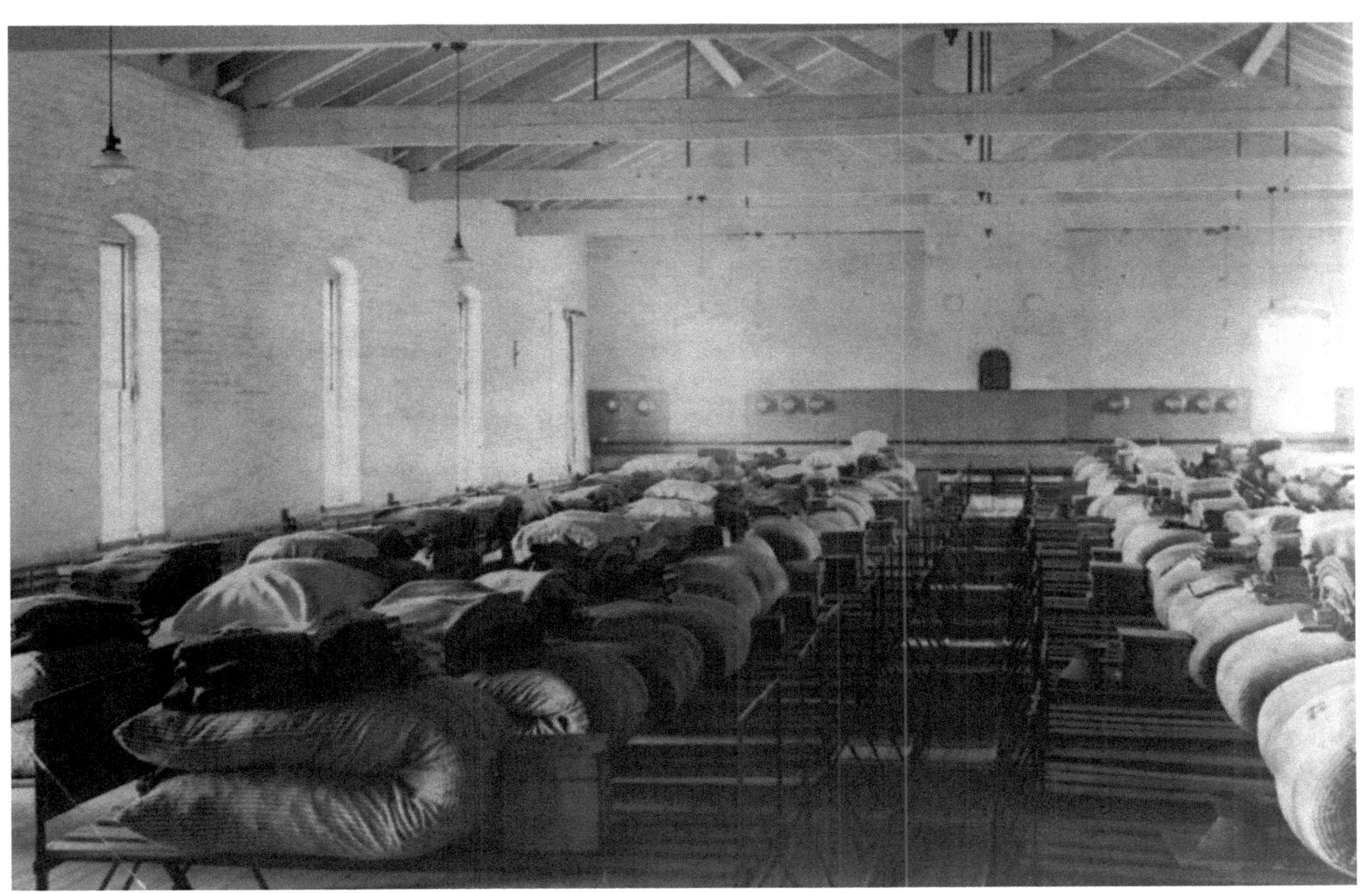

Lower-security prisoners at the U.S. Military Prison in Leavenworth slept in the large dormitory, photographed in 1910.

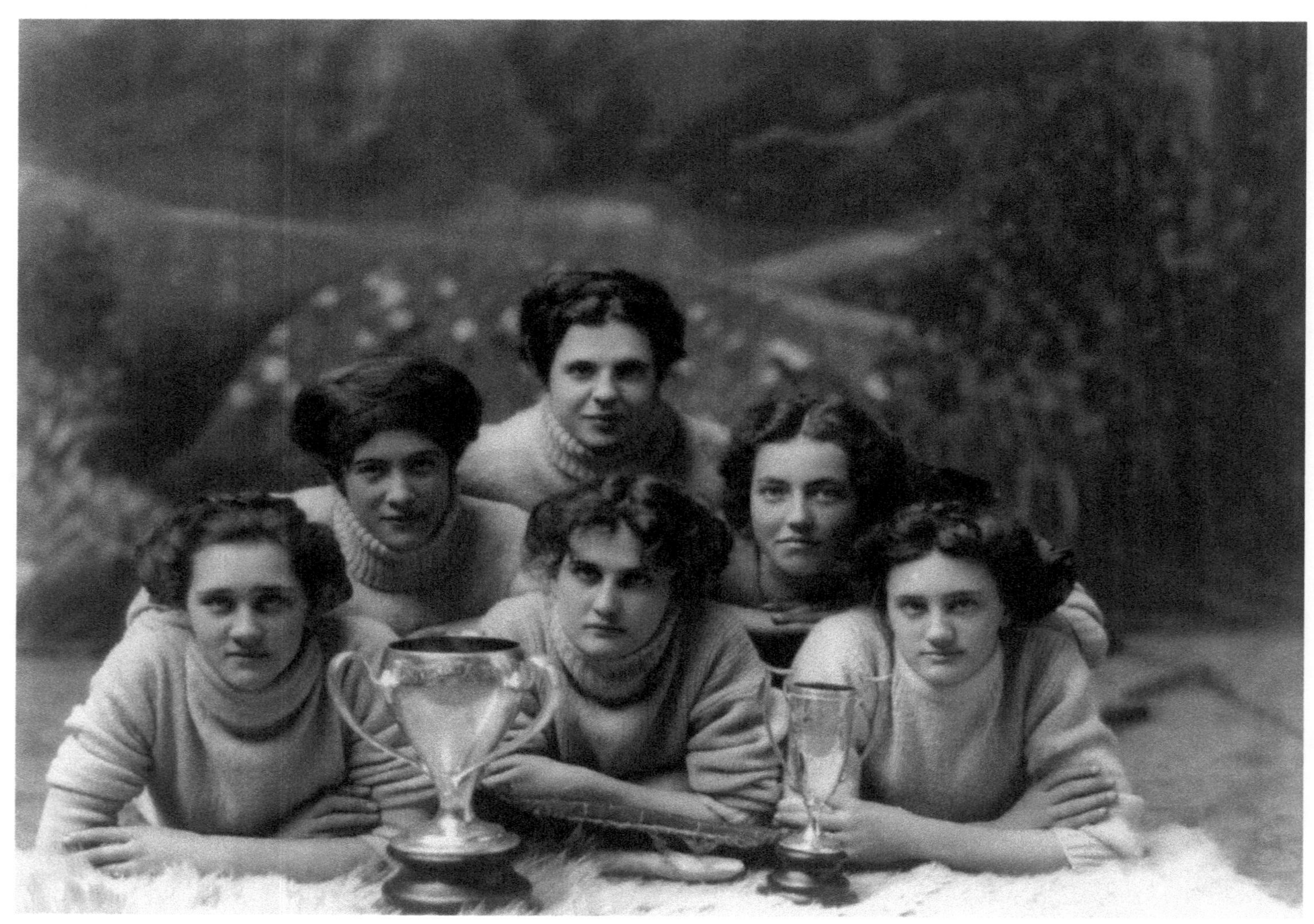

A Chanute photographer recorded this image of the "Championship girls basketball team of Kansas" in 1911. Records indicate that in 1910-11, Chanute defeated Reno County 32–22 to win the Kansas Invitational State Basketball Championship.

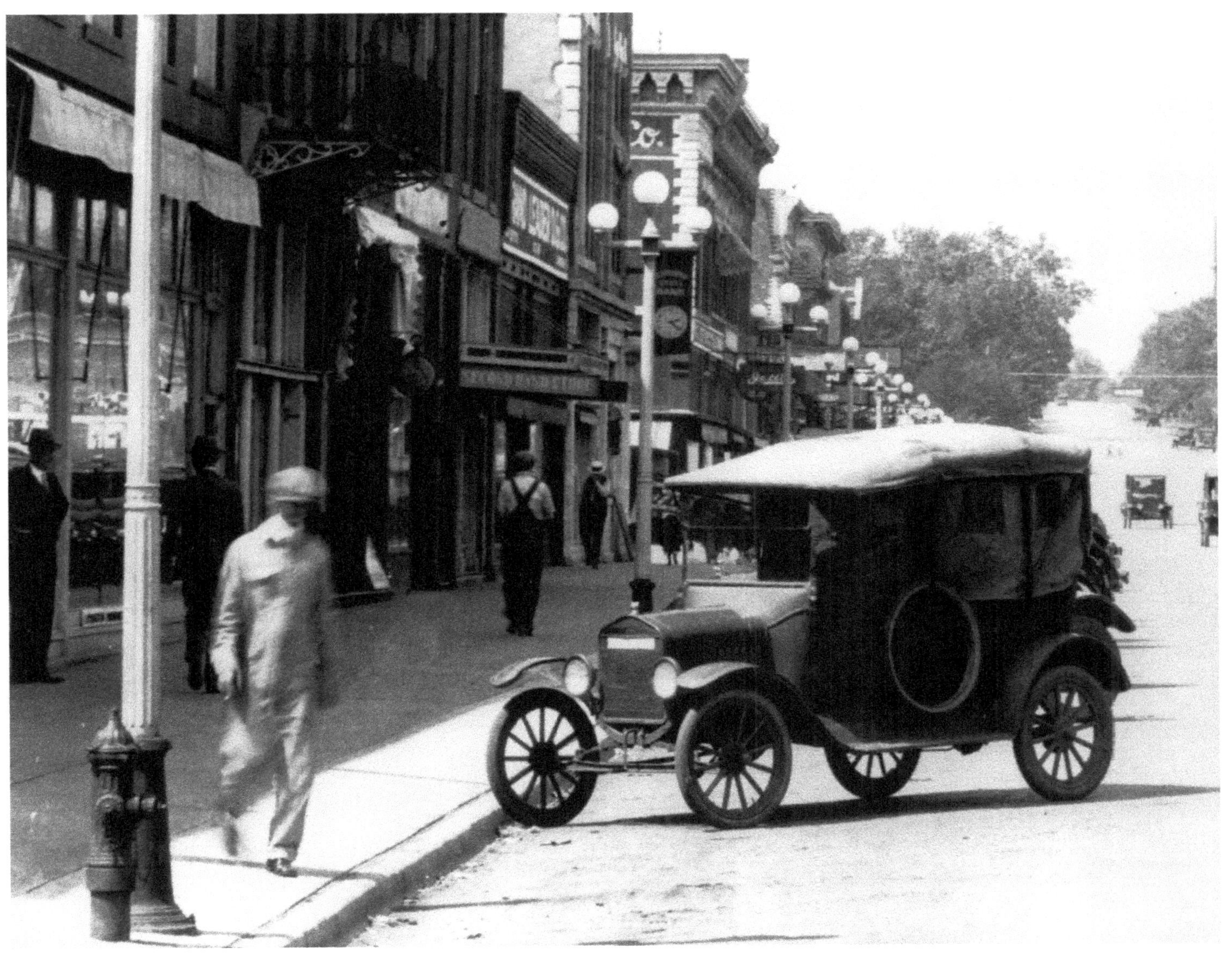

A pedestrian and a car parked diagonally at the curb in Kingman are the focus of a photo taken between 1910 and 1920. It was a busy period for Kansas, once home to famed aviator and businessman Clyde Cessna, who took his first flight over part of the state in 1911.

Where electricity wasn't available, streetcars such as this one in Winfield were mule or horse powered. The streetcar was operated by the Union Street Railway Company.

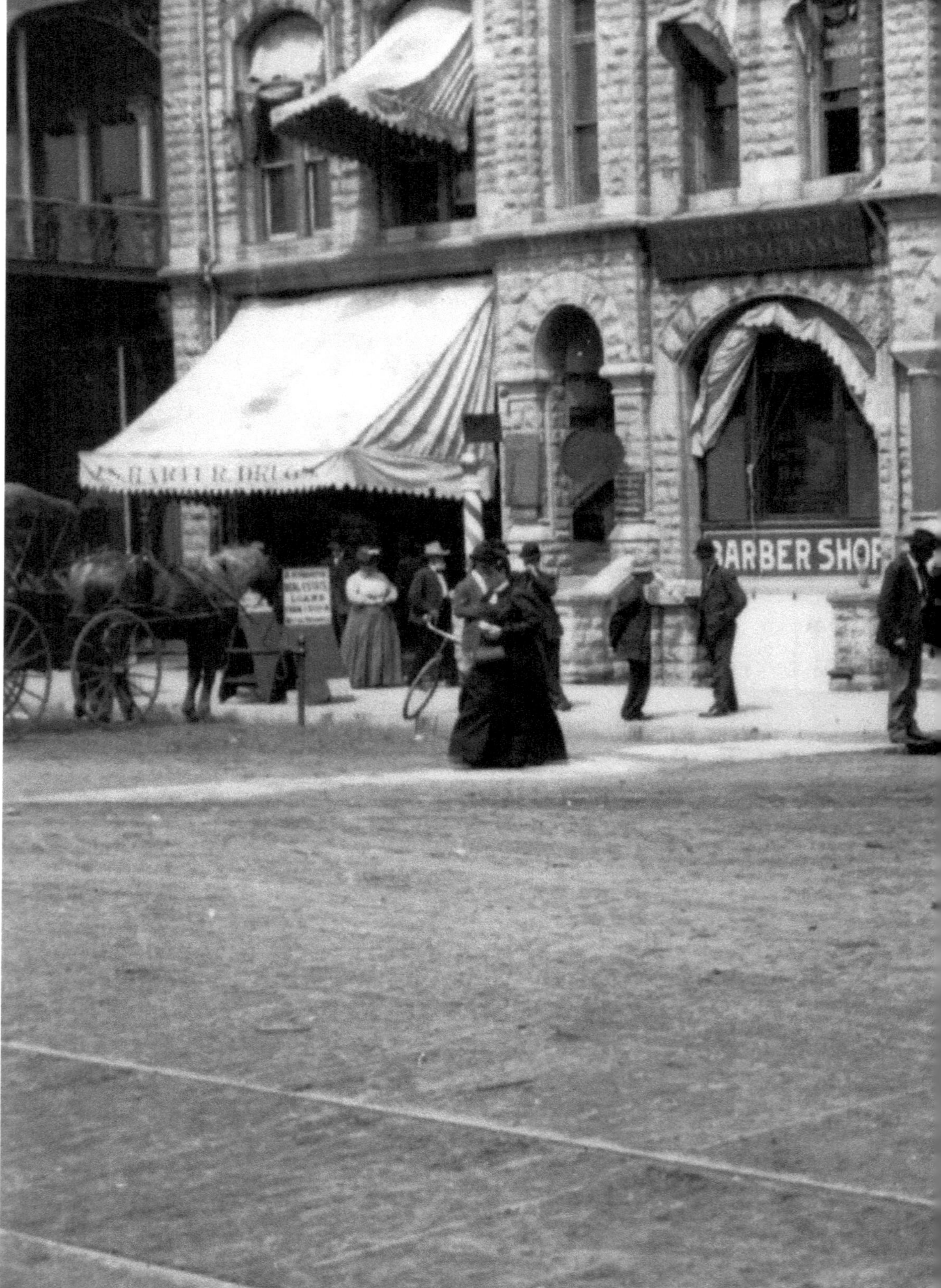

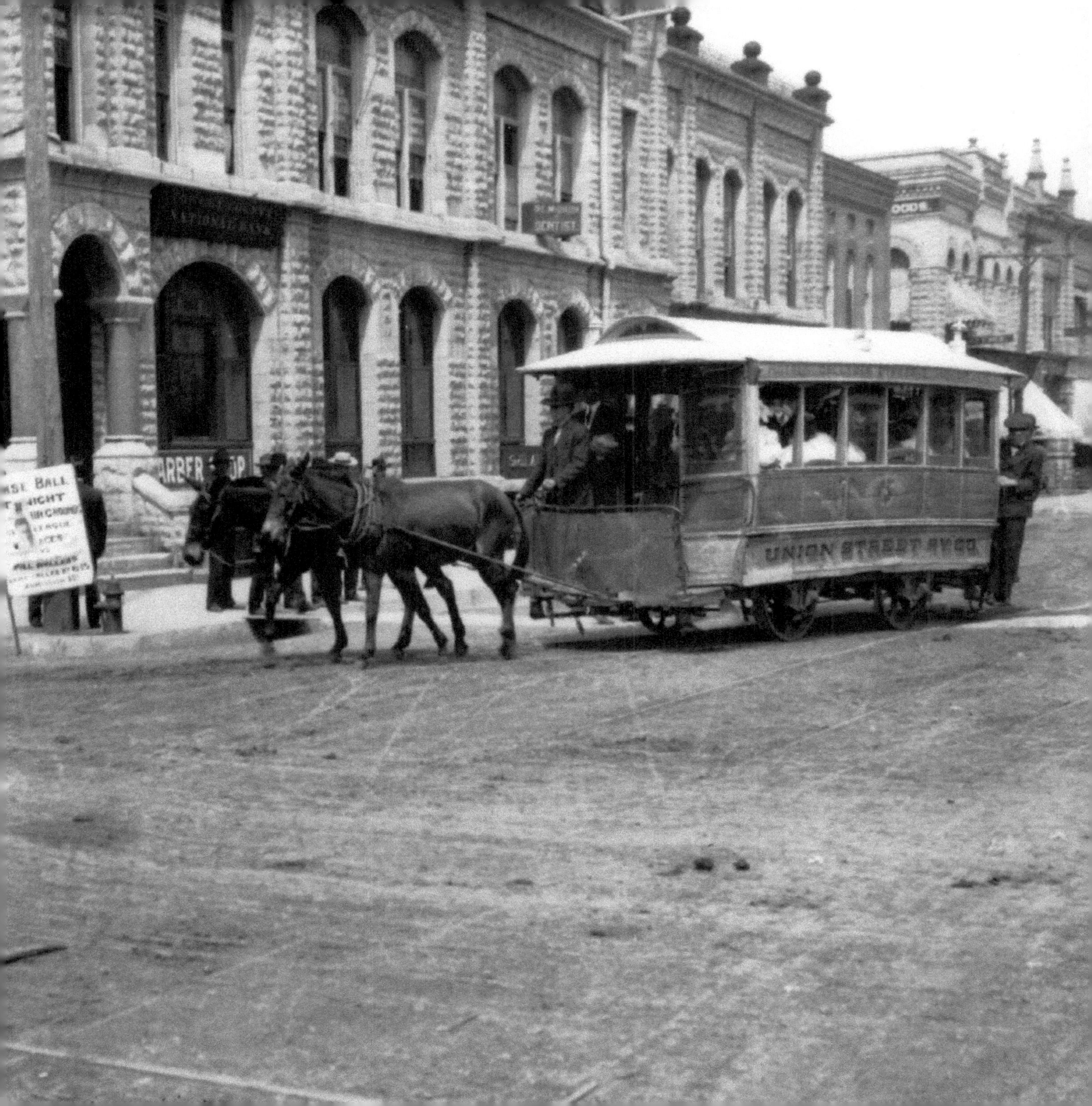
DENTIST
UNION STREET RY CO

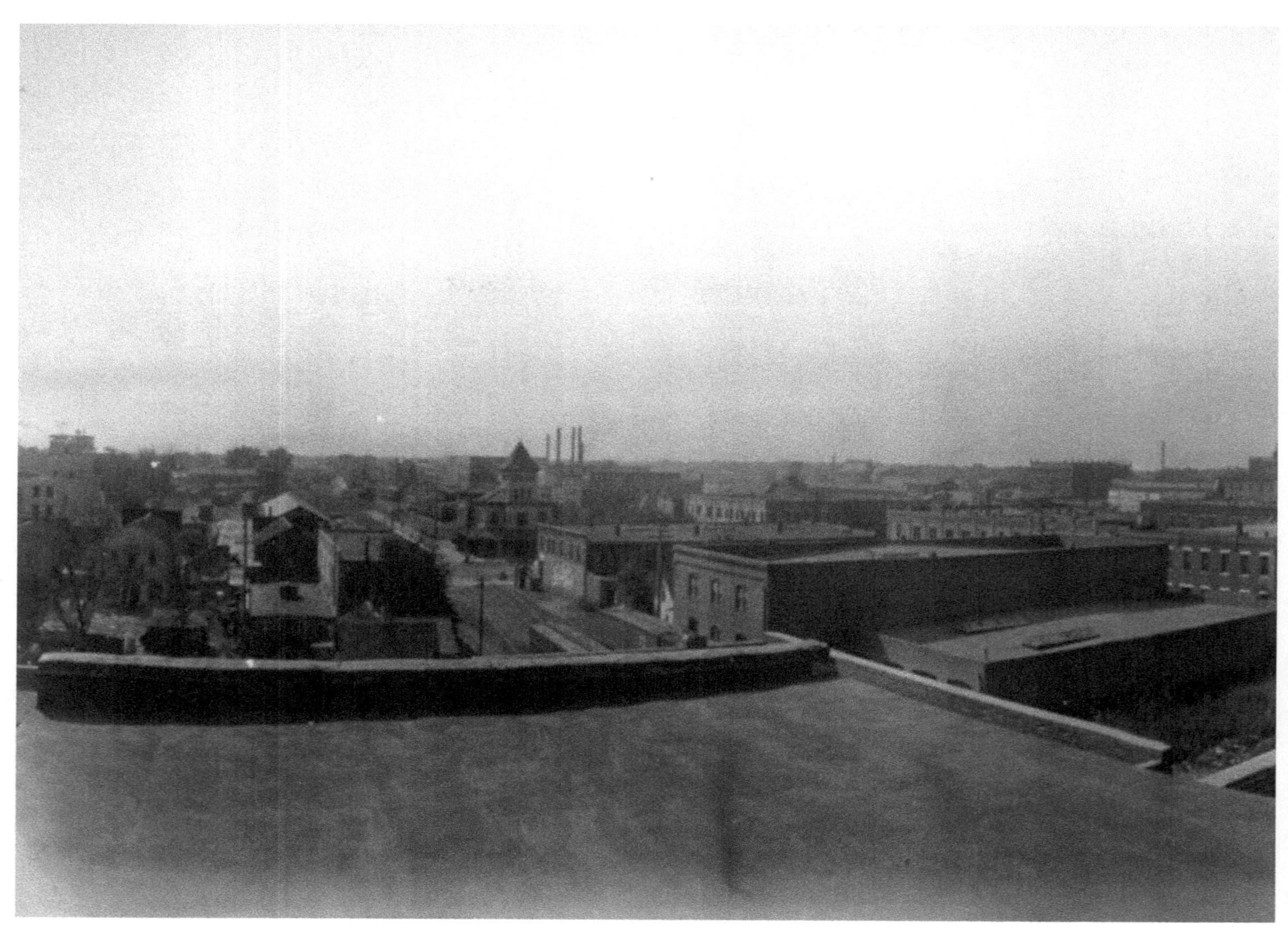

Wichita, Kansas, the most populous city in the state, spreads across the horizon in this rooftop panorama from 1912.

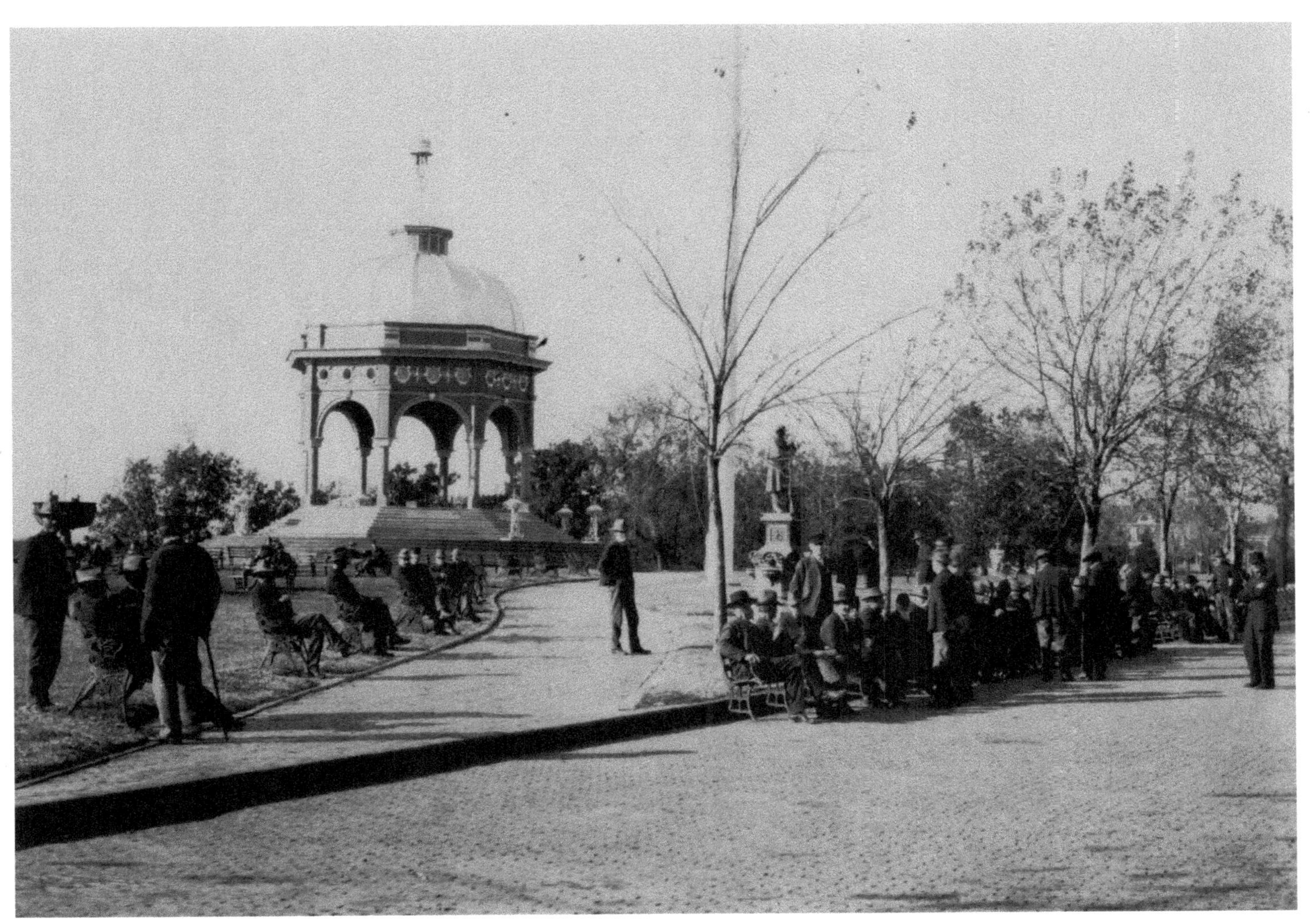

A performance at a bandstand is under way at Leavenworth's National Military Home sometime in the new century.

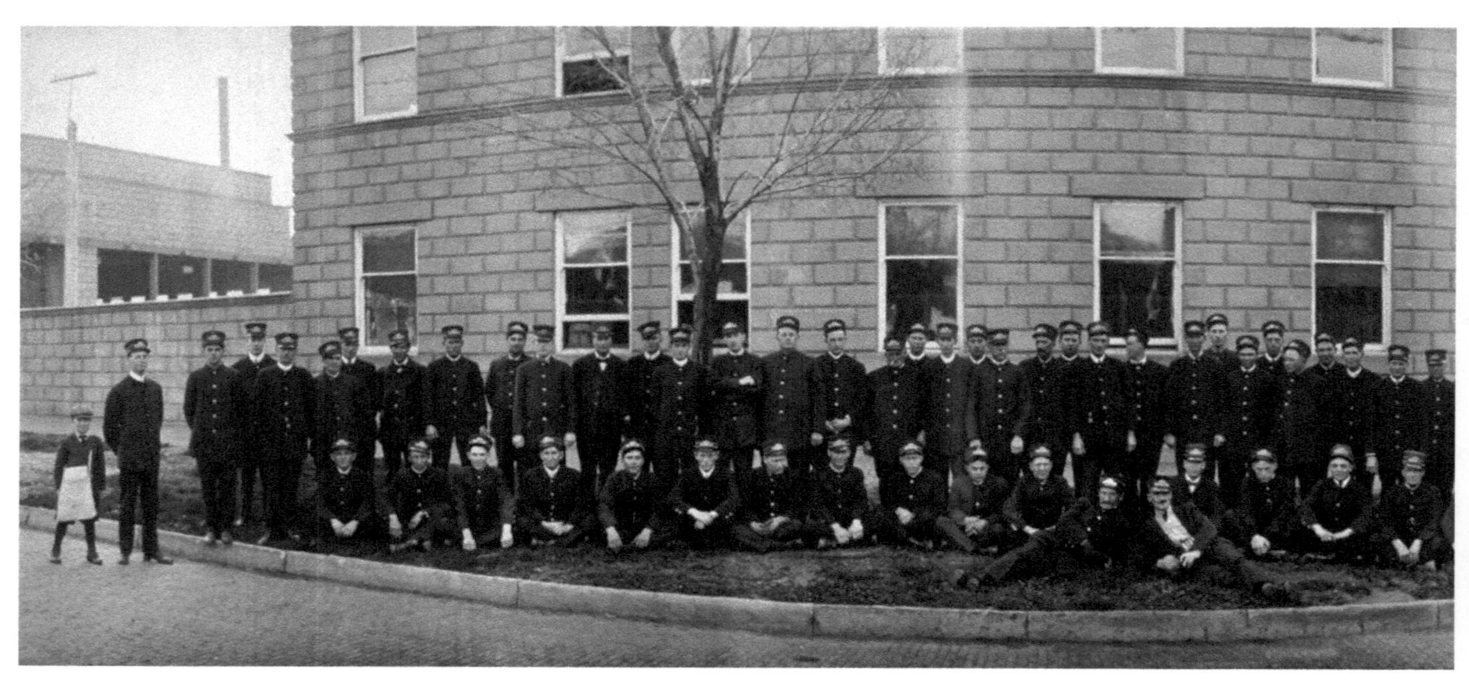

A child joins the group as Topeka Street Railway Company trainmen gather for a group photo on April 27, 1913. Transportation companies included Topeka Railways, which existed between 1892 and 1926; the Topeka City Railway, a mule-pulled car street railway; and the Topeka Rapid Transit Company, a steam-dummy line.

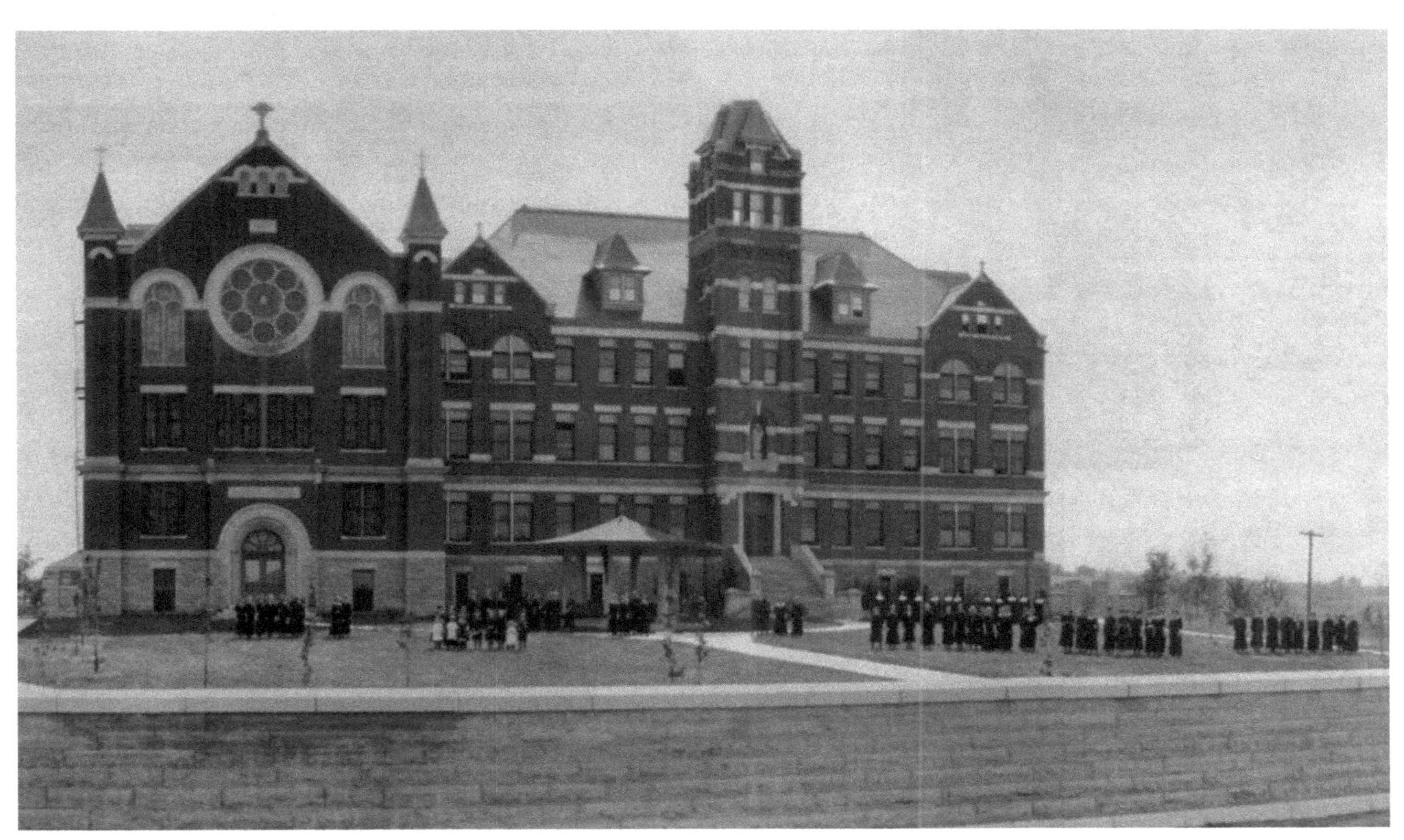

Nazareth Convent and Academy in Concordia was just 10 years old in 1913. The convent, home to the Sisters of St. Joseph, is well known for a stained-glass window that has been referred to as "the beacon of light on Concordia."

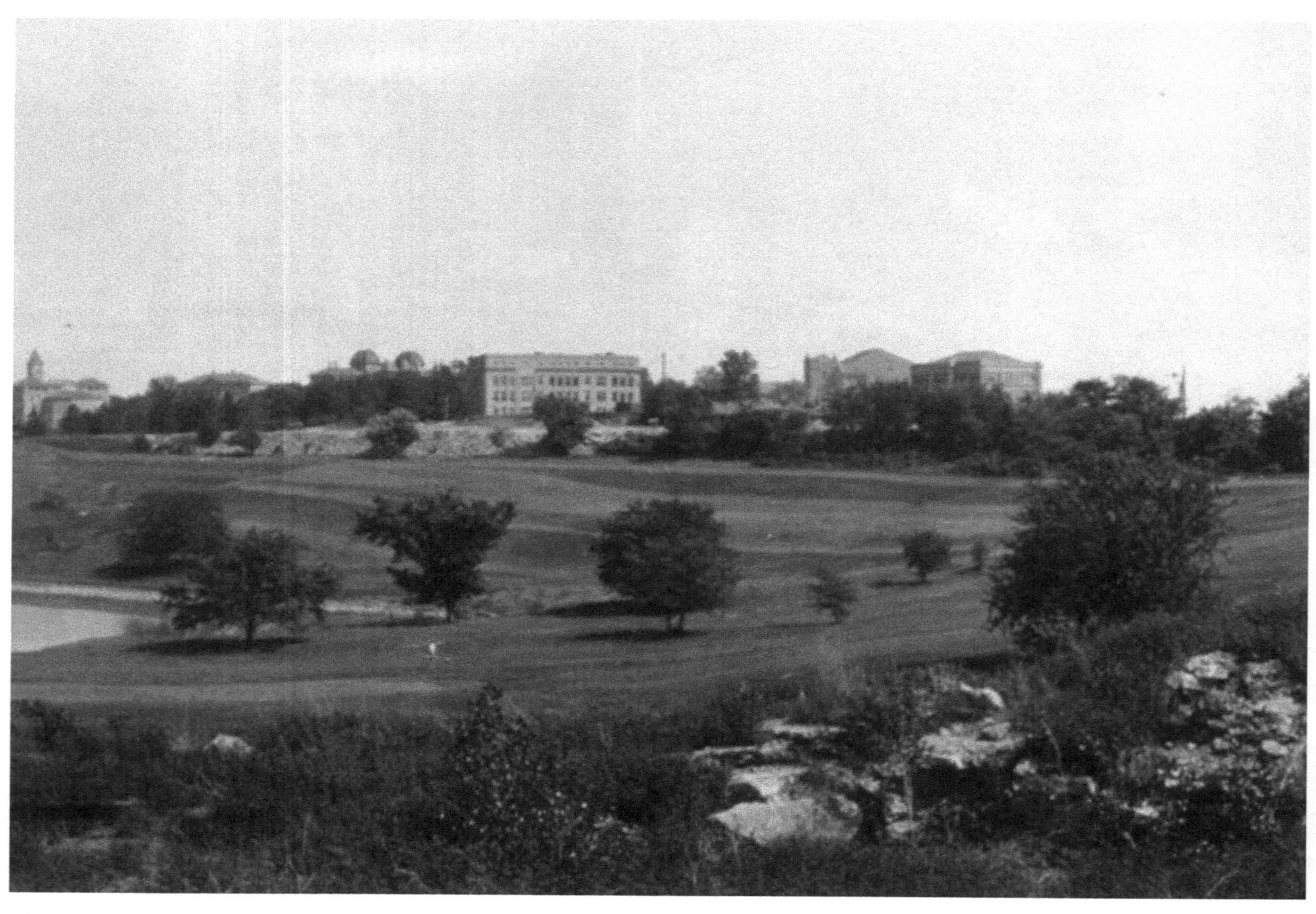

The University of Kansas, located on Mount Oread in Lawrence, is seen here in 1913. The university, established in 1865, for a time was known as Kansas State University.

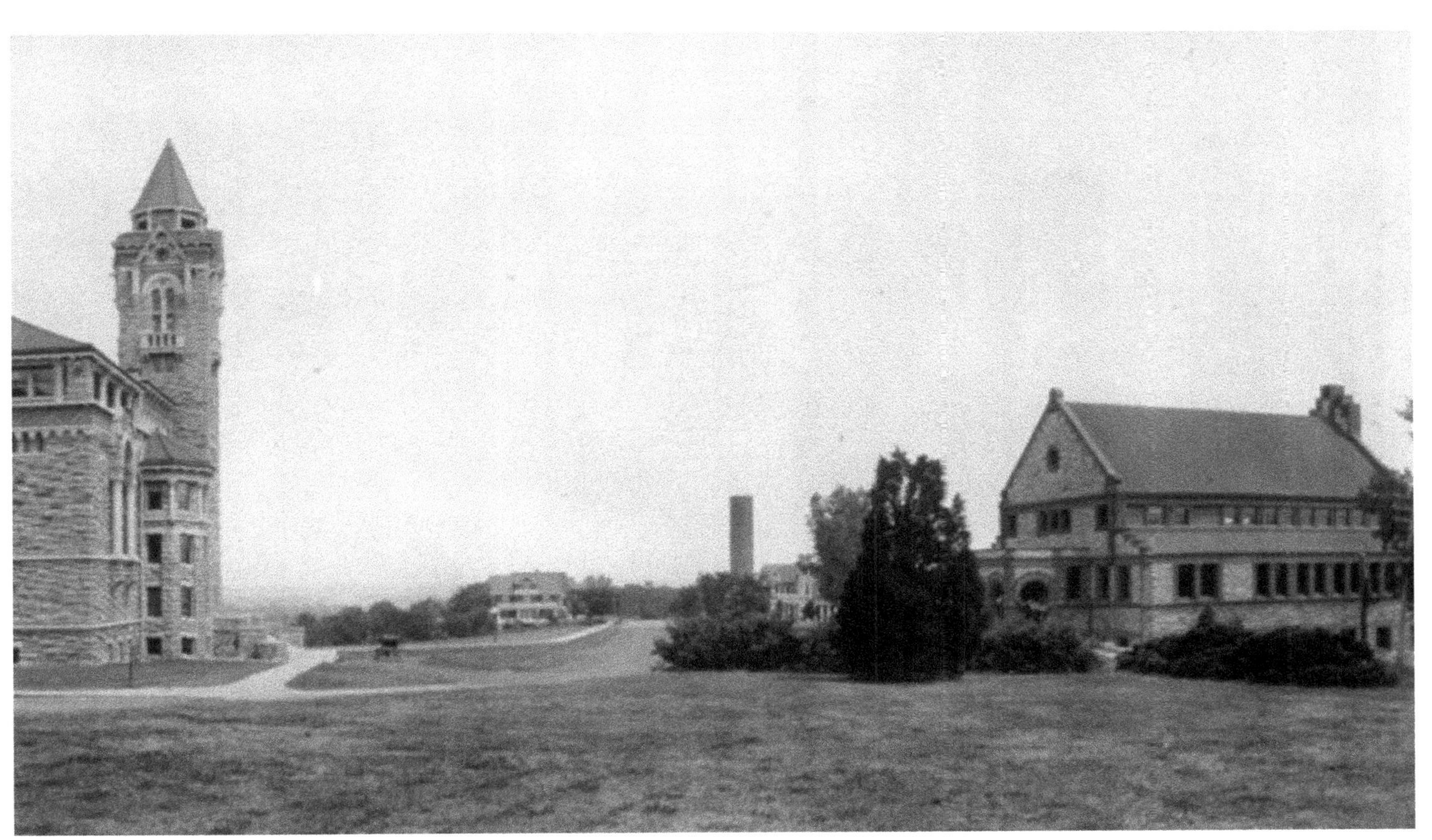

This panorama of the University of Kansas—then called Kansas State University—was recorded in 1913. The buildings at the right and center are not identified, but the building at left is Blake Hall, a physics building named for Professor Lucien I. Blake.

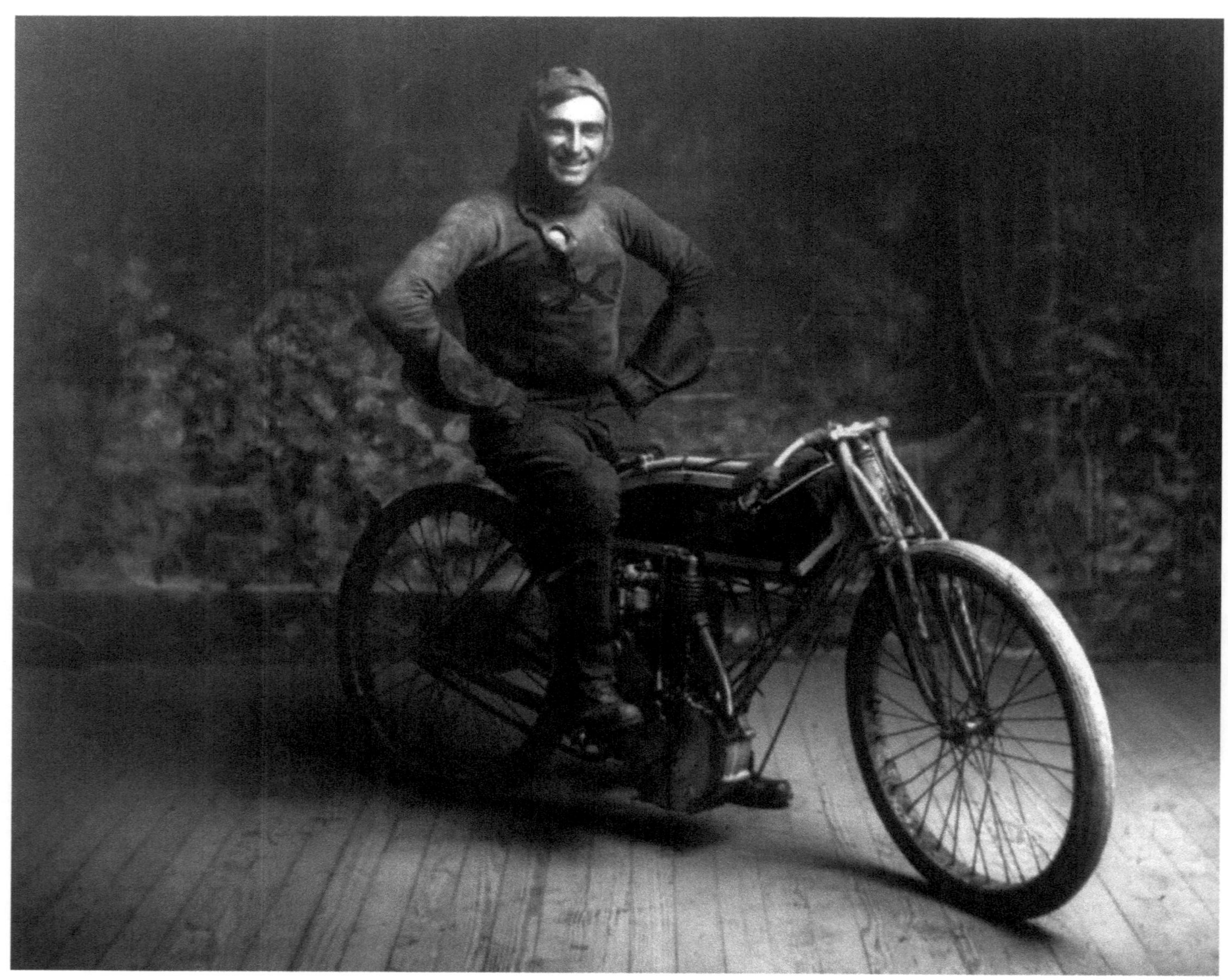

Lawrence Ray Weishaar, identified on the photograph only as "Weishaar," was the winner of a 100-mile motorcycle race in Norton on October 22, 1914. Weishaar's time set a world record, but the renowned rider, known as the "Kansas Cyclone," raced for only ten more years before dying from an injury at a Los Angeles competition.

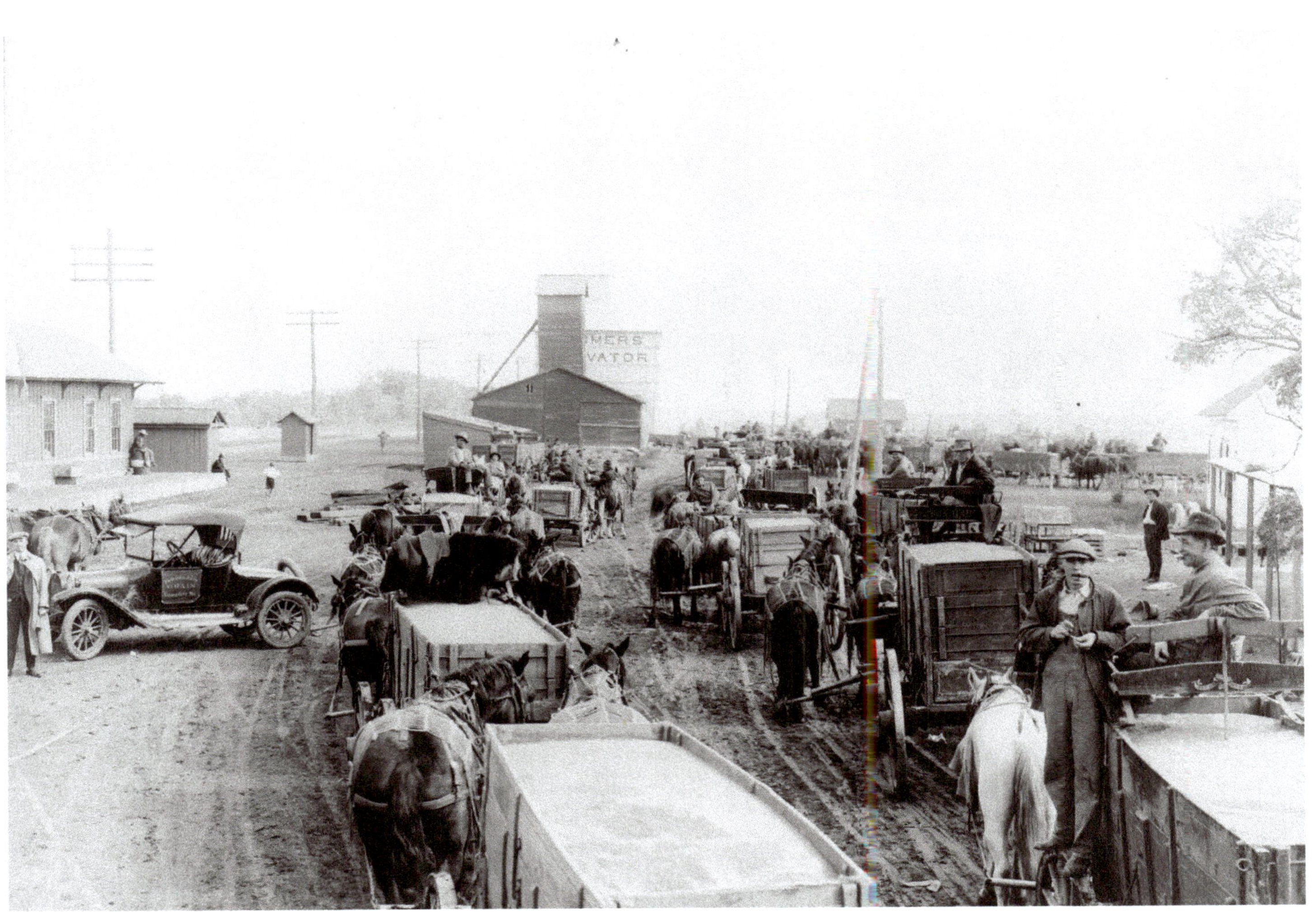

If there's any doubt about the state's prolific crop production, this 1916 photo should dispel it. Wagons line up waiting to deliver wheat to a market in Offerle.

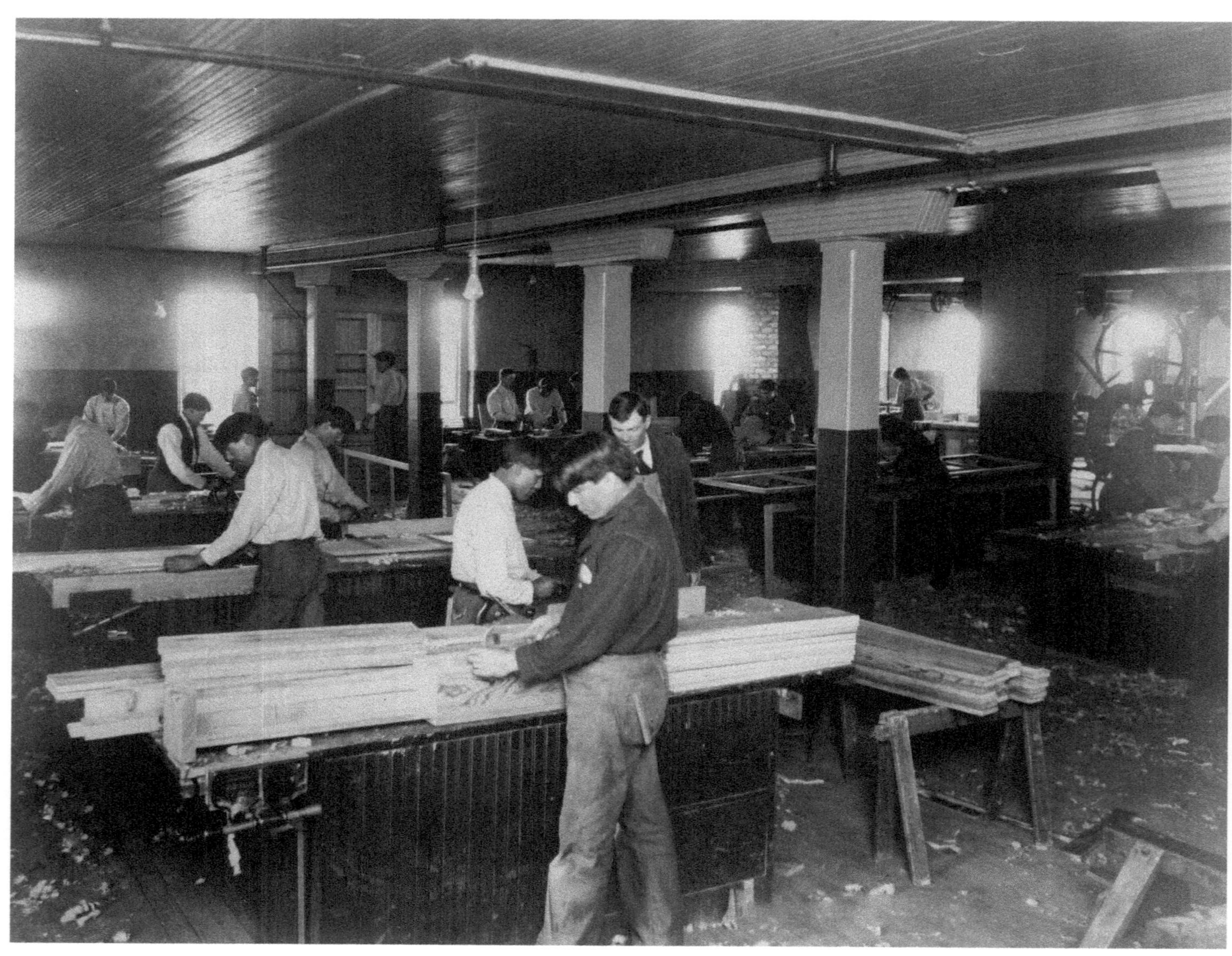

At what was then called Haskell Indian Junior College, students learned vocational and practical skills, such as carpentry, in addition to the usual academic subjects. Founded as a boarding school for Indians from many tribes, the school still exists and is now a university.

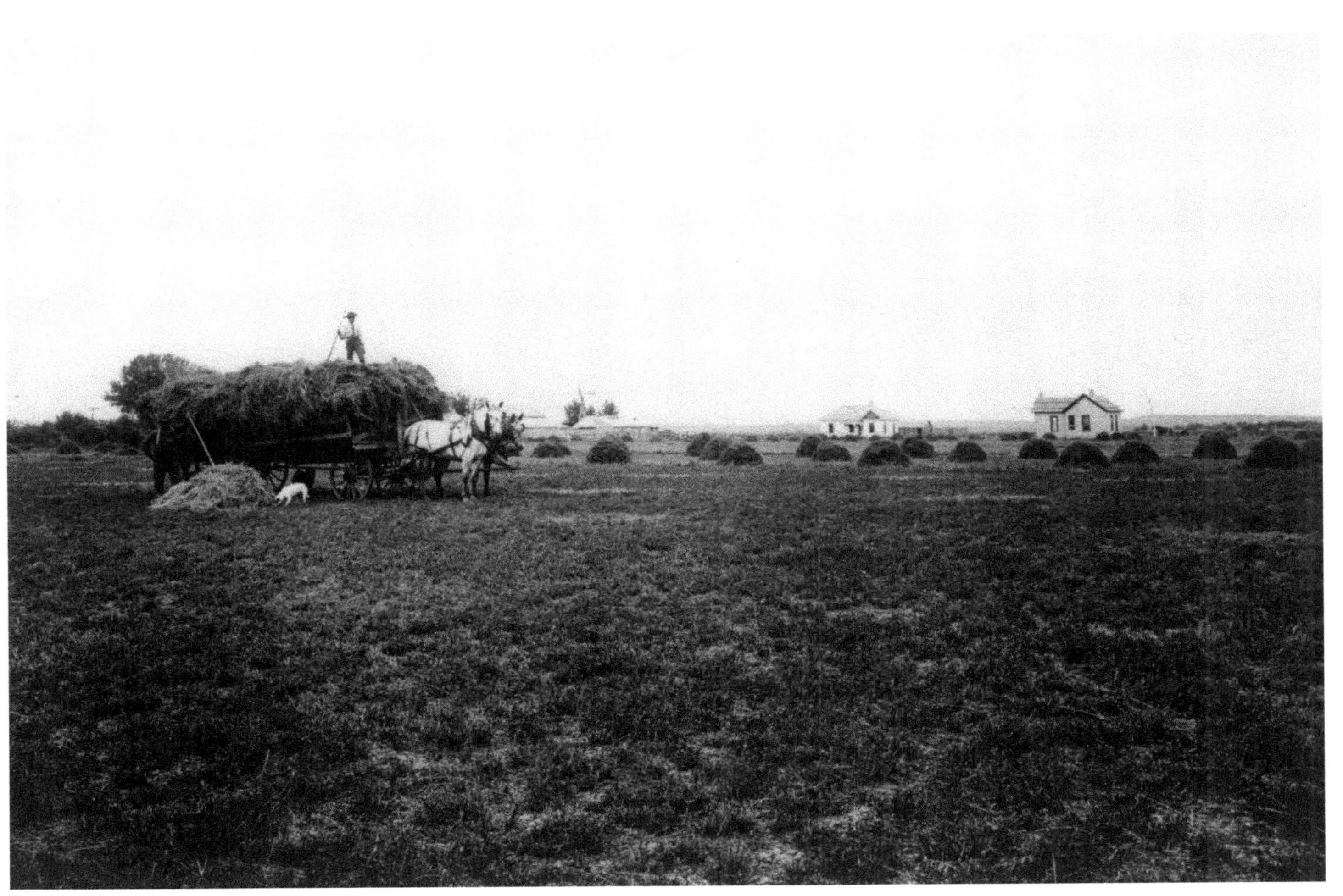

In 1917, this farmer atop a hay wagon stopped long enough to have his picture made.

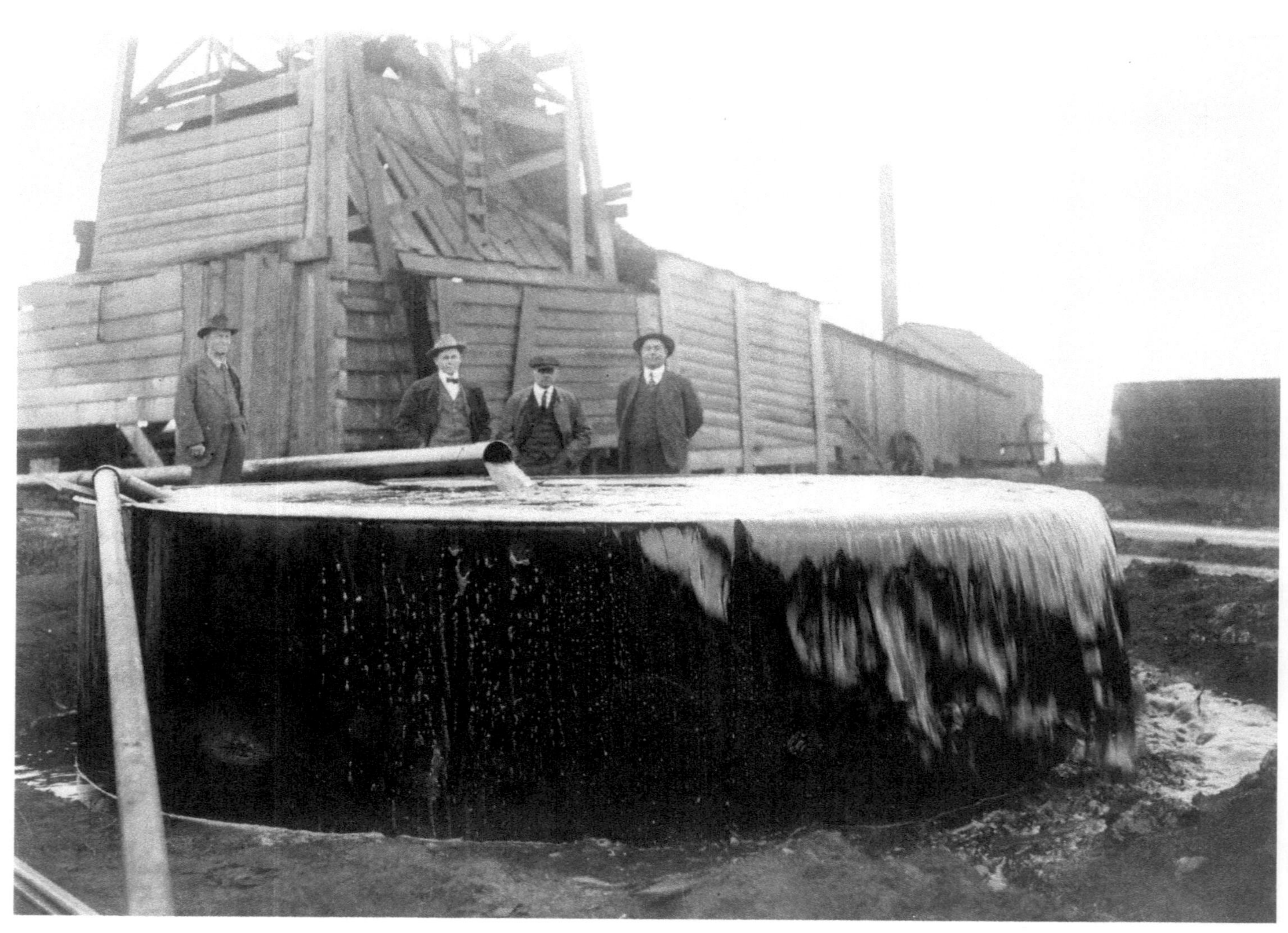

Four men pose for a 1917 photo in El Dorado at the site of Trapshooter's No. 2, an oil drilling operation. The prolific El Dorado oil field covered 34 square miles, used geologic pinpointing to locate oil deposits, and produced 29 million barrels of oil in 1918.

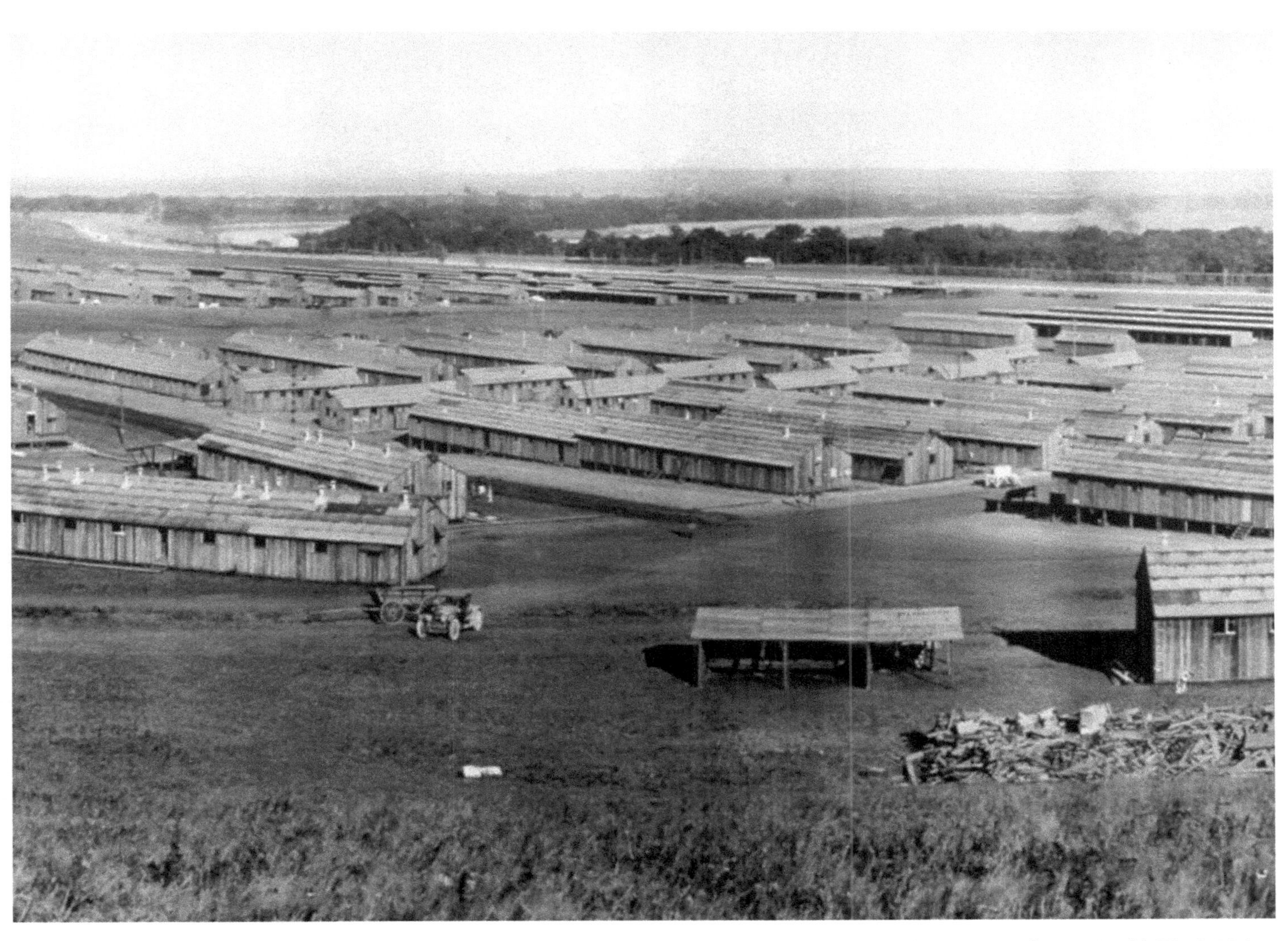

A sprawling cavalry camp occupies an area known as Pawnee Flats near Fort Riley in 1917, during World War I. Union Pacific Railway tracks ran through Pawnee Flats from Junction City, Kansas

Following Spread: The base hospital at Fort Riley is pictured in this 1919 photo by Verne O. Williams, a Kansas City photographer.

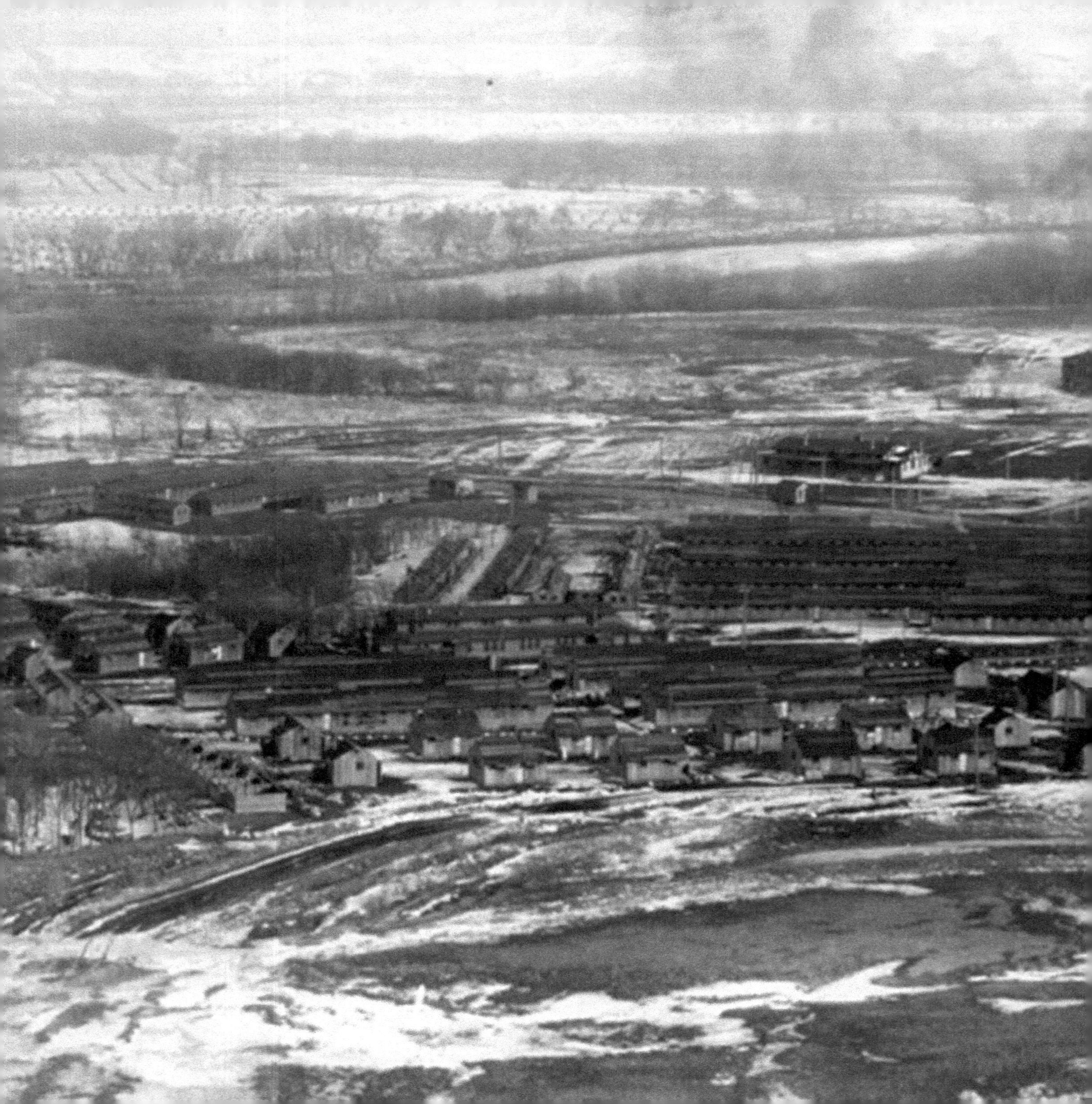

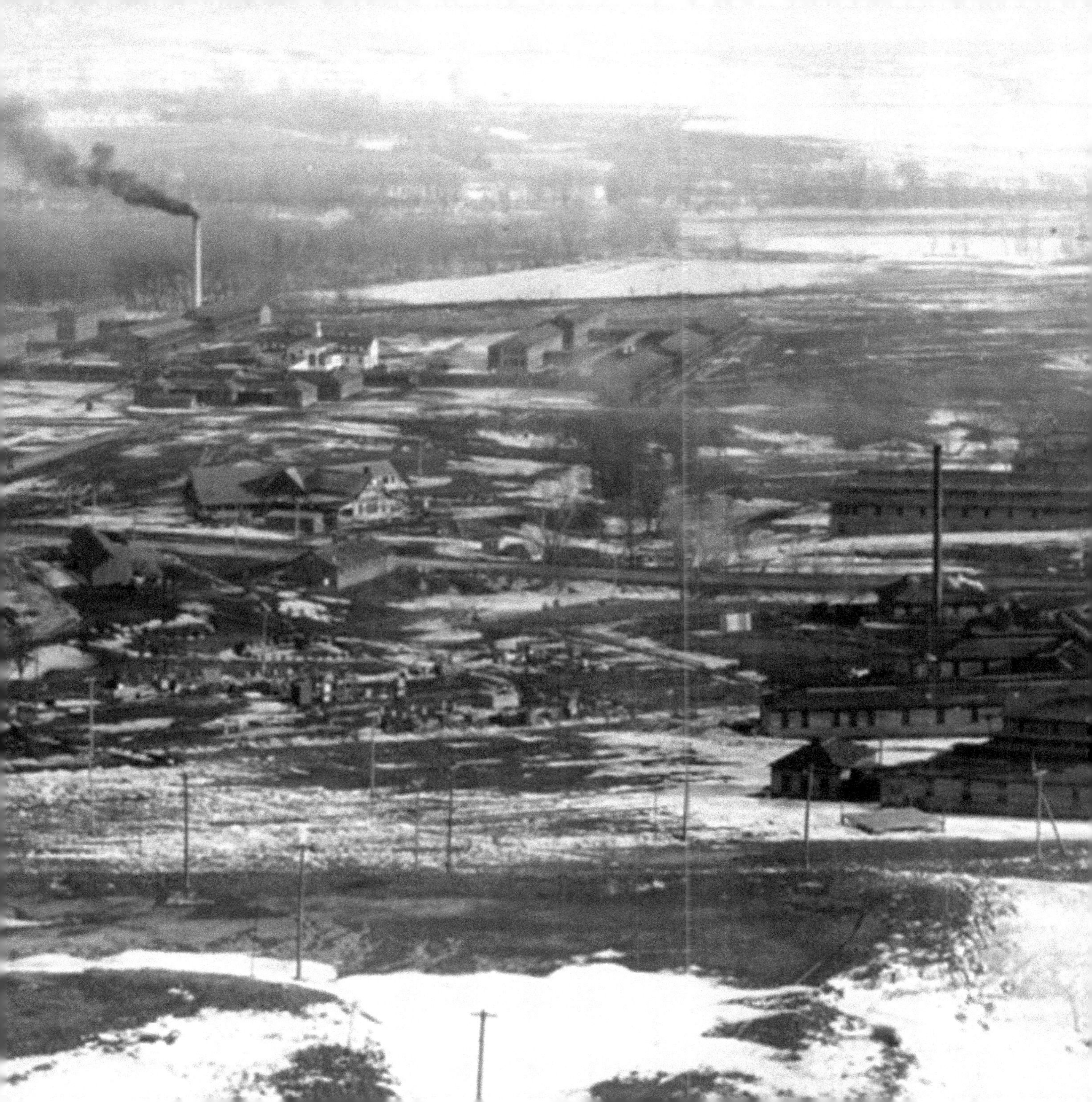

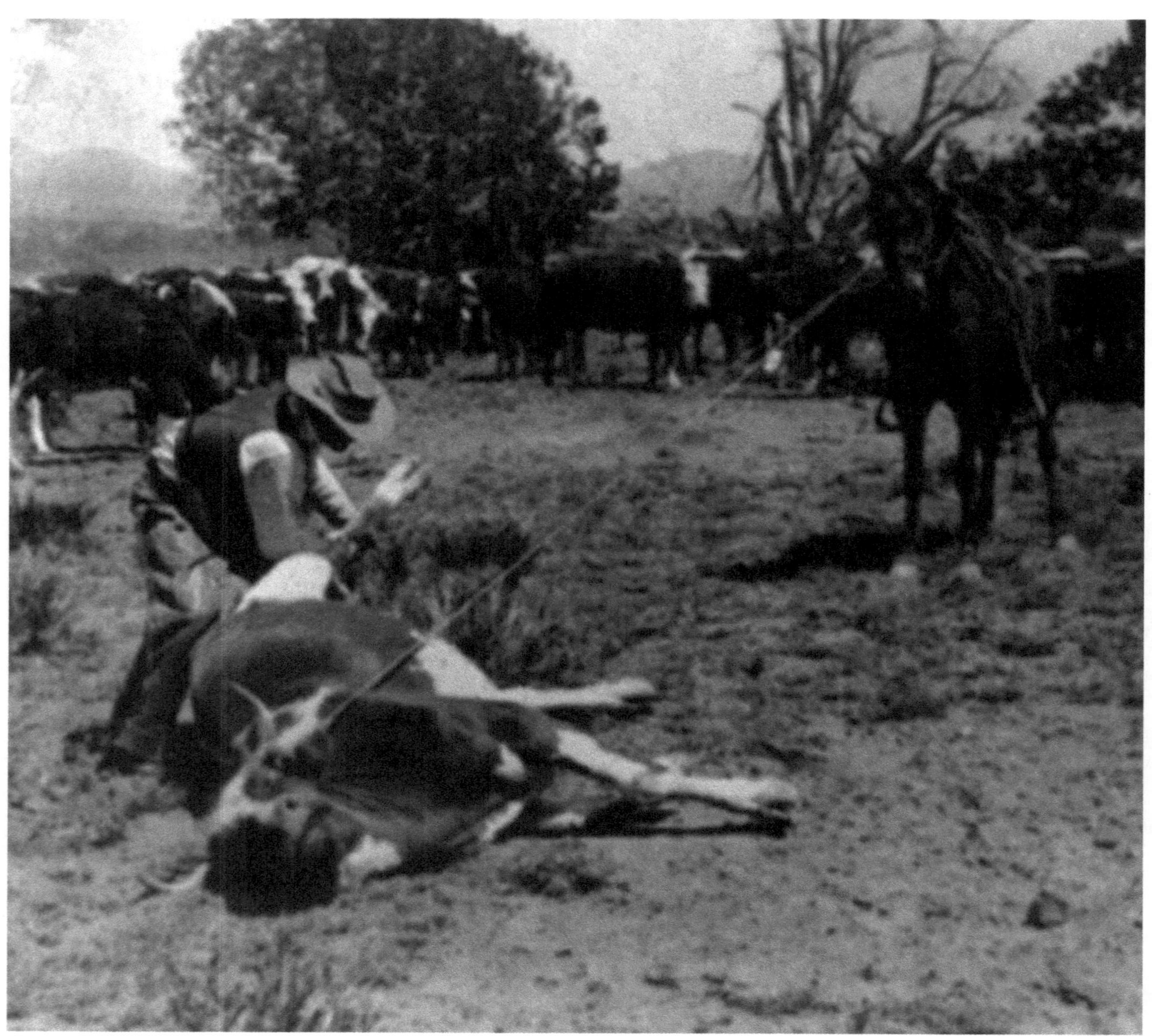

With a cattle herd in the background, a Kansas cowboy ties the hind legs of a lassoed cow in 1919.

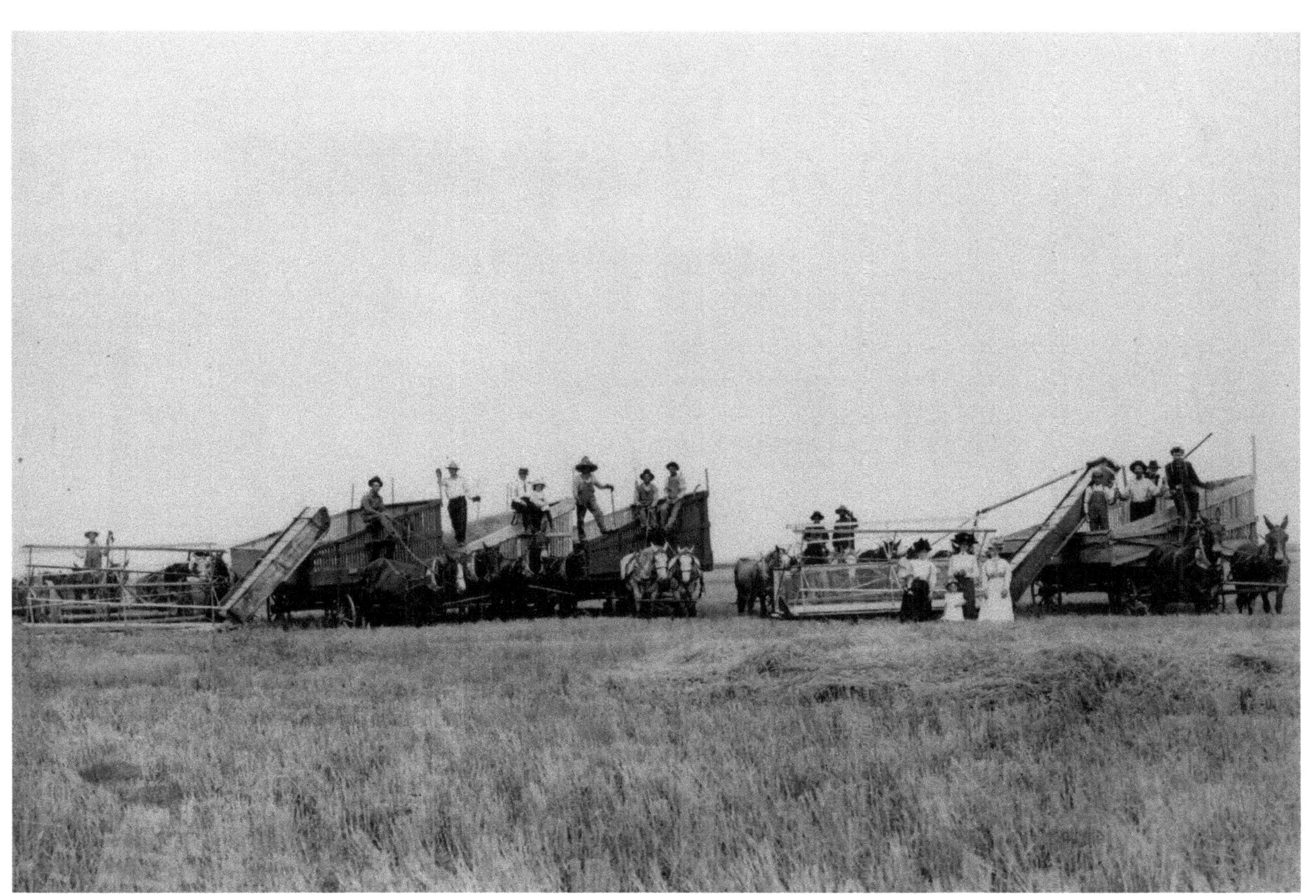

A group of men and women gather in a wheat field during a harvest near Kinsley. Harvesting machinery and horse-drawn wagons are pictured in this photograph from early in the century. The women and girl are dressed in fashionable attire and hats.

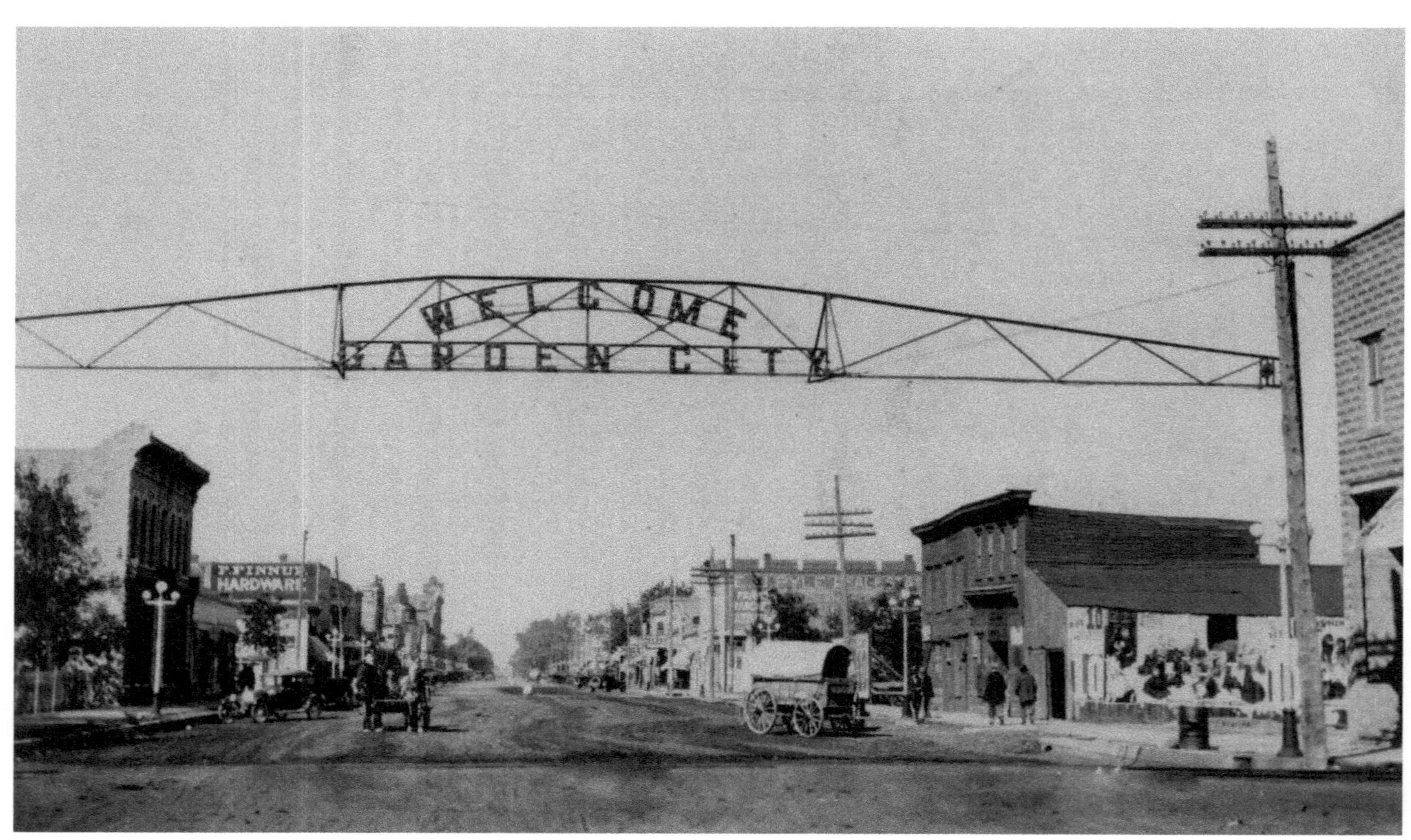

A banner welcomes railroad passengers and other visitors to Garden City's Main Street after 1910. Wagons, carriages, and automobiles leave their tracks on the unpaved road.

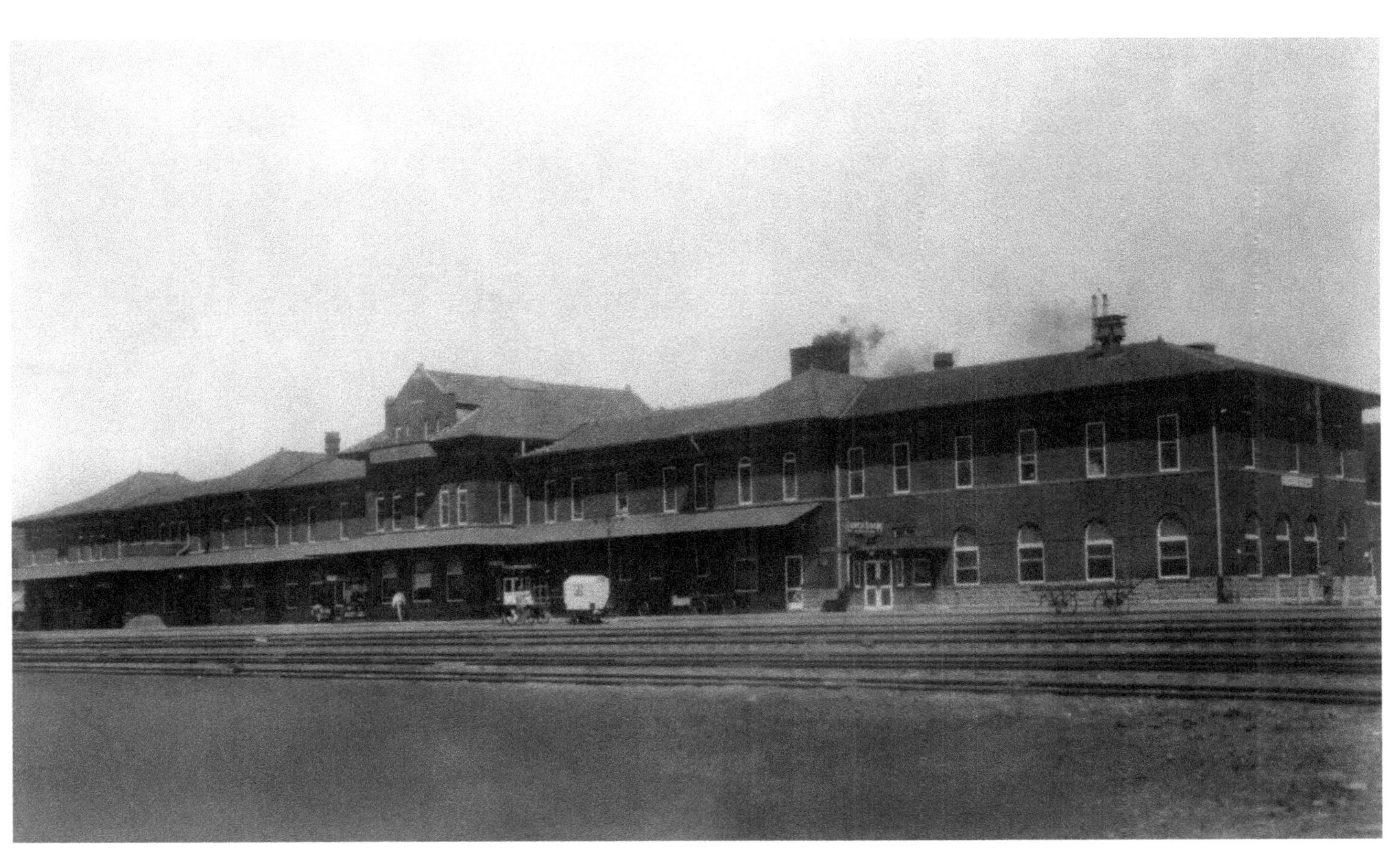

Railroads contributed much to Kansas's development and economic growth. Depots like this one, the Santa Fe Railroad's in Dodge City, often provided overnight accommodations, on site or nearby, and restaurants for travelers.

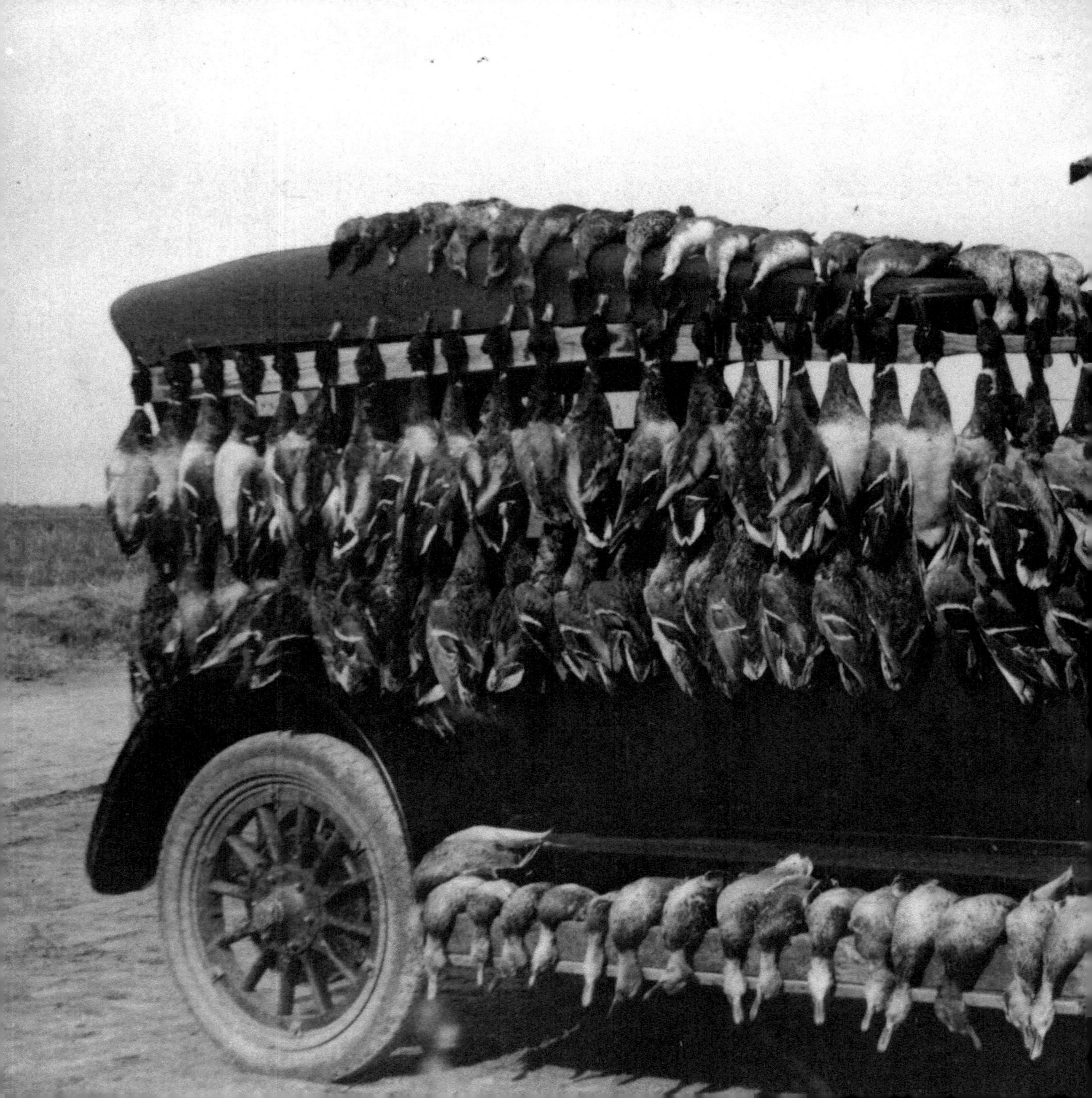

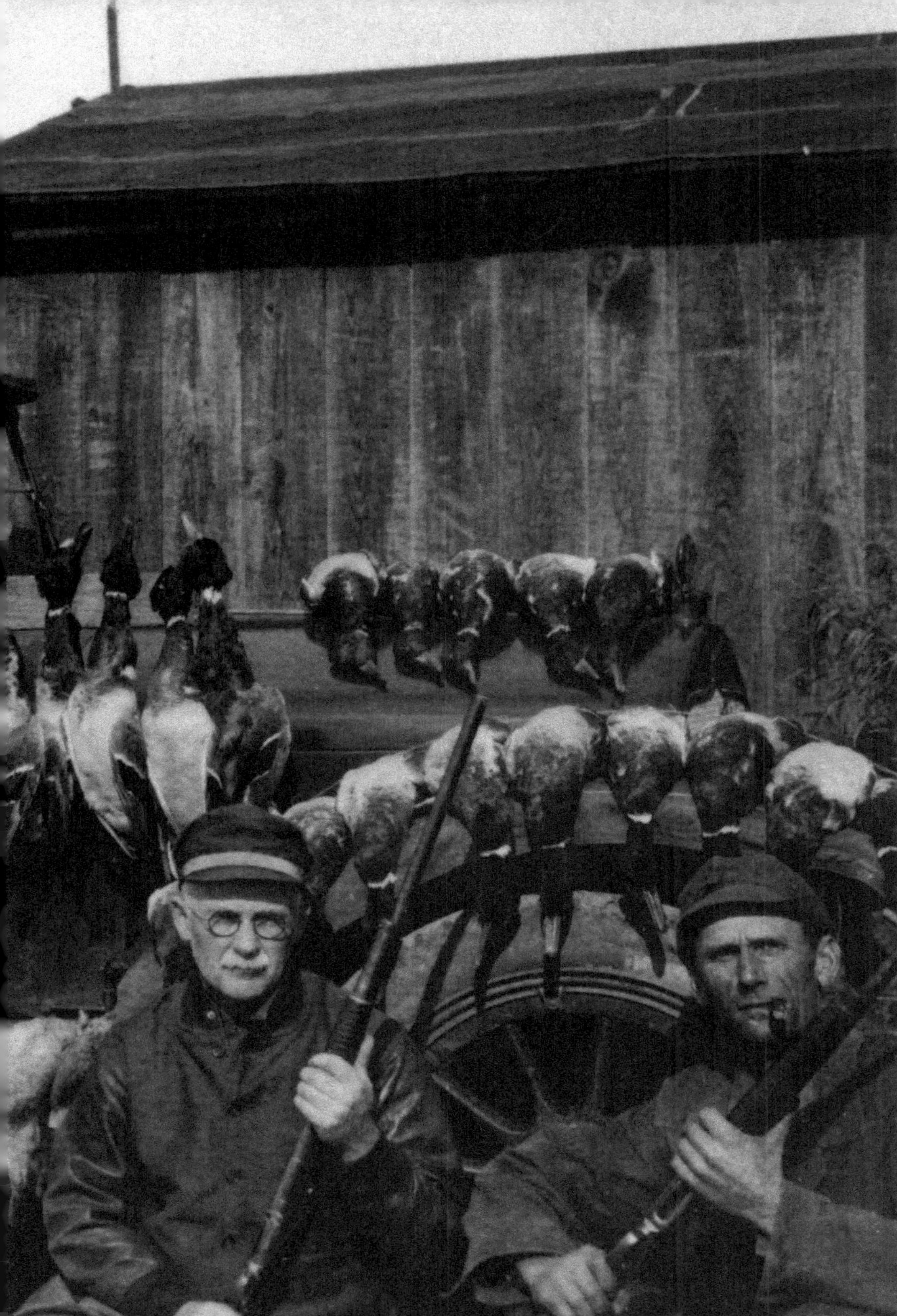

Well before "get all your ducks in a row" became a popular expression, hunters E. A. Detrick, left, and Harry Wanerke display 100 of their web-footed victims after a 1922 hunt in Caldwell.

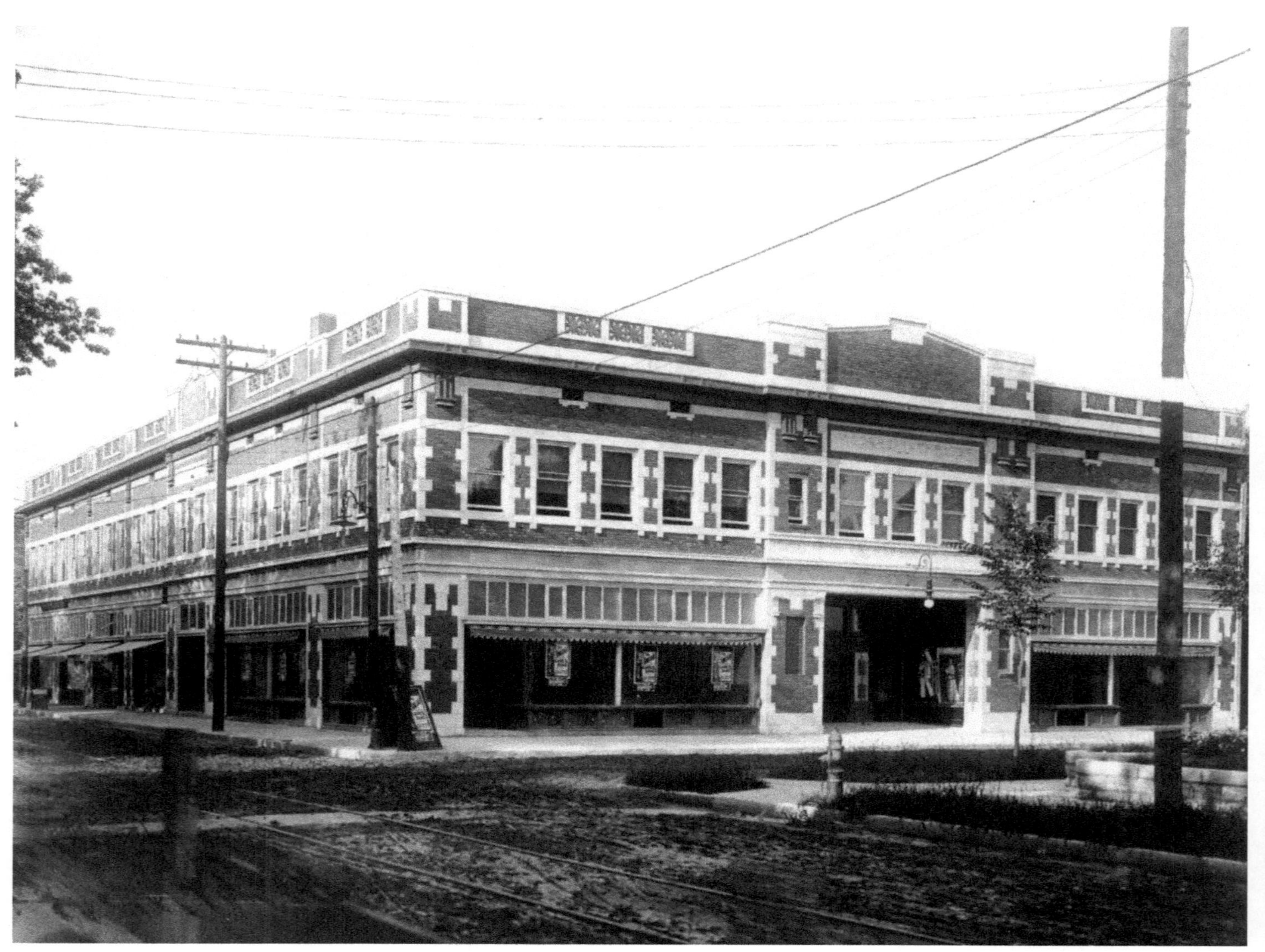

The two-screen Marshall Theatre in Manhattan was acquired by Glen W. Dickinson shortly after he quit a family business in 1920. Dickinson founded the successful Dickinson Theatres chain.

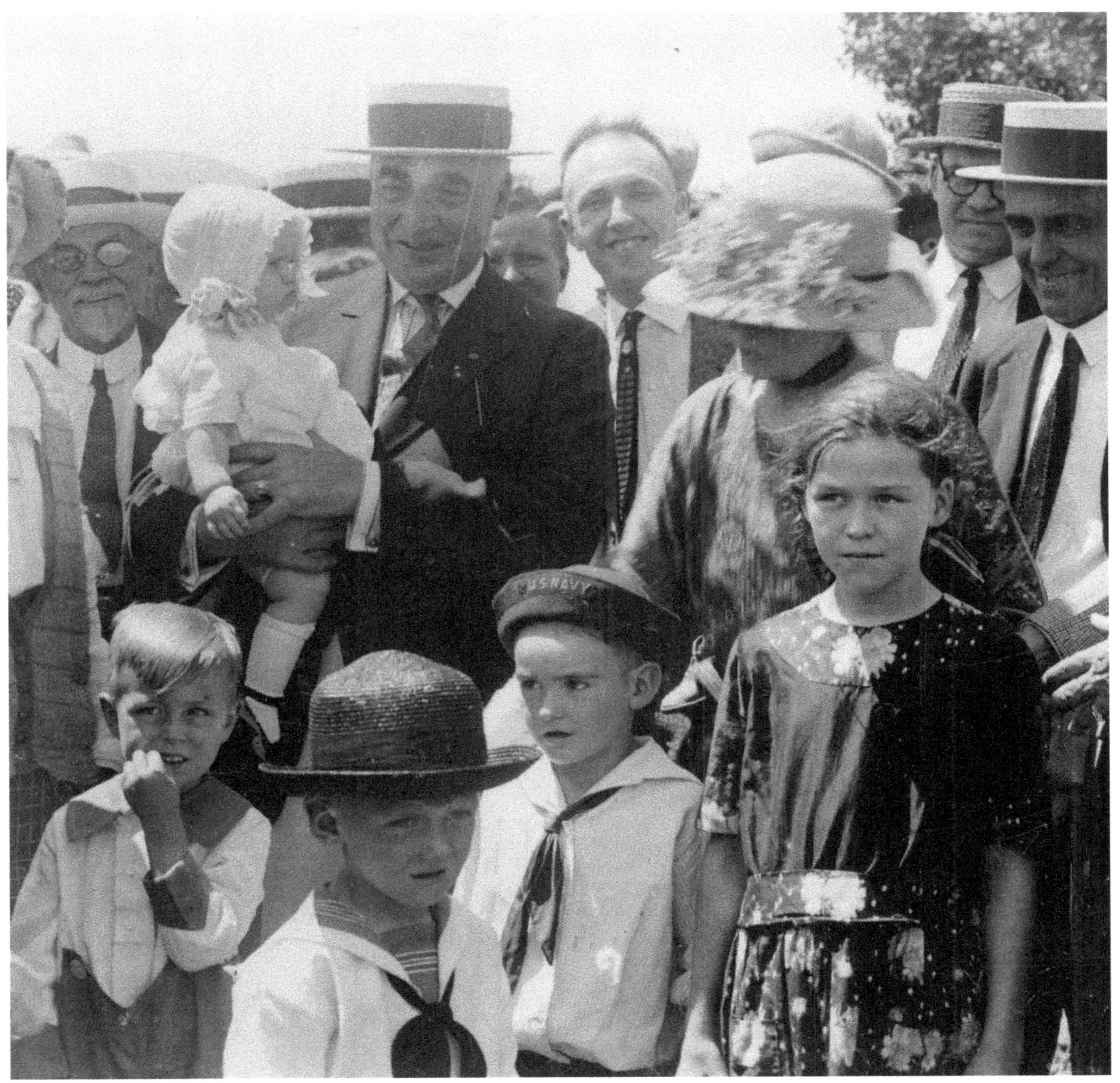

In 1923, President Warren Harding poses with a baby and a group of Hutchinson farmers. Harding, the 29th president, died from the effects of a stroke later that year.

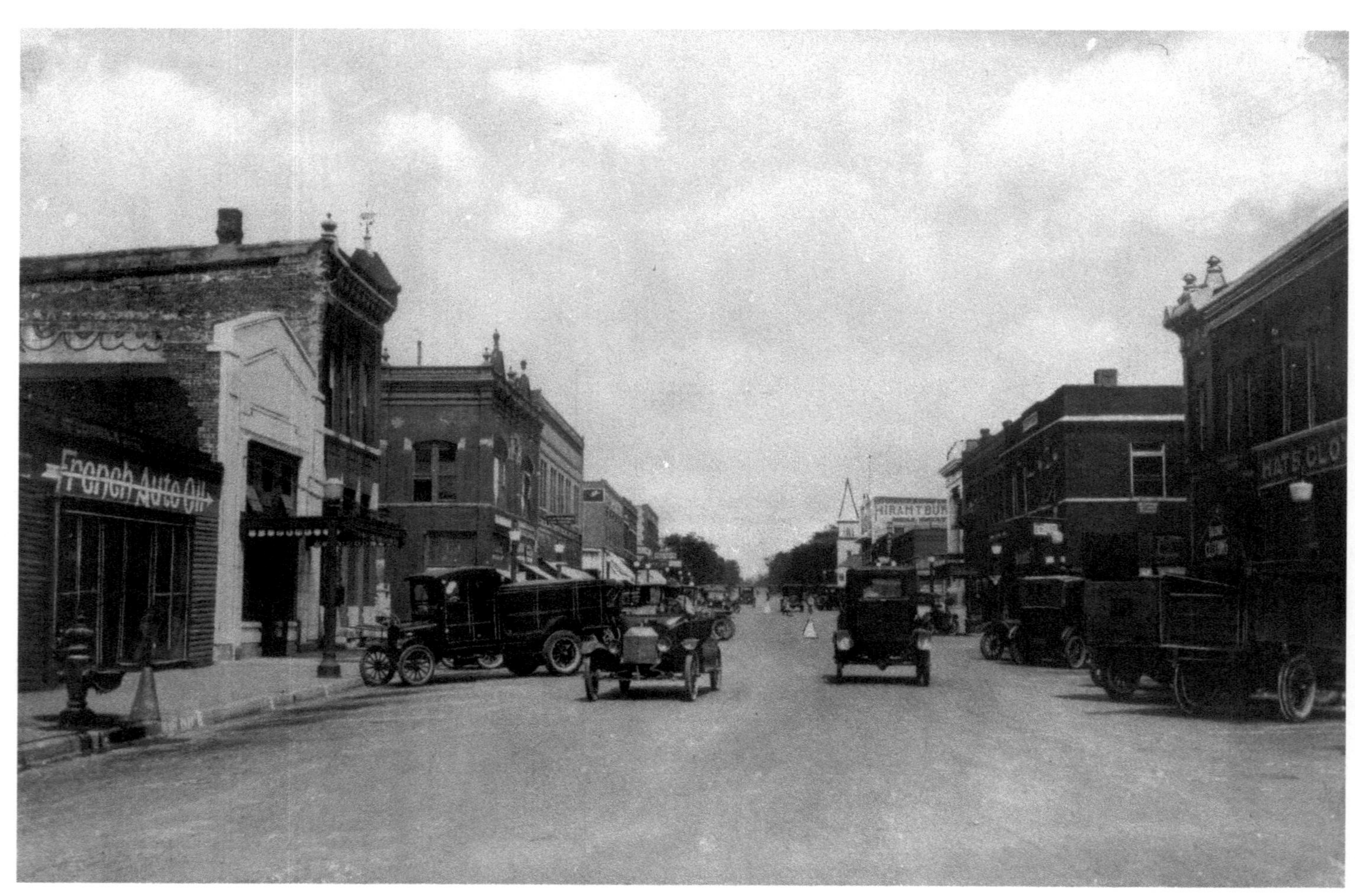

Downtown Hutchinson hums with trucks and automobiles in the 1920s. Across the nation, main thoroughfares such as this one had by now been paved.

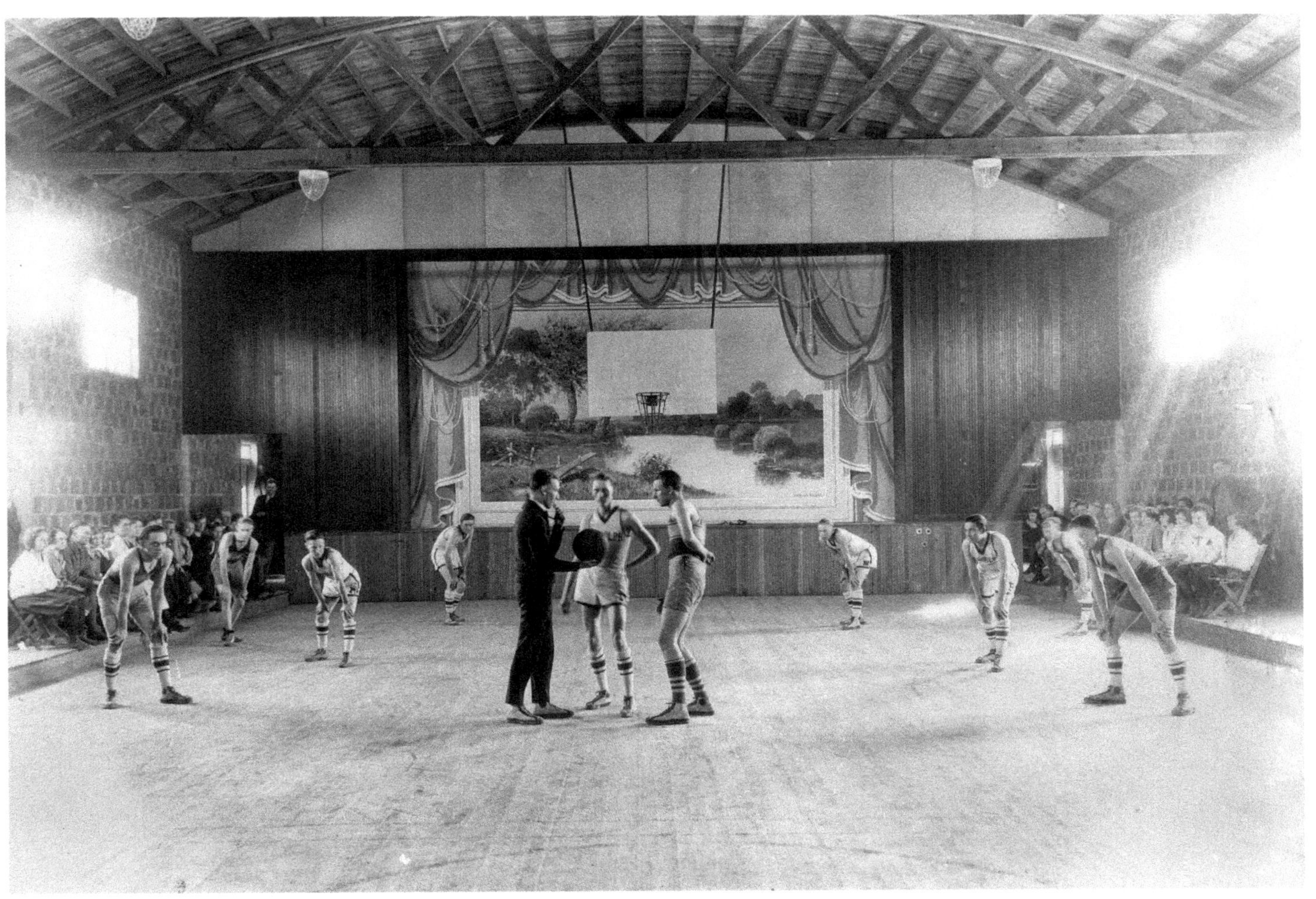

The gyms were less elaborate in the 1920s, but basketball has been a popular sport in the state since its creation in the 1890s by Dr. James Naismith, who began coaching the basketball team at the University of Kansas around the turn of the century. In this photo, player John Marchett waits for a jump ball in the Randolph High School auditorium at the university.

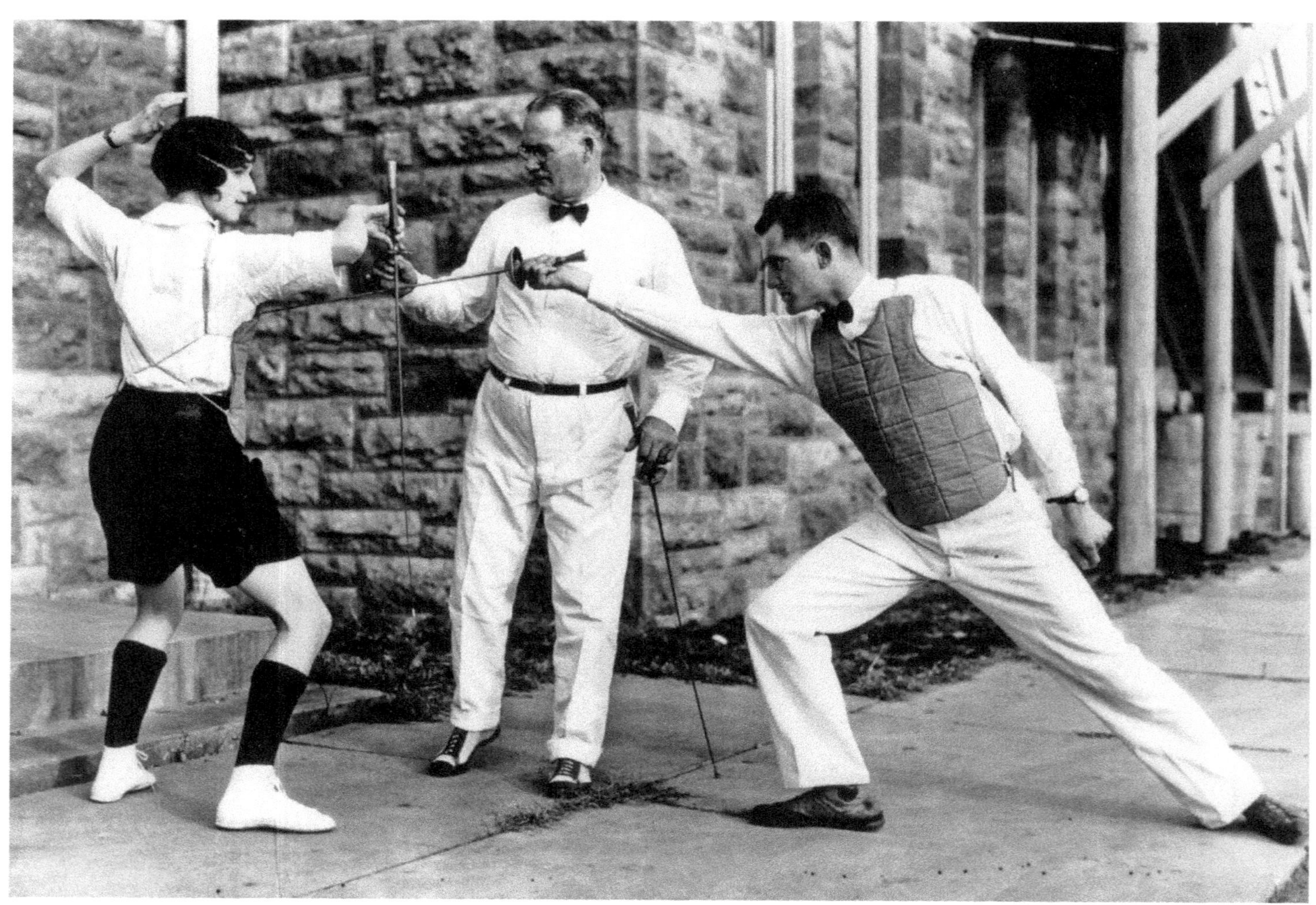

Dr. James Naismith, center, inventor of basketball, was also fencing instructor at the University of Kansas. Naismith supervises as Vera Zscheile, left, takes a defensive position while fellow student Melvin Douglas attempts a thrust. When the photo was taken in the 1920s, Naismith was director of University of Kansas's gym, campus chaplain, and basketball coach.

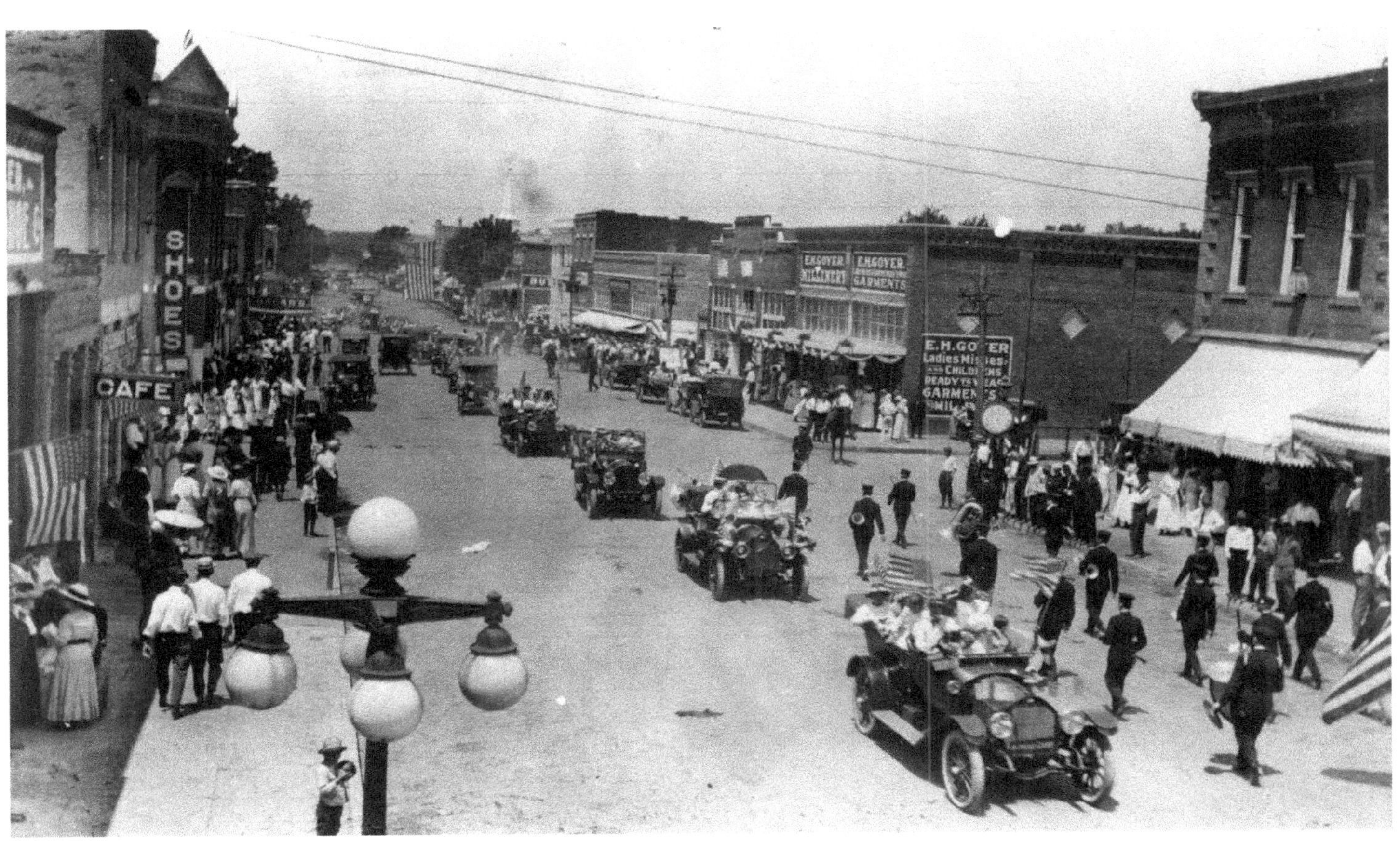

Residents of Neodesha are celebrating the city's 1924 anniversary parade. The parade passes the intersection of Main and 4th streets. In the 1860s, indigenous peoples allowed settlers to establish a trading post on the land that would be incorporated as Neodesha in 1871. Twenty years later, oil was drilled for commercial purposes at a well that later developed into the Mid-continent Oil Field.

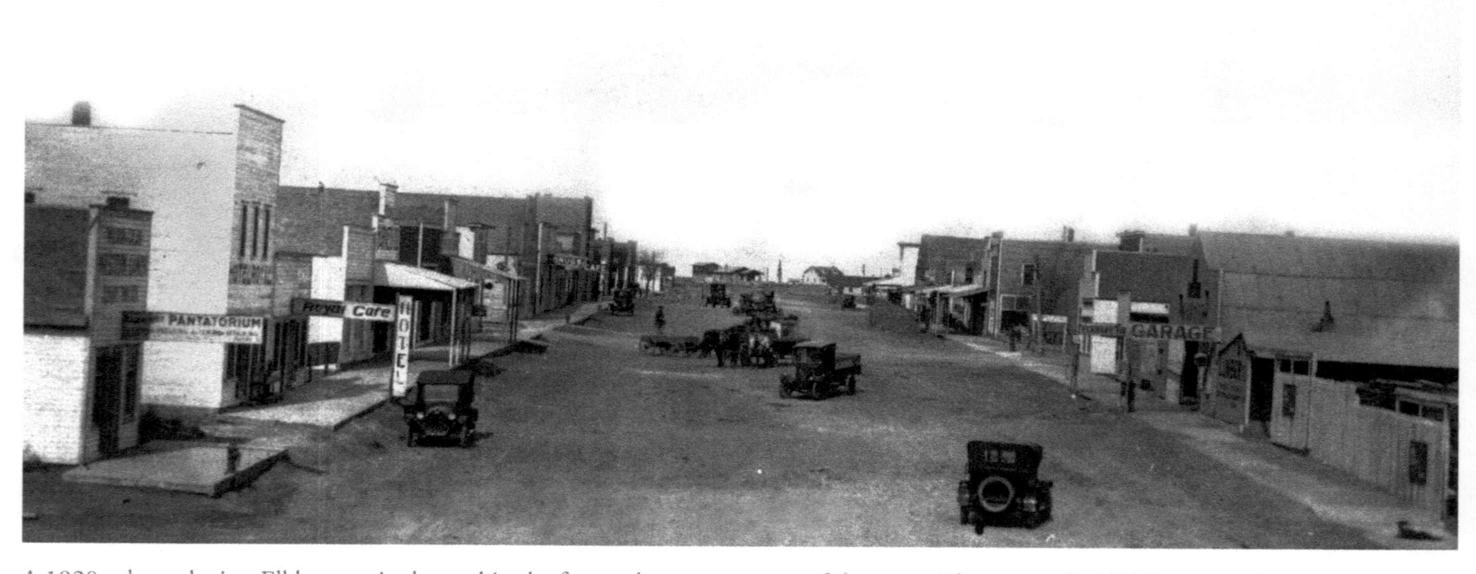

A 1920s photo depicts Elkhart, a city located in the far southwestern corner of the state. Adjacent to the Oklahoma border and eight miles from Colorado, Elkhart is in Morton County, the "Cornerstone of Kansas." Along the unpaved street are several businesses, including cafes, a garage, a drugstore, a hotel, and a pantatorium, at left. A pantatorium specialized in cleaning, dyeing, pressing, repairing, and altering clothing.

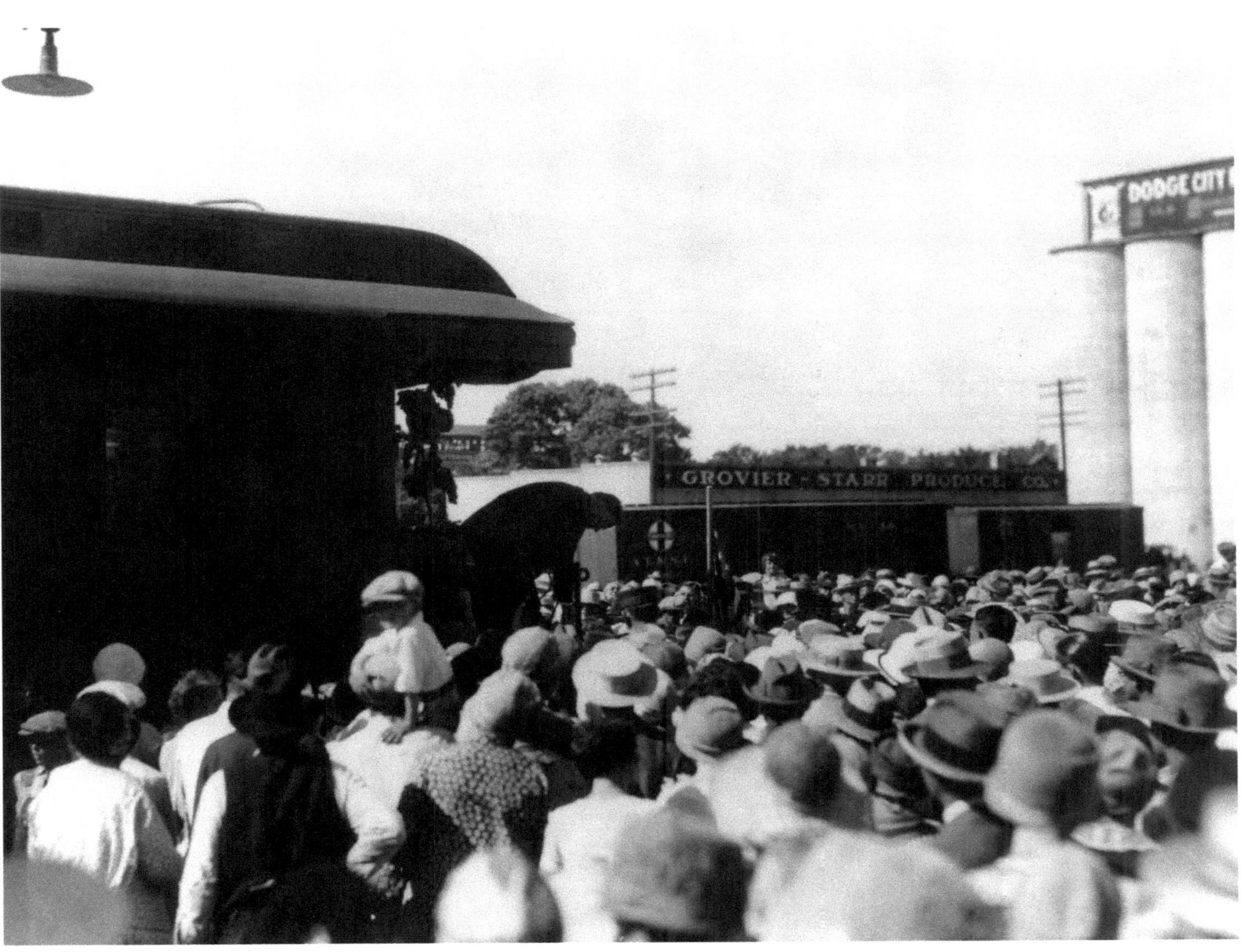

Herbert Hoover campaigns from the back of a train in Dodge City around 1928. Hoover, the 31st president, was in office just eight months wher. the stock market crashed.

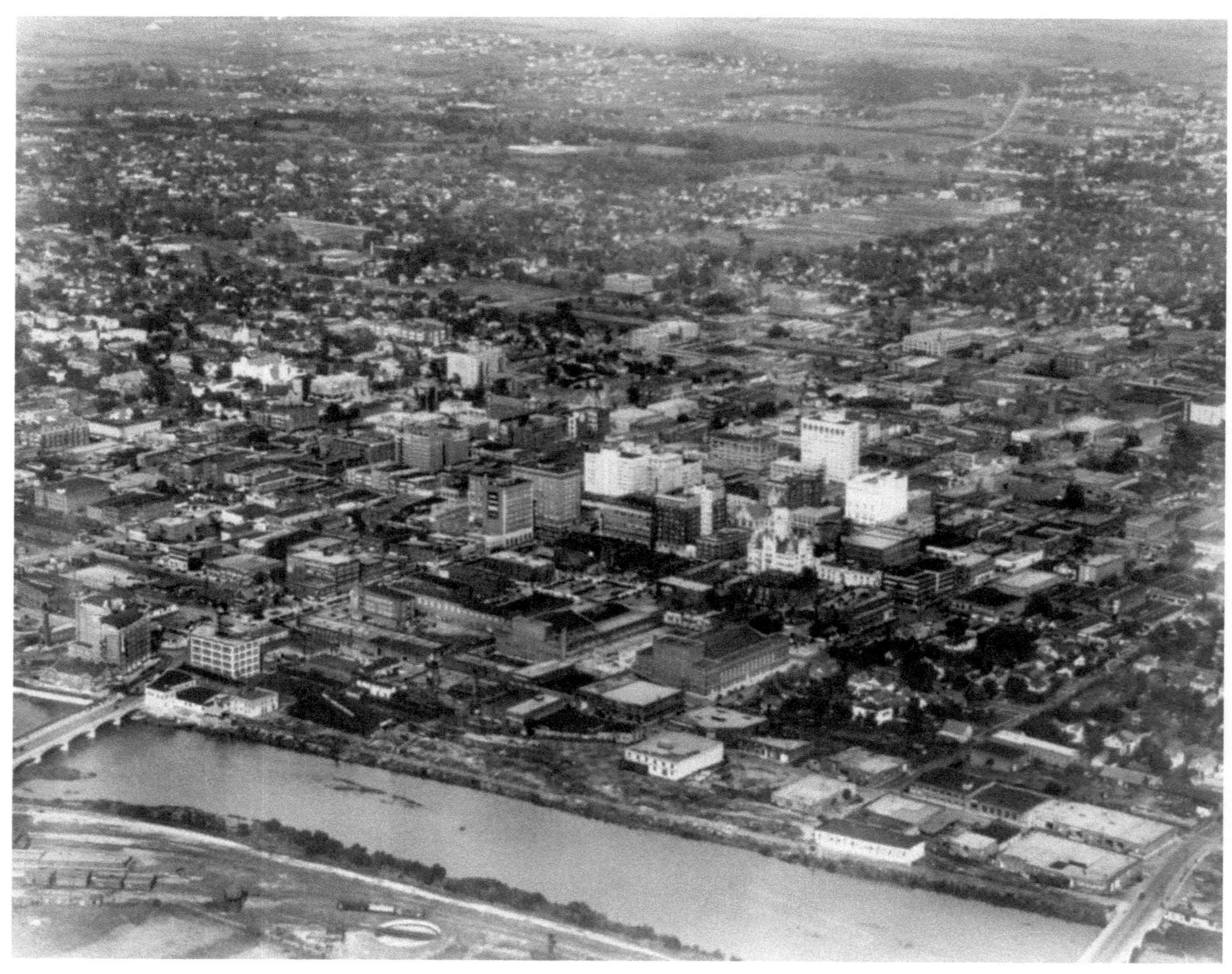

This aerial panorama shows Wichita's emerging downtown and outward growth in 1926. The Arkansas River is visible in the foreground, while farmland can be seen in the background.

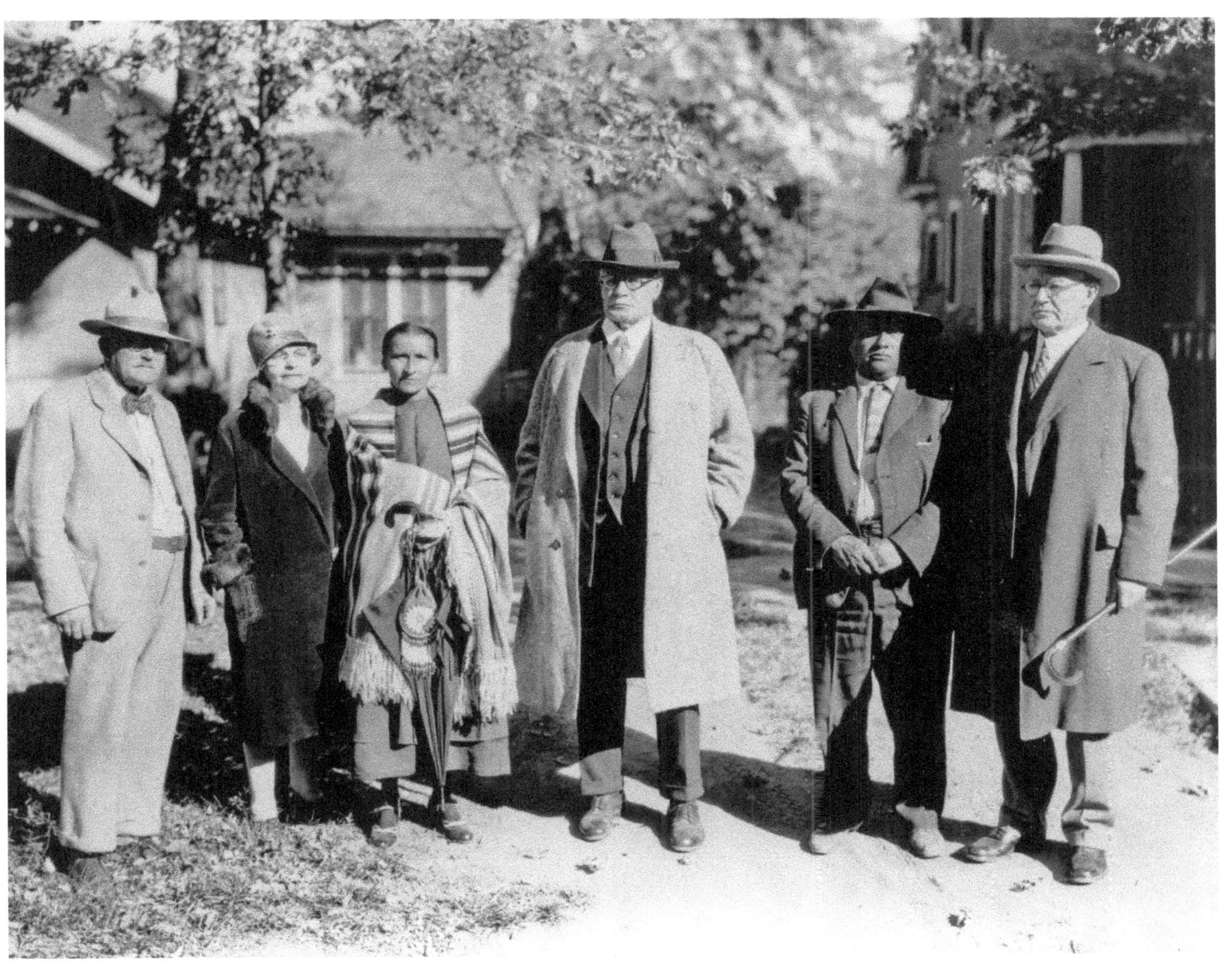

George Hibbard, Mrs. Hibbard, Mrs. George Hunt, General Hugh L. Scott, George Hunt, and General W. H. Sears gather in October of 1927 for a photo in Medicine Lodge. General Scott was an expert in Indian affairs and one-time superintendent of West Point. Scott joined the 7th Cavalry after the Battle of Little Big Horn and is remembered for his notes on the battle.

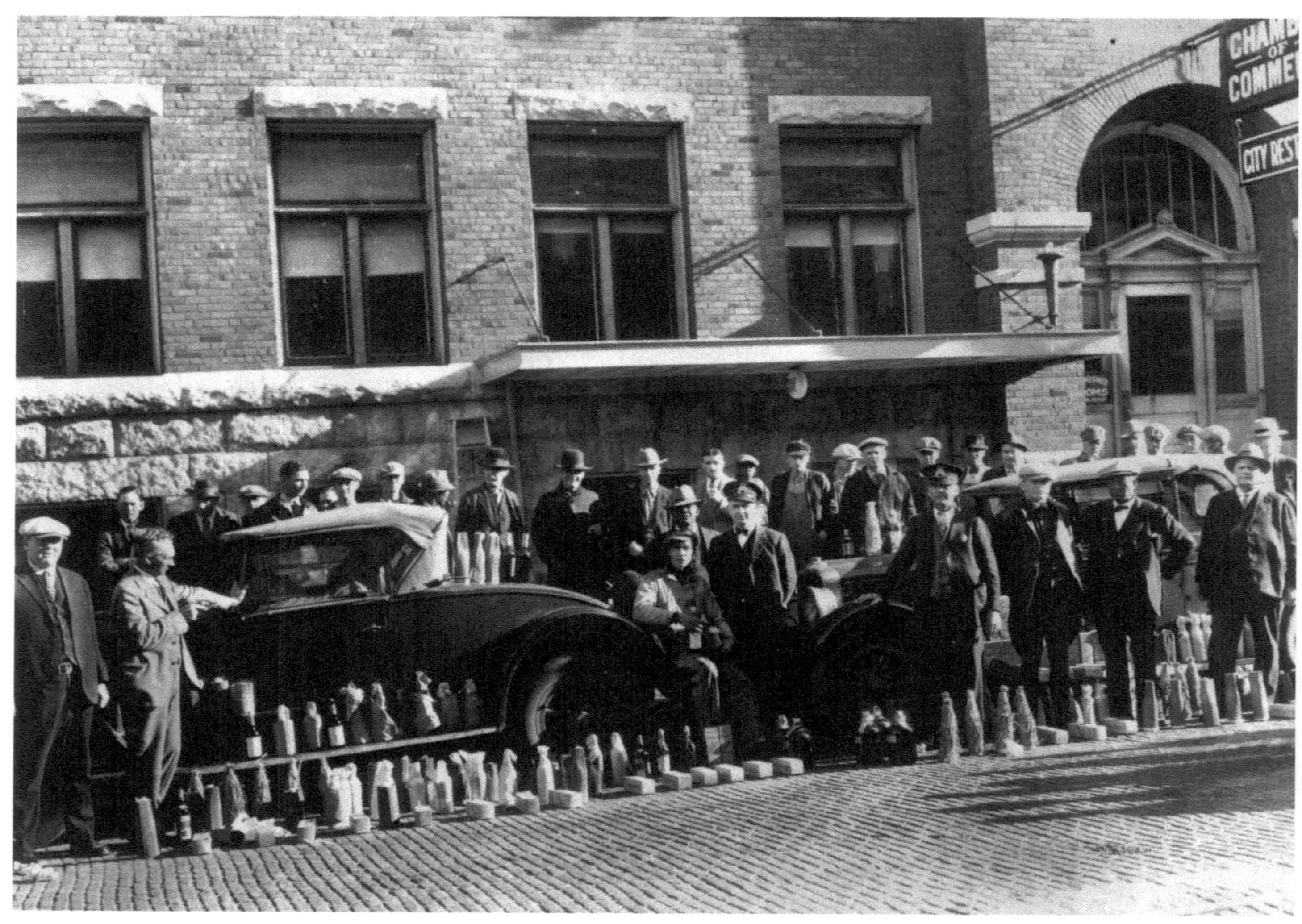

Lawrence police officers display 200 quarts of bootleg alcohol confiscated in raids. The photo was taken in 1927 during Prohibition, which started in 1919 and ended in 1933.

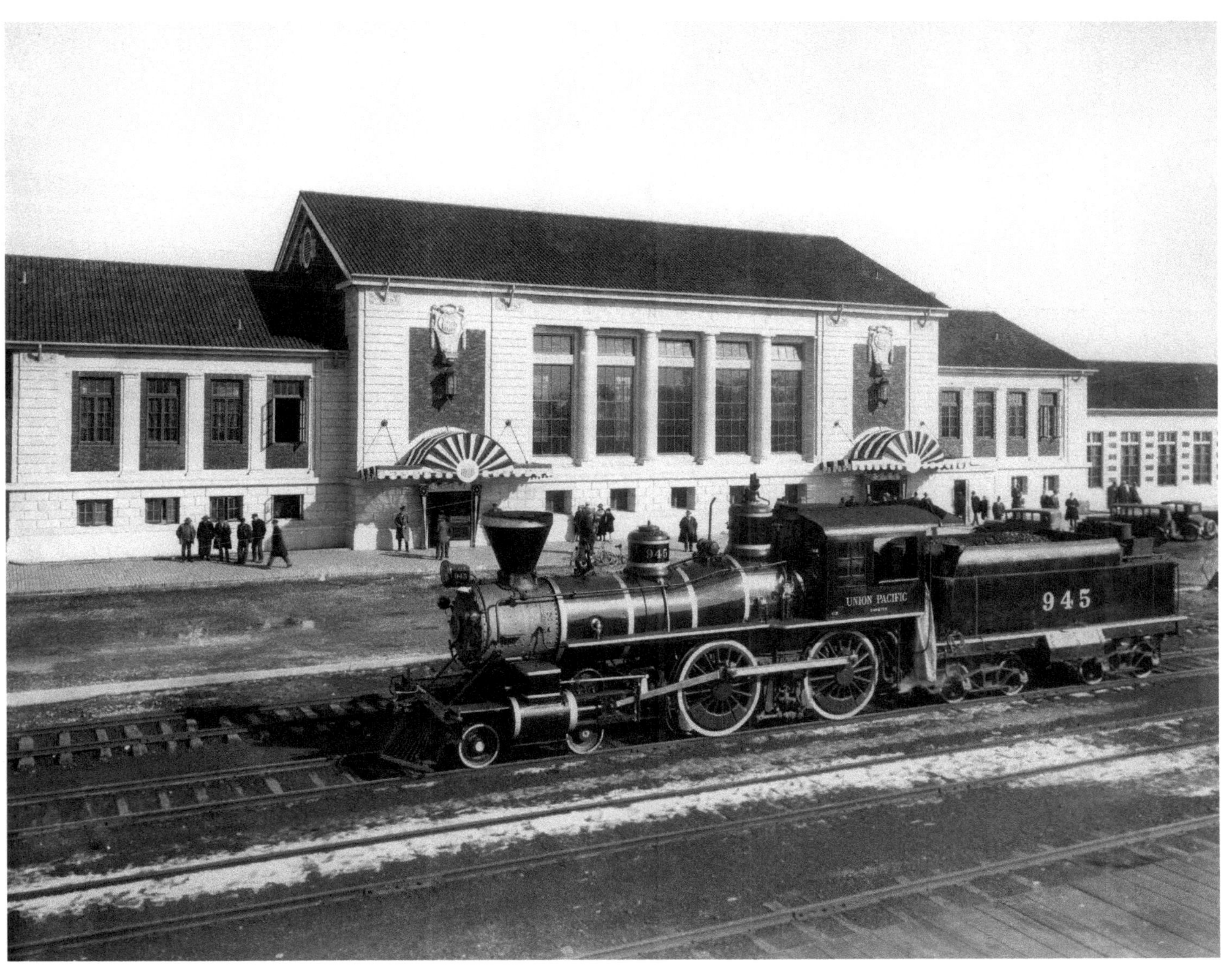

Steam locomotive 945 rests on a track during the 1927 dedication of the Union Pacific Railroad depot in Topeka. The building was listed on the Kansas Register of Historic Places in the 1980s, and in 2002 was granted recognition on the National Register. In 2004, the restored depot opened as the Great Overland Station, a railroad museum and education center.

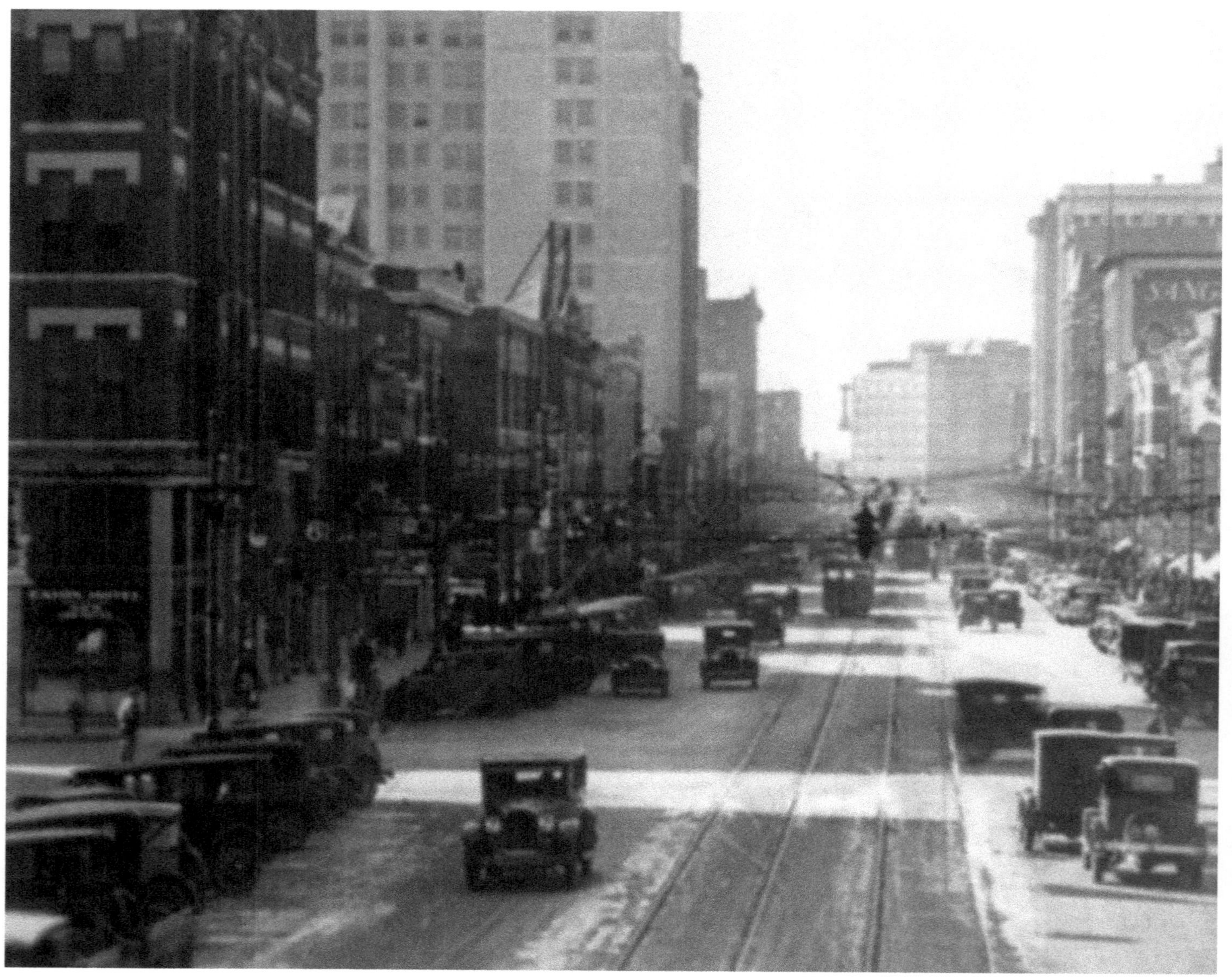

This September 11, 1929, photo looks west on Wichita's Douglas Avenue. Automobiles were already challenging streetcars as the primary mode of transportation.

The Dust Bowl, the Great Depression, and the Allied Cause

(1930–1969)

Kansans have never had it easy—nor, apparently, wanted it so. Unlike other immigrants who arrived before the Civil War, found the weather inhospitable, and left, those who stayed possessed a certain pluck. Given the hot summers and the cold winters, floods and droughts, tornados, sandstorms, and grasshopper plagues, was there ever a choice other than to develop a tough hide?

Kansans would need that strength in the 1930s when the Great Depression and Dust Bowl double-teamed them. Kansas farmers were well acquainted with arid conditions and, under the best of circumstances, had to find ingenious ways to irrigate their crops. When an unusually severe drought struck in 1934, wind combined with sparse vegetation, flat terrain, and poor crop-rotation techniques created "black blizzards," mammoth wind-driven storms of dirt. The storms came in the midst of the Depression, when some Kansans were already receiving federal relief. To a largely agrarian culture steeped in self-sufficiency, aid of any kind—whether justified or not—was viewed as a sign of weakness.

The arrival of the New Deal in the mid-1930s provided a bridge to Kansas's next test: World War II. As is often the case, the war jump-started the economy. An estimated 227,000 Kansans enlisted for military service during the war, while many others manufactured aircraft or trained pilots to fly them. A North American Aviation plant in Kansas City, Kansas, was built to replace a B-25 bomber plant in California that was considered vulnerable to enemy attack.

It was the B-25 that gave the country a needed boost after Pearl Harbor. In April 1942, Lieutenant Colonel Jimmy Doolittle led a group of 16 carrier-launched B-25s on a daring raid on mainland Japan. It was a symbolic victory, but a morale lift for workers at the Fairfax Plant in Kansas City, Kansas, and for the American public at large. In all, the Kansas plant built a total of 6,608 B-25s.

Kansans made the hardware of war, but they also played a key role in training pilots. The United States Army Air Force built 15 bases in the state during the war, while two other cities, Olathe and Hutchinson, were chosen to train Navy pilots.

For Kansans, digging down to cope and contribute has always seemed to come naturally.

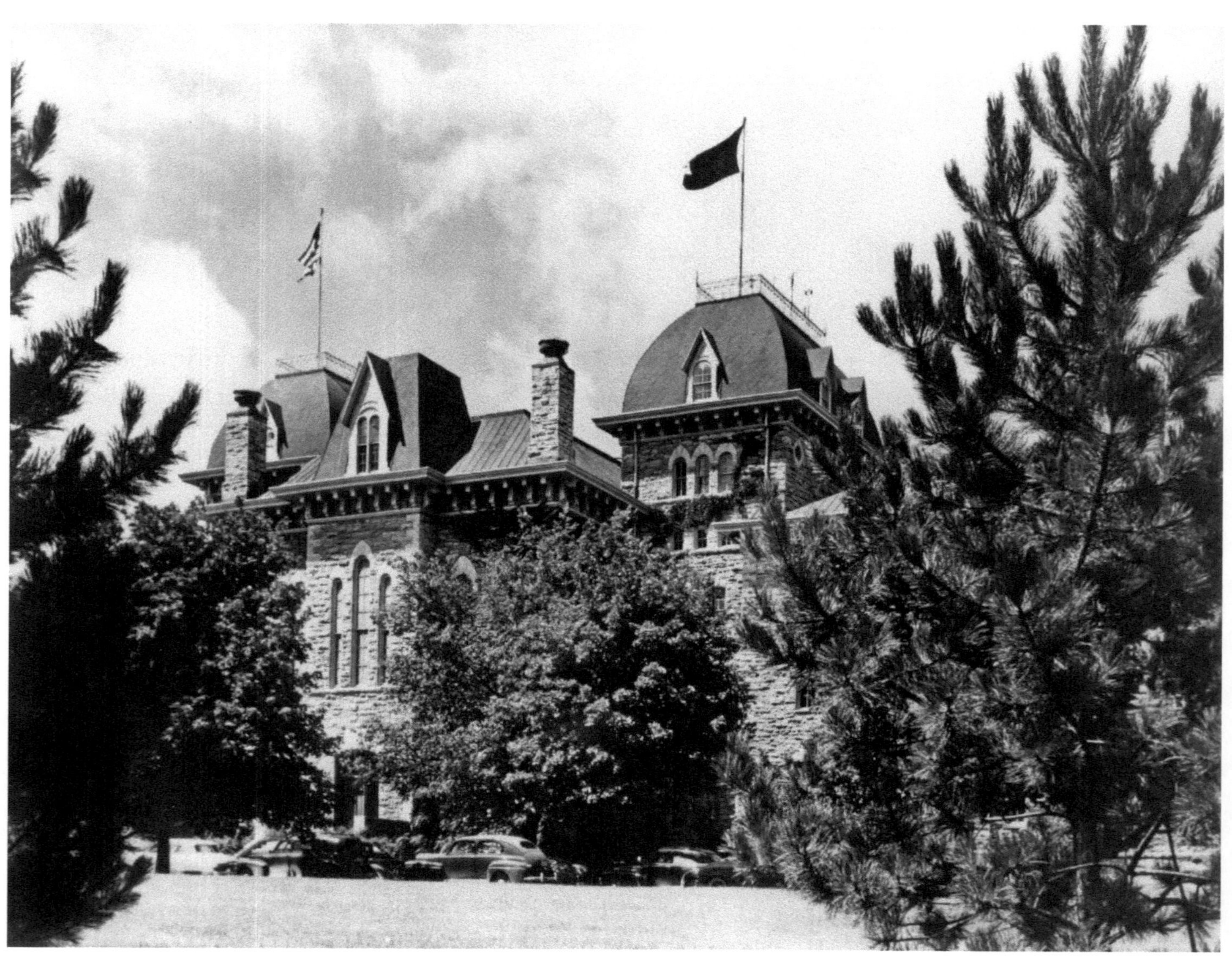

Named for John Fraser, the university's second chancellor, the original Fraser Hall at the University of Kansas was built in 1872. John G. Haskell designed the limestone building, designated the University Building, which was replaced in 1967.

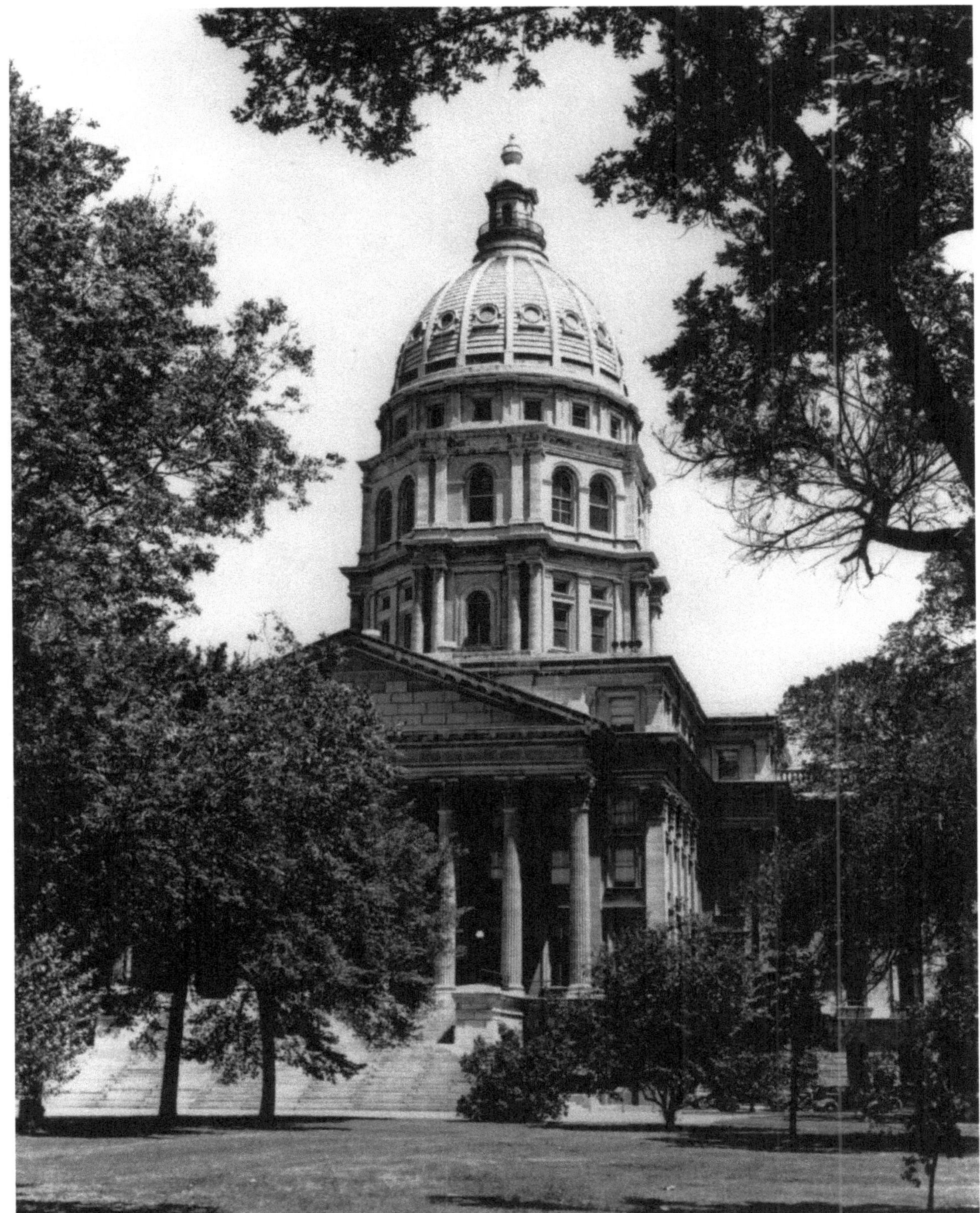

The Kansas State Capitol in Topeka houses the governor's office on the second floor, the House of Representatives Chamber in the west wing, and the Senate Chamber in the east wing. The Capitol was built in stages beginning in 1866 and was recently restored. Its dome is among the nation's largest.

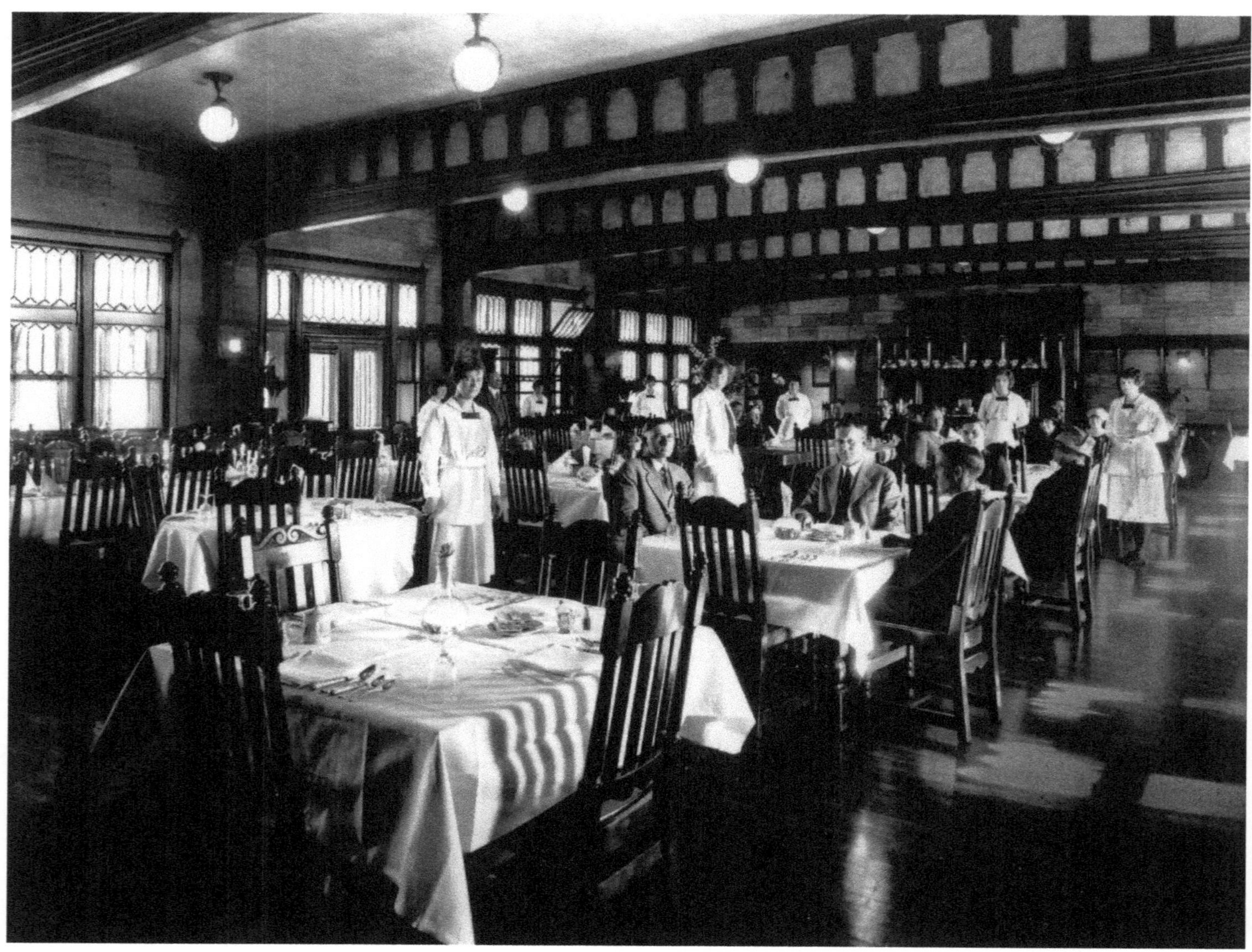

The dining room at the Bisonte Hotel in Hutchinson, managed by the Fred Harvey chain of restaurants, served the Santa Fe Railroad station. Built in 1906, the hotel closed its doors in 1946. One Bisonte employee commented that she and other workers could help themselves to almost anything in the kitchen.

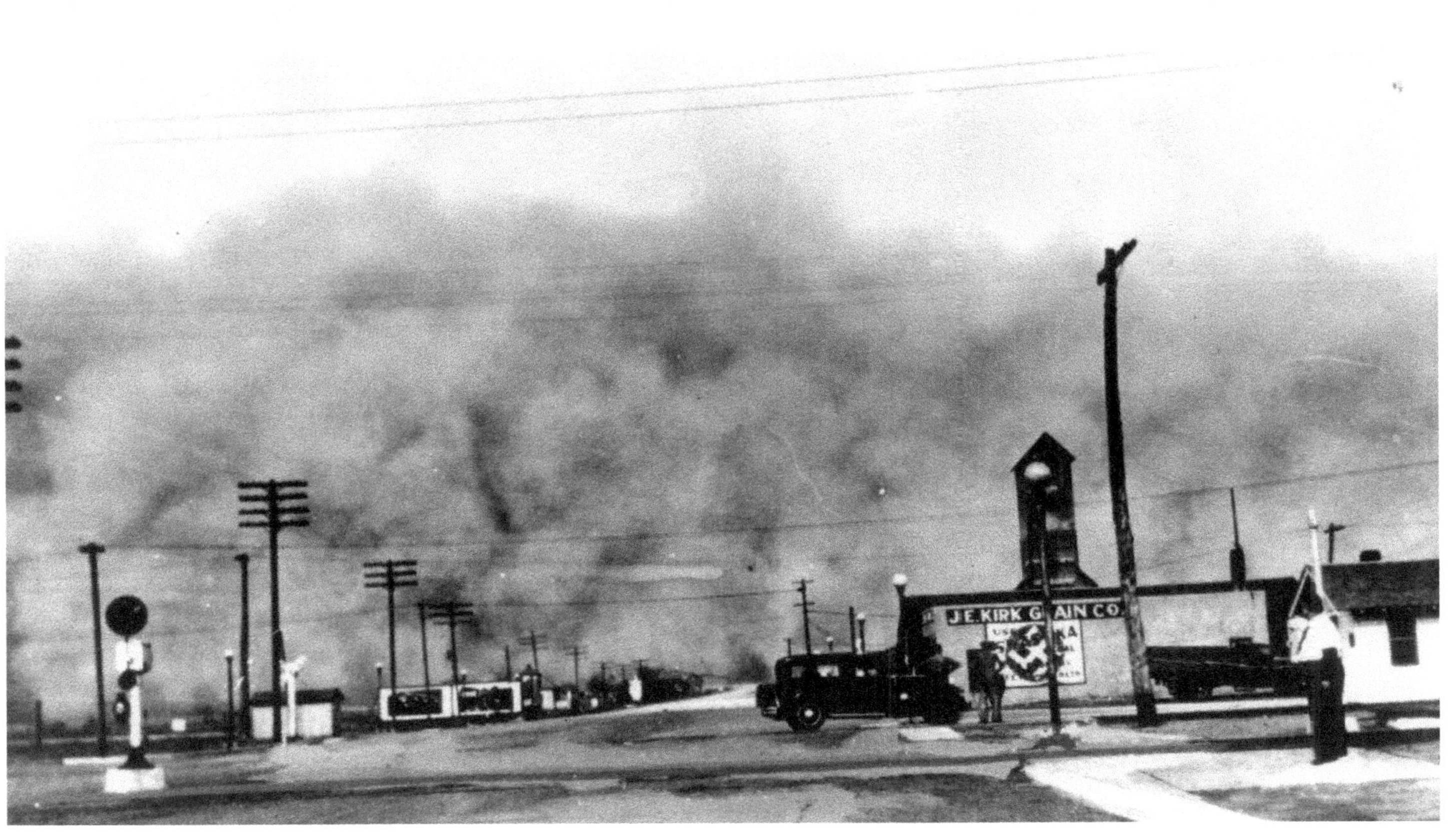

Dust storms like the one pictured in 1935 in Scott City were prevalent in Kansas in the 1930s. Wet sheets were placed on the windows of Scott County Hospital to protect its patients from the dust. Wind, drought, and an often flat terrain contributed to Kansas's dust storms. An advertisement that reads "Use Swastika Coal" from the Swastika Fuel Company is painted on the grain company building at right.

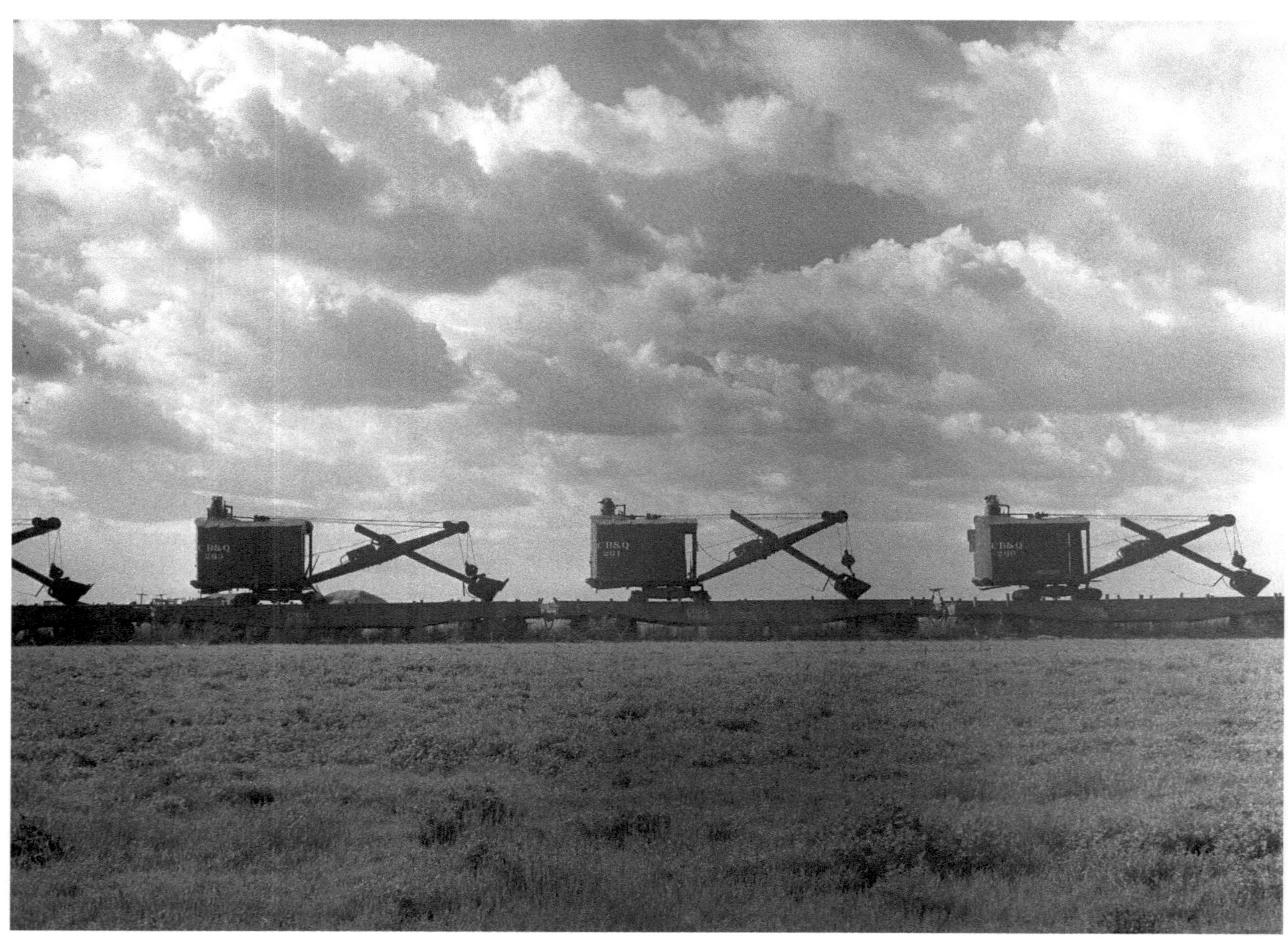

Steam shovels on flat cars create perfect symmetry in this 1936 Arthur Rothstein photo of Cherokee County. During the Depression, Rothstein was one of several nationally prominent photographers hired by the Farm Security Administration to document conditions across the nation.

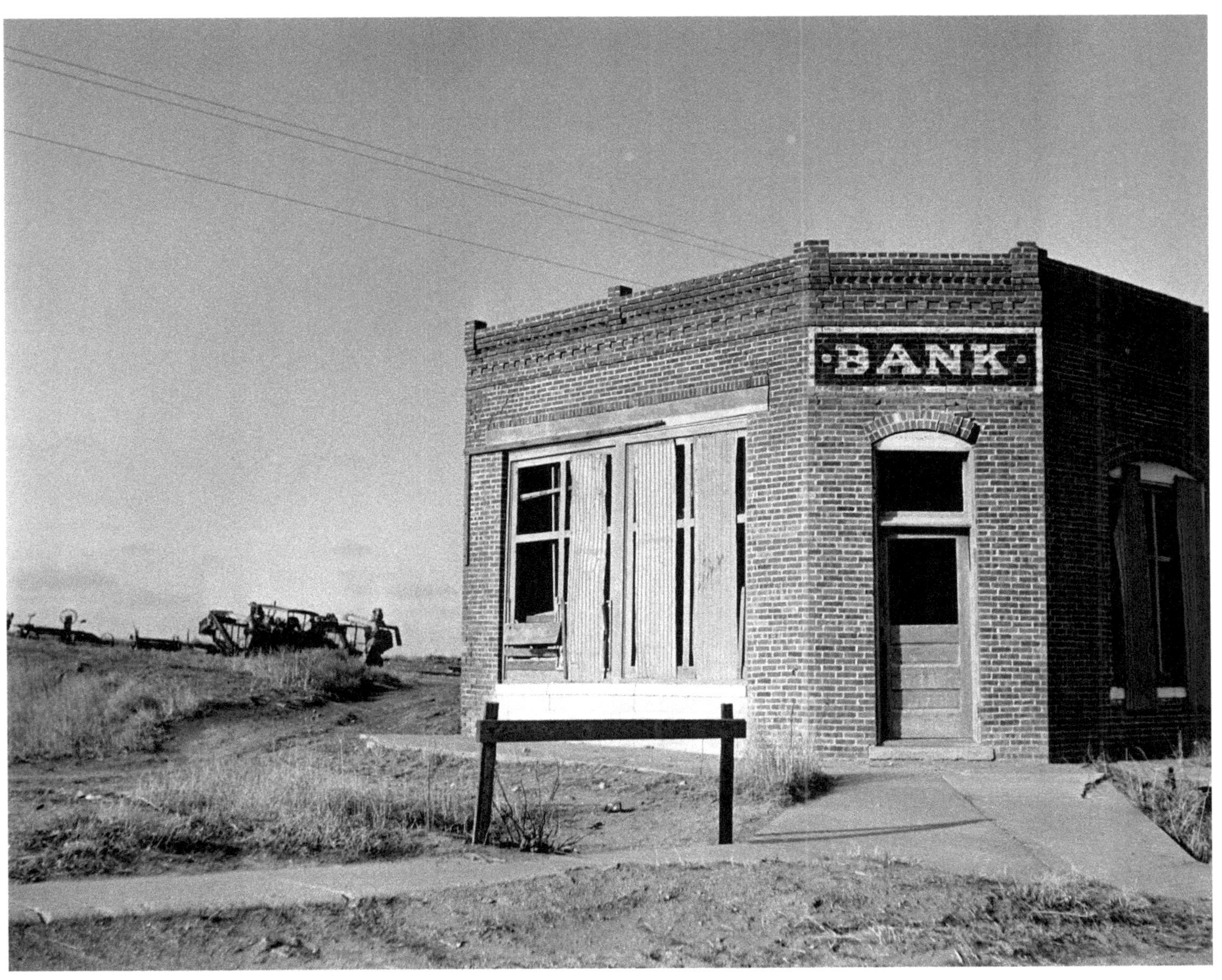

A failed bank in rural Kansas isn't identified, but the photo was taken by a Farm Security Administration photographer in 1936. Farm equipment sits in a field in the background.

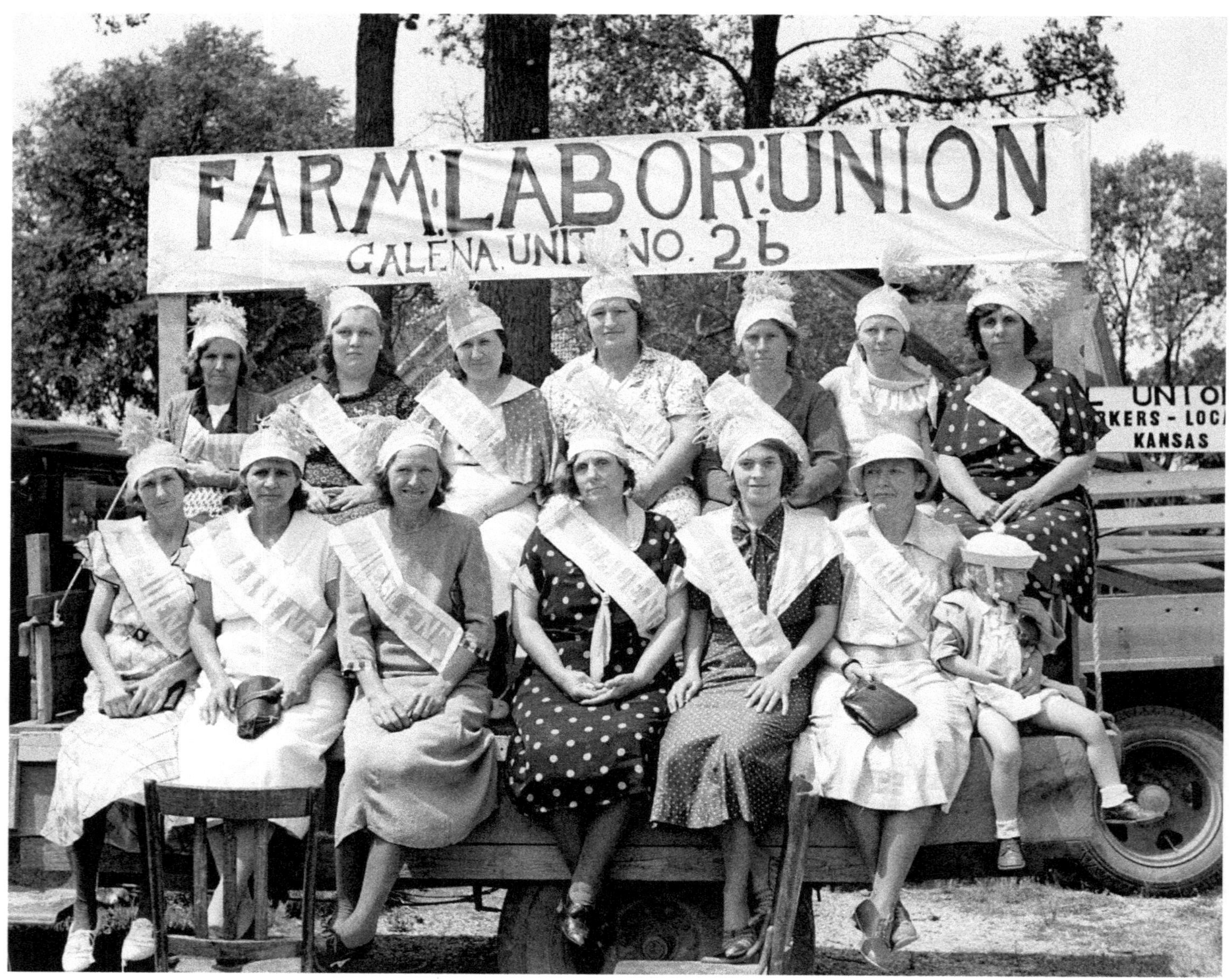

In May 1936, the wives and a child of laborites in the Galena unit of the Farm Laborers Union gathered in Columbus, the county seat of Cherokee County in far southeastern Kansas.

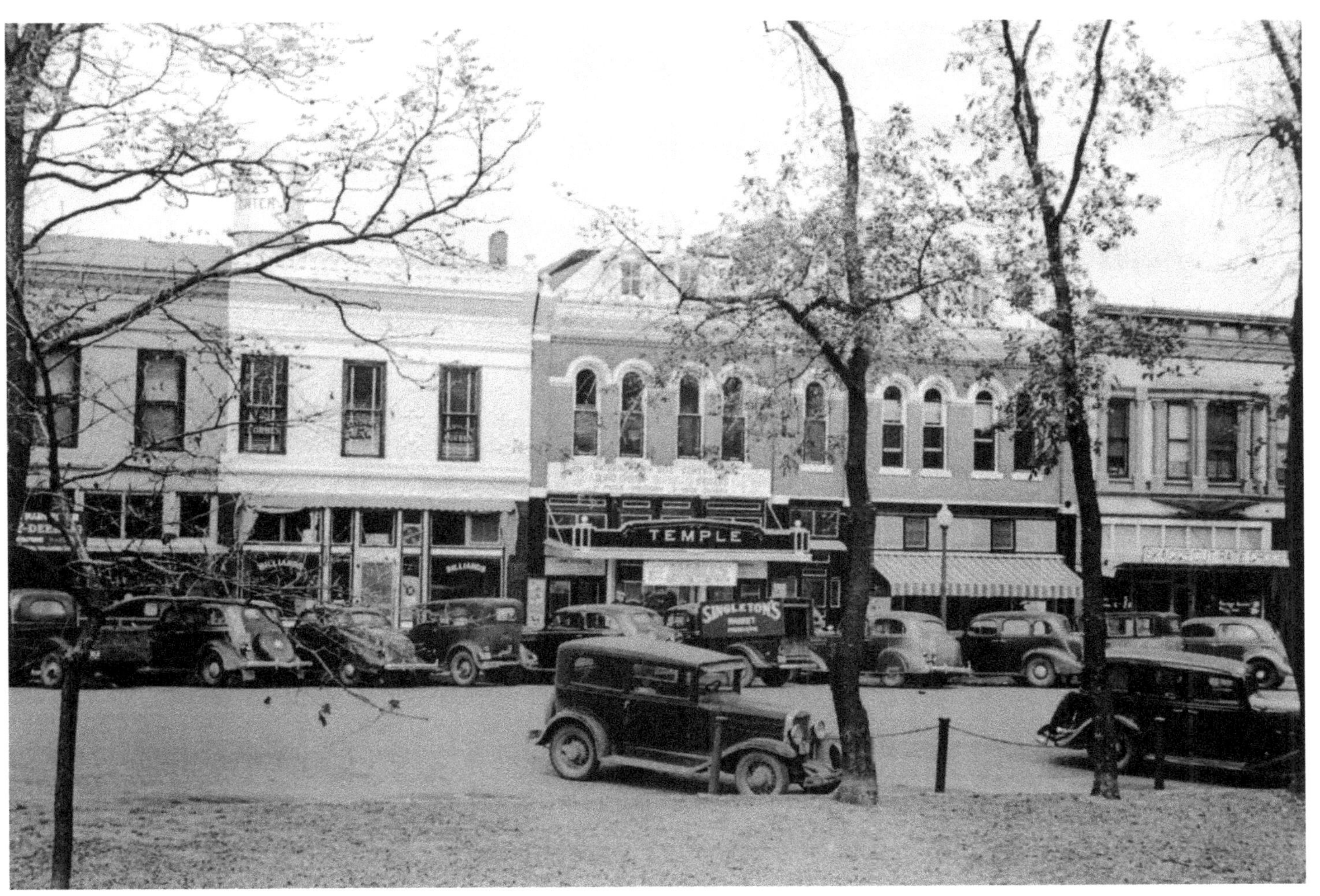

In 1938, cars line the curbs on Main Street in Yates Center. Today, at least 30 businesses in the downtown area are part of the Yates Center Square Historic District.

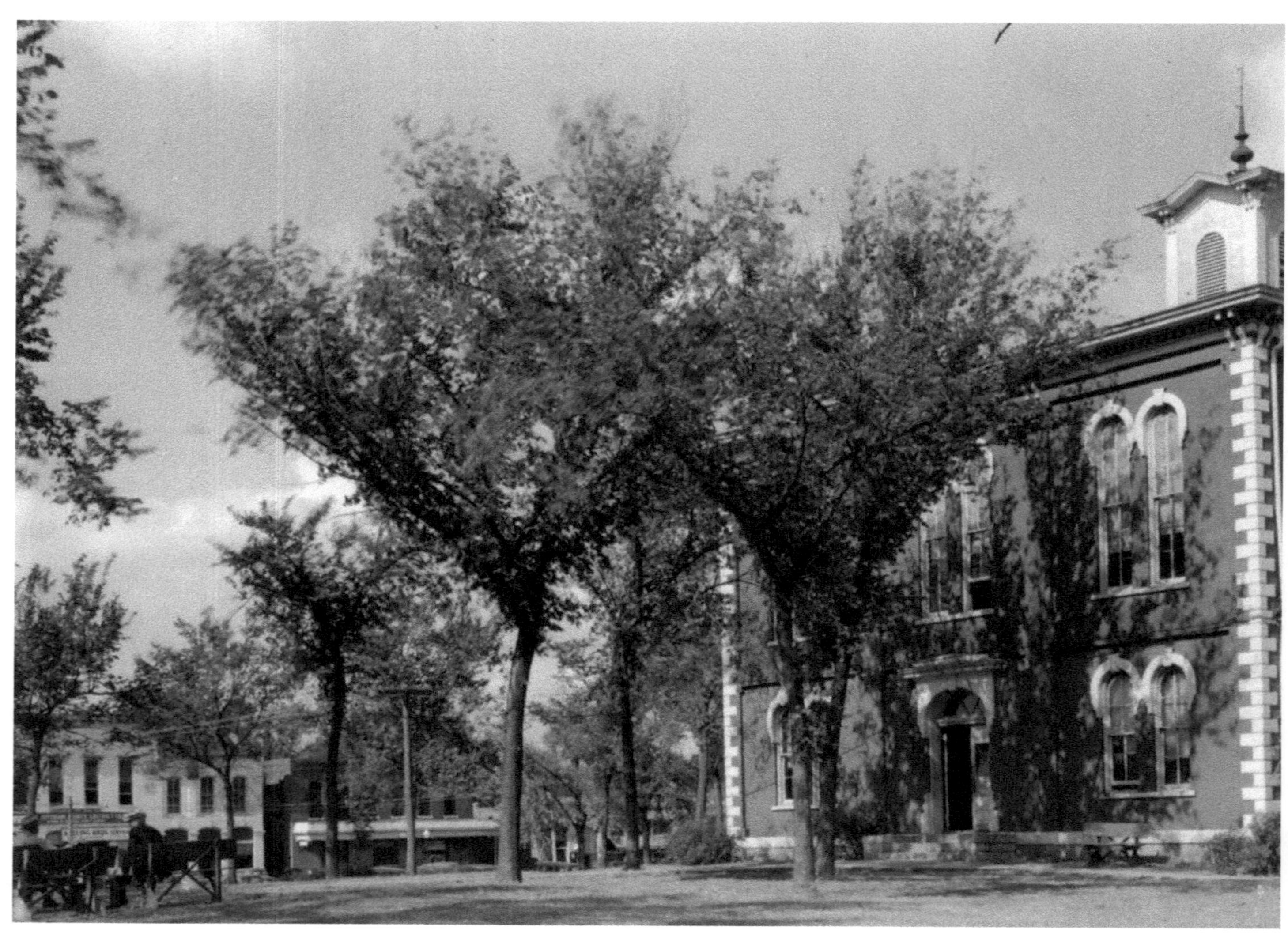

John Vachon photographed the Jefferson County Courthouse in Oskaloosa in 1938. The town is home to the *Oskaloosa Independent,* a weekly newspaper that began publishing in 1860, six months before Kansas became a state.

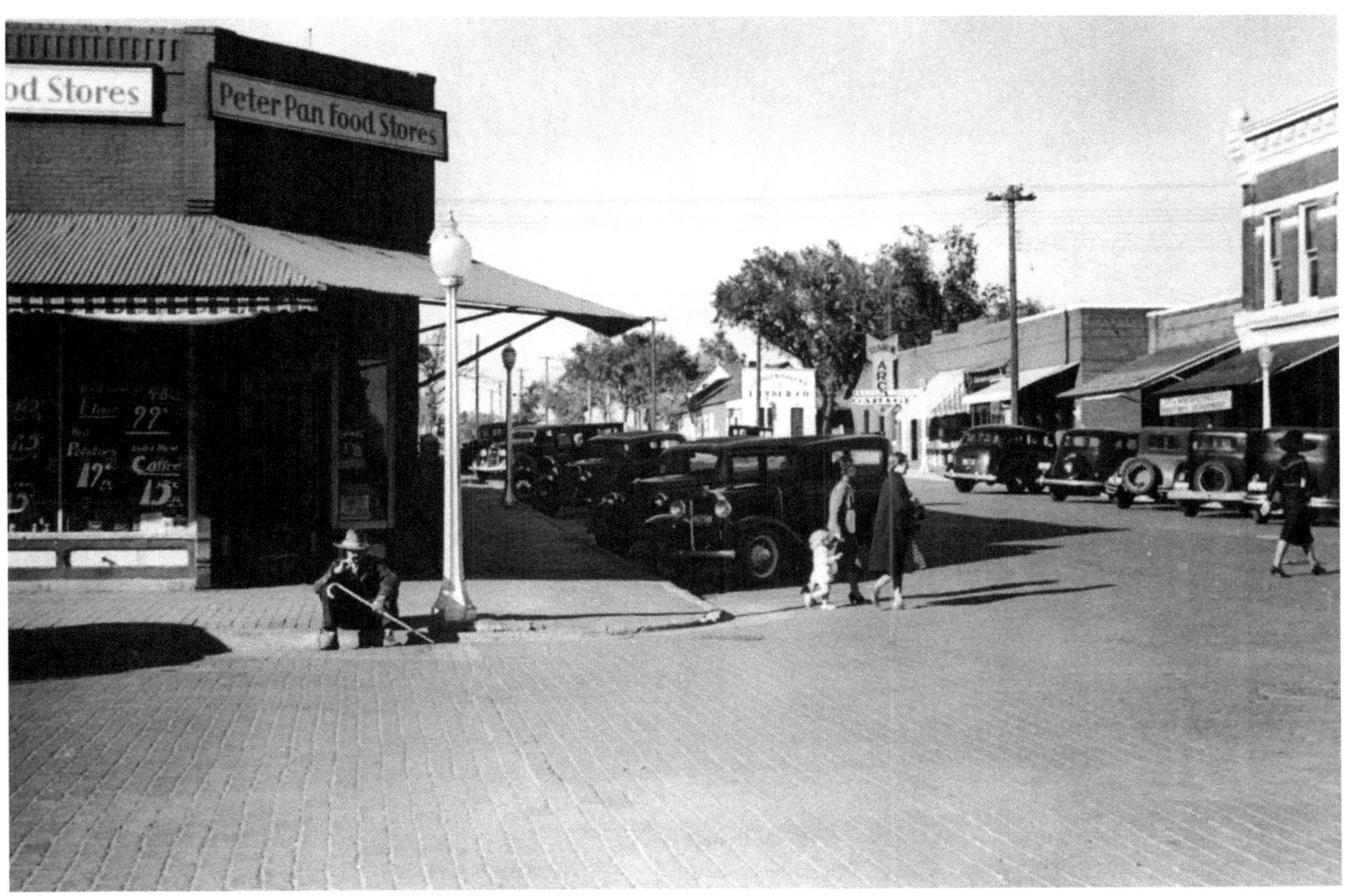

In 1938, Farm Security Administration photographer John Vachon found a man sitting on the curb and pedestrians crossing the street in the Kansas town of Minneapolis. To the left is a Peter Pan Foods grocery store, which advertises coffee for 15 cents a pound.

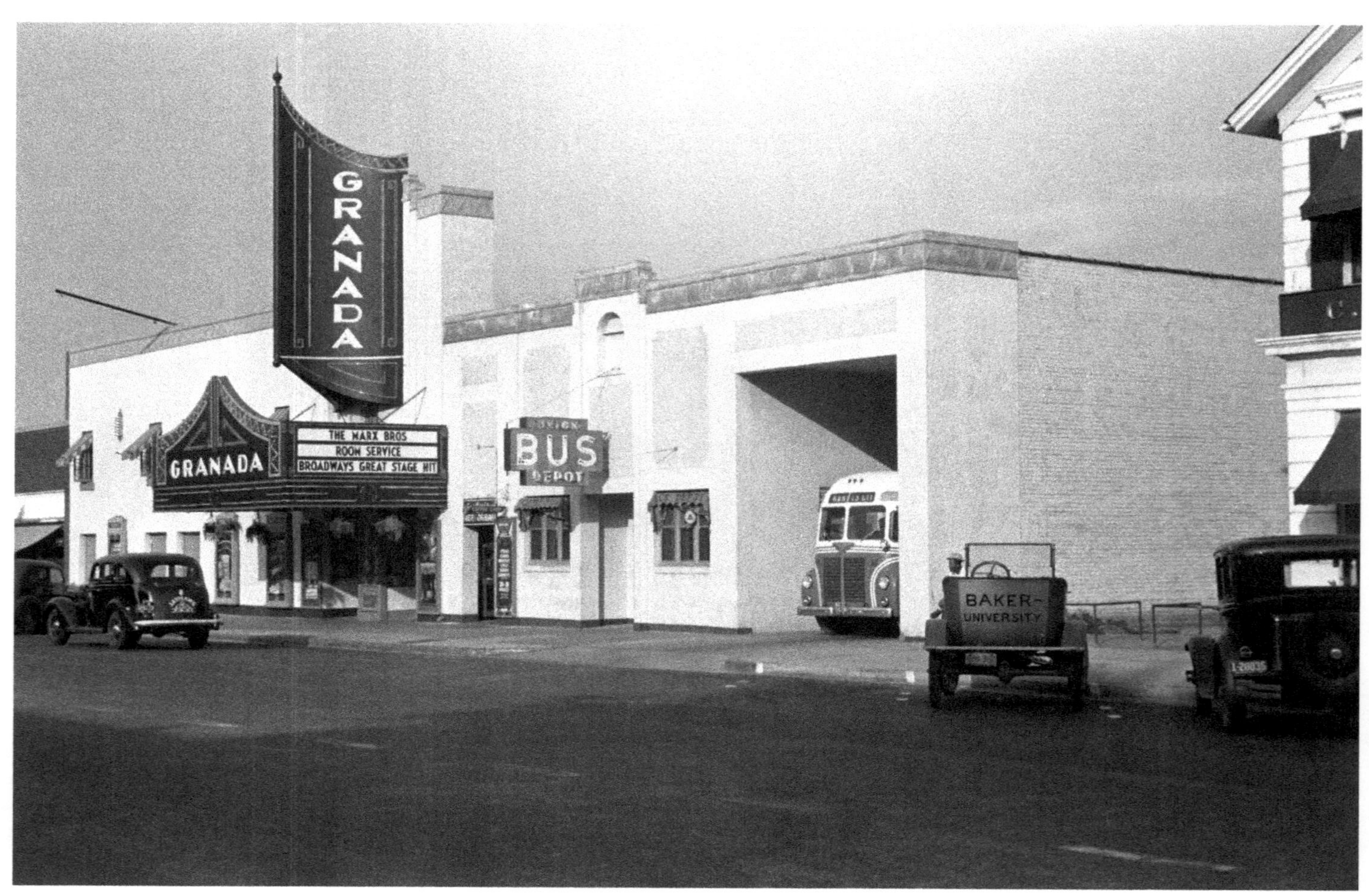

The Granada theater was originally built as a home for vaudeville in Lawrence in 1928. It was designed by the Boller Brothers, an architecture firm that designed several other theaters across the U.S. In 1934, the Granada was converted into a movie theater, and in 1993 it became a venue for comedy and touring musical acts.

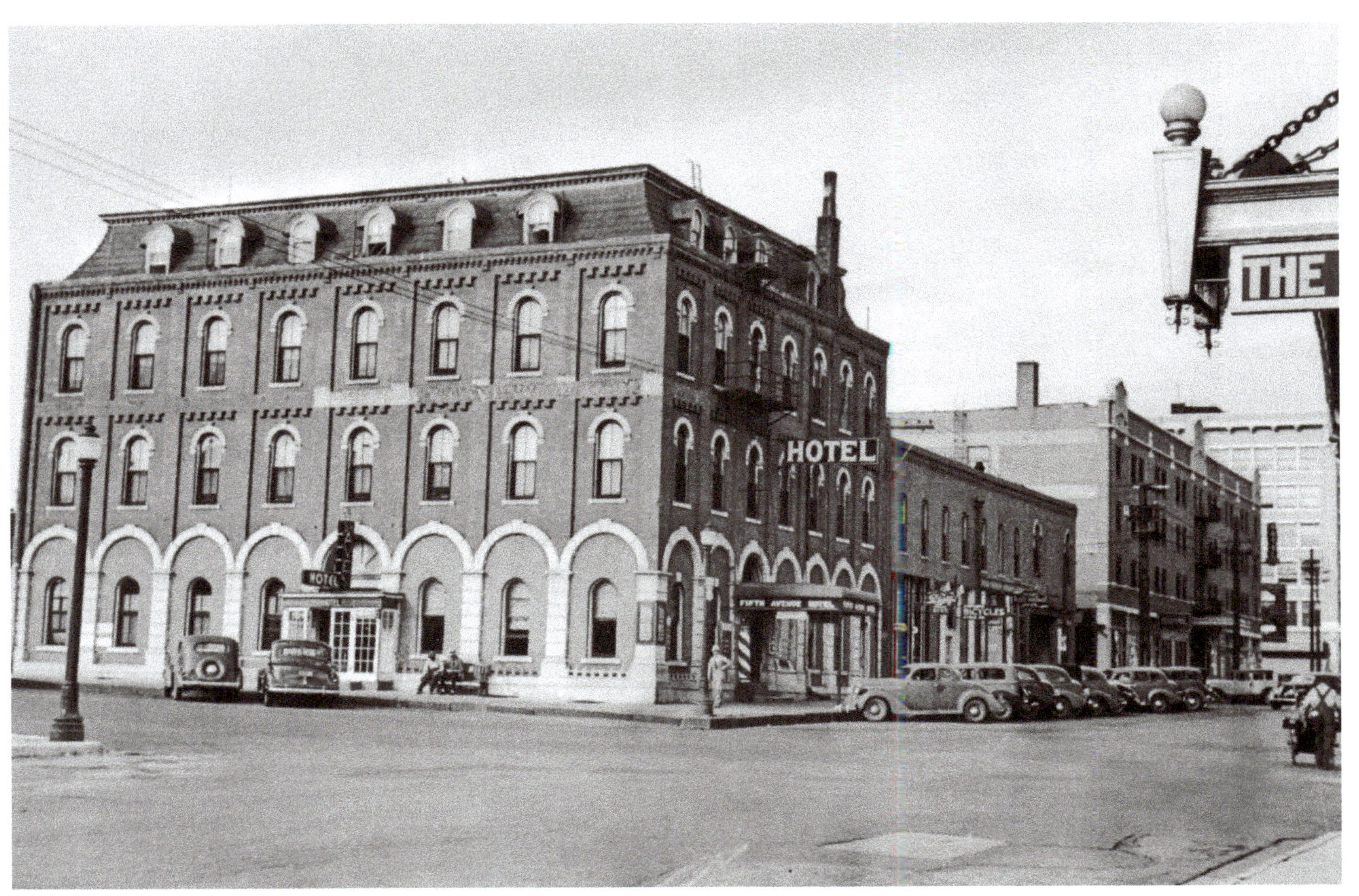

According to the *Topeka Capital-Journal,* the Fifth Avenue Hotel was among the most opulent in the city's early days. Located at 501 S.E. Quincy on the southeast corner of 5th Avenue, it was built in 1869-70 and listed among its guests the Grand Duke Alexis of Russia and General George Custer. The hotel fell into disrepair and was severely damaged by fire in 1951. It was sold in 1960 to make room for a parking lot.

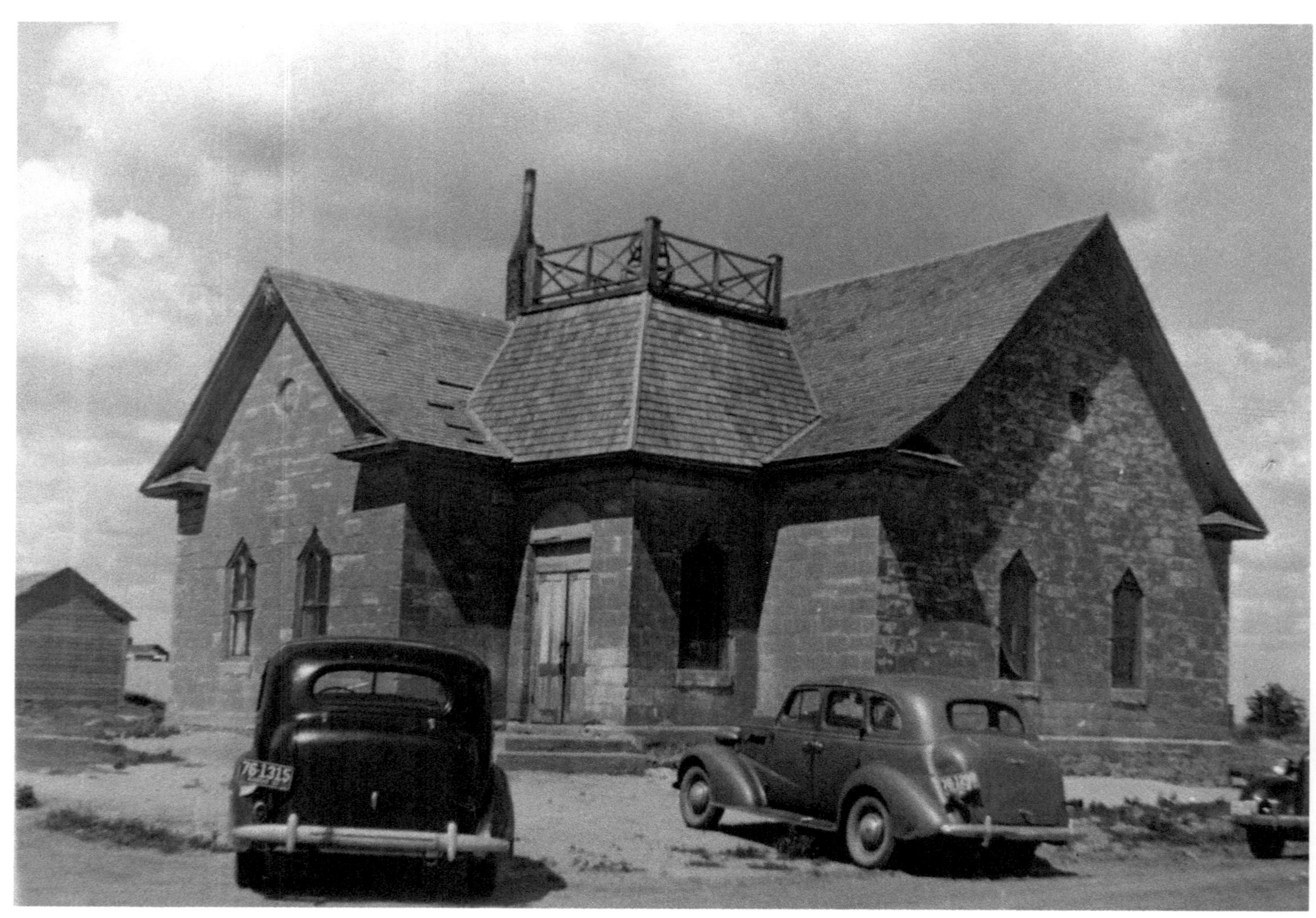

The First Baptist Church is pictured sometime after 1933 at Fourth and Washington streets in Nicodemus. Located in Graham County, the 1907 building has been described as the most enduring congregation existing on the town site since 1878. Nicodemus was settled by Exodusters, freed southern slaves who immigrated to Kansas in 1879 and 1880.

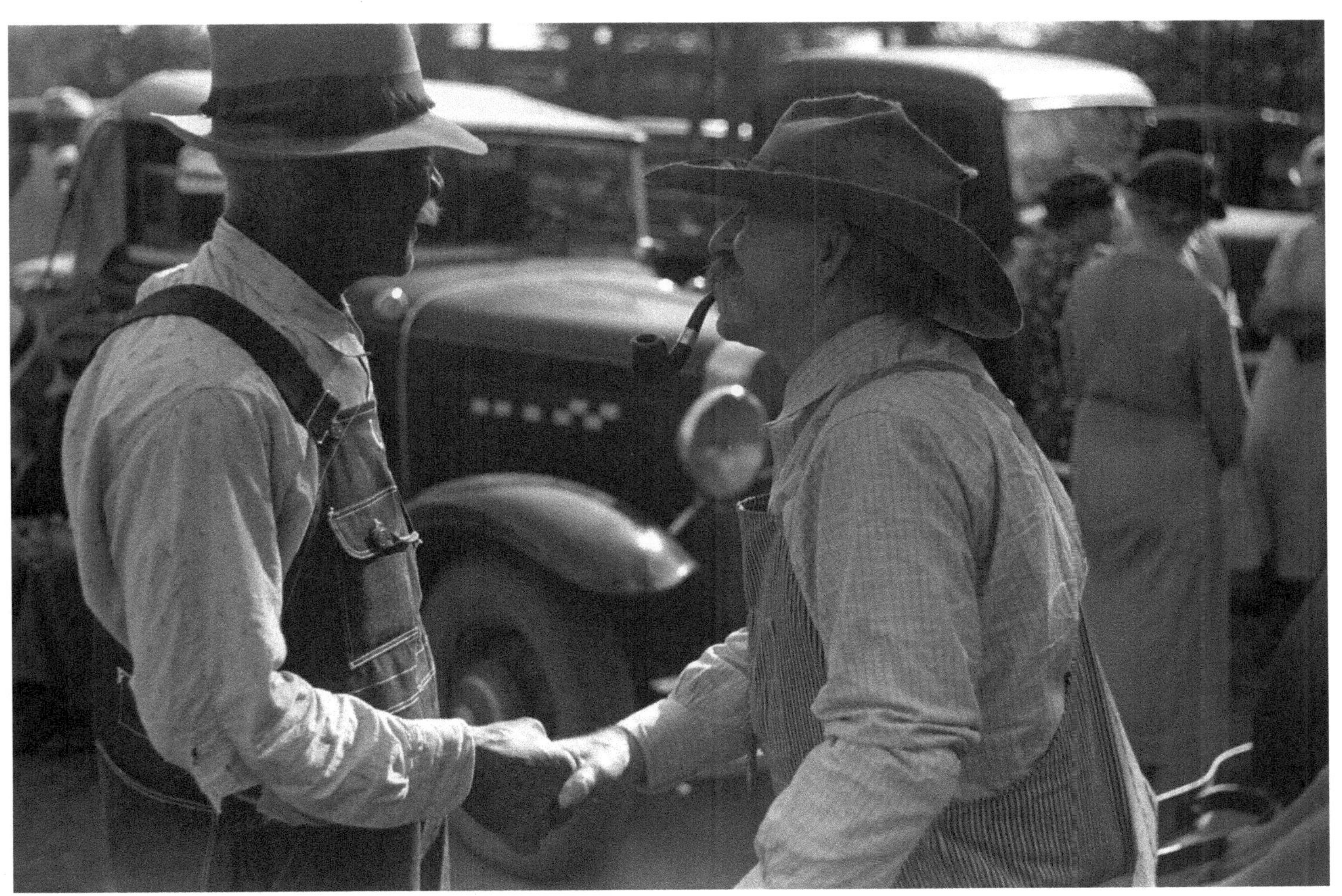

Farming is a solitary occupation, and community events such as this 1938 auction in Oskaloosa were a time to socialize and renew old acquaintances.

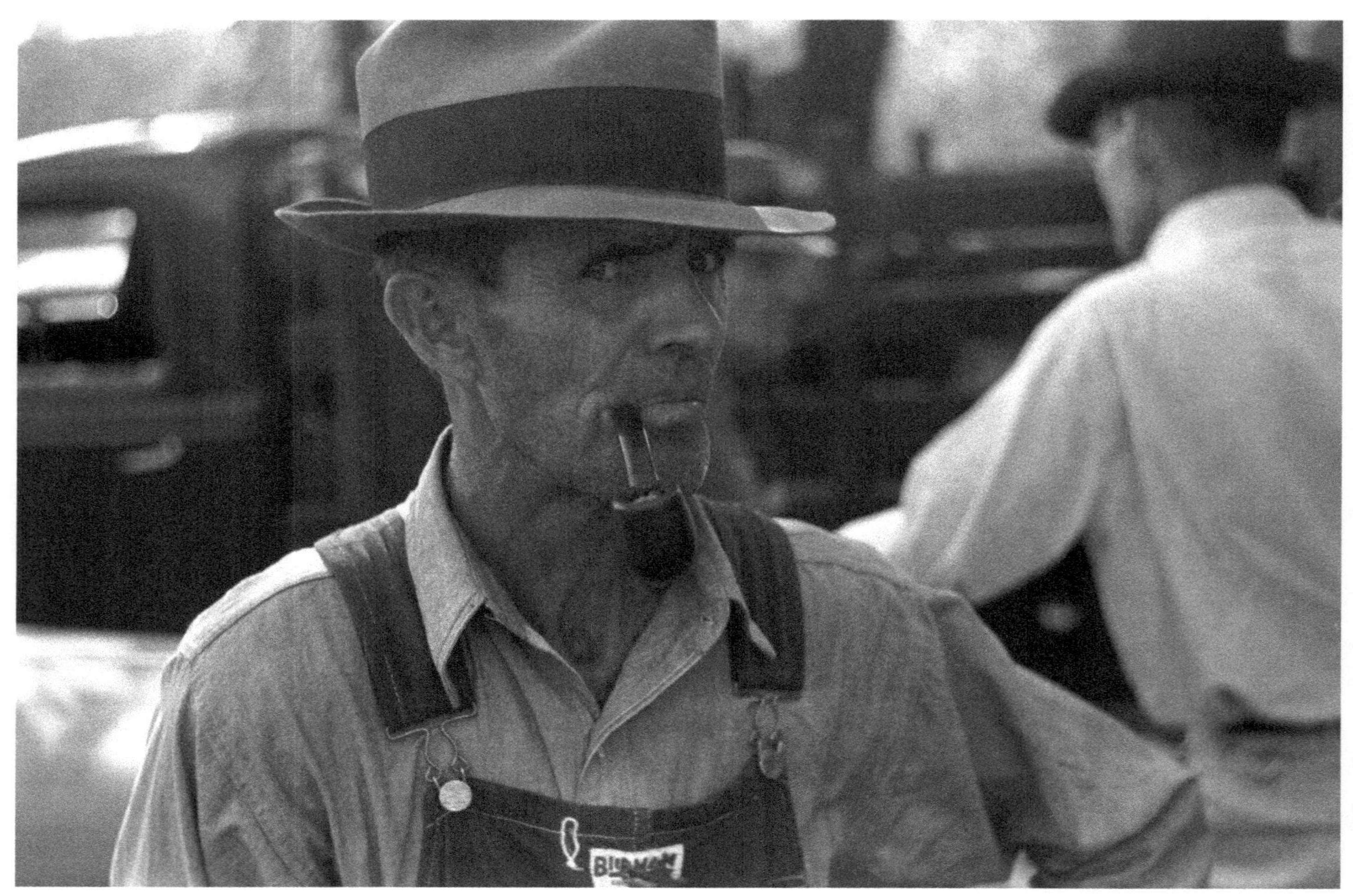

At an Oskaloosa auction, Farm Security Administration photographer John Vachon captured the character of participants, including this wary-eyed man.

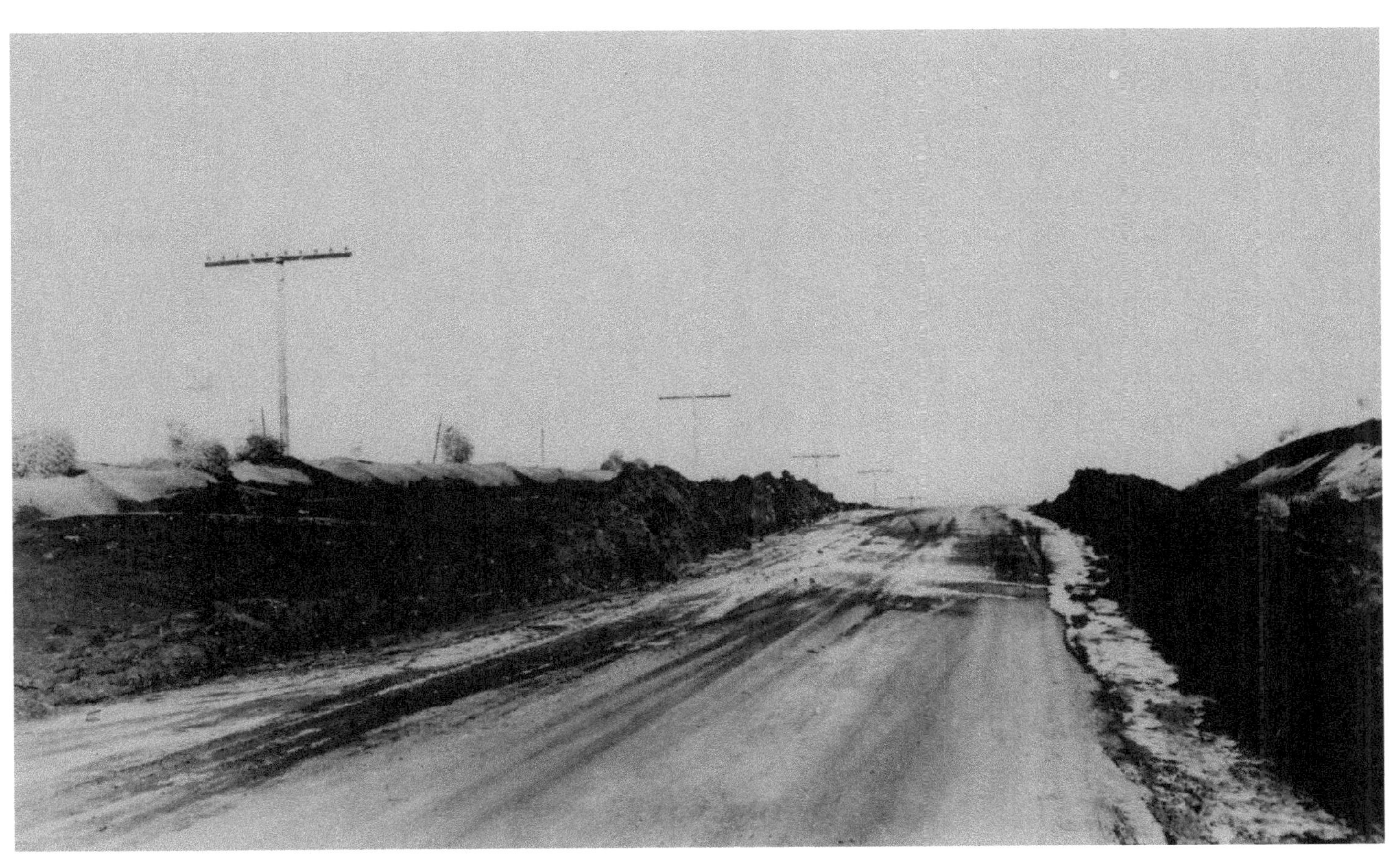

A mixture of dust and light snow is pictured on U.S. Highway 36 during what is described as the blizzard of February 24, 1935. The highway passes through all 13 counties in Kansas that border on Nebraska.

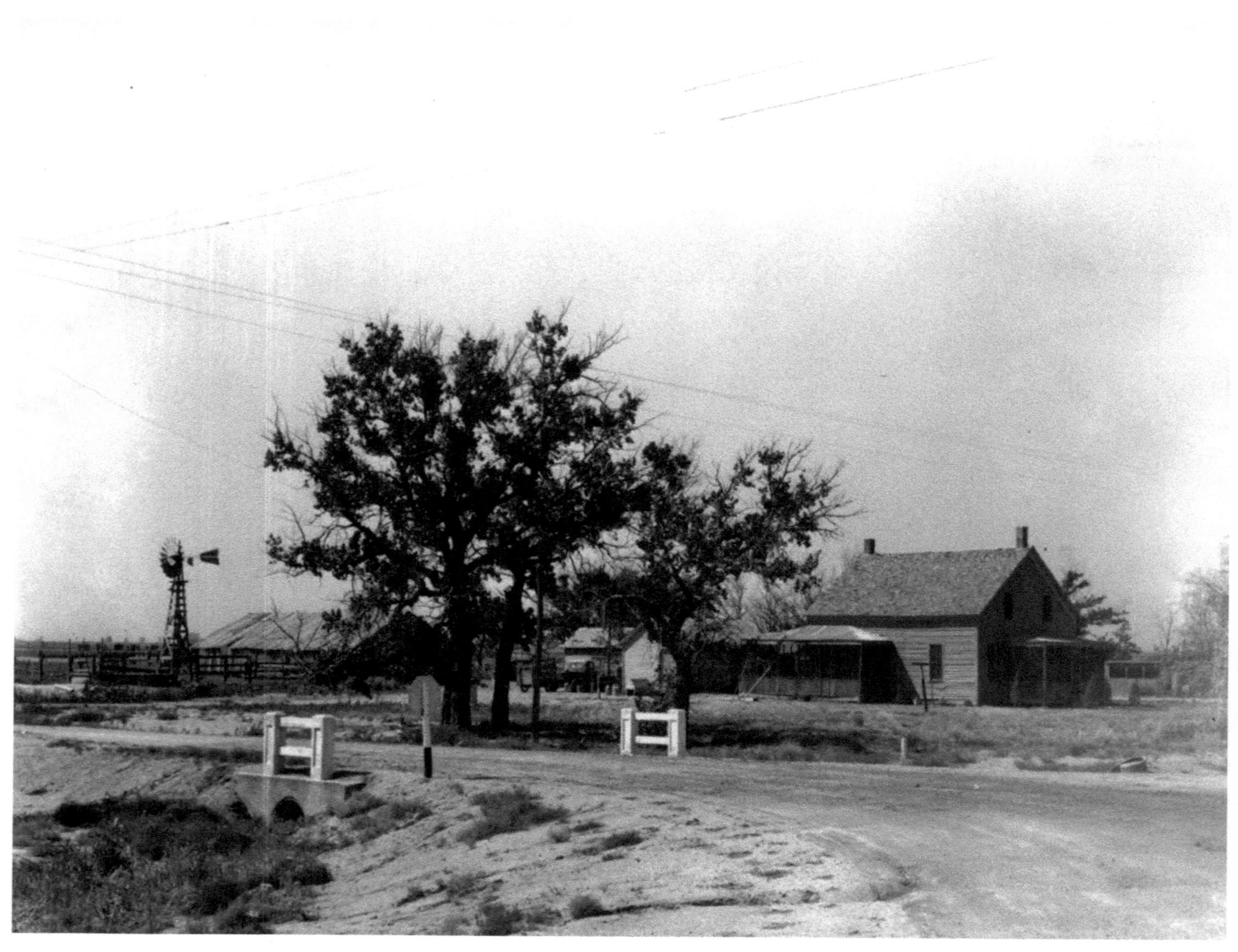

This farmstead in Cimmaron, on the flat plains of Gray County in southeastern Kansas, was photographed in 1939. The functional windmill helped pump well water for use in irrigation.

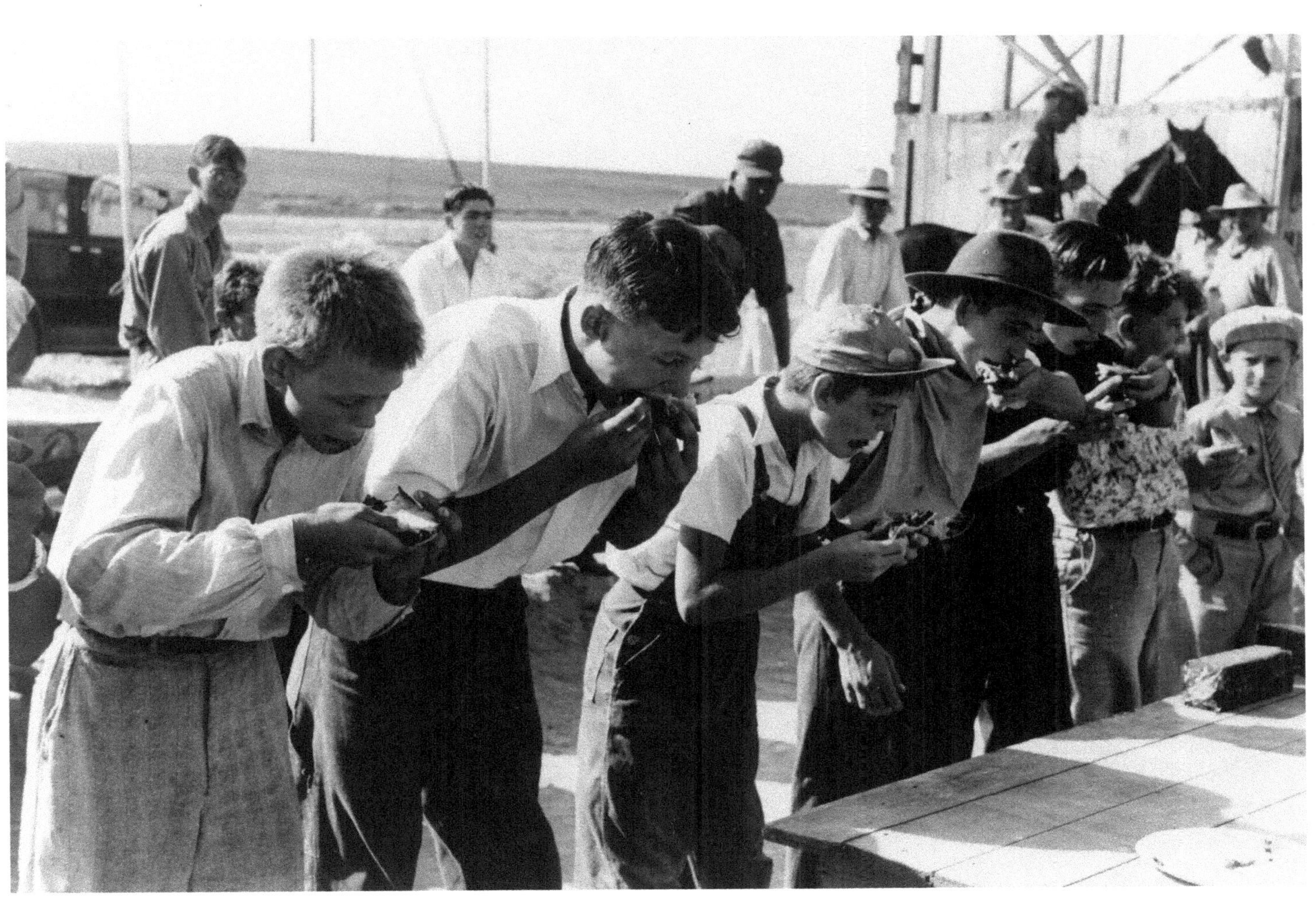

"Hard work, but someone has to do it" might describe the sacrifice contestants are making in a 1939 pie-eating contest at a 4-H club fair in Cimmaron.

A Kansas farmer digs a few inches into the earth looking for moisture. The dry ground—not an unusual circumstance for farmers in the state—was photographed in 1939 in Sheridan County.

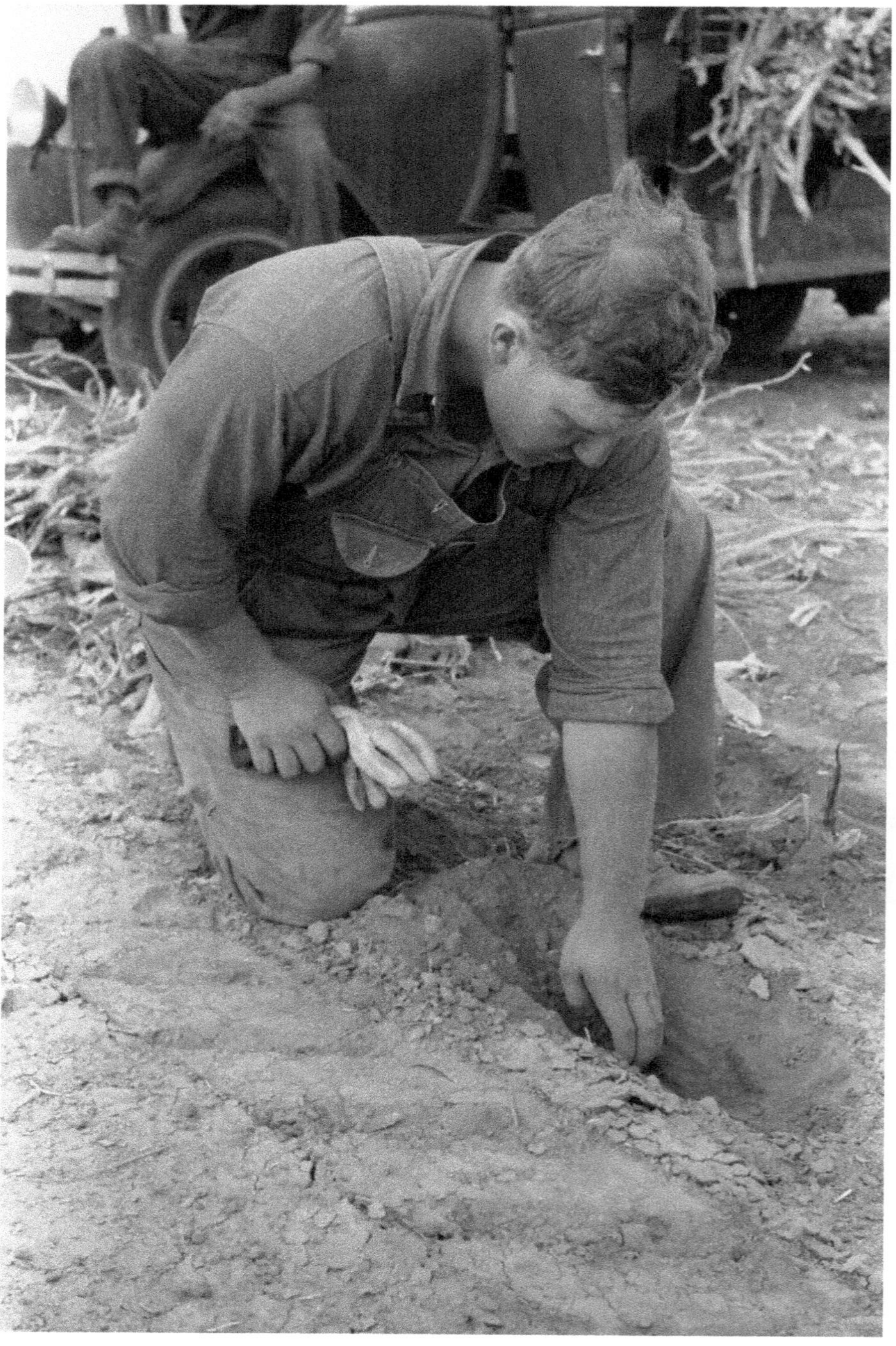

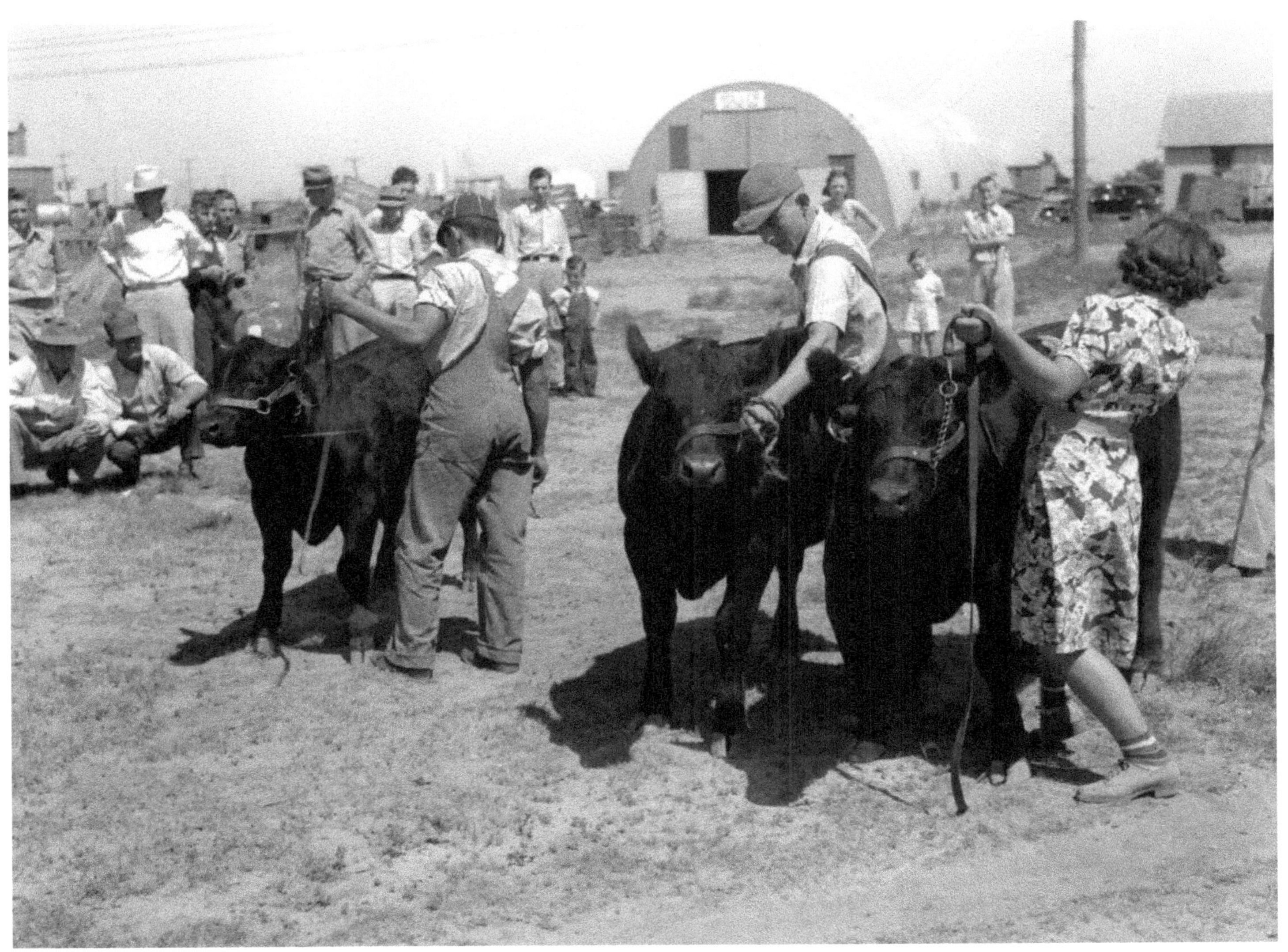

County fairs and 4-H clubs were a staple of recreational and social life for Kansans. In 1939, farmers display their prize bulls at a fair in Sublette. Sublette is the county seat of Haskell County, in far southwestern Kansas.

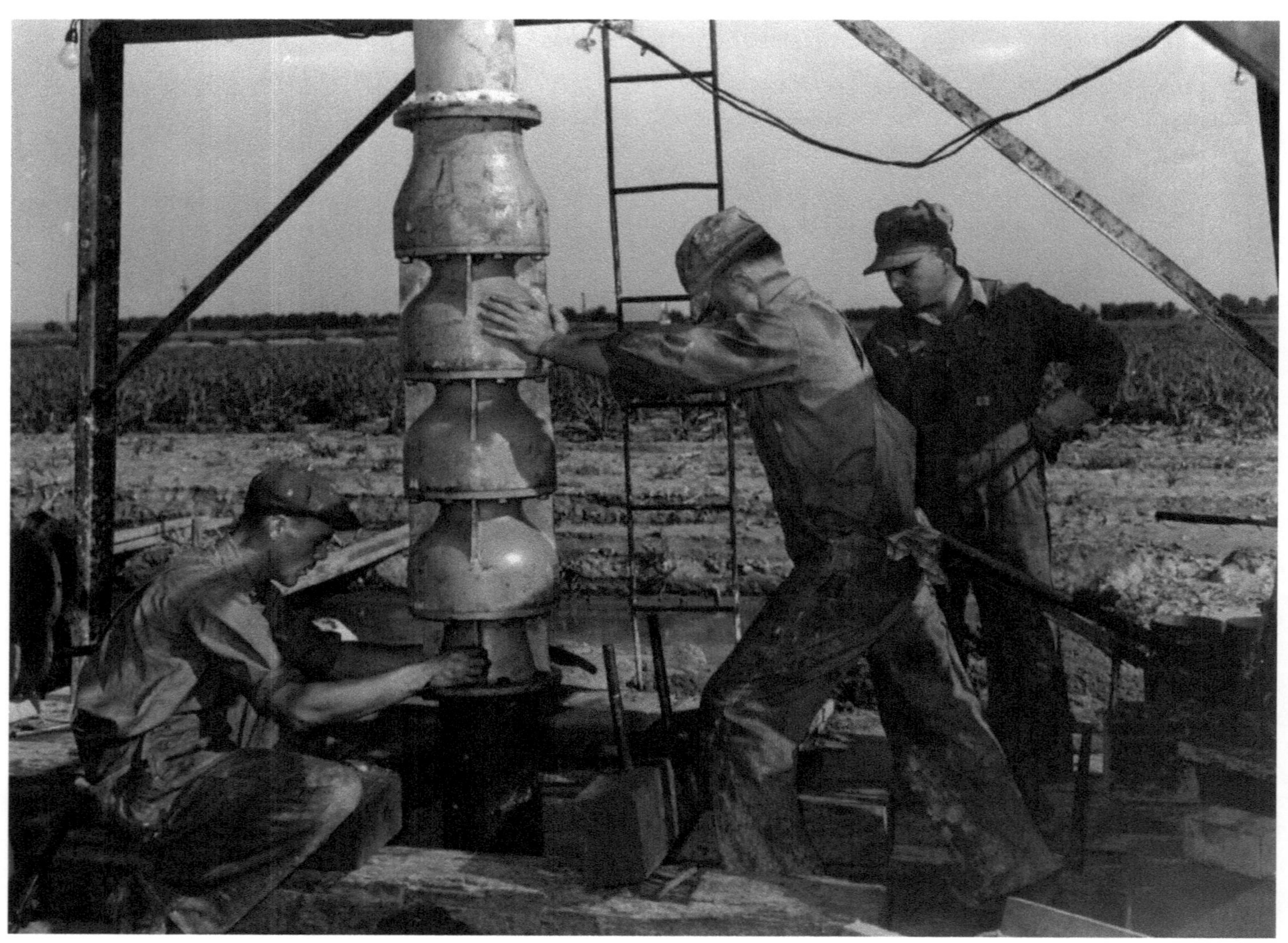

In 1939, workers prepare to install the pumping mechanism of a well used to irrigate crops near Garden City. In a heavily agricultural state, water for irrigation has always been a priority. Finney County, in southwestern Kansas, has the distinction of being one of the most heavily irrigated counties in Kansas.

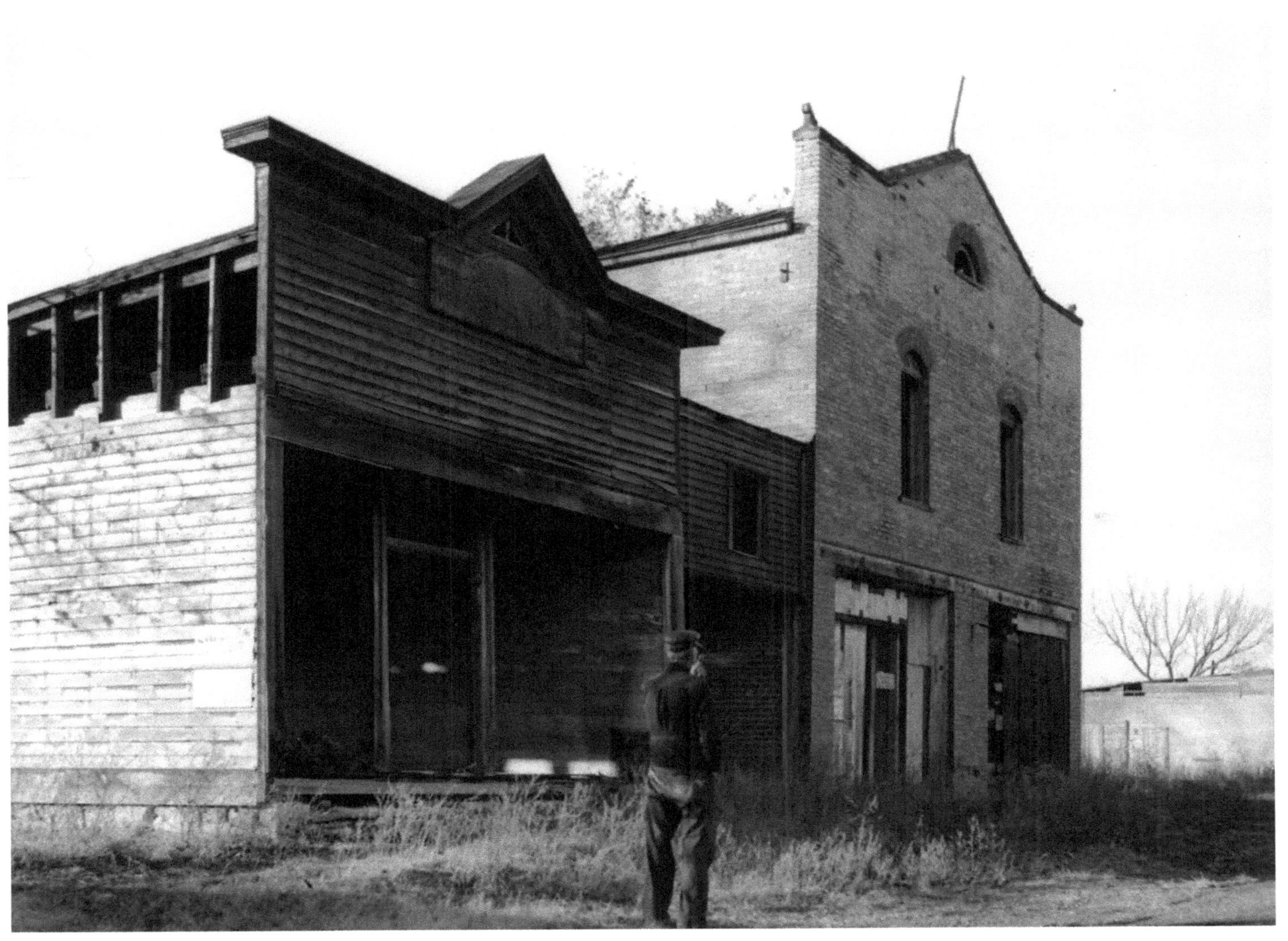

When a Farm Security Administration photographer went to document life in Shaw, Kansas, in 1940, he found abandoned stores in the business district. Shaw, in Neosho County, is southeast of Chanute.

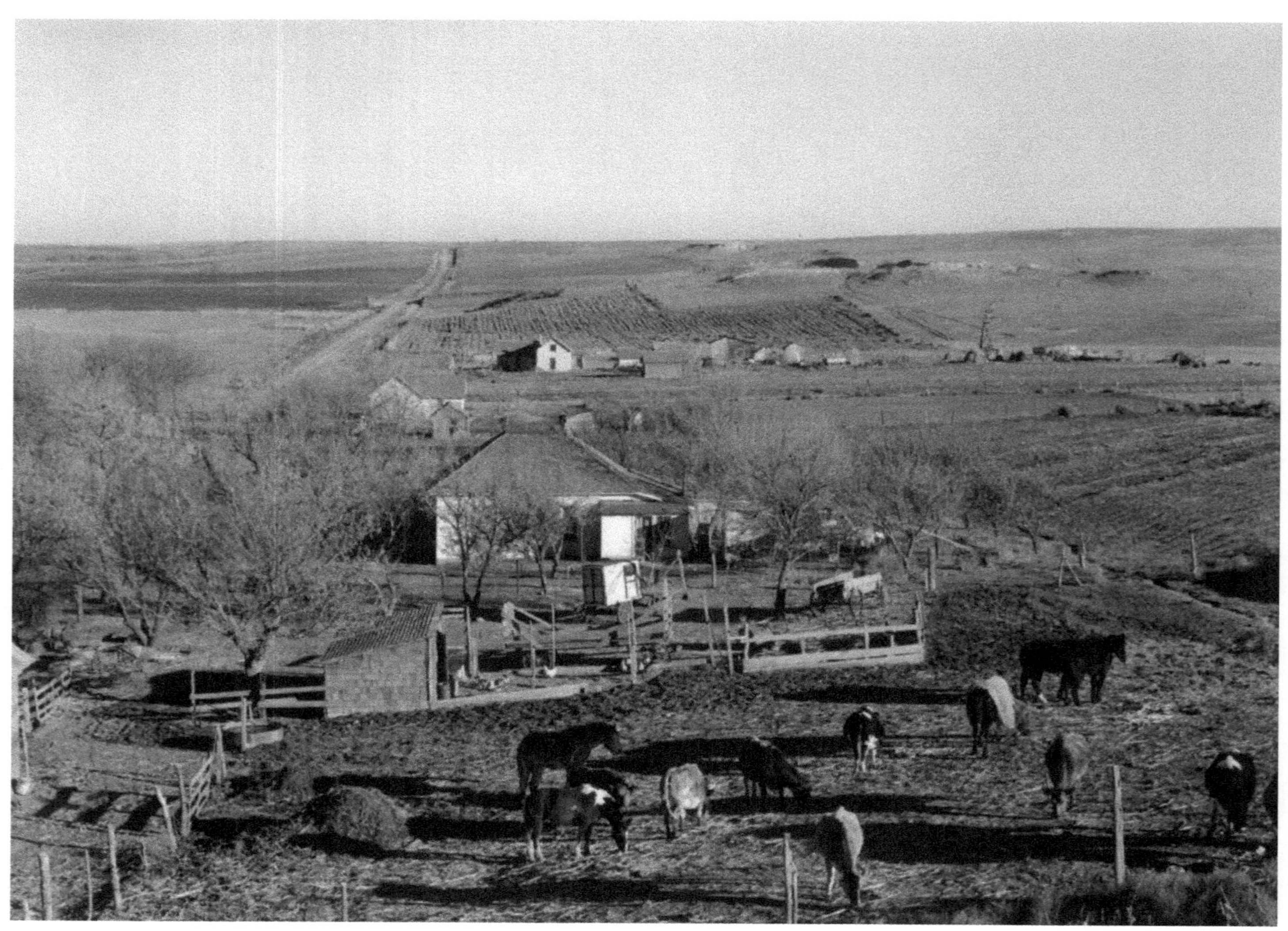

Farmland in Almena, as pictured in 1941, is largely flat and sparsely protected by vegetation. The community is located in what's referred to as the Prairie Dog Valley of Norton County. It had fewer than 500 residents in 2000.

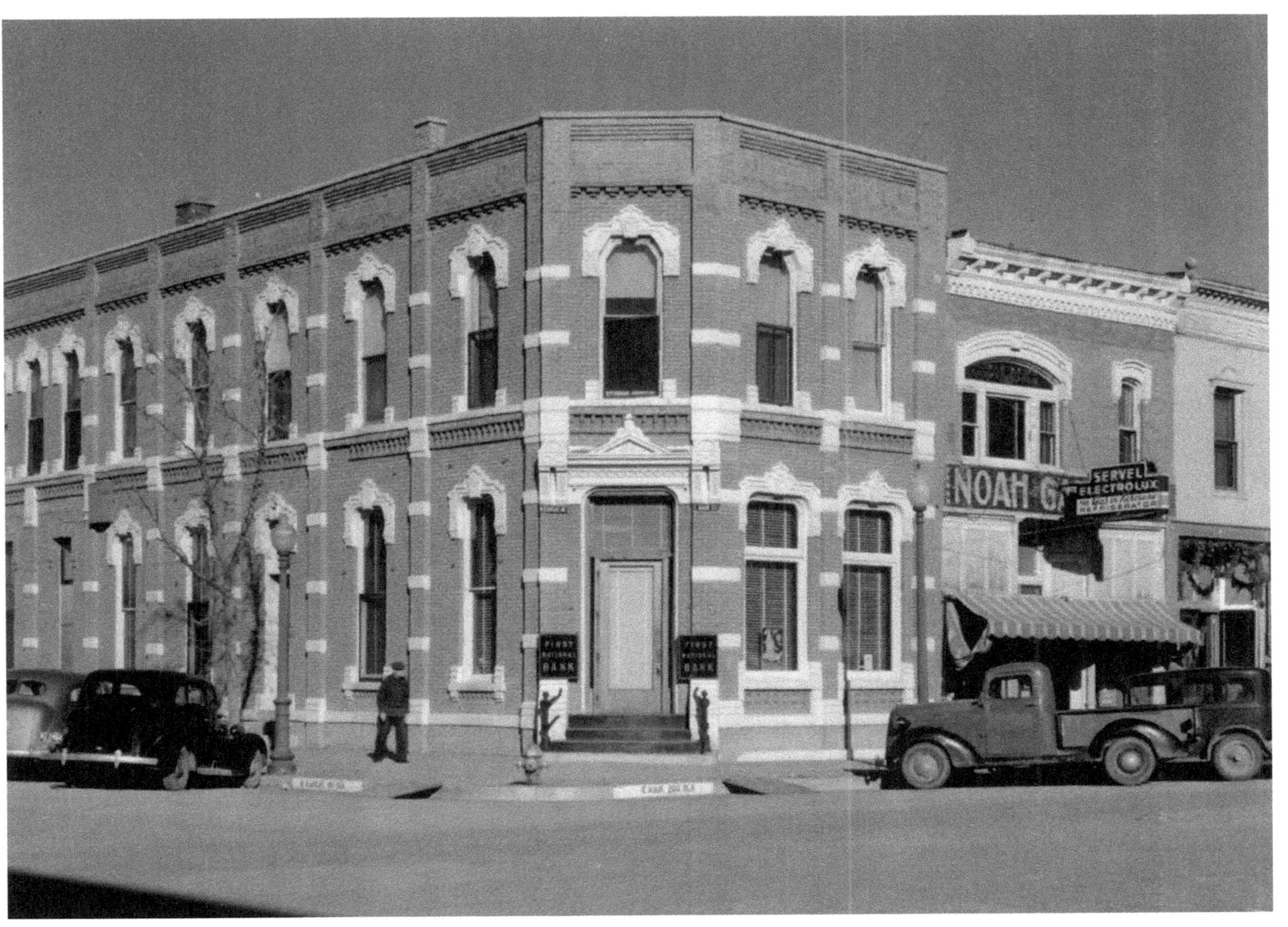

Pearl Harbor had been bombed the month before this photograph was taken, but little about the First National Bank corner in Norton reflected change from life-as-usual.

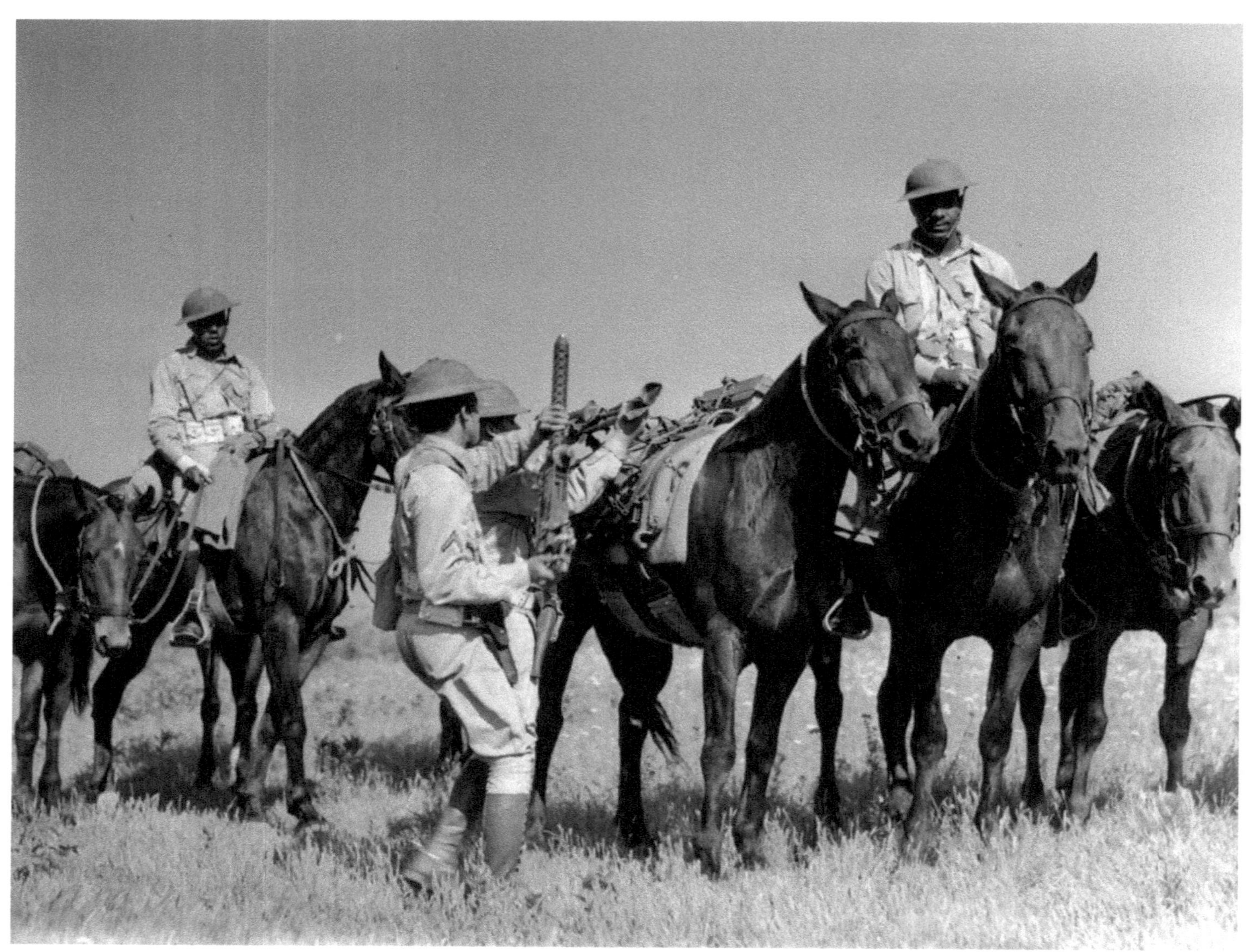

In a stark contrast of military eras, a cavalry unit arrives on horseback to set up a machine gun in a 1942 training exercise at Fort Riley. During most of World War II, African-American troops either served in support roles to white troops or were assigned to segregated units. This photograph was taken by Farm Security Administration photographer Jack Delano.

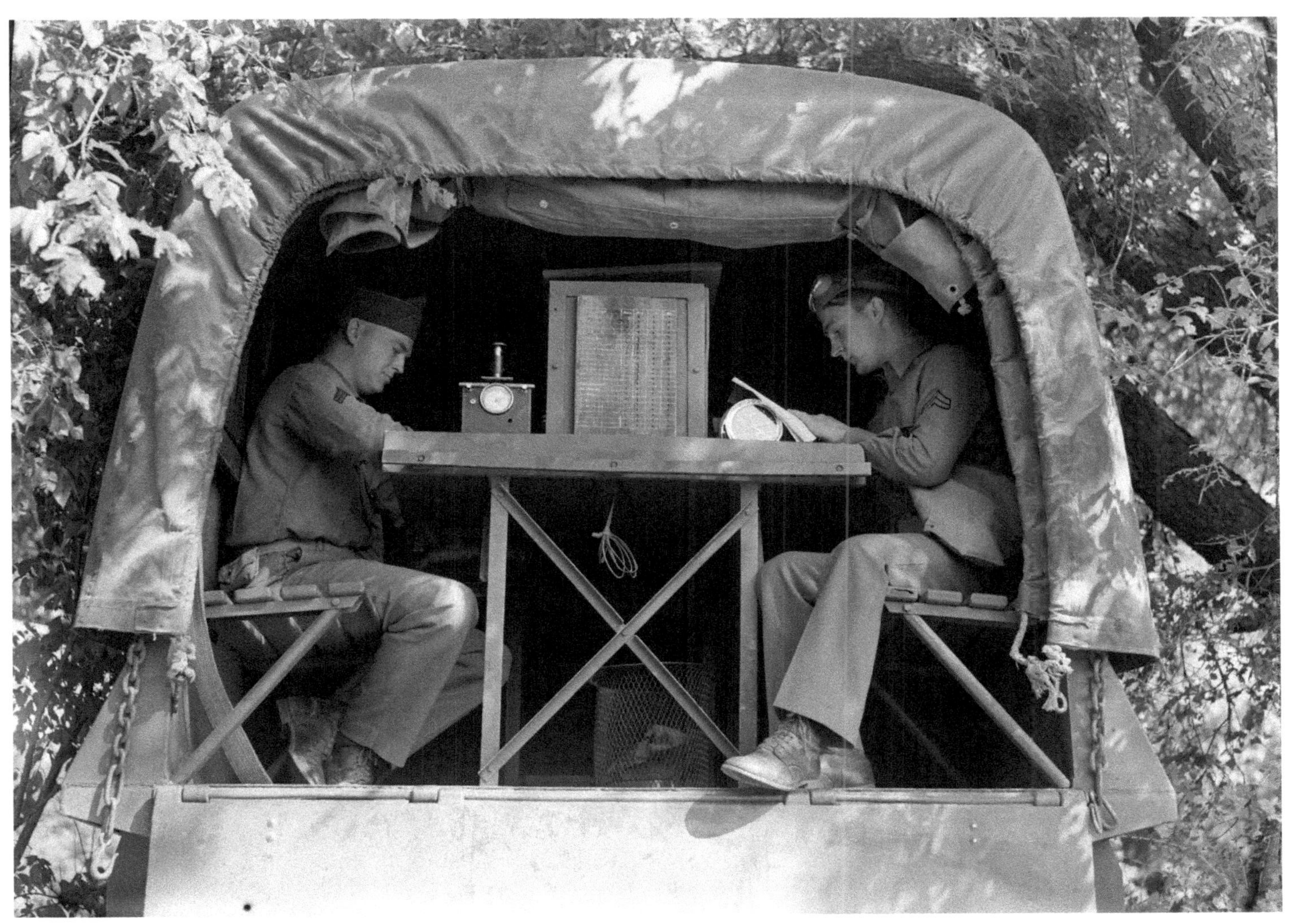

The back of a truck serves as a message center in 1942 for two Signal Corps soldiers training at Fort Riley. In their training for wartime duty, the soldiers have been presented with a battlefield problem to solve in the field.

With most able-bodied men called to military service during World War II, aircraft assembly jobs fell to women such as Mena Weber, who was probably taking five minutes away from her job at Cessna Aircraft Company's Wichita plant to apply makeup. Rosie the Riveter worked hard to help win the war.

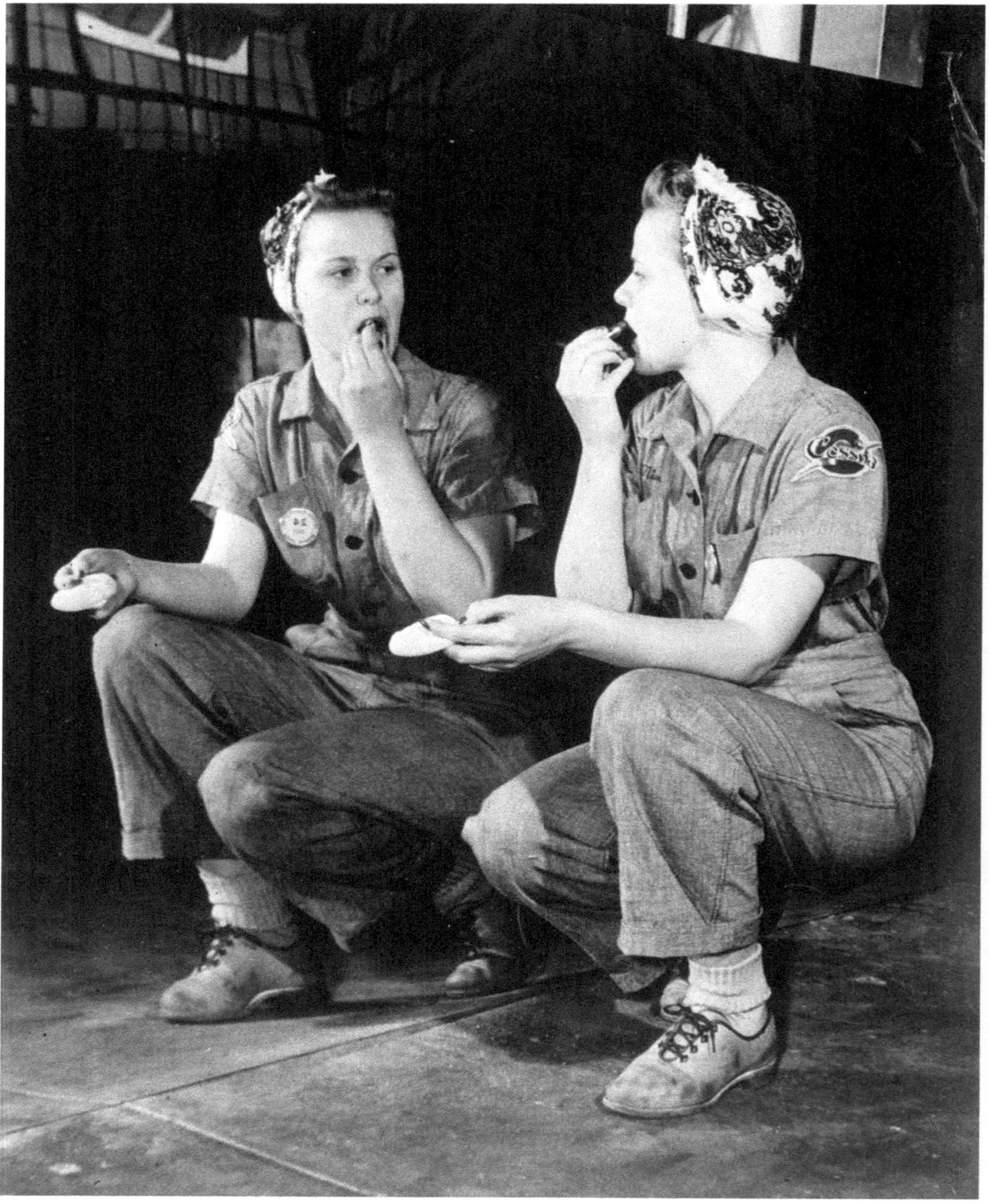

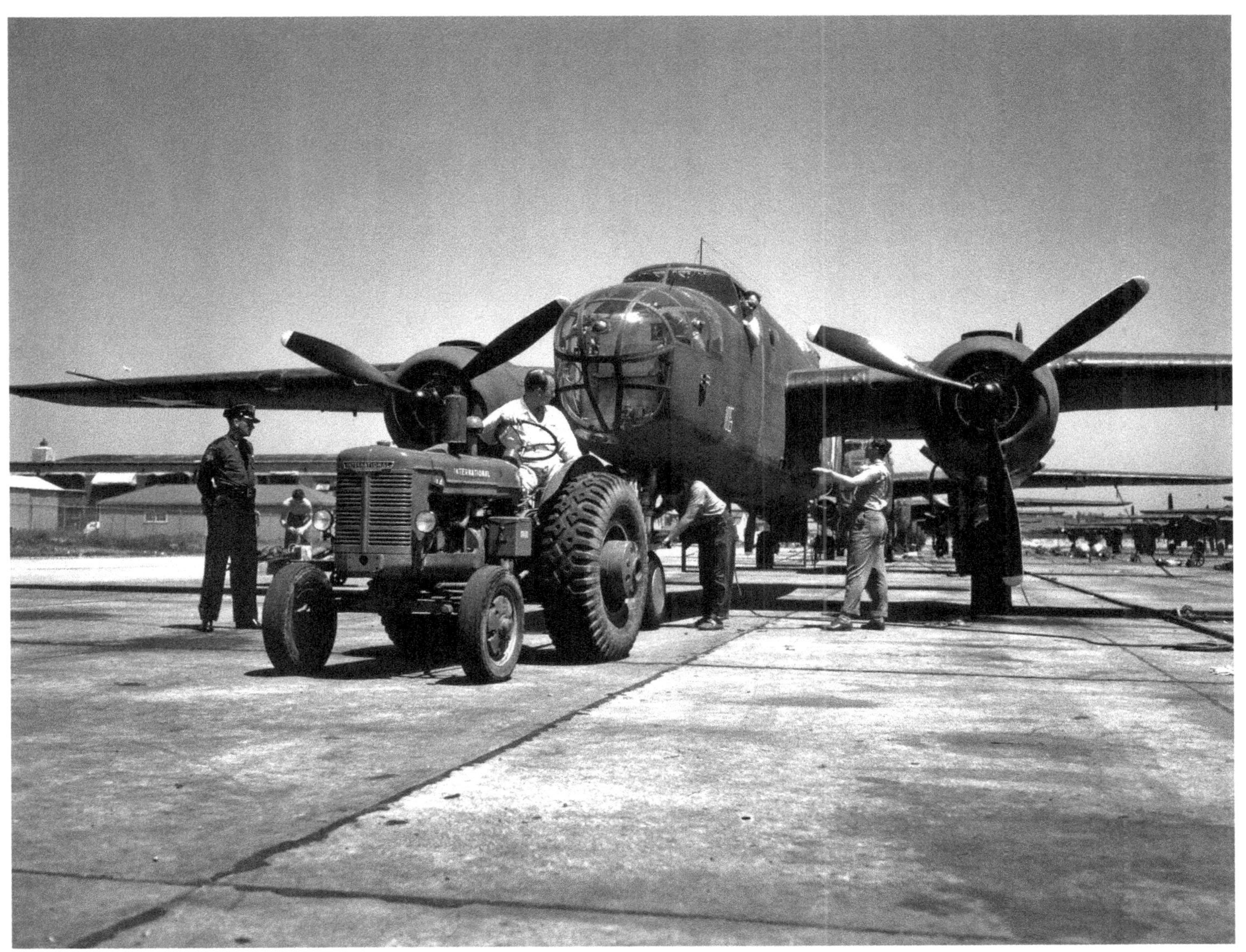

An International tractor pulls a B-25 onto the tarmac at North American Aviation's plant in Kansas City, Kansas. Early in World War II, the primary production site for the B-25 bomber was in Inglewood, California. Seeking a safer inland location, North American Aviation began producing the large majority—6,608—of its B-25s at the Fairfax Plant in Kansas City, Kansas. In all, more than 9,800 of the planes were built during the war.

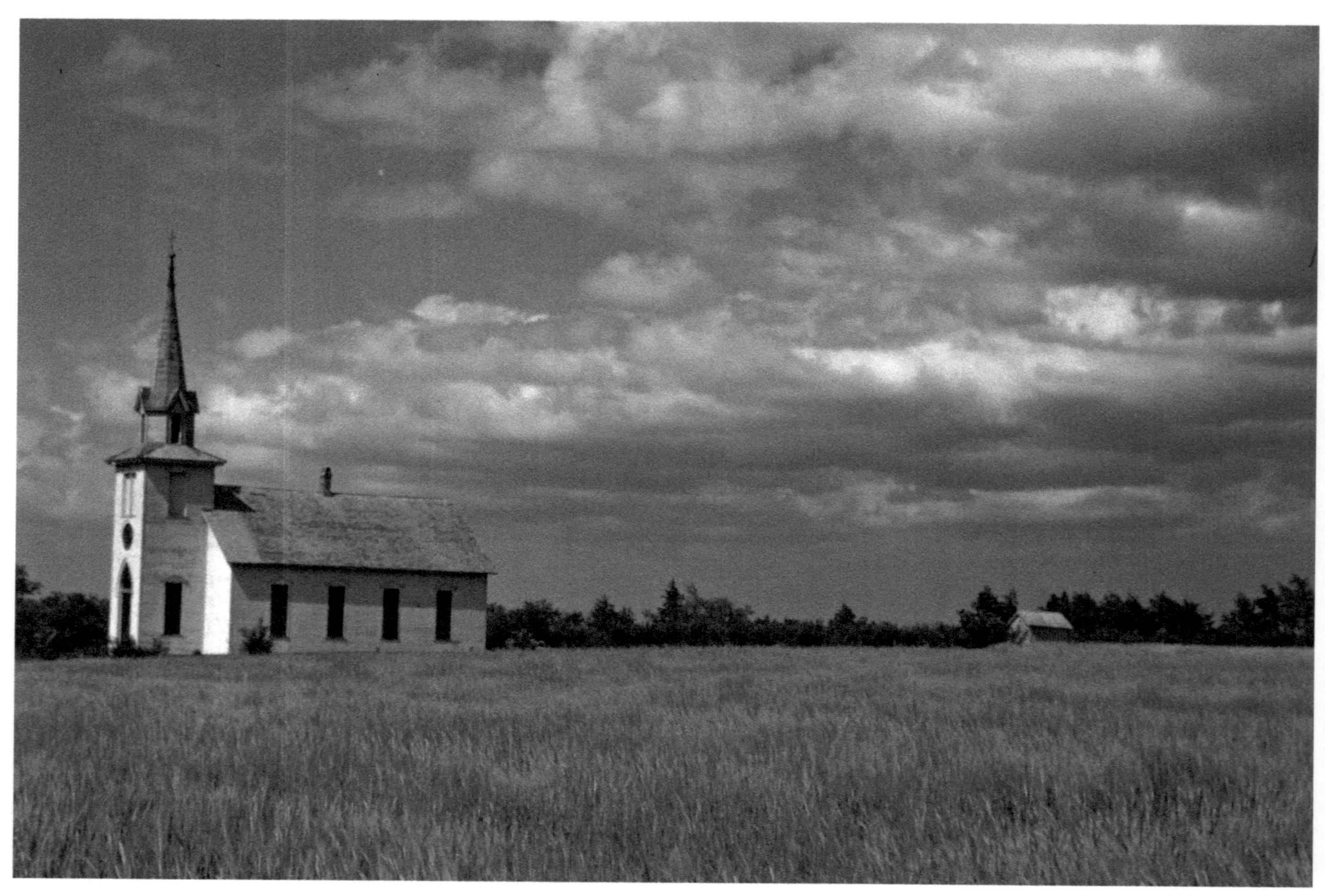

A broad Kansas sky and flat expanse of prairie frame an angular wooden church in Junction City. The scene was photographed by John Vachon in the early 1940s.

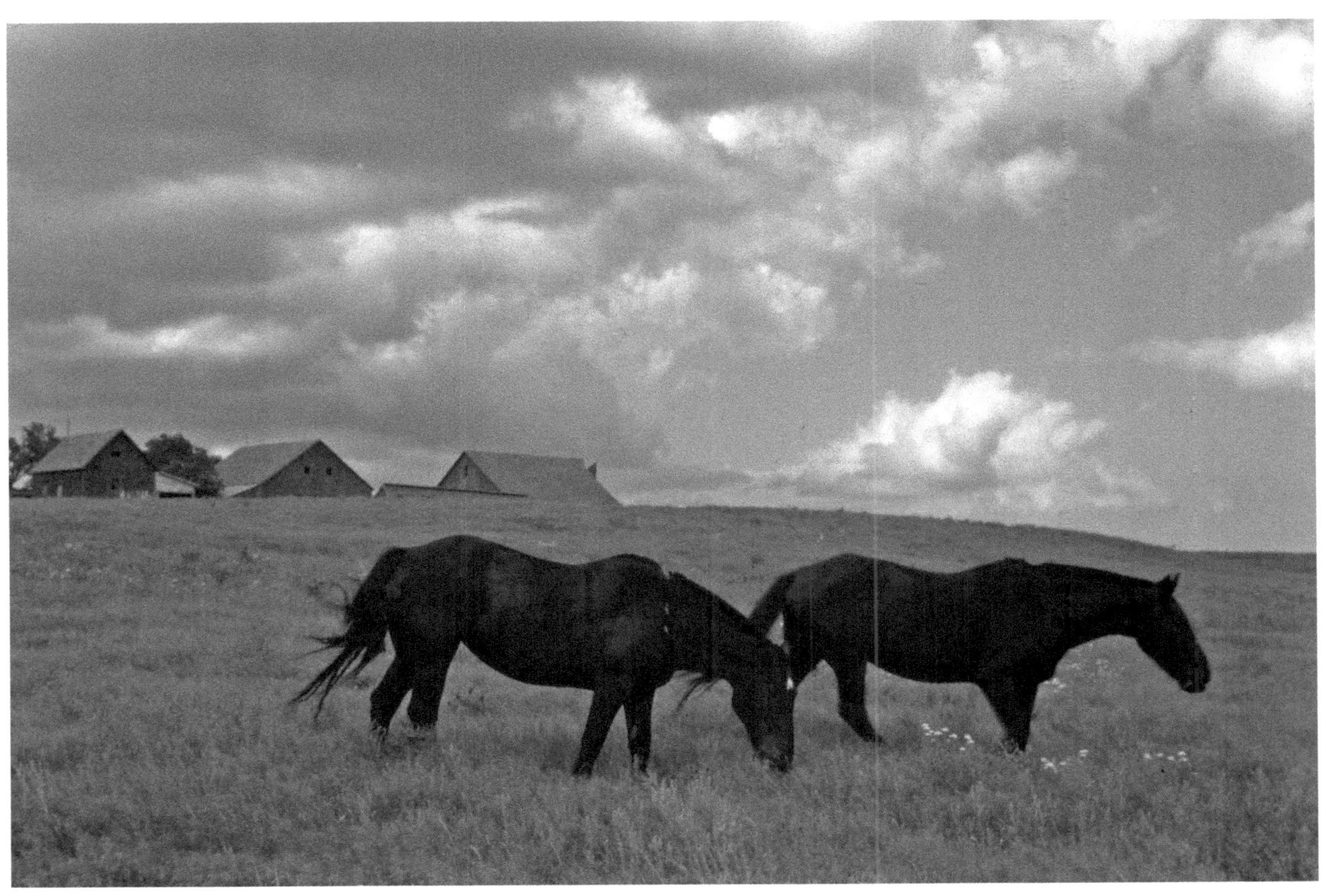

Horses graze on rolling prairie near Junction City. The ominous, heavy skies may be a sign of a tornado developing in the distance. Tornados devastating the state have been recorded since the 1880s, with an average of 50 reported annually. Kansas has more tornados than any other state besides Texas.

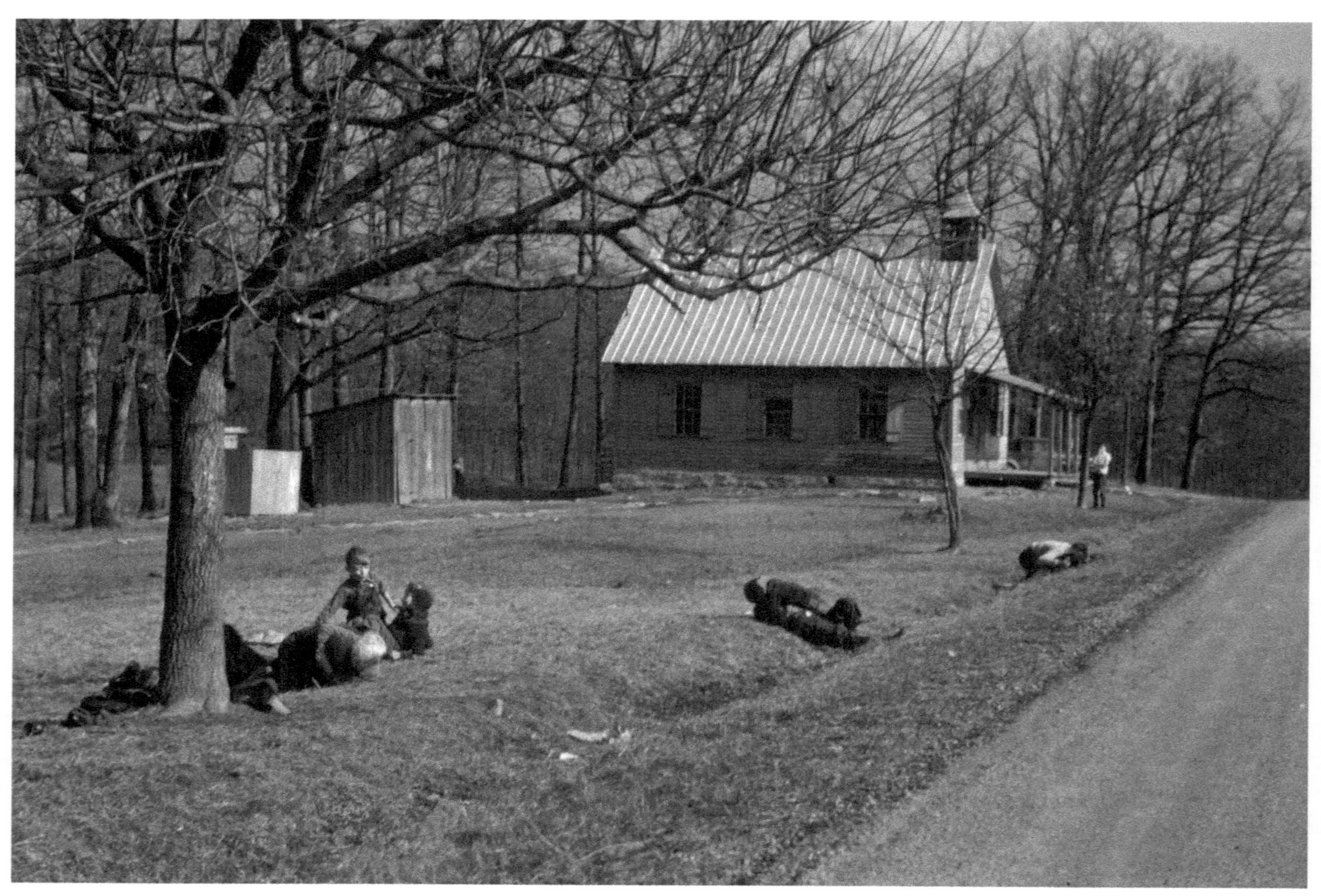

Children play near a schoolhouse on a quiet country road in the 1940s. The school was built with a corrugated metal roof, and the outhouse to the rear of the building was used by the students.

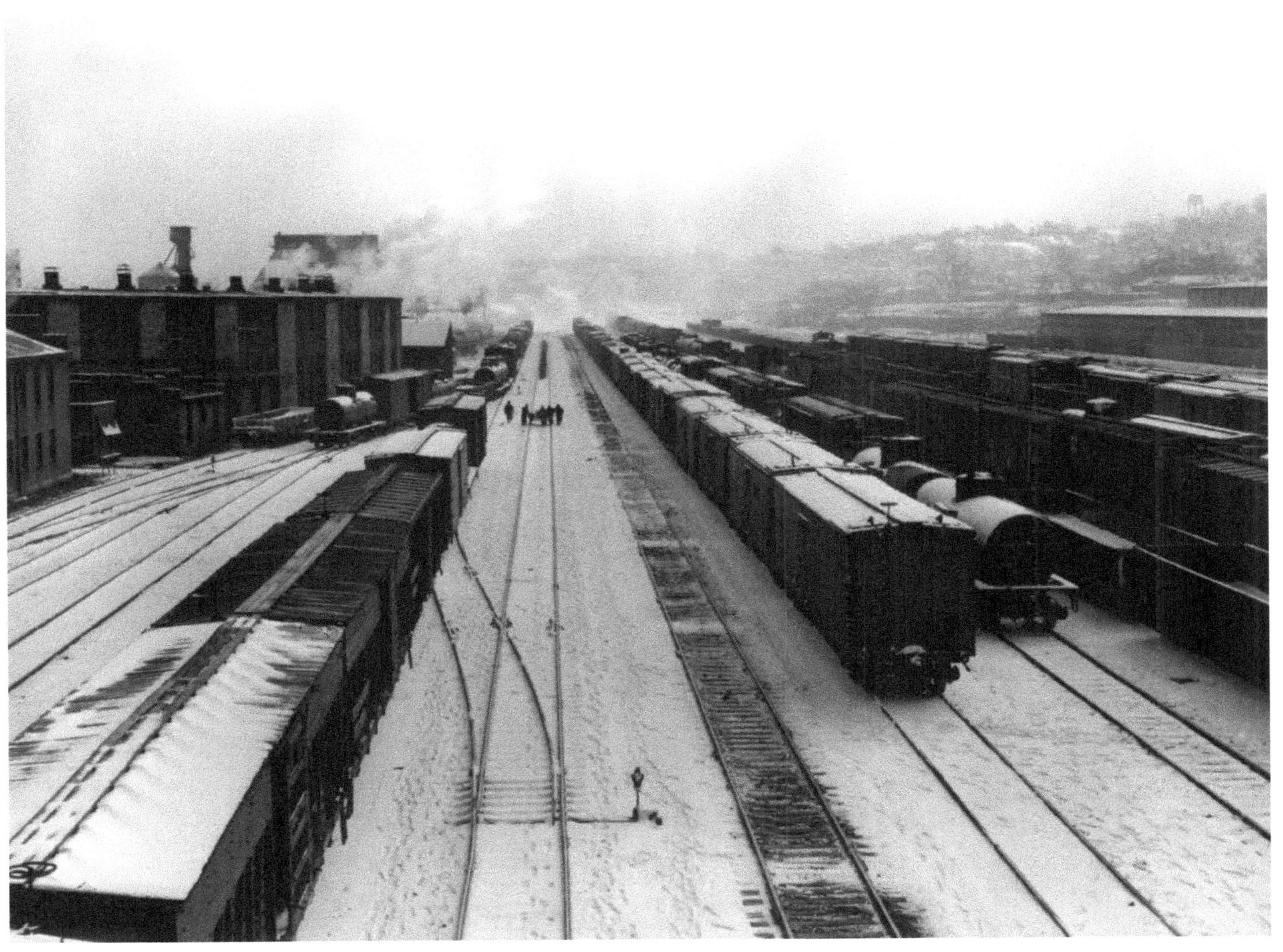

The urban grit of a snow-dusted railroad yard in Kansas City, Kansas, is in stark contrast to the image of a largely rural, agrarian state. Jack Delano photographed the yard, a key connecting point for east-west rail traffic, in March 1943.

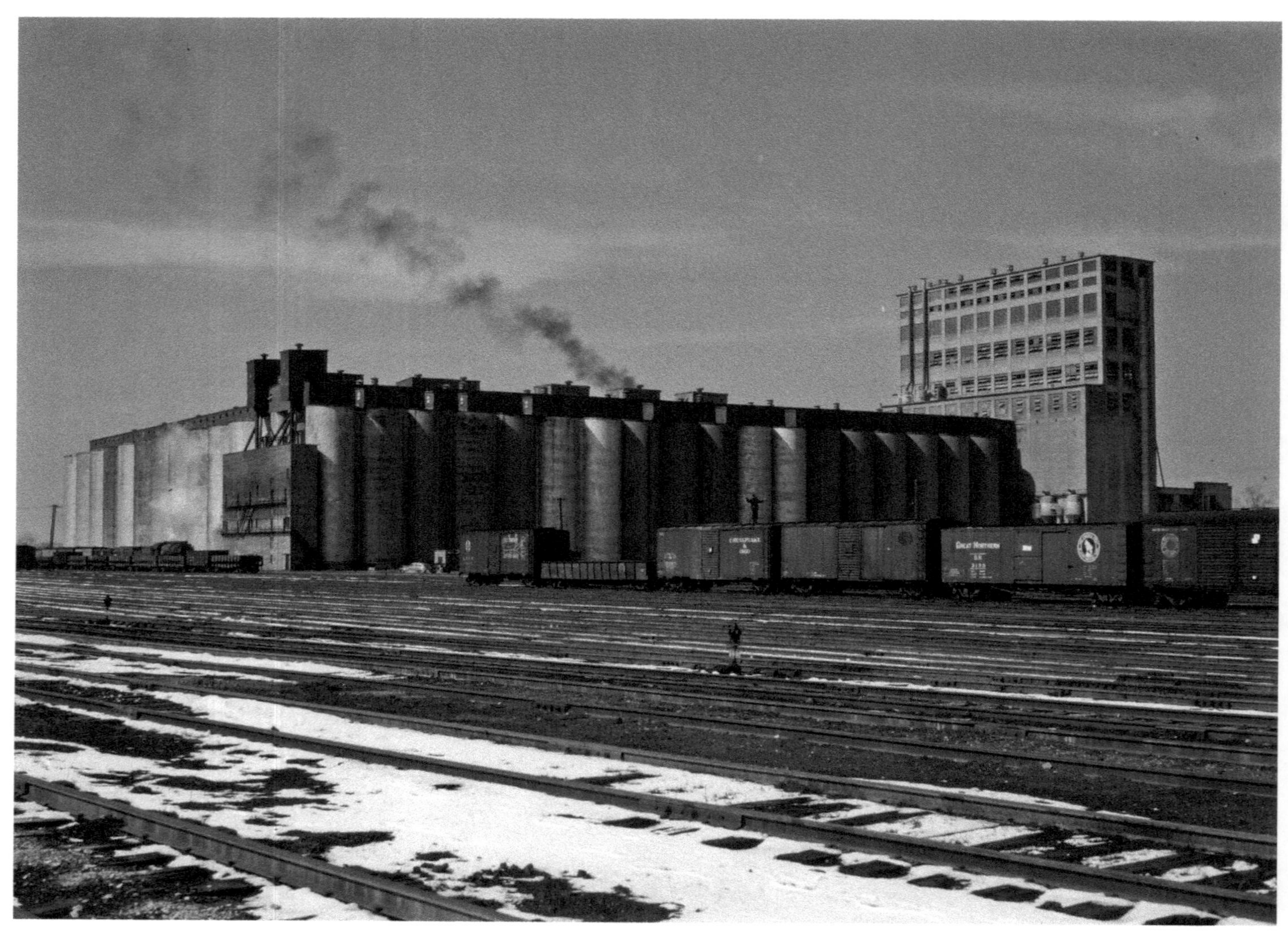

The 10-million-bushel grain elevator operated by the Atchison, Topeka and Santa Fe Railroad at the Argentine Yard in Kansas City, Kansas. Pictured in 1943, the grain elevator was demolished in 1996 and the site covered with new railroad tracks.

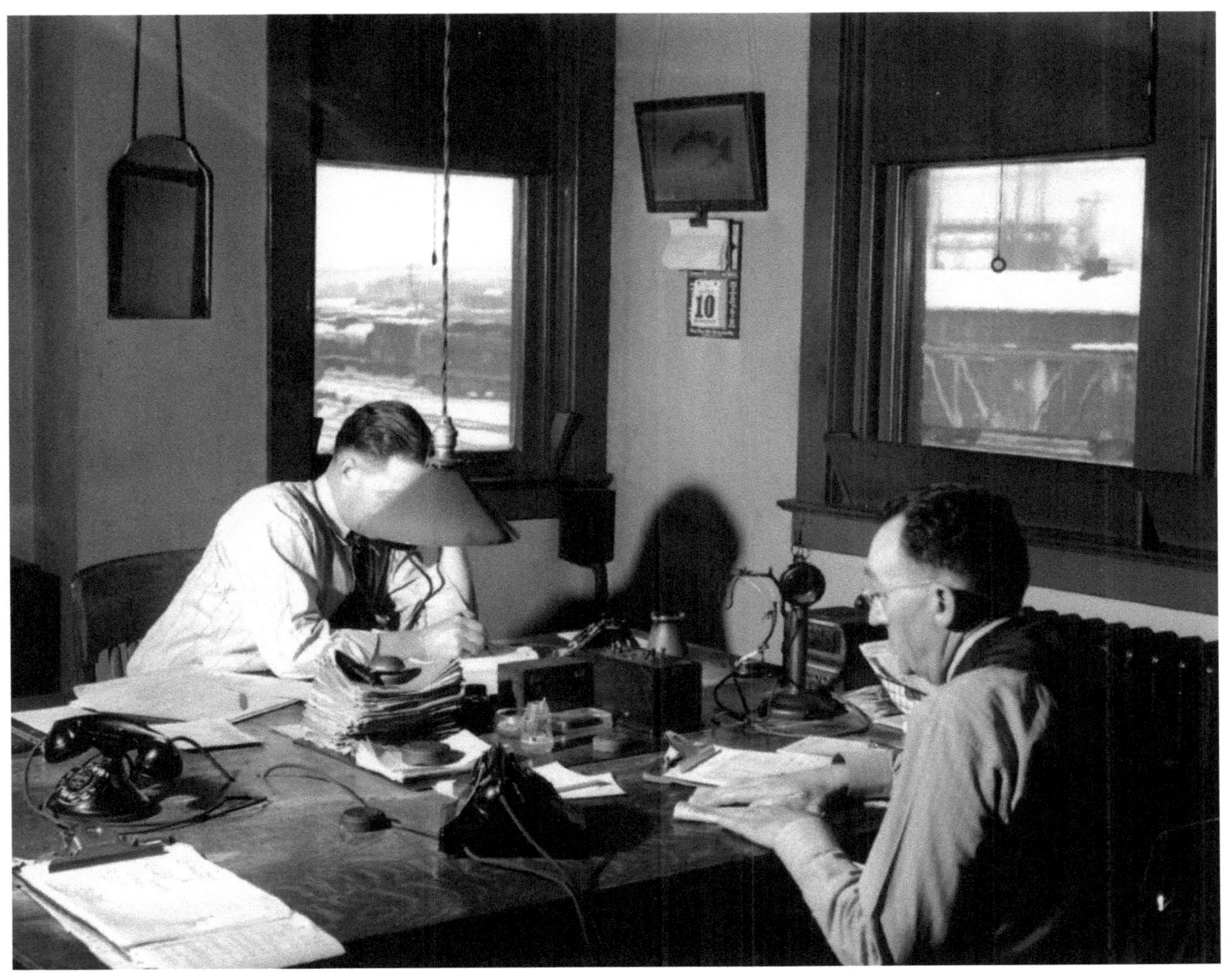

Two trainmasters at Santa Fe Railroad's Argentine Yard work in a dispatch and communications center used to track the heavy volume of rail traffic passing through the Kansas City, Kansas, yard. The Argentine Yard was photographed in March 1943.

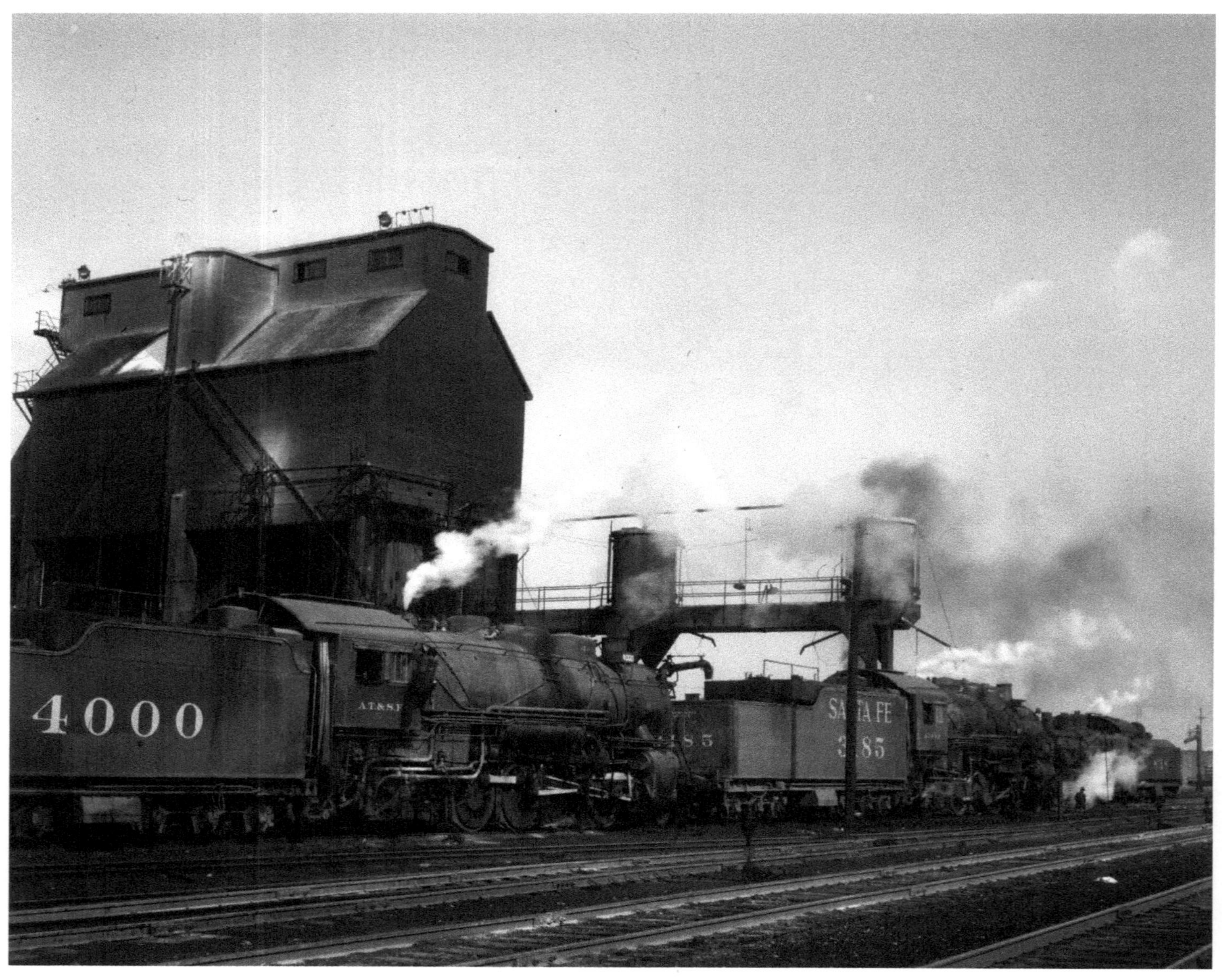

In 1943, locomotives are serviced with coal and sand at Santa Fe Railroad's Argentine Yard in Kansas City. During wartime or peace, the yard's central location made it a key connecting point for rail traffic coming to or from either coast.

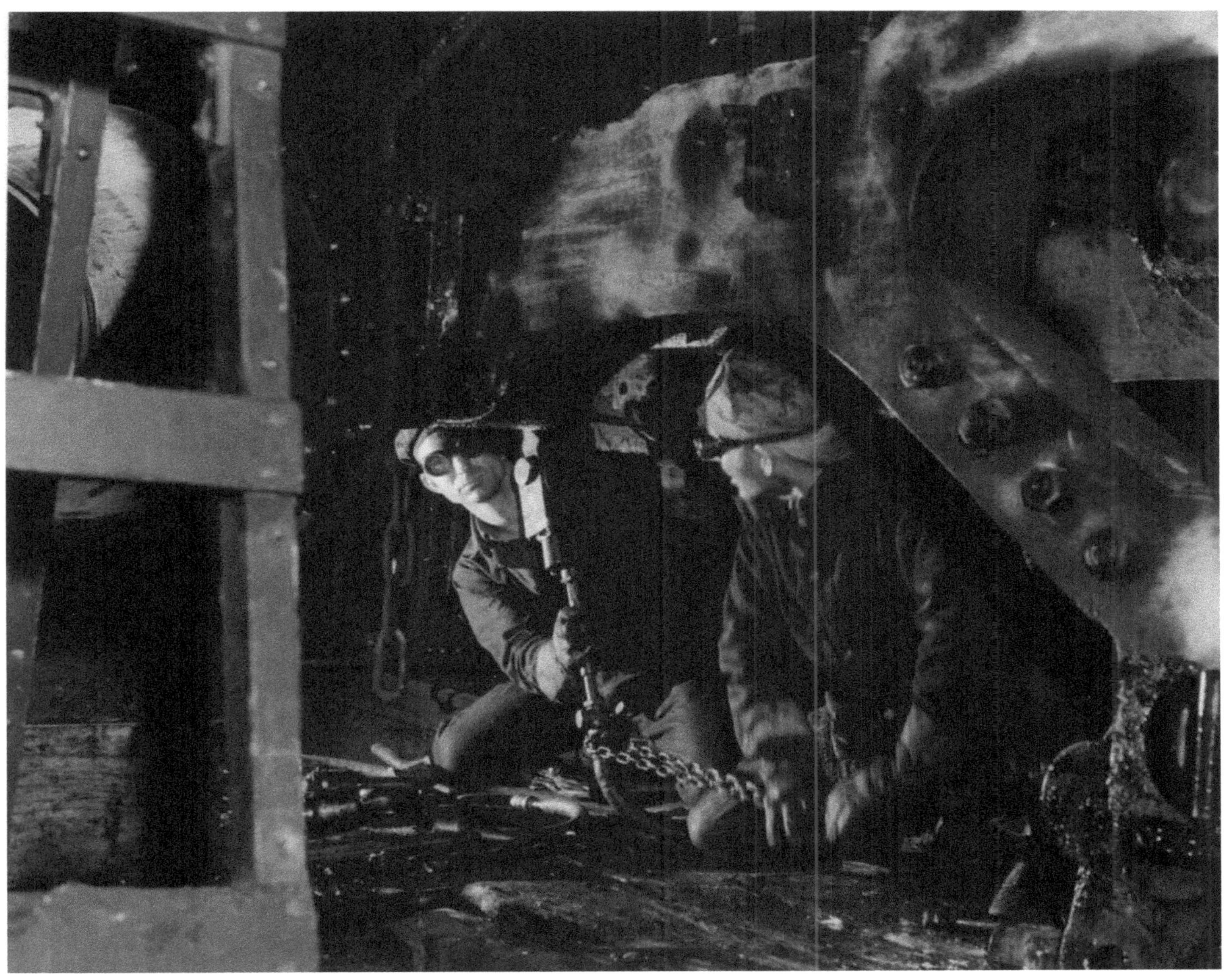

In addition to building rail cars in Topeka, mechanics at the Atchison, Topeka and Santa Fe shop maintained and repaired locomotive engines. This photo was taken in 1943.

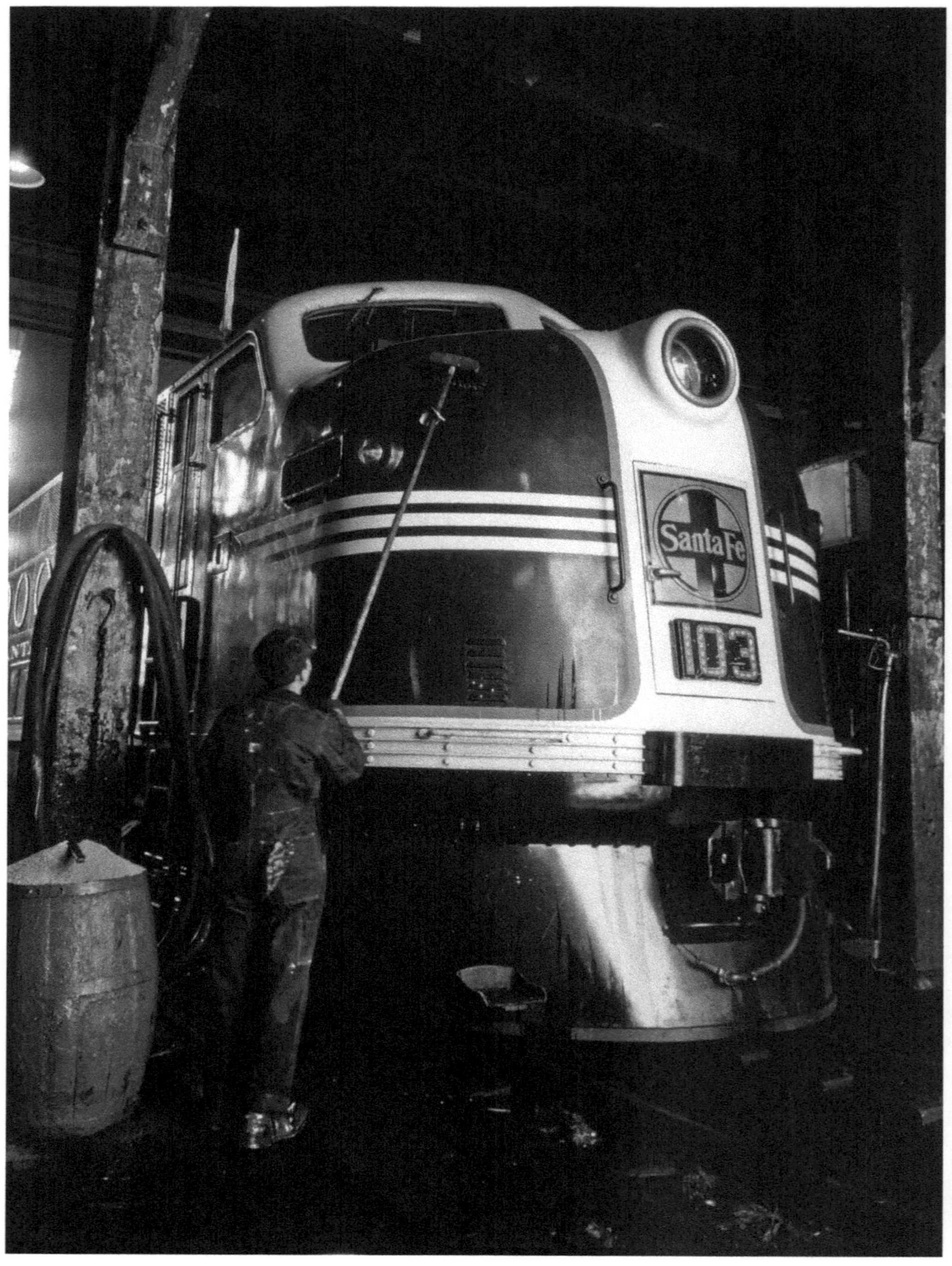

A diesel locomotive is washed in a roundhouse at Santa Fe Railroad's Argentine Yard in Kansas City, Kansas. Developed on 128 acres of Kaw River bottom land between the Argentine and Turner communities in Wyandotte County, the yard was a dense network of terminals, transfer sheds, machine shops, fuel depots, and other service facilities.

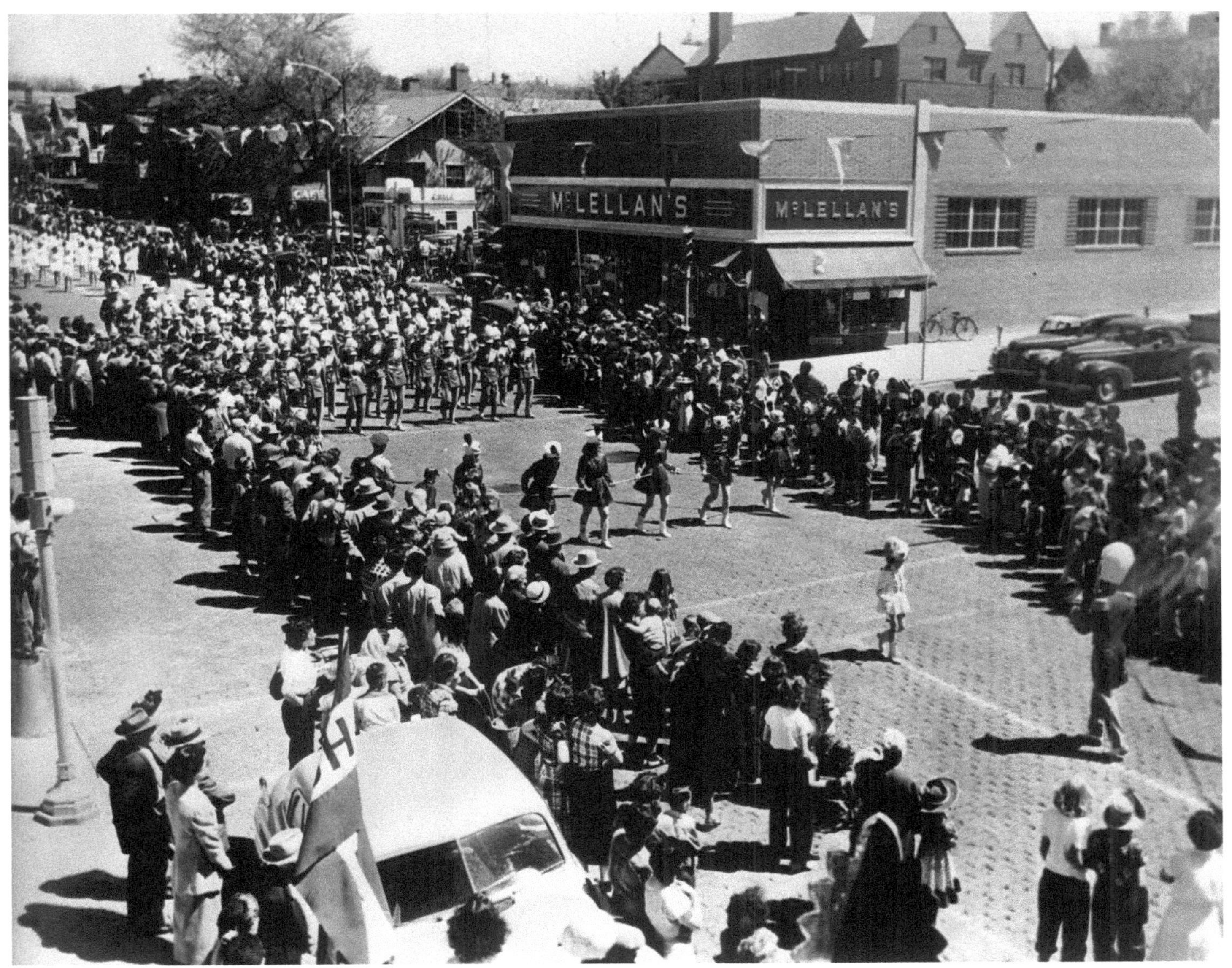

By the time this 1952 photo was taken, parades and marching band competitions had long replaced gunfights in Dodge City. Nevertheless, the Boot Hill Fiesta parade is rooted in the city's colorful and often violent past.

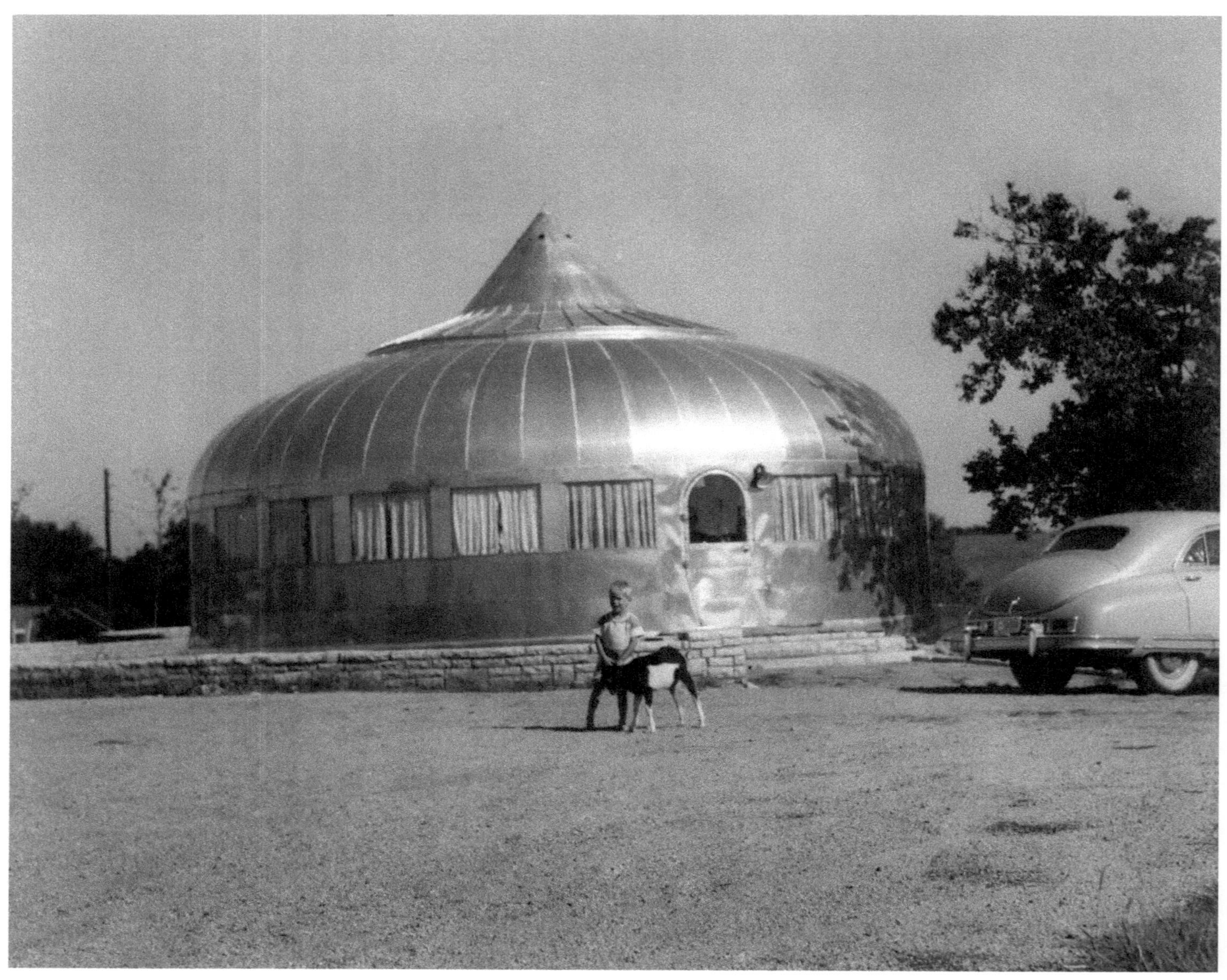

Futurist Buckminster Fuller designed this prototype of the Dymaxion House, which was built in Rose Hill and photographed sometime after 1948. It was made of aluminum and used a tension suspension system from a central mast. Fuller's hope was that the Beech Aircraft plant in Wichita could be converted to mass-produce the homes and provide employment and housing for returning World War II servicemen.

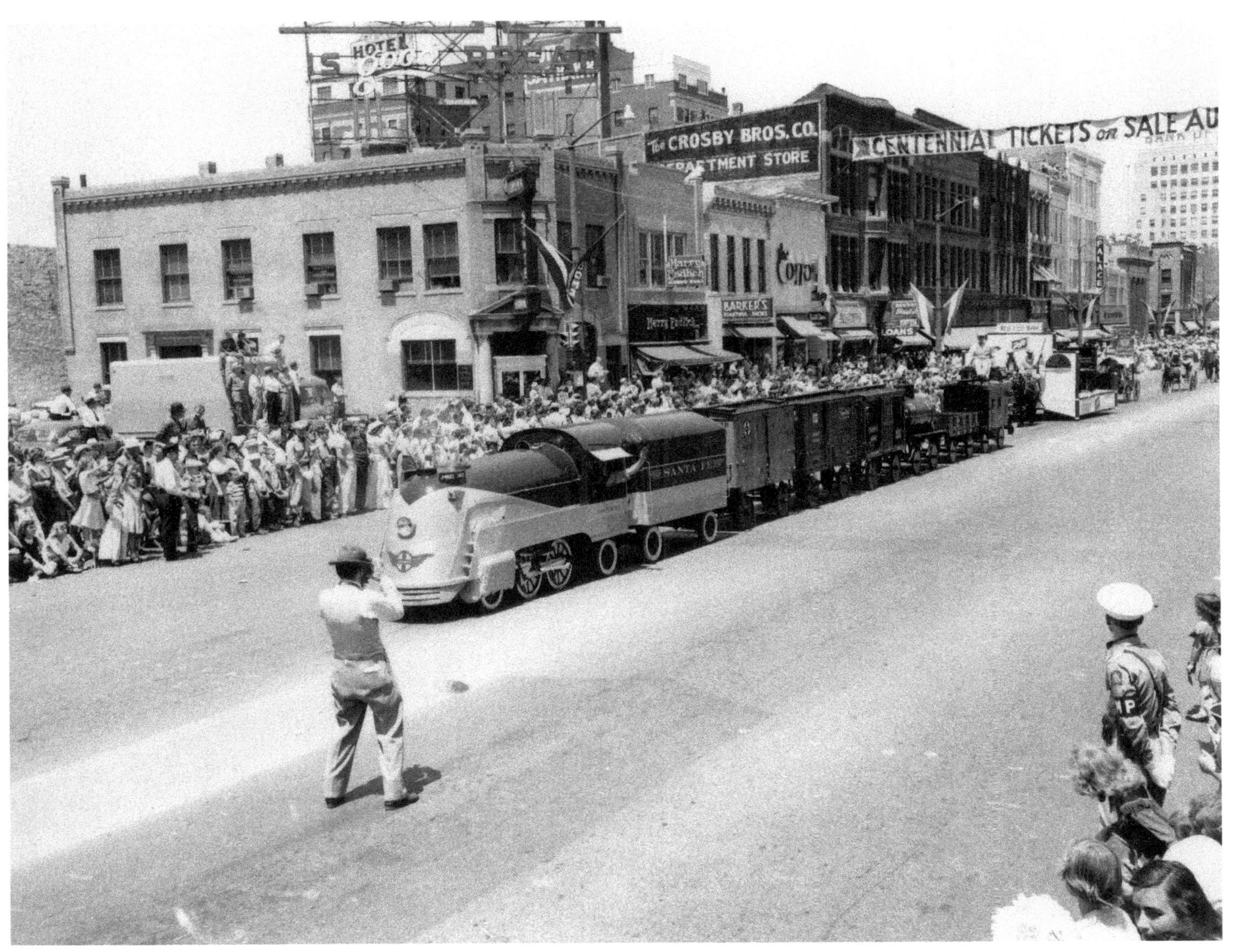

A birthday float and other festivities in Topeka help mark Kansas Territory's centennial in 1954. The state territory was created with passage of the Kansas-Nebraska Act in 1854.

Non-Kansans may associate the Sunflower State with agriculture more than energy, but its production of oil and natural gas has been significant. In this 1954 photo, an unidentified worker labors in a Kansas oil field. The state ranks among the top 10 in crude oil production, is home to one of the nation's top natural gas–producing fields, and is leading the way in renewable energy collection from wind.

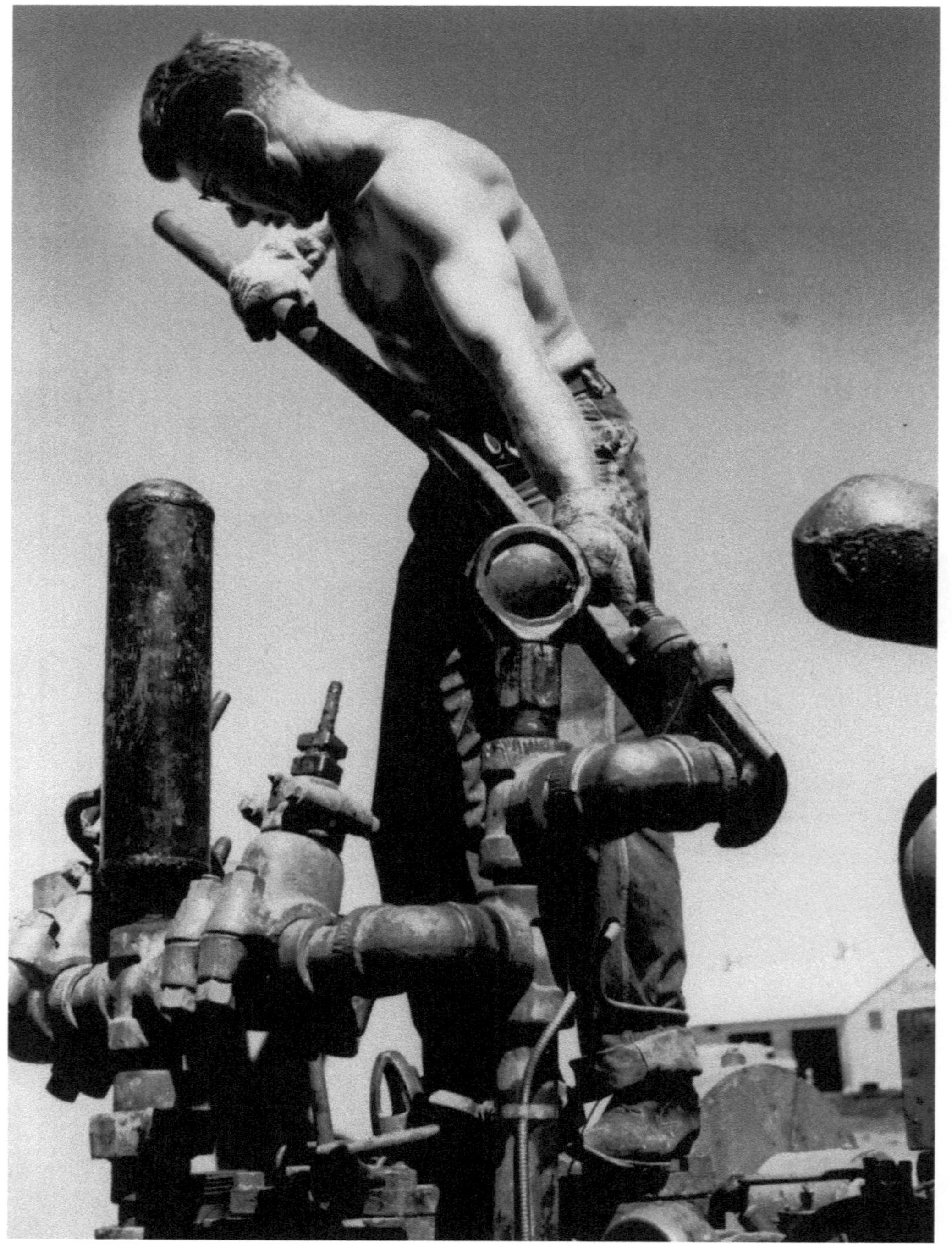

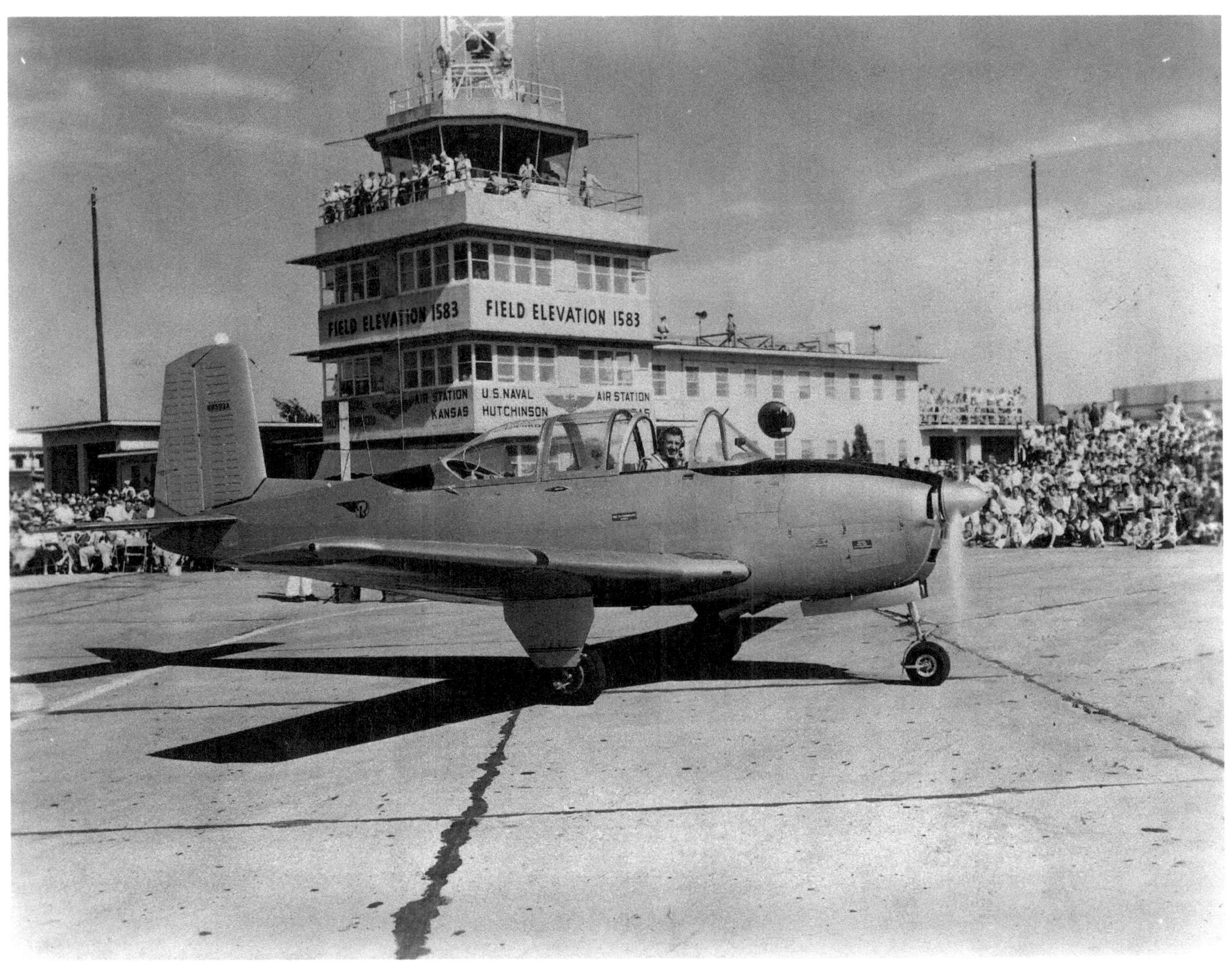

A Beechcraft T-34 aircraft is pictured in 1954 after a demonstration at the Hutchinson Naval Air Station. The base was host to the Navy Relief Kansas Centennial Air Show. Naval air stations were commissioned in both Hutchinson and Olathe, Kansas, to train pilots during World War II.

Pictured in 1955, the General Motors Fairfax Assembly Plant in Kansas City, Kansas, produced Buicks, Oldsmobiles, and Pontiacs. The plant, still in operation at an adjacent location, was built at the site of North American Aviation's B-25 production plant.

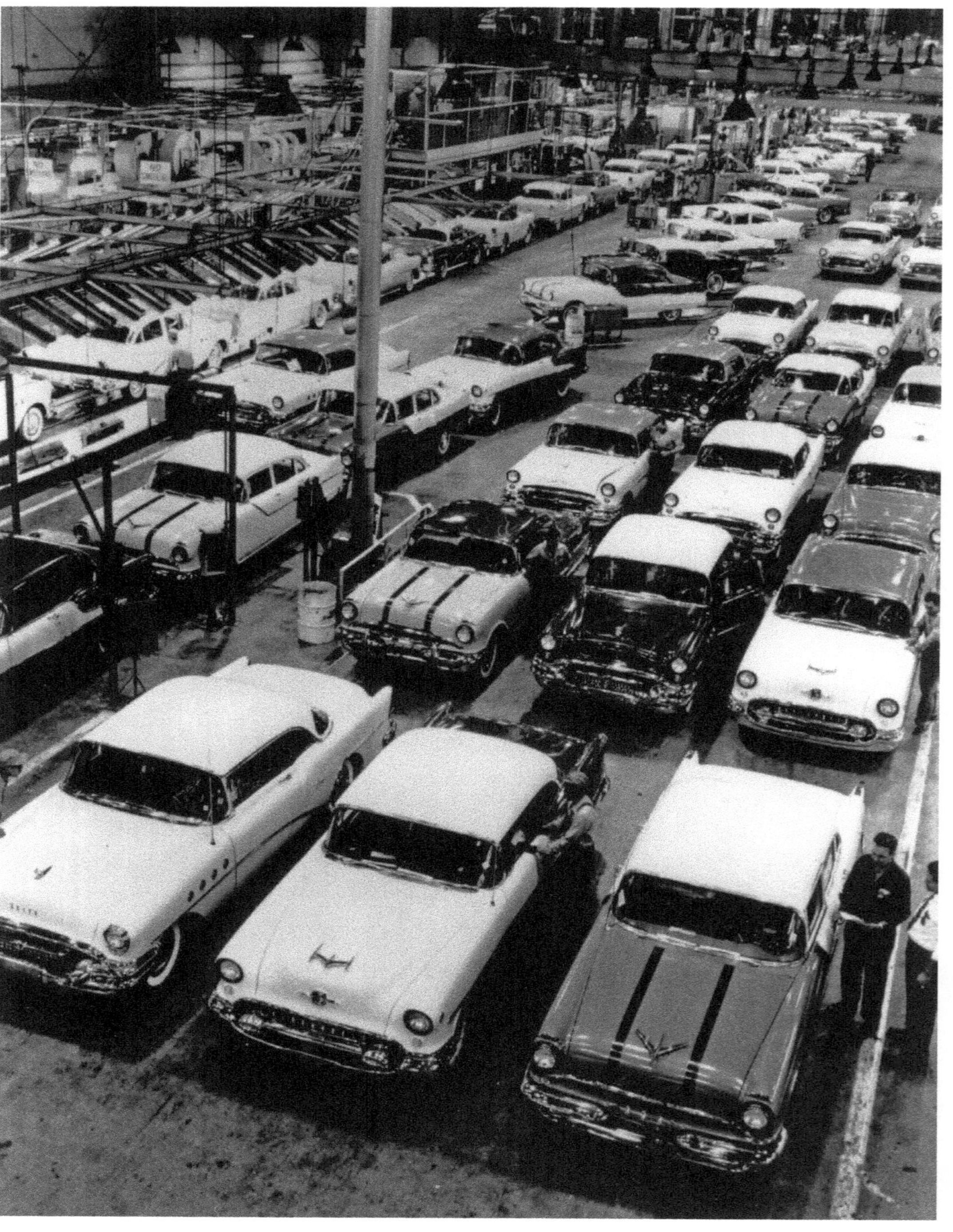

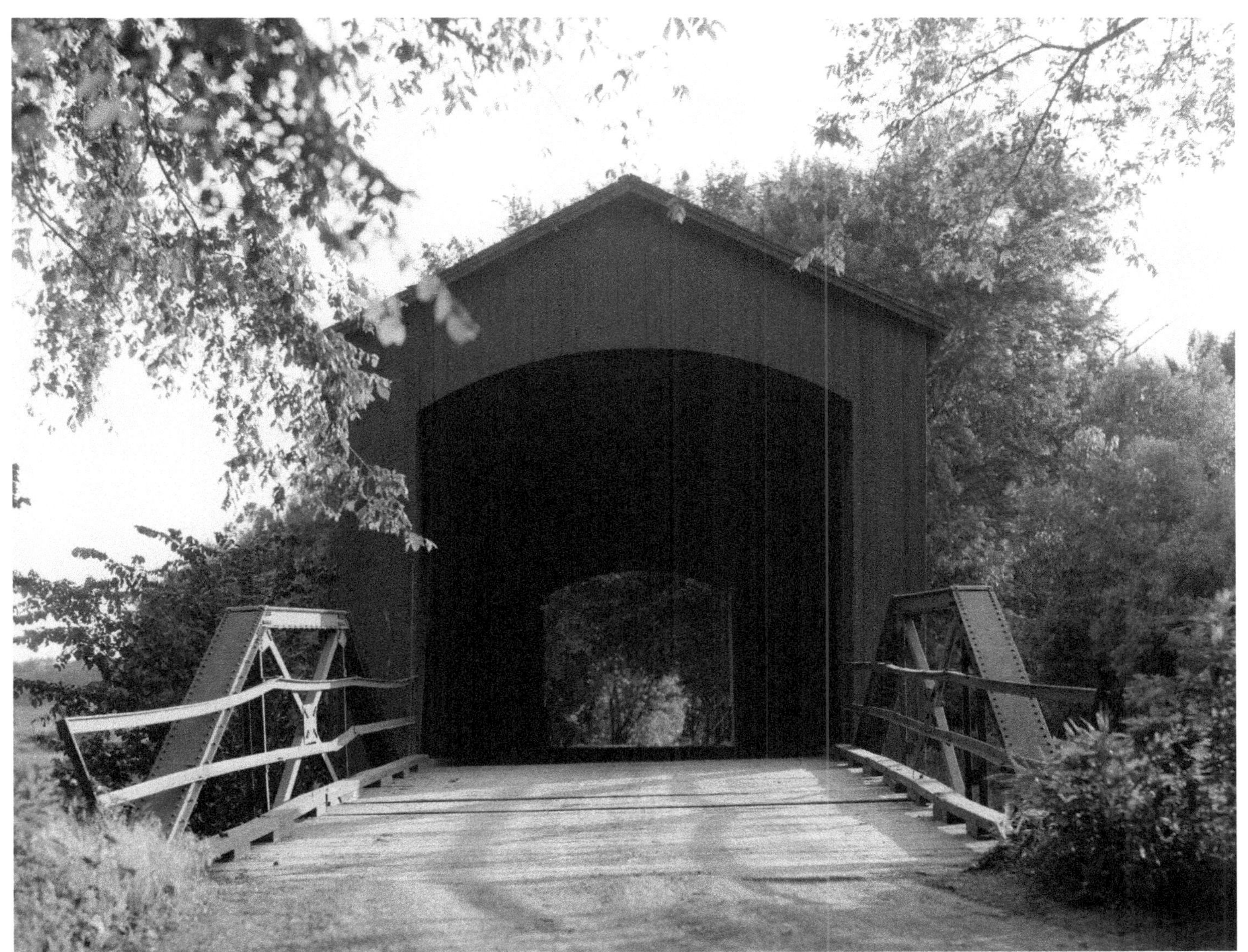

A covered bridge spans Stranger Creek near Kansas Highway 92. According to notes accompanying the 1958 photo, the bridge was originally built in 1859 and then updated in 1946. It was photographed in Leavenworth County near Springdale.

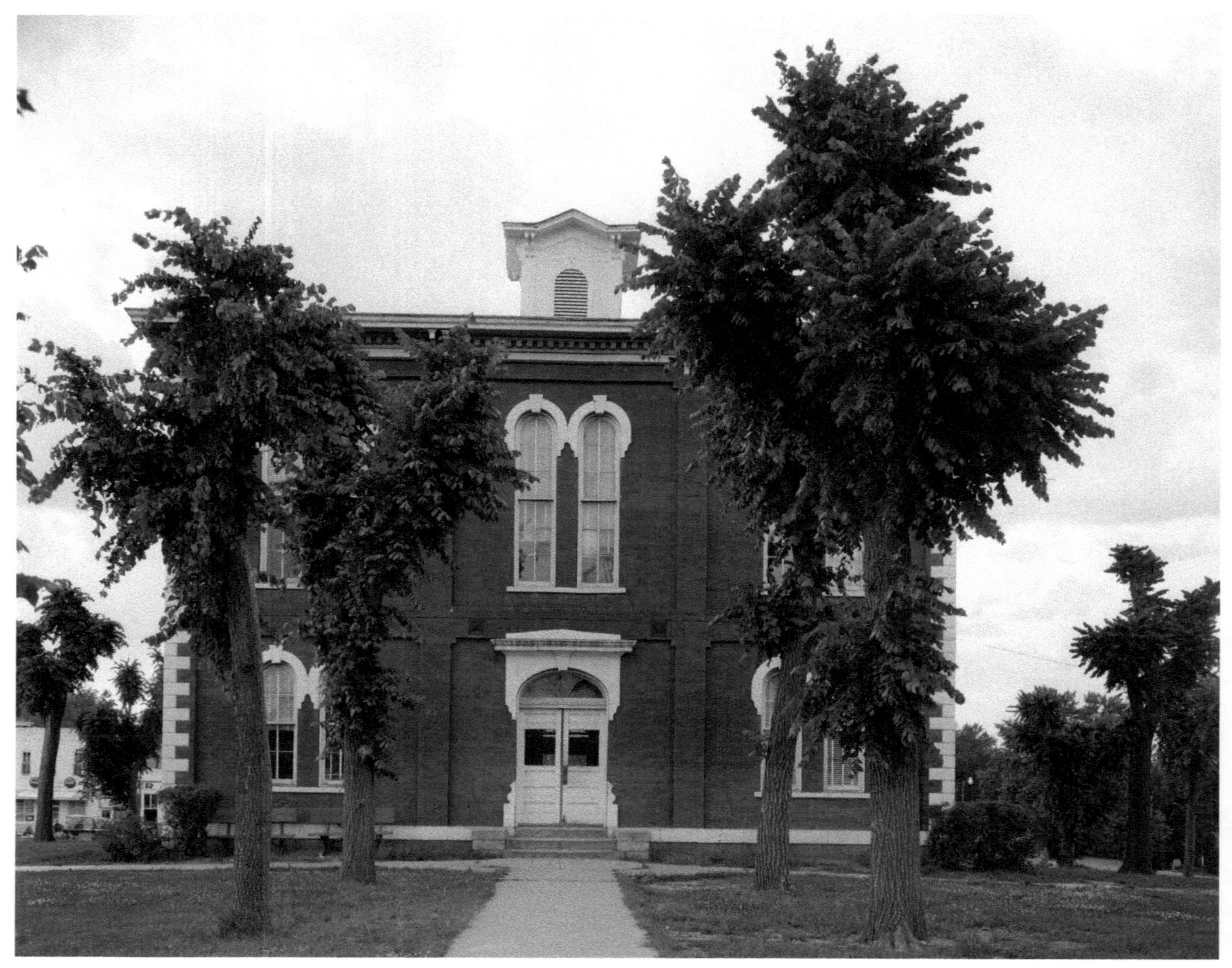

The Oskaloosa Courthouse on the town square in Jefferson County dates to 1867. The building's ornate architectural elements and long life—it is the oldest courthouse still in use in the state—make it especially valuable to historians.

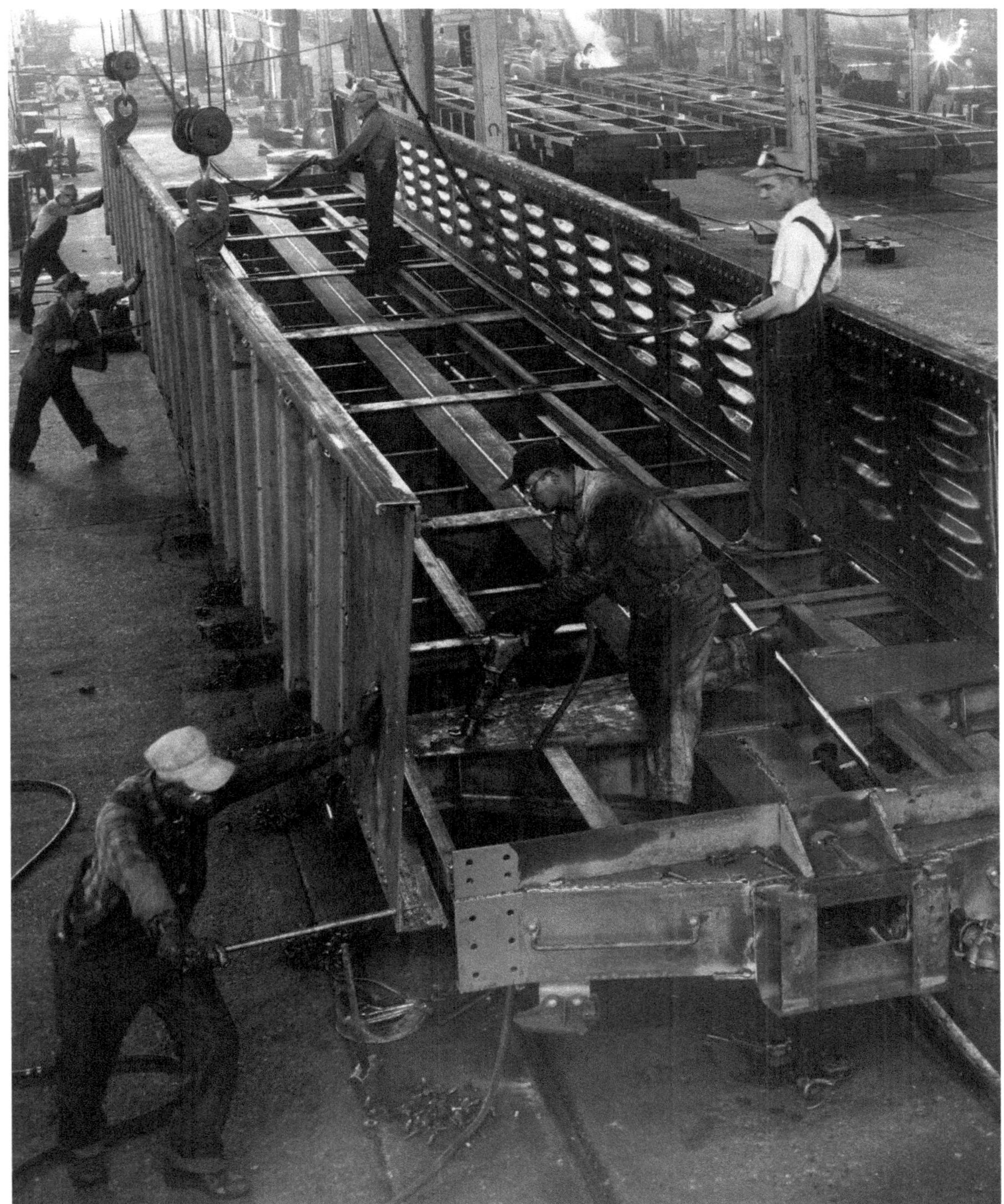

In 1959, workers at the Atchison, Topeka and Santa Fe shop in Topeka build an open gondola car. The cars were designed to haul stone and other loose freight. Railroads, a prime mover in Kansas's development, brought materials and supplies to the West while creating industries, jobs, and communities along the way.

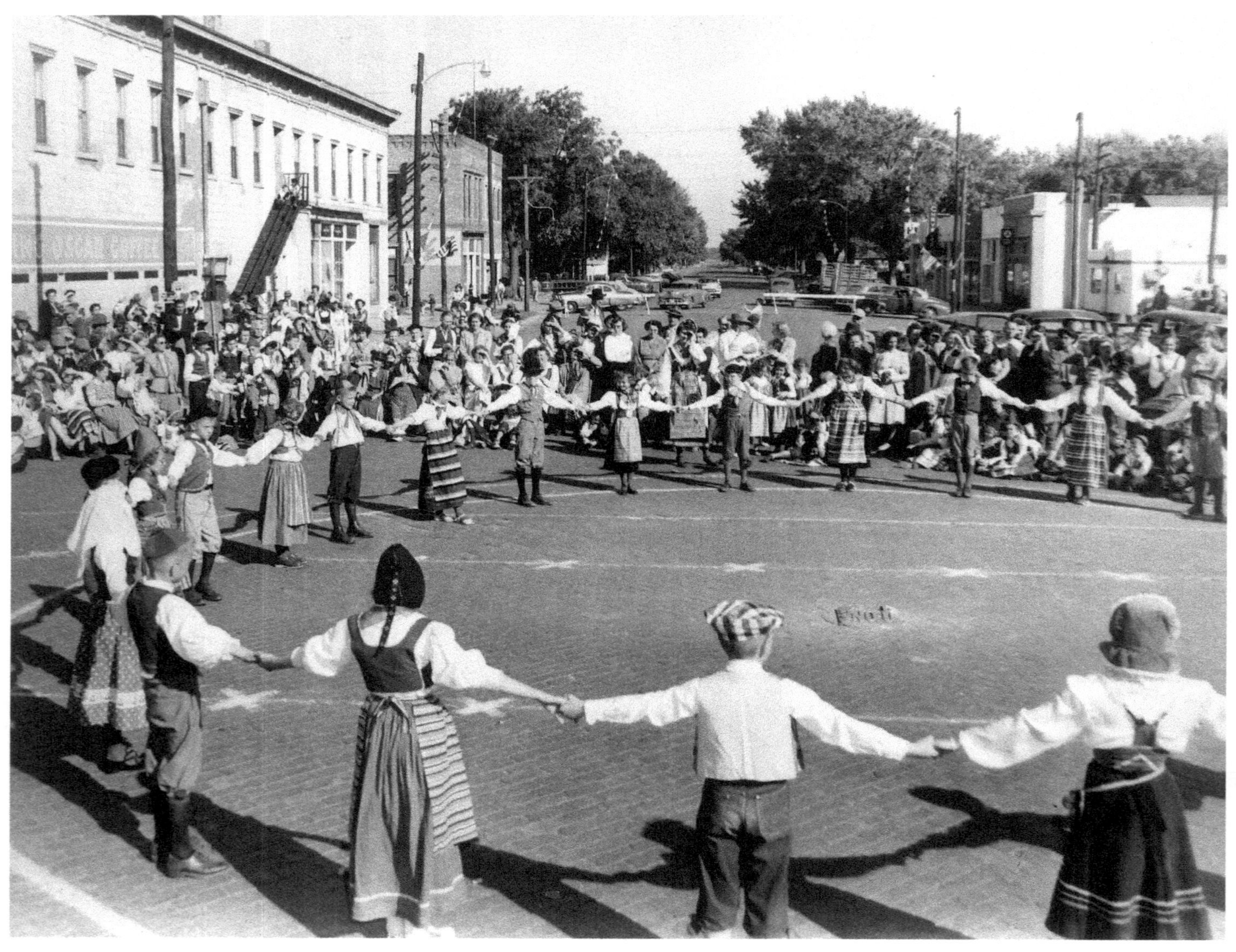

Thanks to ethnic dress and dancing, Lindsborg's Swedish roots are on full display during the Svensk Hyllnings Fest. The biennial festival honors the Swedish immigrants who came to the Smoky Valley in the late 1860s.

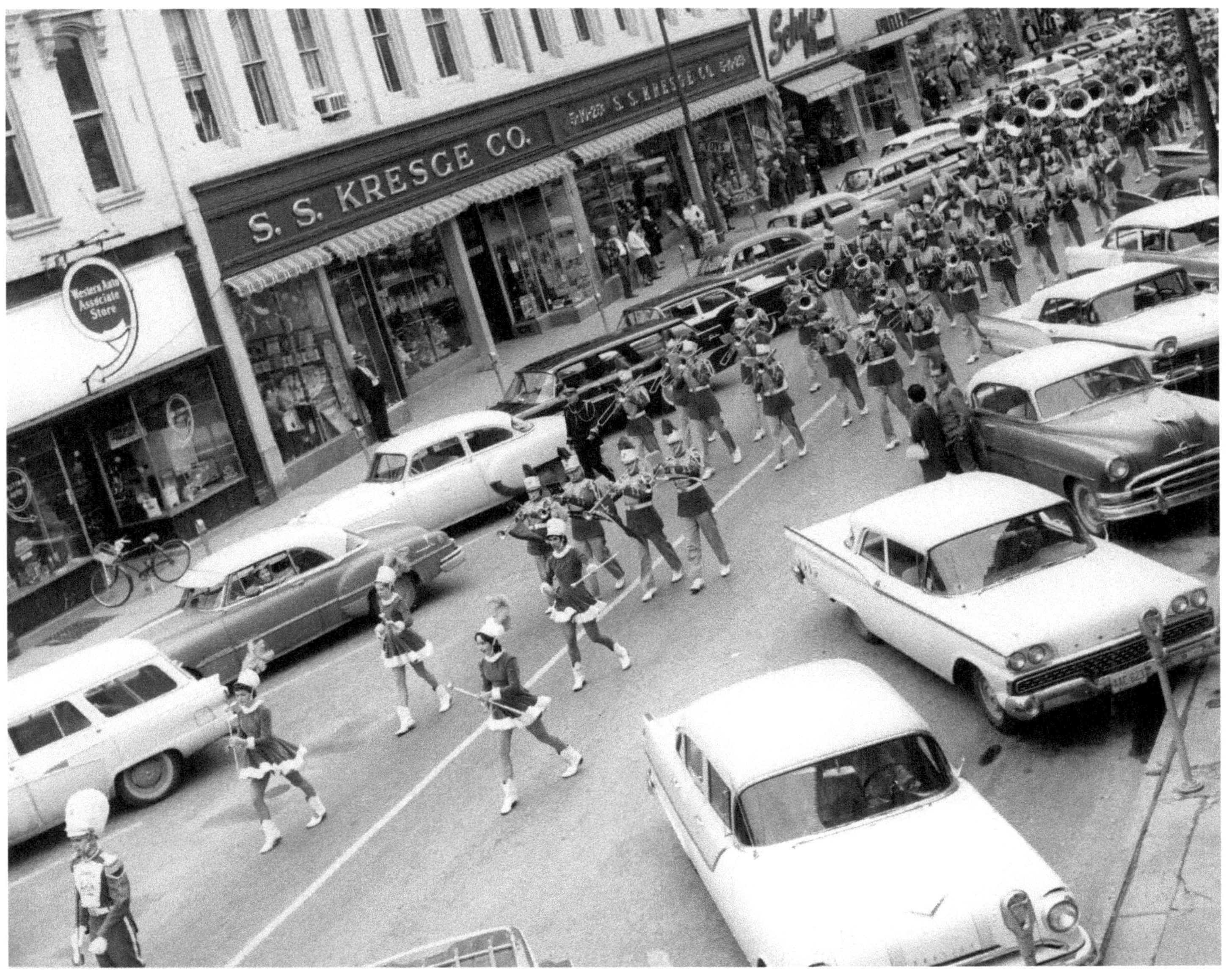

In 1960, a month before John F. Kennedy was elected president, a drum majorette and baton twirlers lead the Leavenworth High School band in a parade through the business district.

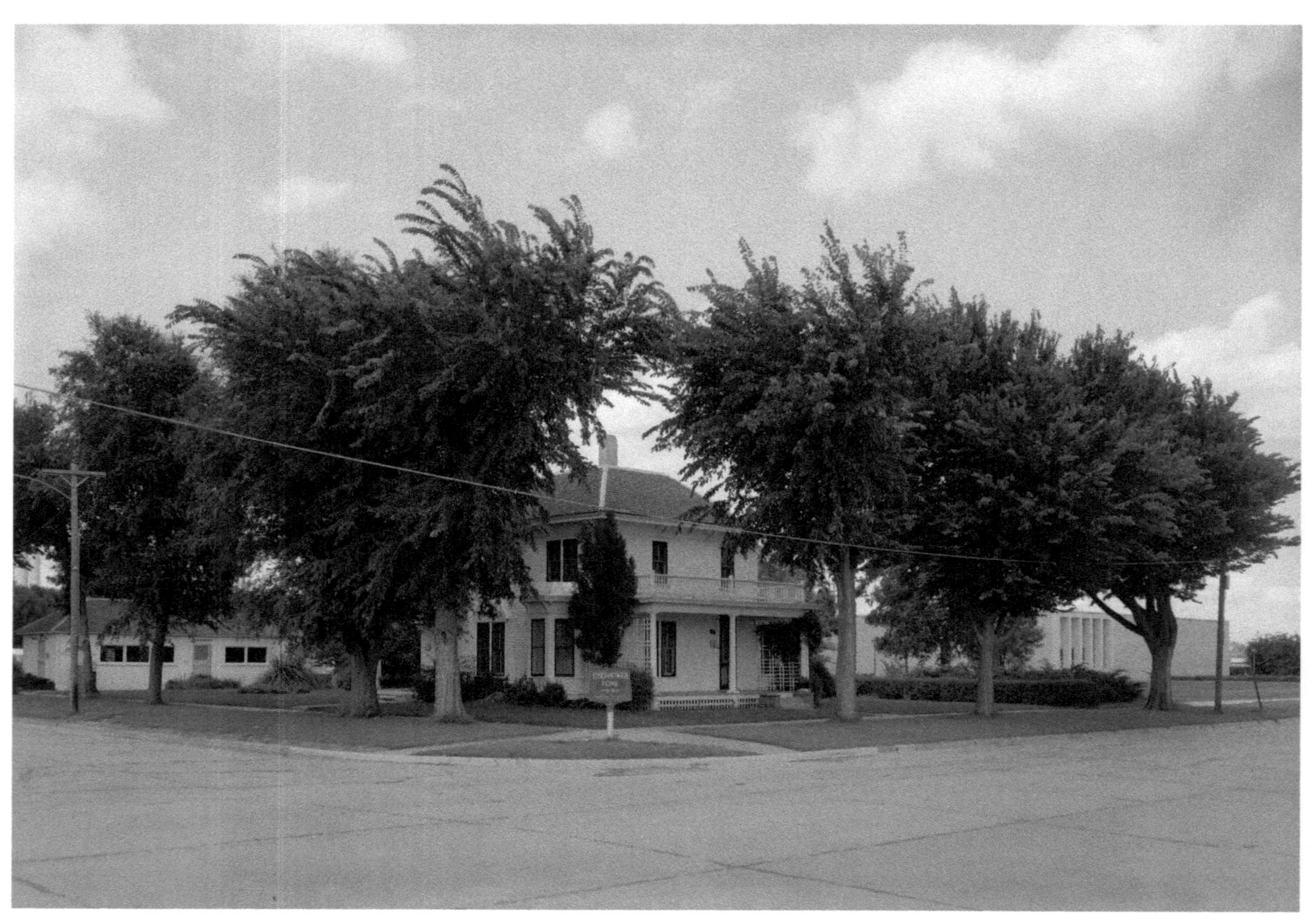

No Kansan is more famous than Dwight David Eisenhower, Commander-in-Chief of Allied forces during the Normandy invasion, and the country's 34th president. His home in Abilene was photographed in 1965.

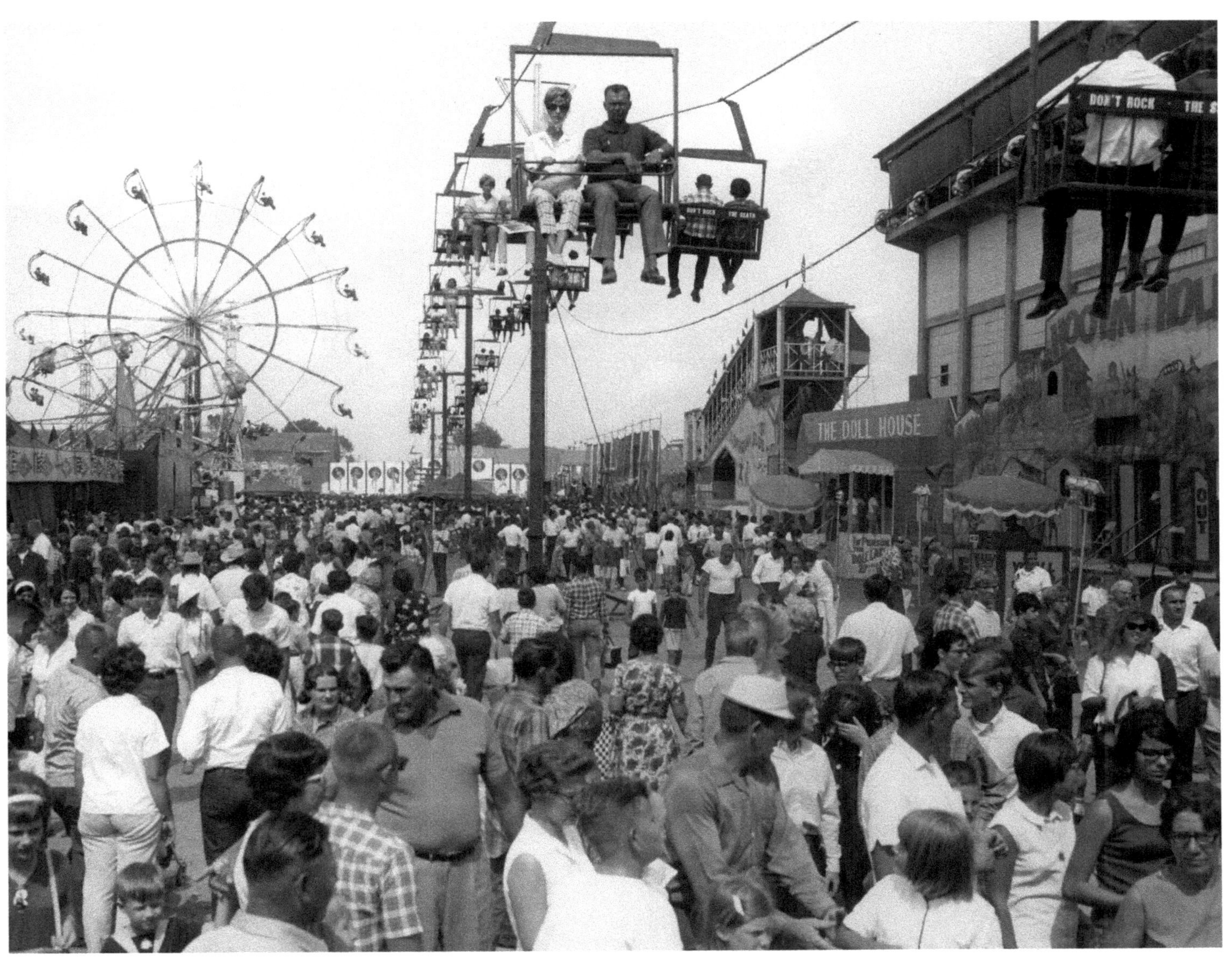

Kansans are known for their work ethic, but they also find time to reward themselves with recreational outlets. Here in the 1960s, aerial tram riders are pictured at the Kansas State Fair carnival in Hutchinson.

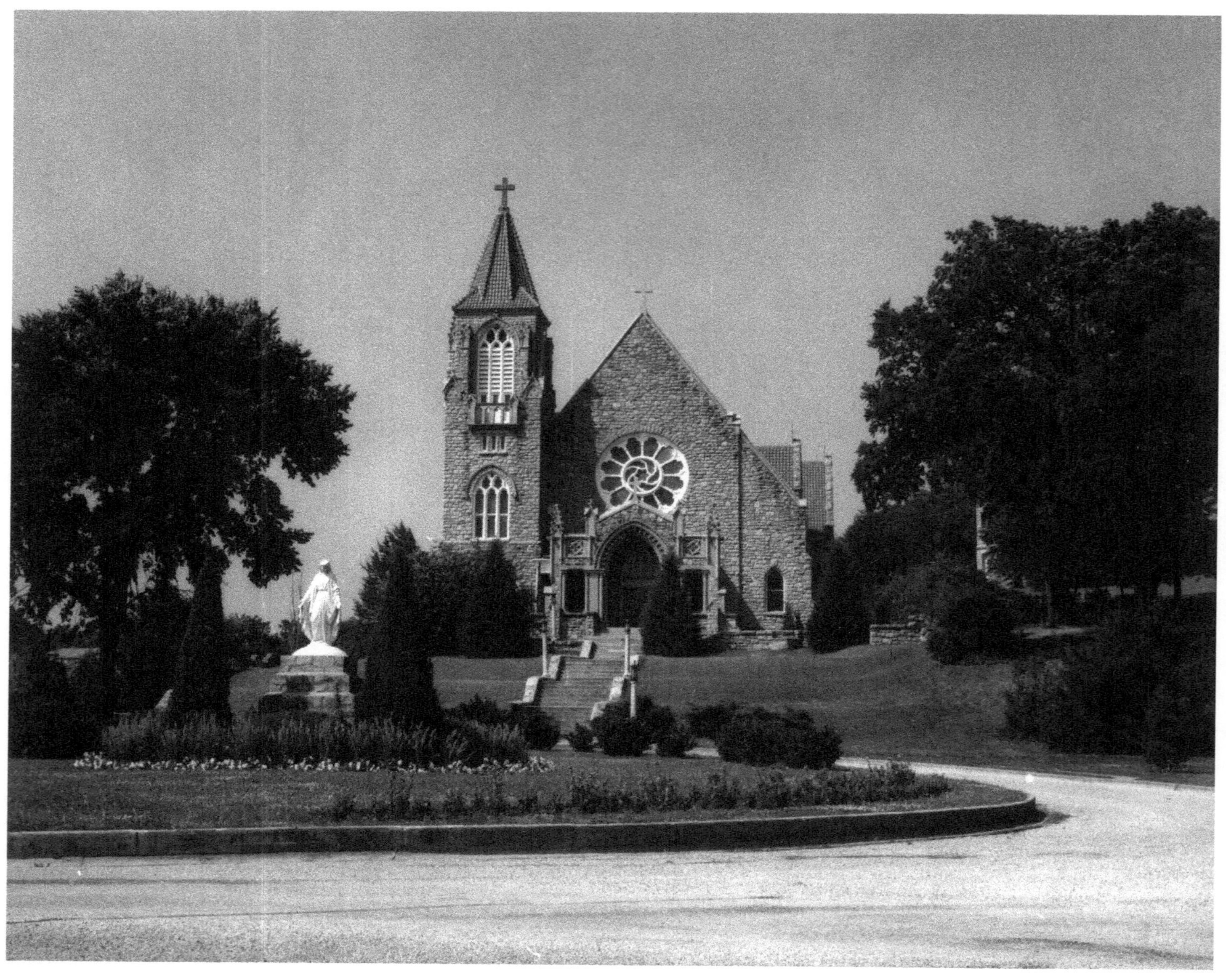

Immaculata Church, on the grounds of St. Mary's Academy and College in Pottawatomie, was built from native limestone. From 1931 to 1967, at least 1,000 theological students were ordained as priests at St. Mary's. In 1978, fire destroyed the church, leaving only the exterior walls standing. The building was completely razed in July 2009.

Notes on the Photographs

These notes, listed by page number, attempt to include all aspects known of the photographs. Each of the photographs is identified by the page number, photograph's title or description, photographer and collection, archive, and call or box number when applicable. Although every attempt was made to collect all data, in some cases complete data may have been unavailable due to the age and condition of some of the photographs and records.

II **East Main Street, Chanute**
Library of Congress
LC-USZ62-090152

VI **Hays City**
Library of Congress
1s00054u

X **Manhattan Milling Company**
Library of Congress
LC-USZ62-090131

2 **Market Square at Fort Scott**
Library of Congress
LC-USZ62-06547

3 **Main Street at Fort Scott**
Library of Congress
LC-USZ62-066545

4 **Rocky Ford Dam**
Library of Congress
ppmsca-19662

5 **Old Fort Well in Fort Scott**
Library of Congress
LC-USZ62-067315

6 **Hotel de Dutton**
Library of Congress
1s00004u

7 **Wyandotte Union Pacific Building**
Library of Congress
1s00006u

8 **1860s Farmhouse**
Library of Congress
1s00003u

9 **Lone Boater on the Kaw**
Library of Congress
1s00009u

10 **Resting on the Curb in Leavenworth**
Library of Congress
1s00025u

11 **Leavenworth Public School**
Library of Congress
1s00026u

12 **Tracks in the Delaware Indian Reservation**
Library of Congress
1s00011u

13 **Delaware Indian Reservation Farm**
Library of Congress
1s00010u

14 **Leavenworth, Lawrence, and Galveston Railroad Bridge**
Library of Congress
1s00014u

15 **Fort Union in Lawrence, 1867**
Library of Congress
1s00020u

16 **Massachusetts Street, Lawrence**
Library of Congress
1s00016u

17 **The Eldridge House**
Library of Congress
1s00017u

18 **The Crandall House**
Library of Congress
1s00012u

19 **Site of Captain Gaius Jenkins Murder**
Library of Congress
1s00021u

20 **Grasshopper Creek**
Library of Congress
1s00033u

21 **Lincoln College**
Library of Congress
1s00037u

22 **"View at Mr. Wetherall's, Topeka"**
Library of Congress
1s00040u

23 **Prairie Hunting**
Library of Congress
1s00038u

24 **Kansas River, Topeka**
Library of Congress
1s00039u

25 **Alexander Gardner at Fort Riley**
Library of Congress
1s00045u

26 **Major E. A. Ogden Monument**
Library of Congress
1s00043u

27 **Junction City's Kansas Pacific Railroad Depot**
Library of Congress
1s00048u

28 **Drover's Cottage at McCoy's Stock Yard**
Library of Congress
1s00052u

29 **"Mushroom Rock"**
Library of Congress
1s00061u

30 **Clear Creek Family with Elk**
Library of Congress
1s01629u

31 **Fort Harker**
Library of Congress
1s00060u

32 **Ellsworth Depot**
Library of Congress
1s00066u

34 **United States Express Stage**
Library of Congress
1s01630u

35 **Central Plains**
Library of Congress
1s00071u

36 **Dodge City**
Kansas Historical Society
64

37 **Dodge City Peace Commission**
Kansas Historical Society
189

38 **Washington Street, Nicodemus**
Library of Congress
069504pu

39 **Exodusters in Nicodemus**
Library of Congress
069503pu

40 **Henry Baden's Grocery and Dry Goods**
Library of Congress
LC-USZ62-090151

42 **E. B. Purcell Trading Company**
Library of Congress
LC-USZ62-090130

43 **Exceptionally Large Potatoes**
Library of Congress
LC-USZ62-104166

44 **"Beantown, U.S.A."**
Library of Congress
3b36520u

46 **Ottawa Business District**
Library of Congress
LC-USZ62-095656

47 **Masonic Temple**
Library of Congress
LC-USZ62-090132

48 **Arkansas City**
Library of Congress
LC-USZ62-095672

50 **The Rasbach**
Library of Congress
LC-USZ62-090133

52 **Hardware Store, Liberal**
Library of Congress
LC-USZ62-102975

53 **Tornado Damage, Wellington**
Library of Congress
3b37815u

54 **Central Avenue, El Dorado**
Library of Congress
LC-USZ62-090150

56 **Harvey Girls at Chanute Santa Fe Station**
Library of Congress
3c18086

57 **"Wm. McLaughlin & Wife, Kansas"**
Library of Congress
07027u

58 **Ponca Sun Dance**
Library of Congress
LC-USZ62-100432

59 **J. B. Watkins Land Company**
Library of Congress
069427pu

60 **West Main Street, Chanute**
Library of Congress
LC-USZ62-047330

62 **Transaction at Watkins National Bank**
Library of Congress
069423pu

63 **Woman in Cornfield**
Library of Congress
3b10549u

64 **Topeka Business District, 1900**
Library of Congress
LC-USZ62-045621

65 **Mules Pulling Streetcars**
Library of Congress
LC-USZ62-045620

66 **1902 Tornado Approaching Lebanon**
Library of Congress
3b37812u

68 **Leavenworth's Carnegie Library**
Library of Congress
15390u

69 **Young Men's Commercial Room**
Library of Congress
LC-USZ62-064629

70 **Northern Surprise and Jessamy**
Library of Congress
3a46724u

71 **An Unlikely Trio**
Library of Congress
3c12635u

72 **"The Garden of the Desert"**
Library of Congress
LC-USZ62-065491

73 **Hunters, Foxhounds, and Prey**
Library of Congress
3b39530

74 **Senate Chamber, 1905**
Library of Congress
6a34891u

75 **Caney Gas Well Ablaze**
Library of Congress
3b13684u

76 **Haskell Institute**
Library of Congress
6a05440u

77 **Pure Milk Company**
Library of Congress
LC-USZ62-133994

78 **Coffeyville, 1907**
Library of Congress
3b23474u

79 **Bethany College Carnegie Library**
Library of Congress
LC-ppmsca-15326

80 **William Howard Taft Address, 1908**
Library of Congress
3b07853u

81 **Goodland Panorama**
Library of Congress
6a05383u

82 **Coffeyville Roller Coaster**
Library of Congress
LC-USZ62-048244

83 **Newton Laborers**
Library of Congress
02210u

84 **Newton Cowboy**
Library of Congress
3b02986u

85 **Gathering to See President Taft**
Library of Congress
02196u

86 **Sod Schoolhouse**
Library of Congress
3c12792u

87 **Octagonal Office**
Library of Congress
3a46419u

88 **Sveadahl Courthouse**
Library of Congress
3b18003u

89 **Atchison Business District**
Library of Congress
6a05261u

90 **Pennsylvania Ave. and Myrtle St., Independence**
Library of Congress
6a05318u

92 **2nd and Main Streets, Ottawa**
Library of Congress
6a05350u

93 **Iola Business District**
Library of Congress
6a05326u

94 **Coffeyville Business District**
Library of Congress
6a05294u

95 **Hiawatha**
Library of Congress
6a05310u

96 **Globe Street, Cherryvale**
Library of Congress
6a05286u

97 **Bird's-eye View, Atchison**
Library of Congress
6a05269u

98 **Main Street, Chanute**
Library of Congress
6a05278u

99 **Globe Office Building, Pittsburg**
Library of Congress
6a05358u

100 **Emporia**
Library of Congress
6a05302u

101 **Olathe**
Library of Congress
6a05334u

102 **Soldier's Home, Leavenworth**
Library of Congress
6a10600u

103 **Downtown Ottawa**
Library of Congress
6a05342u

104 **Belpre Farm Family**
Library of Congress
3a51290u

106 **9th Ave. and Main St., Winfield**
Library of Congress
6a13146u

107 **Ottawa Railroad Works**
Library of Congress
LC-USZ62-41959

108 **Teddy Roosevelt in Baldwin**
Library of Congress
3b25468u

109 **Downtown Winfield**
Library of Congress
6a05373u

110 **U.S. Military Prison**
Library of Congress
3b10968u

111 **U.S. Military Prison Dormitory**
Library of Congress
3a50141u

112 **Chanute Girls Basketball Champions**
Library of Congress
3b36352u

113 **Kingman Street Scene**
Library of Congress
LC-USZ62-092267

114 **Mule-powered Streetcar**
Library of Congress
LC-USZ62-076282

116 **Rooftop View of Wichita, 1912**
Library of Congress
6a05366u

117 **Band Playing at Leavenworth's National Military Home**
Library of Congress
LC-USZ62-053372

118 **Topeka Street Railway Group Portrait, 1913**
Library of Congress
6a25997u

119 **Nazareth Convent and Academy**
Library of Congress
6a05393u

120 **University of Kansas, 1913**
Library of Congress
6a05401u

121 **University of Kansas, 1913 No. 2**
Library of Congress
6a05409u

122 **"Weishaar," World-record Motorcyclist**
Library of Congress
3b03344u

123 Wagons Loading Wheat in Offerle
Library of Congress
3b08882u

124 Carpentry at Haskell Indian Junior College
Library of Congress
3c31955u

125 Farmer on Hay Cart at Harvest
Library of Congress
LC-USZ62-112899

126 Men Posing at El Dorado's Trapshooter's no. 2
Library of Congress
3c12829u

127 Pawnee Flats Cavalry Camp, 1917
Library of Congress
6a31432u

128 Fort Riley Hospital
Library of Congress
6a31077u

130 Cowboy Tying Legs of Lassoed Cow
Library of Congress
3b04627u

131 Harvesters, Kinsley
Library of Congress
LC-USZ62-065174

132 Main Street, Garden City
Library of Congress
LC-USZ62-118796

133 Santa Fe Depot, Garden City
Library of Congress
LC-USZ62-117035

134 "Getting Your Ducks in a Row"
Kansas Historical Society
00088992
Item # 212474

136 Marshall Theatre
Library of Congress
LC-USZ62-135162

137 President Harding with Hutchinson Farmers
Library of Congress
3c16507u

138 Hutchinson Street Scene, 1920s
Kansas Historical Society
00056895
Item # 209627
Call # FK2.F2 D.5 *8

139 Randolph High Basketball Game
Kansas Historical Society
00093585
Item 213122
Call # FK2.R5 R.76 RHS #6

140 Dr. Naismith Supervising Fencing Match
Library of Congress
LC-USZ62-069321

141 1924 Neodesha Anniversary Parade
Kansas Historical Society
00052843
Item # 100271
Call # FK2.W5

142 Elkhart, 1920s
Kansas Historical Society
00110015
Item # 213894
Call # FK2.M9 E.5 MaiS *3

143 Herbert Hoover Campaigning from Train in Dodge City
Library of Congress
LC-USZ62-121935

144 Wichita Aerial Shot
Library of Congress
3b21875u

145 General Scott and Company at Medicine Lodge
Library of Congress
LC-USZ62-092921

146 Bootleg Raid, 1927
Kansas Historical Society
00053434
Item # 208703
Call # FK2.D4 L.77 #4

147 Locomotive 945
Kansas Historical Society
00093948
Item # 213416
Call # FK2.S5 T.74 UP *30

148 Douglas Avenue, Wichita
Library of Congress
3b22762u

150 Fraser Hall at University of Kansas
Library of Congress
LC-USZ62-03939

151 State Capitol
Library of Congress
LC-USZ62-088426

152 Bisonte Hotel Dining Room
Library of Congress
LC-USZ62-091772

153 Scott County Dust Storm, 1935
Library of Congress
LC-USZ62-114845

154 Rothstein's Steam Shovels
Library of Congress
8b27645u

155 Deserted Bank, 1936
Library of Congress
8b27620u

156 Farm Laborers Union, Galena
Library of Congress
8b38311u

157 Main Street, Yates Center
Library of Congress
LC-USF33-T0-01256

158 Oskaloosa Courthouse
Library of Congress
LC-USF34-008715

159 Peter Pan Foods Store, Minneapolis
Library of Congress
LC-USF33-T0-01266

160 Granada Theater
Library of Congress
8a03784u

161 Fifth Avenue Hotel
Library of Congress
LC-USF33-01241

162 First Baptist Church, Nicodemus
Library of Congress
069556pu

163 Oskaloosa Auction, 1938
Library of Congress
8a03787u

164 Oskaloosa Auction, 1938, no. 2
Library of Congress
8a03786u

165 Blizzard 1935
Library of Congress
LC-USZ62-067483

166 Cimmaron Farmstead
Library of Congress
LC-USF34-034023

167 4-H Club Pie-eating Contest, 1939
Library of Congress
3c30594u

168 Farmer Digging in Dry Ground
Library of Congress
8a26889u

169 Sublette Prize Bulls
Library of Congress
LC-USF34-034124

170 Irrigation Machinery
Library of Congress
LC-USF34-034141

171 Abandoned Businesses in Shaw
Library of Congress
LC-USF34-061778

172 Almena Farmland
Library of Congress
LC-USF34-038530

173 First National Bank, Norton
Library of Congress
LC-USF34-038527

174 Fort Riley Cavalry
Library of Congress
LC-USW3-004258

175 Soldiers in Truck Messenger Center
Library of Congress
8d05610u

176 Mena Weber Applying Makeup at Cessna Plant
Library of Congress
8e09024u

177 Tractor Pulling B-25 in Kansas City
Library of Congress
1a35288u

178 Junction City Church in Prairie
Library of Congress
1a34277u

179 Grazing Horses
Library of Congress
1a34280u

180 Children Playing at Schoolhouse
Library of Congress
1a34287u

181 Snowy Railroad, Kansas City
Library of Congress
LC-USW3-019366

182 Grain Elevator
Library of Congress
1a34714u

183 Trainmasters in Dispatch Center
Library of Congress
LC-USW3-019447

184 Trains Being Serviced at Argentine Yard
Library of Congress
1a34716u

185 Mechanics at the Atchison, Topeka and Santa Fe Shop
Library of Congress
LC-USW3-019314

186 Washing a Locomotive
Library of Congress
1a34711u

187 Boot Hill Fiesta Parade, 1952
Kansas Historical Society
00053262

188 Dymaxion House
Kansas Historical Society
00058093

189 Kansas Territory Centennial Parade
Kansas Historical Society
000580645

190 Laboring in Oil Field
Library of Congress
LC-USZ62-077222

191 Beechcraft T-34
Kansas Historical Society
d573
Item #578
Call # FK2.R2, H.8, HNAS, *26

192 General Motors Fairfax Plant
Library of Congress
LC-USZ62-053015

193 Covered Bridge at Stranger Creek
Library of Congress
069893pu

194 Oskaloosa Courthouse no. 2
Library of Congress
069638pu

195 Building a Gondola Car
Kansas Historical Society
00113598
Item # 51755
Call # ATSF Series 2, #424-19

196 Svensk Hyllnings Fest
Kansas Historical Society
00031455
Item # 200214
Call # FK2.M3 L.52.1961

197 Leavenworth Parade
Kansas Historical Society
00058232
Item # 100423
Call # FK2.L3 L.76 LHS #2

198 Eisenhower Home
Library of Congress
069255pu

199 Kansas State Fair
Kansas Historical Society
00052707
Item # 208623, Call # FK2. R2 H.65 F.1965 c *2

200 Immaculata Church
Kansas Historical Society
00093434
Item # 213244, Call # FK2.P3 Sm.71 Cat*10

HISTORIC PHOTOS OF
KANSAS

Positioned in the geographic center of the contiguous 48 states, Kansas has played a vital role in the nation's development. From its Native American roots—the state is named for the Kansa tribe—Kansas has been both eyewitness and participant to history. No state, literally or figuratively, has been more in the middle of America's fascinating story than the Sunflower State.

Culled from Library of Congress and Kansas Historical Society collections, the nearly 200 striking black-and-white images in *Historic Photos of Kansas* trace a progression from "Bleeding Kansas," a period of violent struggle between free-state abolitionists and pro-slavery sympathizers, to the state's many contributions to westward expansion, railroads, agriculture, and America at war.

Although these photos speak for themselves, when combined with captions and chapter introductions, they will transport curious readers to a close-up view of Kansans helping to write history.

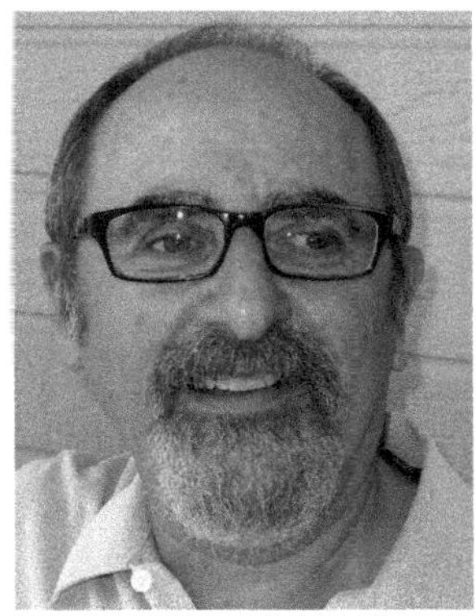

A career newspaper editor and reporter, David Knopf is a freelance journalist, performing songwriter, and soccer coach. He moved to Tulsa, Oklahoma, from the East Coast in 1975, where he met his wife, Marieta, a Kansan. In 1990, the couple settled in Kansas City. They have two children, Sarah and Isaac.

WWW.TURNERPUBLISHING.COM

www.ingramcontent.com/pod-product-compliance
Lightning Source LLC
LaVergne TN
LVHW060604110826
845154LV00003B/37